D0438566

INDIA,
CHINA,
AND THE
UNITED STATES

THIS BRAVE NEW WORLD

ANJA MANUEL

SIMON & SCHUSTER

New York   London   Toronto   Sydney   New Delhi

Simon & Schuster
1230 Avenue of the Americas
New York, NY 10020

Copyright © 2016 by Anja Manuel

First Simon & Schuster hardcover edition May 2016

SIMON & SCHUSTER and colophon are registered trademarks of
Simon & Schuster, Inc.

For information about special discounts for bulk purchases,
please contact Simon & Schuster Special Sales at 1-866-506-1949 or
business@simonandschuster.com.

The Simon & Schuster Speakers Bureau can bring authors to your
live event. For more information or to book an event, contact the
Simon & Schuster Speakers Bureau at 1-866-248-3049 or
visit our website at www.simonspeakers.com.

Map copyright © Jeffrey L. Ward

Book design by Ellen R. Sasahara

Manufactured in the United States of America

1 3 5 7 9 10 8 6 4 2

Library of Congress Cataloging-in-Publication Data is available.

ISBN 978-1-5011-2197-5
ISBN 978-1-5011-2199-9 (ebook)

To my parents, Oma, and Opa,
for believing I can do anything,

to Greg,
for being my partner in everything,

and for Alia and Alexei,
because it is your new world.

O wonder!
How many godly creatures are there here!
   How beauteous mankind is!
O brave new world
That has such people in it!

—William Shakespeare, *The Tempest* (1610–11)

He halted and, with bewildered and horrified eyes,
stared round him. . . . The words mocked him derisively.
"How beauteous mankind is! O brave new world . . ."

—Aldous Huxley, *Brave New World* (1932)

CONTENTS

PART III: STEPPING ONTO THE WORLD STAGE

MAIN CHARACTERS

INDIA

Mohandas Karamchand (the Mahatma) Gandhi (1869–1948) was the preeminent leader of the Indian independence movement and the pioneer of nonviolent civil disobedience, sparking many other such movements around the world. He was a lifelong advocate of religious pluralism and Hindu-Muslim cooperation and for a unified India. He was assassinated in 1948 by a Hindu fanatic.

Jawaharlal Nehru (1889–1964) was a key leader in the Indian independence movement and the Indian National Congress Party along with Mahatma Gandhi. He served as the first prime minister of India from independence in 1947 until his death in 1964. He was a strong supporter of democracy, freedom of religion and expression, and economic assistance to the poor, and is considered a key architect of the modern Indian state.

Muhammad Ali Jinnah (1876–1948) was an Indian Muslim leader who became the founder and first governor-general of Pakistan after Indian Independence, ruling until his early death from illness in 1948. A moderate Muslim who trained as a barrister in London, Jinnah later became concerned with how Muslims would be treated in a Hindu-dominated India and became a key figure in the creation of Pakistan in 1947.

Sonia Gandhi (1946–) is an Italian-born Indian politician who has served as president of the Indian National Congress Party since 1998. A strong advocate for India's poor and rural voters, she is the daughter-in-law of former Prime Minister Indira Gandhi* and widow of former Prime Minister Rajiv Gandhi.

---

* Indira Gandhi was the daughter of Prime Minister Nehru. She happened to marry a man named Gandhi, but is not related to Mahatma Gandhi.

Manmohan Singh (1932–) is an Indian economist who served as the prime minister of India from 2004 to 2014 as part of the Congress Party, the first Sikh to hold the office. Prior to that, as finance minister from 1991 to 1996, Singh carried out important structural reforms that liberalized India's economy.

Montek Singh Ahluwalia (1943–) is an Indian economist and senior civil servant who was one of former Prime Minister Manmohan Singh's most trusted advisers. He served as the top economic advisor to Singh from 2004 to 2014. Ahluwalia consistently pushed for inclusive growth and a more open economy, which some in the left-leaning Congress Party opposed.

Kapil Sibal (1948–) is a senior Indian Congress Party politician. He led multiple ministries in the Indian government under Prime Minister Singh, including Science and Technology, Human Resource Development, Communications and Information Technology, and Law and Justice; at times, he led several ministries simultaneously.

Narendra Modi (1950–) has served as the prime minister of India since May 2014. Modi, a leader of the Hindu nationalist Bharatiya Janata Party (BJP), was the chief minister of Gujarat from 2001 to 2014, where he was known for his pro-business economic growth agenda.

Arun Jaitley (1952–) is a senior member of Bharatiya Janata Party (BJP) and one of Prime Minister Modi's most trusted senior leaders. He has been finance minister of India since 2014, for a time serving simultaneously as defense minister. Jaitley held multiple cabinet level positions between 1999 and 2014 and was also leader of the opposition in the Rajya Sabha from 2009 to 2014.

Kisan Baburao "Anna" Hazare (1937–) is an Indian social activist who led movements to promote rural development and increase government transparency. Most recently he led mass protests around India to establish a national ombudsman (or "Jan Lokpal") to investigate and punish corruption in public life.

Nandan Nilekani (1955–) is an Indian entrepreneur. He is a cofounder of Infosys, one of India's preeminent IT companies, and in 2009 led the creation of India's biometric identification program, Aadhaar, which was created to generate a national identity number for every Indian and to make government services and subsidies more transparent. Nearly 1 billion Indians have voluntarily signed up.

CHINA

Mao Zedong (1893–1976) was an early leader of the Chinese Communist Party whose forces won the civil war against the nationalist Kuomintang Party (KMT). He became the founding father of the People's Republic of China and led the country from 1949 until his death in 1976. Mao is still revered by many Chinese for modernizing China and improving livelihoods. At the same time, his dramatically failed policies, such as the Great Leap Forward, the Cultural Revolution, and other missteps, are thought to have cost between 40 and 70 million lives.

Chiang Kai-Shek (1887–1975) led the centrist, nationalist Kuomintang Party (KMT) in the civil war against Mao's Communist forces and later led China's defense against the Japanese invasion in 1937. Despite help from the United States, a drained KMT lost the civil war in 1949, and Chiang and his allies fled to Taiwan island, where his KMT Party is still a serious political force today.

Deng Xiaoping (1904–1997) was a key Communist Party revolutionary and economic reformer who was China's paramount leader from 1978 through the early 1990s. He led the opening of China's economy, dismantling China's immense agricultural communes and creating "Special Economic Zones," and became the father of China's economic miracle. He also presided over a gradual political opening, which ended abruptly with the Tiananmen Square crackdown in 1989.

Hu Jintao (1942–) was China's president from 2003 to 2013. He worked his way up through China's bureaucracy as a technocrat, was known for his emphasis on consensus-based rule, and is associated with the "Communist Youth League" or "populist" faction in Chinese politics.

Xi Jinping (1953–) has been general secretary of the Chinese Communist Party since 2012 and China's president since 2013. Xi is associated with the "princeling faction" in Chinese politics and is known as a strong, assertive leader who has implemented a tough anticorruption crackdown, as well as economic and military reforms.

Li Keqiang (1955–) has been China's premier since 2013. An economist by training, he heads the state bureaucracy, including the State Council. He is the only Hu Jintao protégé currently on China's powerful Politburo Standing Committee.

Liu He (1952–) is President Xi Jinping's closest economic advisor. He leads the general office of the Leading Group for Financial and Economic Affairs and is responsible for China's most important economic reforms.

Wang Qishan (1948–) is another of President Xi's closest advisors, a former banker, mayor of Beijing, and one of the key organizers of the Beijing Olympics. Since late 2012 he has been leading China's anticorruption drive as head of China's fearsome Central Commission for Discipline Inspection.

Bo Xilai (1949–) is the former Chongqing Party Secretary. He was a prominent, charismatic, ambitious politician, but his political career came to an abrupt end in a high-profile corruption scandal also involving his wife. He has been stripped of all Party offices and is now serving a life prison sentence.

Zhou Yongkang (1942–) is China's former security chief and a member of the elite Politburo Standing Committee. He was one of the most high-profile targets of Xi Jinping's anticorruption campaign. He was convicted in 2015 of bribery, abuse of power, and disclosure of state secrets. He is the highest-level Party official to be expelled since immediately after the Cultural Revolution, and he is serving a life sentence.

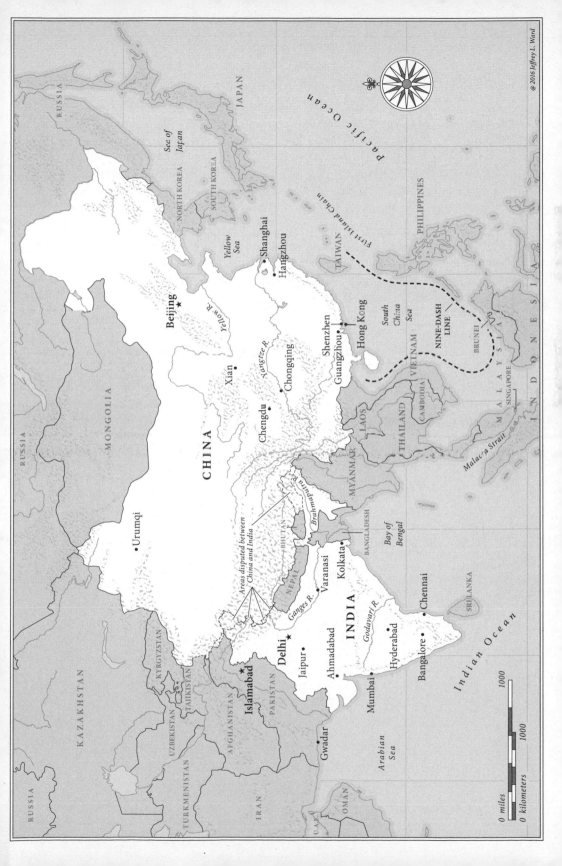

INTRODUCTION

China Flexes Its Military Muscle—Bloomberg

China Fears Sink Markets Again—Wall Street Journal

It's Time to Get Tough on China—Washington Post

China, a Wounded Tiger, Could Lash Out—Los Angeles Times

T HE HEADLINES leading up to Chinese President Xi Jinping's visit to the United States in September 2015 were scathing. Washington threatened to impose sanctions for Chinese computer hacking. Some presidential candidates called for President Obama to cancel the state visit.

I was among the hundreds who stood politely to applaud Xi's speech to the American business community in Seattle during that visit. It was an impressive affair. Entrepreneurs sipped wine and made polite conversation with Chinese officials. Xi is a statesman and looked it, in a crisp dark suit and tie. He struck all the right notes: assuring us that China will create a level playing field for U.S. companies, crack down on commercial cyber-theft, and cooperate with us on issues ranging from Iran to global financial stability. He encouraged the United States and China to "work together" on our future. Yet underneath the ceremony, there was an air of formality, and even discomfort. We had waited in line for more than an hour to go through a security screening. Most of the Chinese and Americans sat at separate tables, scarcely interacting with each other. Some American CEOs fretted about the negative news coverage they would receive for being seen hobnobbing with the Chinese president.

The atmosphere at a Silicon Valley dinner for Indian prime minister Narendra Modi a few days later was entirely different. The prime minister was an hour late. Indians, Americans, and Indian-Americans mingled happily in the banquet room and, in many cases, no one quite knew who belonged to which country. There was such loud, happy chatter that the organizers repeatedly had to ask us to sit down. Most of the Americans onstage, including the CEOs of Google, Microsoft, and Adobe Systems, were born in India. Prime Minister Modi, in a beige traditional Indian Nehru jacket, gave a less formal speech than Xi. He spoke in English, told jokes, shared stories of technology connecting Indian grandmothers to their grandchildren working in San Francisco, sketched his vision for a digitally empowered India, and called the India-U.S. relationship the "defining partnership of this century." In contrast to that of President Xi, Modi's visit received very little news coverage.

The dinners are a snapshot of the state of our relations with Asia's rising giants. We respect China, our commercial ties bind us, but difficult geopolitics and a slew of bilateral disagreements lurk beneath the surface. As we listen politely to Xi Jinping, we don't always trust his words. We are "working hard" to get along with the Chinese, but it is not easy. Some would describe us as "frenemies." Relations with India are much more affable and comfortable. It is far behind China by most economic and development metrics, but has long-term strengths such as real rule of law and democracy. India doesn't get much attention in our press. We assume that we share values and already have a strong "partnership" in most areas. Yet we tend to underestimate India's size and future power.

★   ★   ★

The axial shift of power from the United States and Europe to China and India is unrelenting. By 2030, just fourteen short years from now, Asia will surpass the *combined* power of North America and Europe in economic might, population size, and military spending. The United States will still be the most powerful international player, but China and India will increasingly dictate the terms of global governance. Along with the United States and Europe, they will become the new indispensable powers—whether they rise peacefully or not.

The lion's share of public attention is focused on China. We are obsessed with the Asian goliath and fear that it will replace America's preeminent power. This insecurity misses the larger picture. Due to their size and economic might, *both* India and China will have veto power over most international decisions, from climate change, to the openness of global trade, to nuclear policy, to human rights and business norms. India will be the most important country outside the West to shape the rise of China. We must stop our hand-wringing about China and seek instead to forge harmonious relationships with both giants, and thus bravely create the new world.

More attention has been paid to China's ascent because its boom started earlier and many predict it will be the world's largest economy by 2030 (if measured by purchasing power, it already is). Our news coverage of China is filled with breathless statistics: it already has more megacities than anywhere else on earth; it has promised pensions to more retirees than the total U.S. population; its cars and smokestacks gush almost twice as much CO2 into the atmosphere as the United States; it has more Internet users than the United States and Europe combined, and 2 million censors monitoring them. The list goes on. Sometimes we describe China as an unstoppable juggernaut, ready to dominate the world. A few days later the papers are filled with stories of its impending economic doom and potential political collapse. The truth, of course, lies somewhere in between. China's economy, might, and influence are trending up, but they will not follow a straight-line trajectory.

Many still doubt the relevance of India as a global power. They should not. India will likely be the world's most populous country before 2030, with at least 100 million *more* citizens than China. India will be adding more people than China to the world's middle class, so our companies will strive to please both Indian and Chinese consumers. By 2030, India will lead the world in energy demand. It will be the world's second-largest emitter of carbon, third-largest source of investment in the world, and third-largest economy after China and the United States. It is true that in many areas, especially economic development, India will lag behind the United States and China. Some question whether India's economy will grow enough for it to become a great power, and discount its international role. This misses the point. India is so large that it will impact us whether or not it lifts millions more out of poverty. If it does not grow, international concerns like climate change will only become worse. We need India's help to solve global problems and to shape China's rise, so we want it to succeed.

The interaction between these two Asian giants will impact the United States. Disputes between China and India could force us to take sides, possibly even militarily, since our interests will more likely align with India's. China and India increasingly compete for oil, coal, and other natural resources around the world, and their decades-old dispute over where their Himalayan border lies could turn ugly. India's nuclear program is primarily a hedge against China's larger military. As China extends its sphere of influence south and India east, the two are more likely to come into conflict, and may draw us into their disagreements.

Conversely, the two countries sometimes cooperate in ways we do not like—by setting up a New Development Bank with Brazil, Russia, and South Africa to compete with the World Bank, by refusing to join American-led free trade negotiations, or by India joining China's new Asian Infrastructure Investment Bank. For years China and India argued in concert that they had less responsibility than the West to lower carbon emissions because their economies were less developed, and thus demonstrated that they have absolute veto power on this critical issue. Fortunately, both have recently begun to cooperate with the West. As Chinese and Indian companies become some of the world's largest investors, they will influence global business practices from bribery to environmental stewardship and labor standards.

I have been lucky to have a front-row view of this colossal shift in power, and a small role in shaping it. At the U.S. State Department from 2005 to 2007, I was part of our internal deliberations to create a new strategic partnership with India, and I watched as we struggled to encourage China to become a "responsible stakeholder" in the world system. In the faded splendor of India's foreign ministry, I helped negotiate a civil nuclear accord with Indian officials, which fostered mutual trust that unlocked cooperation in other areas. In a glorious gilded French palace I observed the "new China"—in the form of then foreign minister Li Zhaoxing—flexing its diplomatic muscle by refusing to agree to additional sanctions on Iran. For the past six years, the consultancy I cofounded and manage with former cabinet-level government officials has helped American companies expand into emerging markets. While we focus on the whole world, the two countries that matter most to our clients are China and India. With my clients, on a daily basis I live through the trials of selling to tough Indian and Chinese negotiators or managing unruly subsidiaries in cities from Beijing to Bangalore.

★ ★ ★

To sharpen our perspective on what's at stake for the United States as this power shift progresses, and how critical India will be in shaping China's rise, one can paint two dramatically different portraits of the world in 2030.

First, picture the worst case, a world divided by a twenty-first-century cold war:

China's insatiable demand for resources has caused it to ally with resource-rich countries throughout the world, corrupting their governments, propping up dictators, and exploiting the local population. China's economic power and lavish infrastructure spending has made its Asian neighbors heavily dependent on Chinese trade and investment and effectively "purchased" their acquiescence to China's regional hegemony. Russia has become a junior partner in a China/Russia axis that confronts American policy at every turn. In part to divert attention from their slowing economies, together they work to undermine "western" principles and to dismantle the post–World War II international order established and maintained by the United States. The Mainland has coerced Taiwan into accepting its domination and future control. The South China Sea and its oil are now Chinese territory. China launches constant, low-level cyberattacks against the United States. India and China have had several military skirmishes in the Himalayas and over control of Tibetan rivers, which China wants to divert to water its increasingly parched northern territory.

In this scenario, India's fear of China has brought it into a close military alignment with the United States, Japan, and Australia, and into closer cooperation with Europe. As these opposing coalitions form, an arms race increases military spending. That escalation diverts much-needed funds from social services, improvements in education, and vital infrastructure projects in the United States, China, and India. While China still trades with the West, it does not open its economy further and it increasingly uses its market clout to favor allies and punish adversaries, all weakening western influence. India, despite its alignment with the West, resists open trade. These new divisions bring the influence of institutions such as World Bank and the United Nations to an all-time low.

To prevent unrest over stagnating wages, the Chinese government becomes more authoritarian and represses dissent. India fails to reform its political system, is still plagued by a byzantine bureaucracy and corruption, and economic growth stalls. Its education system remains third-rate, and millions who might have risen out of poverty are still mired in it. India's and China's immense carbon emissions have led to irreversible climate change.*

Alternatively, imagine an optimistic, best-case scenario:

Goods, services, and people flow fairly openly between China, India, the United States, and Europe, making all of these regions more prosperous. India and China agree to share water resources from Tibet and settle their Himalayan border dispute. China accepts the status quo with Taiwan, leaving its ultimate status for future generations. While India, China, and the United States maintain some of the largest militaries in the world, increased cooperation among them, including sharing responsibility for securing the key sea-lanes in the South China Sea and Indian Ocean, allows them to restrain military spending.

---

*One can imagine several variants of this worst-case scenario: An actual short, hot war between the United States and China could ensue if China forcibly seeks to take the Diaoyu islands from Japan, a U.S. treaty ally. Or suppose that Chinese growth stalls, and President Xi Jinping is overthrown in an internal coup, led by Communist Party leaders unhappy with the vast scale of his anticorruption crackdown. This leads to chaos in China, stagnation in the Chinese economy, and, because many countries like Australia, Korea, the United States, and India are dependent on exports to China, a world economic recession.

As a result, each can devote more funds to shoring up pension systems and improving health care, especially pressing needs in rapidly aging China and in the United States. India invests to improve its education system, vital to equipping its fast-growing young population with job skills. Many millions are lifted out of poverty in both India and China. This new cooperation creates space to reform the UN, World Bank, and World Trade Organization (WTO) to make each more inclusive and effective.

The Chinese government introduces some public accountability and creates institutions that uphold the rule of law. Chinese citizens win cases against the government to fight land grabs, for example, and feel generally more empowered. In India, sweeping reforms clean up graft and make government processes more efficient, leading to strong growth. The United States, India, and China—the world's largest "carbon sinners"—sign substantive agreements to combat global warming and together keep greenhouse gas levels below the tipping point.

★   ★   ★

No one can predict with certainty which future will emerge. The outlier scenarios above demonstrate what could happen if we mismanage—or handle perfectly—these two critical diplomatic relationships. Straight-line predictions are invariably inaccurate, and many countries and factors outside America's control will also shape the giants' paths. As the largest power, however, the United States has a special obligation to seek the right trajectory by getting our relations with *both* Asian giants exactly right. This will require subtle, patient long-term diplomacy, not something democracies such as ours are particularly good at, especially during election season.

To do this, we must understand how both societies operate on more than a superficial level. This book addresses that. The first chapter describes the history that the Chinese and Indians tell themselves: the stories that frame how they see their place in the world and how they approach relations with the West. Chapters 2 and 3 illustrate how each country's political and economic system developed, how it works today, and how this will likely affect the pace and character of change over the coming decades.

Chapters 4 through 9 look at the key internal challenges India and

China face on their way to great power status, and how each is grappling with these issues: from income disparity and corruption to massive demographic upheavals, environmental degradation, and the treatment of women, and how each copes with internal dissent. We want both giants to succeed. If China does not manage these problems well, it could fabricate a foreign crisis to placate its public and shore up the Communist Party's legitimacy. If India fails, it would not have the internal strength to help the West shape and moderate Chinese actions on the world stage. A weak India and China would have less bandwidth to tackle global problems such as climate change and terrorism. While we cannot solve their internal problems, the U.S. government, companies, and citizens can cooperate with India and China to help us all achieve the positive vision of 2030.

Chapters 10 through 12 look at the prominent role India and China are beginning to play on the broader world scene. We are seeing this already with the military buildup in both countries; massive Chinese infrastructure investment in Africa, Latin America, and other resource-rich areas of the world; Indian lobbying for a permanent UN Security Council seat; and both countries' negotiation of regional trade agreements that sometimes exclude the West. The United States can help guide both countries' foray into the world into constructive channels.

★　★　★

Some argue that the international system cannot shift peacefully to accommodate new large powers. I disagree.

We have the power to shape this century. To do so we must help influence China's and India's emergence as great powers. Instead of worrying unduly about China and largely ignoring India, we need to get busy working with both on a world order that suits everyone. We have real differences with China in particular that will make its rise complex, and we do not want China or India to replace us as world leader.

This doesn't require us to ignore our interests, or accept without complaint actions we find unacceptable. It does require us to believe that a prosperous, confident China and India are good for the United States. It requires us to tolerate some diplomatic missteps and accommodate their legitimate concerns, while stating clearly what lines cannot be crossed.

It requires us to treat goodwill as a major diplomatic priority. We must coax each giant, through patient interaction and cooperation, to accept a responsible international role. To extend a world order based on American values, we must bring China and India along rather than alienating one or both.

The phrase "brave new world" has famously been used twice. William Shakespeare coined the expression when his heroine Miranda paints a rosy picture of the future in *The Tempest*, a play that reacted to the discovery of the new world. Aldous Huxley later used the words ironically to describe the dystopian world in his novel *Brave New World,* set in the year 2540. We have the power to choose which perspective we want to pursue and promote. In this context, the word *brave* is crucial. Our leadership must be confident. Our strategy must be subtle. Our diplomacy must be resolute. There is reason to hope that with thoughtful, steady policies by the United States, China, and India, this time the world can peacefully accommodate the ascent of two new great powers.

PART I

★ ★ ★

SETTING
THE SCENE

1 | LONG MEMORIES

FIFTEEN THOUSAND performers crowded onto the vast floor of Beijing's "Bird's Nest" stadium in July 2008. Three thousand young "disciples of Confucius," dressed in flowing black and white robes, danced with scrolls and recited ancient proverbs. With impressive pomp and precision, the four-hour Olympic opening ceremony took spectators on a journey across China's early history: the invention of the compass, gunpowder, paper, and movable type, the traders of the Silk Road, and Zheng He's fourteenth-century sea voyages, which explored the world as far as Africa. There the history abruptly stopped, and the ceremony jumped to modern or cultural topics.

Olympic opening ceremonies say a lot about how a country views itself, or how it wants to be seen. Beijing's 2008 opening was a spectacle with no match. It celebrated China's glorious early achievements. It skipped neatly over the centuries of its domination by western powers, its brutal civil war, and the painful paroxysms of the Mao era, and declared boldly that now the Middle Kingdom is back, in the center of world affairs, where it belongs.

The Chinese have not forgotten more painful aspects of their past, but they keep them mostly private. Over a glass of rice wine in a small group, even senior officials have told me of their own suffering during the terrifying purges of the Cultural Revolution, for example, and explained that this created their whole generation's yearning for political stability above all else. They are unlikely to share this in public.

India's yearly Republic Day ceremony reflects a nation more comfortable with both the splendid and more difficult episodes of its history. On Republic Day, thousands of military personnel parade by to raucous marching bands or ride orange-clad camels. Their traditional regalia recalls both the Hindu Rajputs and Indian colonial-era regiments, although many suffered under colonialism. Colorful, noisy floats depict the diversity of Indian culture and religion. In contrast to the joyous pomp, the prime minister opens the day by laying a wreath for those who lost their lives in India's long struggle for independence. Many onlookers barely hold back tears. For most of India's current leaders, the key memory was the trauma they experienced as children in 1947, when they witnessed the country's independence, forced division, and the mass killings that followed. The day reflects both the victories and defeats of this great nation, and an optimistic view about its future.

★   ★   ★

History is malleable. Every country—including the United States and European nations—reinterprets its history. Many of India's and China's actions on the world stage are framed by what they consider their shameful recent pasts, and their glorious distant history. Both were repressed by outside powers in the nineteenth century, and their nations were born amid chaos in the twentieth. They draw very different conclusions from these similar trajectories.

Many excellent volumes have been written on Chinese and Indian history. Here I will highlight only the history that Chinese and Indians tell themselves: the key events that frame how they see their place and approach relations with the world.

The great religions and philosophies founded in India and China influence their societies and politics to this day. In broad brushstrokes, Indian empires assimilated outside cultures and religions more than their Chinese counterparts, and some Chinese emperors strictly limited their subjects' interactions with the world beyond the Great Wall. Some of this distrust of outsiders still exists in China today. The glories of China's imperial dynasties loom large in China's imagination, especially in contrast to its perceived humiliation at the hands of the Europeans and Japanese in the nineteenth and twentieth centuries. China has some lingering resentment toward the West and is eager to recover its great power status. India, under oppressive British colonial rule for two hundred years, seems less compelled to prove that it can compete with the West.

Both countries struggled in the early twentieth century to create their current regimes—communism under Mao in China, and democracy on the model of Gandhi and Nehru in India. These struggles have left their mark. Gandhi and Nehru's legacy is a pluralist, gentle one, and Gandhi especially is universally revered in India. By contrast, Chinese modernizers would like to forget Mao and the atrocities he committed, yet he retains symbolic power as the man who made China great again. As an Italian journalist once memorably put it, "At the center of China lies a corpse that nobody dares remove." China is now "communist" in name only, so the Party is struggling to find a new unifying narrative and must dust off Confucianism and other homegrown philosophies in order to find a modern way to interpret Mao's long reign.

For China, its history creates a combination of insecurity and bravado. We will see how this plays out later in China's nationalism, its tough stance on the South China Sea, the Himalayan border dispute with India, and countless other diplomatic issues that should be easier to resolve than they are.

India is now more at peace with its past. After independence in 1947, it initially reacted to colonialism by closing its economy to what it perceived as western exploitation. It refused to align with any major power, and instead chose to speak for other downtrodden countries as the leader of the "nonaligned movement." Some of its older diplomats retain a latent distrust of any large power, including the United States. This pendulum is slowly swinging back to the center with a more open economy and a closer partnership with the West.

To better understand India and China as they return to their historic place as great powers, and to persuade both to help bring about the positive scenario for 2030, we must appreciate the lenses through which each sees the world.

★   ★   ★

Once over a twelve-course banquet, an erudite Chinese diplomat told me, "Confucius is making a comeback." It seemed an odd phrase to me at the time, but he was right. After a century of trying to purge Confucius because his legacy was seen as backward-looking and hierarchical, the Chinese Communist Party now seems eager to resurrect him. He had a starring role in the Olympic opening ceremony. Confucius is China's way to emphasize its native philosophy and avoid western ideologies that could undermine the Party.

The life of Confucius, the philosopher and teacher who lived in the sixth century BCE, is shrouded in mystery. Stripping away the myth from his real life is nearly impossible. His sayings have been interpreted and reinterpreted over time to suit the political winds. Confucianism emerged at a time of internal divisions and war in China, and its goal is social harmony and order. Confucius taught that the way to achieve this is through ritual and ethical behavior, and by putting the greater good of the group ahead of individual desires.

Most Chinese are still deeply influenced by Confucian ethics, for example by emphasizing the importance of family and education and feeling great responsibility to care for aging relatives. On the darker side, many argue that Confucius's philosophy emphasizes the superiority of fathers, husbands, and rulers over children, wives, and citizens, who are relegated to subordinate status.

China's leaders have recently made a concerted effort to reintroduce Confucianism outside the family and spiritual sphere, and into politics. After China's revolution, Mao vilified Confucius as a symbol holding China back, so the Communist Party closed or destroyed many shrines to him. This abruptly changed about a decade ago. Many shrines have reopened, and the government added a stop in Confucius's hometown, Qufu, to the high-speed trains that run from Shanghai to Beijing. President Xi and other party leaders make pilgrimages there. Chinese professors of Confucian studies—once not much in demand—are now giving frequent lectures to senior party officials, and many government workers liberally lace their speeches with Confucian quotes.

Why this sudden interest in an ancient philosopher? Confucian emphasis on stability and social harmony helps the modern Communist Party maintain order. Scholar Michael Schuman and others also argue that "having replaced Marxism with capitalism . . . the leaders of modern China have been left scrambling for an alternative governing ideology to legitimize their rule." In the late 1980s, too many of China's young people were drawn to western ideals of democracy and individualism, and this resulted in the Tiananmen Square uprising—the student protests and violent government crackdown on them in 1989. For the Party, western liberal ideals are dangerous, and Confucius is a native substitute for imported ideologies that could threaten their rule.

★   ★   ★

As with Confucianism in China, most Indians are still deeply steeped in the culture of their religion, even if they are not themselves religious. Hinduism, Buddhism, and Islam came at different times to the Indian subcontinent. Each left a potent imprint and affects the current world outlook of its followers. While India's constitution emphasizes religious pluralism and tolerance, the election of Hindu nationalist Narendra Modi as prime minister has inflamed some tensions between Hindus and Muslims and provoked a national debate on the role of religion in Indian public life.

Many scholars consider Hinduism, which developed around 3,500 years ago, the world's oldest religion. Hinduism has many gods, and unlike Islam and Christianity, it does not have a clear founding date, founder, or basic text like the Bible or Koran. It teaches its followers that their behavior in this life has implications for the next (karma), and that the only way to escape the cycle of rebirth is to let go of the ego and merge with the universal soul.

Hinduism is present in the daily lives of 900 million Indians today. Most have shrines to some gods in their homes and make small offerings to them daily. Prime Minister Modi has called Hinduism not a religion, but a "way of life." He, along with millions of other Hindus, performs yoga and breathing exercises every day and speaks regularly to Hindu gurus for advice.

Hindus learn from childhood the stories of the *Ramayana* and the

Mahabharata—epic poems written more than 2,000 years ago whose moral lessons remain relevant. In the late 1980s, a seventy-eight-part Indian television series on the *Ramayana* drew more than 100 million viewers and essentially brought India to a standstill for an hour each week: government meetings were rescheduled and buses stopped as dozens gathered around television sets to witness the gods and demons play out their destinies.

Compared to the rushed individualism and constant striving of the western world, Hindus can seem more relaxed about their place in the universe. The Hindu acceptance of what is—whether it's one's caste or adverse events fate throws one's way—can sometimes seem bizarre to Americans. An American friend doing business in India was once told by an employee that he couldn't finish a critical assignment for the CEO because "the universe just said no."

The founders of independent India were committed to religious tolerance. India's first prime minister, Jawaharlal Nehru, himself was fairly secular and India today is a country of tremendous religious diversity. But in recent decades, Hinduism has become an increasing part of India's public identity especially since the successful election of the openly Hindu party—the Bharatiya Janata Party, or BJP, and its current leader, Prime Minister Narendra Modi.

From a young age, Modi volunteered with the Hindu nationalist group Rashtriya Swayamsevak Sangh (RSS), as did many other BJP leaders. Defenders of the RSS argue that it is a sort of Boy Scout organization for teens and adults that teaches discipline, good values, unity among Hindus of all castes, and Indian patriotism. Yet many secular, liberal Indians distrust Modi's government for being too close to the RSS. To its detractors it looks more like the "Hitler Jugend," as one liberal journalist put it to me. Some RSS members take part in military drills and exercises, and its critics argue that the RSS wants an India that is more openly Hindu and militarized.

The RSS and Modi also played a role in a symbolic issue that has bedeviled Hindu-Muslim relations in India for decades: a conflict over a small house of worship in the town of Ayodhya—a mosque to some, a Hindu temple to others. Some sources say Hindu Lord Rama was born at this site where a mosque was built centuries later. In 1990, BJP leader L. K. Advani marched on Ayodhya with an army of 75,000 Hindu volunteers to tear down the mosque and erect a temple to Lord Rama. Twenty thousand Indian police met the marchers and, after days of fighting, stopped the onslaught. Two years later, however, other hard-line Hindu activists descended on Ayodhya and within a few hours tore down the mosque with hand axes, sticks, and their bare hands, setting off interreligious riots across India.

In 2002, Modi had just been elected chief minister of the state of Gujarat when Muslims on a train in his state murdered fifty-eight Hindu pilgrims returning from Ayodhya. When Modi declared a day of mourning for the slain pilgrims, Hindu fanatics used the opportunity to butcher four thousand Muslims in revenge, while police largely stood by. Several independent inquiries have cleared Modi of all wrongdoing in the riots. Yet the U.S. State Department denied Modi a visa to travel to the United States for a decade due to this incident, which means that most U.S. diplomats don't know him well. After this massacre, Modi kept the RSS on a tight leash in Gujarat. Yet questions about his commitment to religious tolerance remain.

Since Modi became prime minister in 2014, India has had a heated internal debate about the role of Hinduism in public life that is not yet resolved. Hindu nationalist ministers sometimes make outrageous comments that inflame interreligious tensions, such as when a BJP chief minister suggested in late 2015—after a horrid killing of a Muslim man by a Hindu mob for eating beef—that Muslims are only welcome in India if they stop eating cows. Hindu nationalists in Modi's cabinet also advocate for a more muscular and military-focused foreign policy, and a harder line toward China.

While Hinduism is a native religion, Islam came to India peacefully by way of Muslim traders along the Sindi coasts about a thousand years ago. In the sixteenth century, Islam came again, this time through Mughal invaders from the high plains of Kabul, in what is now Afghanistan. Their empire united most of north and central India for several hundred years. Although these Sunni Muslims believed in one god, Allah, and their faith had little in common with the polytheistic Hinduism, the Mughal conquerors mostly coexisted in harmony with other religions.

Indian Islam today is on the whole more moderate than that in the Persian Gulf states or Pakistan. Many of the Muslim traders who plied the Indian coasts were Sufis who integrated with other religions and adopted some of their cultural practices. Many Indian temples and mosques feature both Hindu and Muslim symbols. Pakistan, by contrast, defined itself as a Muslim state, got much aid from conservative Wahhabist groups in Saudi Arabia, and sends many migrants to the Sunni Gulf states. It has grown increasingly conservative since the 1980s. The Indian state, with its fear of Pakistani terrorism, closely watches its own madrassas. India's more than 130 million Muslims are also spread throughout the country, so they are a sizable minority everywhere, and a majority almost nowhere. This encourages people to make coexistence work. India's lively democracy, secular constitution, and welfare schemes to assist poor Muslims also contribute to most Indian Muslims feeling comfortable and proud to be Indian. Violence with Hindus is still infrequent, although it has risen slightly since the Hindu BJP-led government took office.

While most Indians are Hindus or Muslims, there are more than 20 million Christians, a similar number of Sikhs, and almost 10 million Buddhists. Chinese and Indian leaders today are fond of pointing out how Buddhism in particular unites them.

Buddhism was born from the teachings of Prince Gautama Buddha, who lived in northern India in the sixth century BCE. In the centuries after its founding, monks migrated over the Himalayas to spread its influence to Tibet, China, and eventually Japan and much of Southeast Asia.

During his first visit to India in 2014, Chinese president Xi Jinping emphasized these ties: "the relationship between China and India dates back over 2,000 years. Buddhism was born in ancient India, and thrived in ancient China." What Xi diplomatically failed to mention is that this peaceful religion is the source of an insoluble current conflict between

China and India. India has sheltered the Dalai Lama, leader of Tibetan Buddhism, and hundreds of thousands of his followers, since they were attacked and driven out by the Chinese state in 1959. While both India and China avoid griping at each other over this issue in public, it is clearly a thorn in their relationship.

★   ★   ★

Over the centuries, kingdoms in both China and India grew and shrank. For several centuries a dynasty was able to unify large parts of each country, and then a period of war and disunity followed. Both countries have been invaded many times. Kublai Khan rode across the Mongolian plains to conquer and rule central China in the thirteenth century. Muslim invaders swooped down several times from what is now Afghanistan and Pakistan to conquer the relative lowlands of Delhi and central India starting in the tenth century. The Muslim Mughals ruled their great empire from Delhi, and left India and Pakistan some of their most enduring monuments, including the Taj Mahal and the Jama Masjid, Delhi's central mosque.

The two societies reacted differently to invaders, and this helps explain their reactions to outside influences today. Indian culture generally absorbed invaders into a colorful mosaic of religions and cultures. The Muslim leader Akbar the Great, who reigned from 1556 to 1605, studied other religions and surrounded himself with a nobility composed of Indian Rajputs, Hindus, as well as Afghans, Persians, Uzbeks, and Turks, and integrated them into his rule.

The Ming dynasty in China took a different approach. It overthrew Kublai Khan's heirs and united China by riding a wave of public antagonism to foreign rule. It built the Great Wall and controlled any contact its citizens had with the outside world, including by forbidding them to travel. China's leaders were not all such isolationists. The earlier Tang and Song dynasties were more cosmopolitan. Yet in general Indian kingdoms were more accepting of outside influence. When Indians tell me the stories of their civilization, they tell a story of assimilation. As one senior Indian politician explained: "Historically, India has been a fundamentally 'open' society. It has received and absorbed major influences from outside, like Islam and Christianity, and radiated cultural influences, outward." The Chinese tell a different story. It is of their former dominant place at the center of world history.

As historian Jonathan Spence explains, between the fourteenth and seventeenth centuries, the Ming Empire became "the largest and most sophisticated of all the unified realms on earth." With a population of some 120 million it was far larger than all European countries combined.

Under the Ming, China projected its power to its neighbors and beyond. This period produced another hero who is often invoked by Chinese leaders today: the maritime explorer Zheng He. Chinese leaders have recently resurrected him as a symbol of the country's historic influence around the world and of its peaceful, benign foreign policy.

Like Confucius, Zheng He played a starring role in the 2008 Beijing Olympics opening ceremony. Hundreds of sailors dressed in bright blue gracefully maneuvered oars twice their height in a procession celebrating his legacy.

Zheng He led several expeditions by the Chinese fleet to South Asia and, eventually, all the way to East Africa, decades before Columbus reached America. He carried treasures such as porcelain, silks, and musical instruments from China to the world. The Ming emperor wanted Zheng's voyages to dramatize China's role as the most powerful nation on earth, to encourage Southeast Asian nations to pay tribute to the Chinese, and others to establish trade and diplomatic relations.

Centuries later, in the 1930s, both Chinese nationalists and communists proclaimed Zheng a Chinese hero to stoke national pride after a century of humiliation by western powers. In the mid-1980s, Chinese leader Deng Xiaoping began to invoke Zheng to emphasize a slightly different point: he was the flag-bearer of an educated, advanced civilization, equal to the West. Deng also used Zheng as historical proof that diplomatic opening and economic liberalization, which Deng was pursuing at the time, was a wise decision.

The Chinese have continued to glorify Zheng He. In 2005 the government organized a vast exhibition about him in Beijing, which underplayed Zheng's mission to force countries to pay tribute to China and instead emphasized his interest in trade and peaceful relations. In 2009 a television series about his life aired to great audience acclaim. As China's trade with South Asia and Africa has grown, Chinese diplomats in Africa regularly cite his voyages as the start of friendly ties, and as a way to differentiate themselves from the West. China's ambassador to South Africa remarked: "Instead of establishing colonies or engaging in slave trade like western colonists of the time, Zheng He traded goods with local people and introduced the Chinese culture."

After the glories of Zheng He, the Ming dynasty turned inward, preoccupied with defending their land from renewed northern Mongol threats. After a succession of weak Ming emperors, the Qing dynasty took over in 1644. The Qing were also largely uninterested in the outside world, which caused problems when the West showed up at China's door.

In 1793 a British envoy arrived at the Qing court, bearing gifts and a proposal to trade. China then accounted for about a third of the global economy. Europeans and Americans bought many Chinese goods, such as silks, porcelains, and tea, which led to a serious trade deficit and a constant flow of silver to China. The emperor swatted the barbarians, in the form of the British envoy, away. The Chinese do not have "the slightest need of your country's manufactures," he wrote to King George III. So the British returned a few decades later with gunboats to force trade open.

Thus began the "century of humiliation," as China calls it. It casts a long shadow on China's interpretation of its history, and on Chinese self-confidence on the world stage. Many of China's diplomatic actions now stem from a desire never to repeat China's nineteenth-century helplessness at the hands of foreigners. Domination by western powers also intertwined the fates of China and India, sometimes in tragic ways.

In spite of its dominant economic position, by the early nineteenth century, China faced growing internal pressures: there were too many people with not enough agricultural land and industry to absorb their labor, which led to unrest. The Portuguese, Dutch, Spanish, British, and French had arrived to trade and proselytize, but the Chinese largely rebuffed them.

The British began planting opium in large amounts in their Indian colonies as a cash crop, starting in the mid-nineteenth century. Eventually opium accounted for almost 20 percent of British revenues from India. The British sold opium primarily to China, where addiction to the drug skyrocketed. Worried about his citizens, the Chinese emperor wisely outlawed its use. To stop this policy, British warships arrived in 1830 and a decade later conquered the struggling Chinese navy in the first Opium Wars. Under a draconian "peace" treaty, China had to pay reparations to England, five cities were opened to the British for trade, and Hong Kong was ceded to the British. Similar "unequal treaties" with France, the United States, Russia, and Japan followed. Foreigners gradually encroached deeper and deeper into what was previously Chinese territory by forcibly opening new "treaty ports" and later conquering territories, such as Vietnam, Cambodia, Burma, Korea, and Manchuria, which had all previously been part of China or paid tribute to the emperor.

As the Qing dynasty weakened and its economy stalled, there were powerful internal rebellions against the emperor. The British and French preferred to deal with the Qing emperor, rather than the rebels, so they helped to suppress some of these uprisings. Tens of millions of Chinese were killed or displaced in these wars, which lasted twenty-five years. It was a dark period in Chinese history.

The Communist Party continues to emphasize China's ability to overcome this exploitation by foreigners. A vast exhibition at Beijing's National Museum, called China's "Road to Revival," follows the struggles against imperialist oppression. President Xi used the exhibition as a symbolic backdrop for his famous "Chinese Dream" speech in 2012. A 2003 fifty-part television series portrays the Chinese diplomat who signed the treaties as a tragic hero who was forced to capitulate to foreign aggression. Civil society groups have created "Internet memorials" online with patriotic materials about the unequal treaties. The Party encourages these nationalistic reactions. They reflect China's desire to be beholden to no one and its desire for power and respect on the global stage.

The constant reminder about their past shame, and their duty to overcome it, makes Chinese diplomats prickly when discussing topics from democracy in Hong Kong, to who owns certain islands in the South China Sea, and especially China's conflicts with Japan over the Diaoyu islands, which the Japanese call the Senkaku. After Japan's victory over China in a war in 1894–95, Japan forced a number of concessions and established de facto control over the uninhabited rocks of the Diaoyu. China aggressively asserts that they are Chinese in part to rectify this past defeat. One midlevel Chinese military commander told me in 2012: "We are no longer weak. We will risk war with Japan and the United States, but we will get the Diaoyu back."

★   ★   ★

India also suffered at the hands of the West. It has a dark view of its colonial period, yet that has not resulted in the nationalistic and anti-foreign flavor this sometimes takes on in China. Most Indians I speak to are proud of their independent, unruly democracy and its rising status in the world, without the hard-bitten determination of the Chinese to redress past humiliations.

Amitav Ghosh, one of India's most acclaimed novelists, describes the popular view: "Before the British came, India was one of the world's great economies. For 200 years India dwindled and dwindled into almost nothing. Fifty years after they left we have finally begun to reclaim our place in the world." Many in the Indian elite share Ghosh's harsh view of British influence, even those whose offices are housed in the lovely red-stone government buildings in Delhi that the British Raj built.

As in China, internal weakness and fighting between Indian princes contributed to the rise of colonialism in India. Britain initially sought trade: it imported vast amounts of textiles from India, and paid for them in silver, thus draining its own treasury. This made it attractive to conquer the source of the products, rather than paying for them. By the eighteenth century, Britain's East India Company (and in some cases its French counterpart) was adept at playing Indian rulers and merchants off against each other to gain greater control. In the 1750s, for example, the company built fortifications in Calcutta, in Bengal state, intended to keep out the French East India Company. The young, inexperienced Bengali ruler told the British to stop. He also taxed his merchants more to build up his own army. The British allied with the disaffected merchants, who then convinced part of the Bengali army to defect, thus handing the British a

major victory. Although many Indian states fought valiantly and successfully against the British, the British East India Company used variations
of this divide-and-conquer tactic to great effect across India, ultimately
capturing Delhi in 1803.

Initially the East India Company created its own bureaucracy to gov-
ern India, while taking a large portion of Indian tax revenue to pay for the
textiles it was exporting to Europe. Rebellions against British rule were
frequent. In 1857 a massive mutiny of Indian soldiers nearly succeeded
in ousting the company. The British government had to intervene and
crushed the revolt at great expense in men and treasure. After this debacle,
the British Crown pushed the East India Company aside and ruled India
directly until its independence in 1947.

The British kept the trappings of the Mughal and other Indian emperors, even though they were rulers in name only. On the positive side,
they transformed the somewhat flexible legal code into written law and
introduced railways, telegraphs, and the postal system. More harmful was
the favoritism the Brits showed some castes and religions over others to
rule a large continent. They emphasized religious differences and caste
hierarchies in ways that are still felt today. Britain also deforested much
of India's jungle to start coffee and tea plantations. Many leading Indian
economists maintain that this colonial system—which increasingly ex-
ported India's raw resources and reimported manufactured goods from
Britain—led to India's failure to industrialize.

While India suffered from colonialism as much as China, it hasn't felt
the need to "prove itself" on the international stage to overcome this legacy. India has had the opposite reaction. It defines itself as a peace-loving
nation, in contrast to aggressive colonialist powers. When visiting the
United States in 1949, independent India's first prime minister, Jawaharlal
Nehru, made this point beautifully. His country, he said,

> is not fettered by the past, by old enmities. . . . Even against her
> former rulers there is no bitterness left. . . . The main objectives of
> [her] policy are: the pursuit of peace, not through alignment with
> any major power [] but through an independent approach . . . the
> liberation of subject peoples [] and the elimination of want, dis-

ease and ignorance. . . . It is clear that all remaining vestiges of imperialism and colonialism will have to disappear.

India sees itself as a soft power advocate for a more just future. China sees itself as a country resuming its rightful place as the most powerful and influential of nations.

Modern Chinese and Indian leaders refer to their ability to overcome western oppression as a point they have in common, although India is friendly to the United States, while China remains somewhat skeptical. It is telling that Chinese leaders are more likely to make this point. "Historically," said Mao Zedong, when he met Prime Minister Nehru for the first time in 1954, "we Eastern countries have been humiliated by Western countries. . . . Although we have many differences of thought and social system," he continued, "we have one big point in common: that is, we all want to oppose imperialism." At the first meeting between Xi and Modi sixty years later, Xi struck a more optimistic note on the same theme: "I have been especially interested in India's colonial history. . . . Chinese and Indian people have . . . supported each other's efforts for [ ] liberation. . . . India cheered for China during our anti-opium war, and China encouraged India's independence movement."

In the same week that Xi gave this friendly speech about Indian-Chinese unity, Chinese troops crossed the disputed Himalayan border into India, reportedly even trying to build a road there. Chinese incursions like this are becoming more common. Indians are thus increasingly skeptical about China's proclamations of friendship and anti-western unity. Speeches notwithstanding, China's belligerent attitude is driving India closer to the United States.

★   ★   ★

Nearly two hundred of China's best actors, including Chow Yun Fat and Jackie Chan, paraded across the screen in period costumes. In 2009 and 2011, China's propagandists made two epic films—*The Founding of a Republic* and *The Beginning of the Great Revival*—to commemorate the founding of the People's Republic of China. The films begin with the 1911 revolution that toppled the Qing dynasty and continue through the civil war and the glorious rise to power of the Chinese Communist Party. The films portray a soft-filter, idealistic version of twentieth-century Chinese history. Mao Zedong, Communist China's founding father, is a good-looking, idealistic young revolutionary, and a romantic frolicking in the snow with his beloved wife. They feel like Chinese versions of *Dr. Zhivago* meets *Pearl Harbor*.

Government offices and schools bought tickets in bulk and organized viewing trips in the middle of the workday. At the grand conclusion of the second film, with text superimposed on a Tiananmen Square flooded with computer-generated fans of communism, the Party spells out the theme: "Under the leadership of the Communist Party, China has been on a glorious path of ethnic independence, liberation, national wealth, and strength." Audience reaction was mixed. Some students who saw the films cried at the scenes of student and worker protests. Others reacted cynically, commenting on social media that many theaters were empty, or the audiences looked bored.

China has had a turbulent last century. Many of its current leaders were directly involved in the Communist Party's march to power, or are the direct descendants of those who were. The glorious rise of the Communist Party is an ever-present theme in the Party's dialogue, and the Party uses films such as the ones above to try to instill patriotism in the younger generation.

After the Qing dynasty fell in 1911, the early decades of the twentieth century in China were marked by near-constant civil war between the centrist, nationalist Kuomintang Party (KMT), led by Chiang Kai-shek, and the Chinese Communist Party, led by Mao Zedong. During the civil war that began in the 1920s and continued for two decades, the KMT and communists allied briefly but then formed two bitterly warring factions.

By late 1934, Chiang Kai-shek had Mao and his communists cornered. To avoid annihilation, the communists evacuated their tiny stronghold in Jiangxi province and fled six thousand miles, marching for more than a year over icy mountains, with limited food, and at times slept standing up. About 90 percent perished in the snow. Only about eight thousand communists survived the "Long March"—the crucible of China's Communist

Party. Chinese leaders Zhou Enlai and Deng Xiaoping were Long Marchers. Many in today's Chinese elite—including President Xi Jinping and the recently disgraced Bo Xilai—are direct descendants of Mao's closest associates who supported him and survived this darkest hour.

The Long March looms large in the Chinese view of itself, especially for the older generation. President Xi has visited key sites along the route and alludes frequently to the Party's early "glory days." Ordinary Chinese react differently depending on their generation. When an American journalist motorbiked the entire route recently, older Chinese—reflecting the nationalist propaganda of their upbringing—lauded his patriotic spirit. Young people, preoccupied with forging their own future, seemed baffled by his desire to investigate the Long March. One asked him, "Don't you have better things to do with your time?"

In July 1937, the Japanese invaded China, and committed mass atrocities, including the rape, burning, and killing of tens of thousands in Nanjing. Japanese soldiers killed a staggering 14 million Chinese during the war, while fewer than 500,000 Japanese soldiers died in China. The conflict became part of World War II when the United States declared war on Japan in 1941 and actively began to help the Chinese Kuomintang against Japan.

When the war ended in 1945, the Kuomintang fighters were exhausted, and their government weakened by corruption and infighting. Meanwhile the communists had developed bases behind Japanese lines and strengthened their popular support in the countryside. The civil war resumed. On October 1, 1949, despite help from the United States, a drained Chiang Kai-shek and his remaining Kuomintang loyalists fled to Taiwan Island, and Mao Zedong raised the red flag of the People's Republic of China.

Like American stories about the revolution and Declaration of Independence, these epic battles loom large in the story line of the Chinese Communist Party today. In 1991, in an effort to inspire patriotism after the Tiananmen Square massacre, the propagandists went into overdrive. They produced another epic film depicting the civil war as a triumph of the heroic Communist Party against terrible KMT foes. More than one hundred thousand Chinese army soldiers served as extras, and the film portrayed many of China's present leaders, not surprisingly, as dashing, courageous young men.

For decades Chinese history books have taught a biased version of these events. They describe the hardships of the Long March and the courage of the communist rebels in detail. Many books ignore the massive war effort by the United States or the Kuomintang's valiant fight against Japan. One widely used textbook says, misleadingly, that China won Word War II because "the Chinese Communist Party became the core power that united the nation." Most Chinese students finish high school convinced that the Communist Party defeated internal and external foes single-handedly, and that China has only ever fought in self-defense. Public figures reiterate this view. In September 2015, on the seventieth anniversary of the end of World War II, President Xi staged a twelve-thousand-troop parade through the streets of Beijing and in a speech recalled the Chinese Communist Party's defeat of the Japanese aggressors.

Less prominent on Chinese movie screens and school books is the history of China under Mao's leadership from 1949 to 1976. Initially the communists implemented fairly moderate social and economic policies, such as laws to make women more equal, and land reform that gave peasants more rights.

By the early 1950s, however, the Party was emulating the Soviet Union. It nationalized industry and forced peasants to merge their small farms into cooperatives. When the first Five Year Plan to accelerate growth fell short, in 1958 Mao launched an attempt to greatly increase output of farming and industry, called the "Great Leap Forward." It was a disaster. Farm output declined drastically, and an estimated 20 million people in China died in a three-year, catastrophic famine.

As a result of these tragedies, more judicious leaders tried to move Mao aside and implement more realistic economic planning. But Mao Zedong was not easily sidelined. To stage a political comeback, in 1965 he launched a campaign to overcome "capitalist" trends in China. Together with his fearsome allies, known as the Gang of Four, he recruited students to criticize older party members for not being sufficiently communist.

He forced intellectuals and educated youths into manual labor in the countryside. The orgy of political violence that followed—known as the Cultural Revolution —killed between 750,000 and 1.5 million people. It did not subside until the early 1970s. In 1976 Mao died, and after a brief power struggle, economic reformer Deng Xiaoping came to power. He would become the father of China's economic miracle.

Burned into the early memories of many of China's current leaders, these traumatic events have largely disappeared from China's official history. High school history textbooks cover the Great Leap Forward and Cultural Revolution in a few brief and vague sentences. Some students say their teachers explain that these were "mistakes" by Mao, but not serious ones. Information about these events is not hidden—Chinese can access plenty of information online if they are interested—but it is not emphasized. The books also barely mention the Chinese army crackdown on peaceful prodemocracy demonstrators in Tiananmen Square in 1989, and, as we will see later, the government has done much to wipe clean any references to this incident.

Mao remains a strange figure in China—at once a god and a discredited despot. Many well-educated Chinese see him as a deeply flawed figure who nevertheless achieved some great things. Yet he retains a loyal fan club. Lower- and middle-class Chinese in particular revere him. At the extreme are leftist/Maoists who operate scores of websites to celebrate his legacy, with names like "MaoZedongFlag" and "RedChina." For many citizens, Mao is a symbol of days when society was more equal, and people had free, basic social services and were protected from cruel market forces.

Inching through the endless line at Mao's grandiose, columned mausoleum in the center of Tiananmen Square, I was surrounded by Mao fans. Hundreds of thousands of Chinese and foreigners a year visit Mao's corpse to pay their respects. A young woman supporting her grandmother's arm explained that it was the older lady's dying wish to see the great leader, because, as the dutiful granddaughter translated, "He is the father of China. We owe him everything." After an hour, I caught a brief glimpse of the Chairman's embalmed corpse, neat, ashen-faced, and frowning, as it rested uncomfortably under a draped Chinese flag. My elderly neighbor bowed her head in reverence and cried as one might in a church. Her granddaughter seemed less impressed. She quickly took a picture and then continued to WeChat with her friends on her phone.

While many Chinese modernizers would like to forget Mao and his atrocities and move on, his symbolic power remains. With the original Communist Party philosophy that he stood for dead, Mao's symbolism as a man who navigated China back toward the center of world affairs is all that remains.

★   ★   ★

The central character in India's stormy recent history is easier to revere: the great Mahatma Gandhi. The last home of Gandhiji (as Indians call him out of respect) in Delhi is not grandiose. There are no lines, just a scattering of mostly silent visitors. I was blissfully alone inside the cool walls of the great Mahatma's bedroom on a sweltering Tuesday. A white mattress on the floor, a small desk, and his spinning wheel were the only furnishings. Here he met with world leaders and tried in vain to stop the millions of mass murders that his fellow Indians were committing against each other. In this quiet garden, a Hindu fanatic assassinated him for pushing for the peaceful coexistence of all religions. I bowed my head in respect.

The stories of India's great independence leaders, Gandhi, Nehru, and Muhammad Ali Jinnah, the Indian Muslim leader who became the father of Pakistan, are emblematic of India's painful birth as a country. They were moderates. All three were born to middle-class or wealthy families, were very bright, and trained as lawyers in Britain. All three—and their Indian National Congress Party—initially had moderate aims. They merely wanted to reform the British colonial system and make it fair for ordinary Indians.

Calls for independence from Britain, and Jinnah's push to establish Pakistan as a separate country for Indian Muslims, came only after the British repeatedly rebuffed ideas for legitimate political reforms and crushed all dissent. After many Indians fought on behalf of Britain in World War I, Britain failed to give these soldiers enough food and medicine, creating yet more legitimate anger.

Born in 1869, Gandhi was the eldest of the three and the most able to appeal to ordinary Indians. He practiced law for years in South Africa, where the racist apartheid regime led him to develop a strategy of nonviolent protest and boycotts. When he came back to India in 1915, he remained on the periphery of Indian politics for several years but gradually became the face of independence.

In 1919, a British general, who had banned public gatherings, opened fire on and killed four hundred unarmed Indian families, who had merely come to celebrate a fair, in what became known as the Jallianwala Bagh massacre. This and other injustices fueled the independence movement. Gandhi was also adept at mobilizing the public. In 1930 he led a satyagraha (his method of nonviolent civil disobedience) to protest a British tax on salt. Gandhi and his supporters marched 240 miles to the sea and picked up their own salt, to symbolize that salt was free and should not be taxed. Millions read the news reports of the British arresting Gandhi for the peaceful march. Nehru and other independence leaders were also in and out of jail for their political activities during these decades.

The Muslim League also formed during this time. Although Jinnah had been an early Congress Party member, he became convinced the Congress Party of mostly Hindus did not represent the interests of India's Muslim minority. Jinnah gradually concluded that India's Muslims should have independent states in the parts of India where they were the majority population. Gandhi strongly protested, insisting that India's Hindus and Muslims were united by common history and ancestry.

Finally, exhausted from World War II, the British agreed in 1946 to grant India independence as quickly as possible. Despite last-ditch attempts by Gandhi to preserve a unified India (he even offered the presidency to Jinnah, which naturally made Nehru livid), the country was now in virtual civil war, with killings between Muslims and Hindus increasingly common. In April 1947, Nehru reluctantly agreed to an independent Pakistan. Sir Cyril Radcliffe, a well-meaning British bureaucrat who had never been to India, was tasked to make decisions about the two country's borders, using only some outdated maps.

Ten million (!) Hindu and Muslim refugees rushed across the new borders to avoid being caught on the wrong side after partition. No British troops were asked to guard the borders or the refugee trains traveling across them. More than a million people died. A Punjabi journalist described the gruesome scenes he witnessed:

> [A]n empty refugee special steam[ed] into Ferozepur Station. . . . The driver was incoherent with terror, the guard was lying dead. . . . all but two [carriages] were bespattered with blood inside and out; three dead bodies lay in pools of blood. . . . An armed Muslim mob had [] done this neat job of butchery in broad daylight.
>
> There is another sight. . . . A five-mile-long caravan of [twenty thousand] Muslim refugees crawling at a snail's pace into Pakistan. . . . Bullock-carts piled high with pitiful chattels, cattle being driven alongside. Women with babies in their arms . . . all leaving because bands of Hindus and Sikhs . . . had hacked hundreds of Muslims to death and made life impossible for the rest.

At midnight on August 14, 1947, amid terror and bloodshed, independent India and Pakistan were born.

Many films and books describe the fight for independence and horrors of partition, which is the defining trauma in the lives of many of India's current leaders. Many of India's and Pakistan's leaders were born on the "other side" of the border and had to flee as children, or heard gruesome stories from their parents. Former Prime Minister Manmohan Singh and opposition leader L. K. Advani were born in what is now Pakistan. Pakistani dictators Muhammad Zia-ul-Haq and Pervez Musharraf were born in what is now India. The father of Zulfikar Ali Bhutto, one of Pakistan's most revered leaders, was born into a Hindu Rajput family that later adopted Islam.

My old friend and Indian diplomat Raminder Jassal, a Sikh, had to flee from rural Punjab, now in Pakistan, as a small child. He described visiting a bazaar in his former native town decades after partition. This is still an unusual trip for an Indian diplomat because of the countries' fraught relations. When Raminder told the Pakistani Muslim merchants in their humble shops that his family had fled from their town, they pressed their best wares into his hands and refused to be paid. Many ordinary Pakistanis and Indians, like these shopkeepers, would like to put the painful history of the two countries behind them.

Yet the tragedy of partition bedevils India's relations with Pakistan to this day. Gandhi was assassinated in January 1948 because of his perceived sympathies toward India's Muslims. India and Pakistan fought wars over the disputed territory in Kashmir state in 1947, 1965, and 1999. The Kashmir conflict still serves as a justification for Pakistan's support of anti-Indian terrorist groups, as well as for both countries' development of nuclear weapons.

China has been adept at using Pakistan as a strategic hedge against India. In 1950 Pakistan was one of the first countries to recognize Communist China. The partnership gathered momentum after 1962 when China and India fought a brief war over their disputed Himalayan border. After the war, China and Pakistan concluded a trade agreement, settled their territorial disputes, and started building the Karakoram Highway to connect the two countries. Later China also gave military aid and provided key information on nuclear weapons to Pakistani scientists to help them build a bomb. The economic and military ties between China and Pakistan are stronger than ever today, and serve as a way for Pakistan to protect against more powerful India.

In addition to creating a permanent rivalry with Pakistan, the shock of independence fundamentally shaped India's economics and diplomacy. Nehru and his heirs crafted economic policies often in direct opposition to those imposed by the British, including trade barriers to protect its nascent industries, and the elaborate bureaucracy of the "license raj" to keep tight control of its domestic businesses. India is still relatively closed to trade with other nations. This inadvertently shackled the Indian economy for decades, until Finance Minister Manmohan Singh reversed many of them in the 1990s.

After independence, India identified itself as the protector of oppressed and colonized peoples everywhere. Nehru adamantly opposed all alliances with large powers, so India avoided taking sides between the United States and Soviet Union. Instead it became the self-declared leader of the "nonaligned movement." To this day, some of India's diplomats, especially the older ones, are steeped in this tradition. They generally vote against the United States and European nations at the UN and retain a latent distrust of Washington. This is only slowly changing. The younger generation is friendlier to the West due to our many cultural ties and a shared, growing distrust of China.

★   ★   ★

China's reaction to its oppression by outside powers often gives one the feeling that it is trying to reclaim something that is lost and is afraid to give an inch (in the South and East China Sea disputes for example) because it might be seen as weak. This makes it more difficult to establish trust and to integrate it into the existing world order. China's resulting combination of insecurity and bravado also means that the United States doesn't quite take China's words at face value. For example, is China's drive to build infrastructure throughout Asia an altruistic gesture to help its poorer neighbors or a subtle way to reestablish the client states of the Ming era? Only China's leaders know. India is more at peace with its past, but it has only recently come out of the self-imposed distance it created from the West as a reaction to its own colonialist history.

The stories China and India tell themselves about their histories also complicate their relations with each other. Are they partners, struggling to overcome western exploitation and raise their people from poverty? China, and to a lesser extent India, like to use this rhetoric at summit meetings, but neither truly believes it. Are they rivals for dominance in Asia? Neither country would say this openly, and it is also only partially true. Many Chinese leaders do not think of India as powerful enough to be a real rival. India doesn't really want to be a rival to anyone. But Indians worry about China's new assertiveness, from its enormous economic investments in India's region to the Chinese navy's increased interest in the Indian Ocean.

The lessons China and India draw from their own histories, as well as their divergent political and economic systems, which we will explore next, determine much of their behavior today.

2 | THE NATIONS THEY BUILT

W HEN CURRENT Chinese President Xi Jinping was fourteen years old, Red Guards accosted his father. They dragged the old man before a crowd and forced him to declare that he was a horrible person. Then they threw him into prison. The crime: Xi's father, one of the original communist leaders who had followed Mao since the Long March, was now suddenly considered not revolutionary enough.

It was a stunning reversal. Just a few years earlier, the elder Xi had been vice premier and a confidant of Mao. Xi Jinping attended a prestigious school for the children of the elite. Suddenly he was without parents and sent to a village in the countryside to work as a farmer and build dams and roads. As Xi himself explains, he slept on "earth beds," and had no meat in his diet for months at a time. Many teens in this situation would conclude that communism was a dangerous system. Xi begged to join the Communist Youth League and became a lifelong party stalwart.

A few years later, across the Himalayas, India's current prime minister, Narendra Modi, went into hiding to avoid arrest. In 1975 he was a young organizer for the Hindu nationalist organization RSS when the country's prime minister, Indira Gandhi,* suspended India's constitution. She jailed many of her political opponents, including many of Modi's associates.

---

* Despite the name, Indira Gandhi was Jawaharal Nehru's daughter, and not related in any way to the Mahatma Gandhi. By chance, she married a man also named Gandhi.

Disguised as a Sikh with turban, full beard, and sunglasses, Modi continued to distribute banned opposition pamphlets and organize protests. After India's democracy was restored, he ran for political office in his native state, and was ultimately elected prime minister.

In the face of political persecution, these two young leaders responded to these traumatic events very differently. The chaos of China's Cultural Revolution taught Xi and many of his peers to value the stability of the system and economic prosperity above all else, even if it meant sacrificing individual freedoms. Although India's democracy was only two decades old when Indira Gandhi suspended most democratic institutions, it was strong enough to survive. The press defied censorship, police and judiciary refused the government's orders, and opposition parties, including Modi's BJP, banded together to reject authoritarian rule. These divergent reactions explain much about the underlying values in each society that maintain China's and India's political systems today.

★   ★   ★

China and India created dramatically different governments after they cast off the influence of outside powers following World War II. The nature of those systems impacts the likely pace and character of change in each country in the coming decades.

In China's five-thousand-year history there have been no strong, domestically grown ideas about representative government or democracy. There was nothing like the Roman Senate or Magna Carta. Emperors ruled. A strong central government meant the country could prosper and expand. During times of weak leadership, the empire was cut into pieces. So it is not surprising that in China, power is constantly being negotiated: it is not based on the rule of law. The Communist Party is in control, so change happens from the top down. Communist Party leaders debate each other behind the scenes in nontransparent processes. They, along with national ministers, leaders of important provinces, prominent businessmen, entrepreneurs, and senior academics, all have some say in a system that scholar Ken Lieberthal has called "fragmented authoritarianism." Although Party leaders sometimes find it difficult to implement reforms if officials lower down the chain are unwilling, the key official line is harmony. This makes it easier for China to push through difficult internal reforms and to project a unified front, even if that front hides uncomfortable disputes under the surface.

In contrast to China, India has an astonishing diversity of ethnic, religious, geographic, political, and caste affiliations. While the British ruled India with an iron fist, most independence leaders were educated in the political traditions of the West. India's diversity, and its founding fathers' strong belief in political freedoms and democracy, caused Mahatma Gandhi, Jawaharlal Nehru, and their heirs to craft a government with many checks and balances. This led directly to the complex coalition politics and relatively weak central government we see today. Policy change in India often begins through citizens' initiatives, or through its powerful, experimental state governments. Competing factions and the short-term outlook that comes with elected politics makes it more difficult for India to reform and to project a strong image to the world.

To work effectively toward good relations with both India and China, the United States must first appreciate the internal political constraints that often make China's politics difficult to understand, and that hamper India's ability to be more assertive internationally. President Xi Jinping and Prime Minister Modi have personally held key regional and national political posts in their respective governments, so their lives illuminate how each political system developed, and how it operates in practice today.

★　★　★

Xi Jinping is a son of the Chinese Revolution in every way. His career, and that of his father, Xi Zhonghun, reveals how China's communist government was formed, and how it does business now.

Born in 1953 in Beijing, Xi was the third child of Xi Zhonghun. The elder Xi was already China's propaganda minister when his son was born.

As writer Evan Osnos reported in a thoughtful profile on Xi in the *New Yorker*, Xi's father joined the communists as a teenager, and during the Chinese Civil War helped establish a guerrilla base for the Party in northwest Shaanxi Province. At the end of the Long March, this base gave refuge to Mao Zedong and the remnants of his followers. It became the famous Yan'an Soviet, the center of the Chinese Communist Party until it won the revolution in 1949. As a veteran revolutionary, propaganda minister, and, later, vice premier, the elder Xi played an integral role in creating the communist political system.

The new government nominally divided power among three central components: the Communist Party, the formal governmental structure (the "State Council"), and the People's Liberation Army, or PLA. This structure survived the political earthquakes of the Mao era and is still used today.

The Communist Party, or "CCP," supervises all aspects of ideology and gives broad policy direction to the government bureaucracy and the army. The Party has 87 million members, an enormous number, but still less than one-tenth of the Chinese population. Party members are integrated in every institution from government ministries to private businesses. At the bottom, Party membership feels more like belonging to a professional networking organization. Some entrepreneurs have told me they joined only because Party members get easier access to bank loans and contracts with large enterprises, not because they share the ideology. Local Party chapters meet only about once a month, and discuss social outings more often than they study the new government edicts. For its top leaders, however, the Party dominates every aspect of their lives and tends to isolate them from the public. Security guards and staff surround them. It sometimes confuses American businessmen that the Party secretary (head of the Communist Party) in each province is the person who has the final sign-off on all key decisions, rather than the head of the state government or mayor.

The Party leadership operates as a pyramid. Near the top sits a Central Committee of about two hundred members, which includes some provincial governors, regional Party secretaries, military leaders, ministers in the State Council, as well as the leaders of state-owned enterprises, educational institutions, and organizations such as the Communist Youth League. People are promoted to this elite group based on their Party loyalty and how well they performed in lower-level roles. The Central Committee meets in person once a year in the fall at a Plenum, where major policy decisions are announced.

At one Plenum every five years the Central Committee elects from among its members a twenty-five-person Politburo. From the Politburo it chooses an elite seven-member Standing Committee, and from that a general secretary, who serves as the Party's top leader and China's president, currently Xi Jinping. The Politburo Standing Committee is the key entity that rules China. It makes the final decisions on all important policy issues.

While the Standing Committee and senior Party leaders shape China's broad policies, the State Council leads the government bureaucracy, including all the different ministries, and implements these policies. Although there is no western parallel, it serves as a de facto cabinet. The premier—currently Li Keqiang—heads this bureaucracy. The State Council's most senior members, the vice premiers, are simultaneously members of the twenty-five-person Politburo. These overlapping positions are confusing, but they serve an important purpose: they ensure that all leaders of the bureaucracy are loyal to the Party and aligned on major policies.

Xi Jinping's father was a key official in this State Council structure soon after it was formed. When Xi Jinping was five, his father was promoted to vice premier and worked under Zhou Enlai directing the State Council's lawmaking and policy research functions.

In 1954, a year after Xi Jinping's birth, the new regime created a National People's Congress—the NPC. It started as, and still is, a legislature in name only, and does not really serve as a check on the Party's power. Elections are dull: voters usually only have one choice. During a brief thaw in the 1980s, my Chinese colleagues tell me, there were some contested local elections and real political engagement, but the Party put a stop to this after Tiananmen Square. The NPC's nearly three thousand members come from all regions, and include a large delegation of military leaders and successful businessmen. Pony Ma, CEO of Tencent, is a member. The NPC meets once a year in March to sanction decisions already made by the Standing Committee. A smaller subgroup of the NPC meets more often and has real input into the content of laws. A law is only put to a vote once the NPC and other parts of the government reach a rough consensus with the government; thus the National People's Congress has never actually voted down a law that the Party put in front of it.

★ ★ ★

Xi Jinping grew up as part of the privileged Communist Party leadership group. As a vice premier, his father lived in the relatively plush (by Chinese communist standards) Zhongnanhai leadership compound. While his father was in favor with Mao, young Xi Jinping enjoyed all the benefits that came with being the son of a prominent revolutionary. Evan Osnos reports that Xi attended a prestigious school that was nicknamed the *lingxiu yaolan*—the "cradle of leaders." He adds that "the students formed a small, close-knit élite; they lived in the same compounds, summered at the same retreats, and shared a sense of noblesse oblige."

Without elections or other checks on the power of the Party and its chairman, Mao Zedong, high-level officials were subject to Mao's whims. Politically expedient purges were frequent. Xi's father, a loyal communist since he was fifteen years old, was purged in 1962, merely for saying positive things about a book published by another famous communist who had fallen out of favor. Mao saw even this minor expression of independent thought as potentially subversive. The elder Xi was demoted to deputy manager of a tractor factory in Luoyang—far from the center of power in Beijing. Xi's mother was forced to do hard labor on a farm.

The elder Xi had not yet been rehabilitated when the fever of the Cultural Revolution rocked the country in 1966. Osnos reports that Xi Jinping continued on at school and was too young to join the Red Guards, as many of his schoolmates did, and "did not fit cleanly into the role of either aggressor or victim." In January 1967, a group of Red Guards denounced Xi's father, and he was later imprisoned in a military base for years. Xi Jinping's elite birth had become a liability. Xi later described the period—as many Chinese do—as "dystopian collapse of control."

Like most educated, elite children of that era, in 1968 Xi Jinping was "sent down" to the countryside as part of Mao's massive reeducation campaign. There he worked on road construction near the symbolic Yan'an area where his father had helped shelter the Long Marchers. Xi was shocked at how hard he had to work. Since Xi became president, Chinese state media has mythologized this period in his life, with article after article extolling him as a man of the people for his hard manual labor and the fact that he lived with peasants in a cave.

Several reformist Chinese friends chuckle at how the media lionizes Xi for his time in the countryside. They explain that virtually every well-educated teenager was "sent down" and had a similar experience: they worked malaria-infested rice paddies, melted steel, or harvested endless grain under a burning sun. Often, like Xi, they were separated from their parents, who were in political detention, and did not see them for years.

As the Cultural Revolution ebbed, despite the terrible injustice the regime had committed toward his parents, Xi Jinping remained a true believer. He enrolled at prestigious Tsinghua University and repeatedly tried to join the Communist Party Youth League. They finally accepted him after several rejections in 1974, a year before his father was freed.

Xi—and most other current Chinese leaders—experienced firsthand the brutal power politics of the Chinese communist system. His generation's longing for stability and consistent decision making stems from their personal experiences. After the terrifying chaos of the Mao era showed that it was impossible to rule a country based on the whims of one man, China encouraged the idea of "collective leadership." Since Deng Xiaoping's more moderate leadership began in the late 1970s, the men who sit on the Politburo Standing Committee have formed a collective leading team in which each man has a numerical rank, currently from one to seven. Each is responsible for a specific portfolio—such as the economy, propaganda, military, anticorruption and so on—but they make major decisions by consensus. This collective leadership approach is designed to guard against erratic swings in policy, and it has largely worked for four decades.

In the 1970s, Xi Jinping was still far from the lofty heights of the Standing Committee. After finishing university in 1979, he became an aide to Geng Biao, a senior defense official in the PLA who was an old revolution-era friend of his father.

While Xi was able to jump directly into a plush government job because of his family connections, most young Chinese who want to enter the civil service today have to take a very difficult, competitive exam. The exam is a faint echo of China's ancient imperial system. Of the nearly one million applicants, only a tiny percentage receives job offers—3 percent in 2014. Government jobs were long sought after because they come with employment for life, a good pension, and an urban residence permit called *hukou* (which means the official's kids can go to better urban schools, have decent health care, and receive other services). Many Chinese derisively call it the "golden rice bowl." For the first time in years, however, in both 2014 and 2015 the number of applicants for the civil service fell steadily, almost certainly because the government's anticorruption campaign is making these jobs less attractive and more potentially perilous.

Xi's decision to work for the People's Liberation Army (PLA) was a somewhat unusual step for a well-connected young Party member. It has become a key strength for him now. As a young military aide, Xi learned the ways of the PLA and made valuable contacts. This is a key strength that other recent Chinese leaders, like former President Hu Jintao, lacked. The PLA remains one of China's most powerful and opaque institutions. It currently has 2.2 million active personnel and 510,000 reservists.

The PLA reports to a twelve-person Central Military Commission (CMC). Xi Jinping chairs this commission but it is otherwise led by top military brass. Xi is the only civilian with direct control over the military, which gives him considerable influence over China's hard power. As in everything political in China, party ties and loyalty are strong throughout the armed forces. Two senior military leaders are also members of the Politburo. Most rank-and-file PLA members belong to the Communist Party. The PLA is not a national army, but rather an armed wing of the Communist Party.

It is culturally quite separate from the rest of the Party and government. Many military leaders come from multiple generations of military service. They are a cohesive group, often with their own living compounds, schools, and retreats, and don't interact much with China's civilian technocrats. No part of the government bureaucracy scrutinizes the military budget, and from time to time questions arise about how much control China's civilian government has over the military. Since becoming president in 2012, Xi Jinping has moved rapidly to reform the military and fix this, and it is fairly certain that the PLA obeys his orders, as we will see later.

After his three-year stint in the military, Xi Jinping sought administrative experience in China's outer provinces, another step that was considered unusual at the time. He first became deputy to the Party boss in an inconsequential rural country in Hebei. After honing his skills there, he was promoted to other regions, and in 2002 became party secretary of Zhejiang, an economically vibrant southern province. There he helped promote private business, followed instructions from the Party bosses in Beijing, and avoided controversy.

Unlike in federalist United States or India, where many policies are created at the regional level, the role of provincial and local governments in China is to implement policies created in Beijing. The Party sets the directives. Previously this was pretty simple: grow the economy at all costs. Now provincial leaders must also make sure that growth is inclusive and sustainable, for example by reducing carbon emissions. Provincial officials have broad discretion in how to meet these targets. Xi was well aware of this, and by most accounts scrupulously met his growth targets.

In a one-party state, it is not surprising that in each region or city the Communist Party secretary is the most important person. Unlike the mayor, who reports to the State Council and its bureaucracy, the local party secretary reports directly to the Politburo, and the party secretaries of important regions are often Politburo members themselves.

The Party ensures that provincial leaders are loyal to Beijing partly by rotating leaders and generally not permitting anyone to rule in his home province. As Xi knew, serving loyally in the provinces is a stepping-stone to greater things. About three-quarters of recent Politburo members have served as provincial chiefs and this number is increasing.

Some party secretaries wield enormous personal power and oversee subregions larger than most European countries. A classic example of this is Bo Xilai before his fall from power in the region of Chongqing. Chongqing, small by Chinese standards, has almost 30 million people and a GDP of $235 billion a year, similar to that of Portugal, with an astounding

11 percent annual economic growth rate. As long as Bo loyally implemented Beijing's orders, he was a star. But when he veered from the Party script and tried to amass his own power base after 2007 with populist projects such as providing public housing and convening public gatherings to sing revolutionary songs, the Party realized that he could threaten them directly and ousted him. While Bo was convicted of bribery and embezzlement (hardly unheard-of in the Communist Party), the state-owned news service Xinhua summed up the real reason for his removal: "[The Party] will not tolerate defiance of discipline . . . [or] allowing Party members to *go their separate ways and do what they want*." Bo was handsome, ambitious, articulate, and building a personal following instead of toeing the Party line. In China, this is a jailing offense.

Xi Jinping was more politically adept than Bo. In 2007 he was sent to Shanghai to take over as party secretary, the most powerful office in that region. There a corruption scandal had implicated associates of Jiang Zemin, the powerful former president, who served from 1989 to 2002. As Osnos reports, it gave Xi an opportunity to show his political skills. He reassured officials that there would not be a large-scale purge and thus raised morale, but also projected toughness on corruption to the public, all without alienating Jiang. Xi also modestly rejected his official villa and instead made it a retirement home for PLA veterans.

As a reward for Xi's excellent work in Zhejiang and Shanghai, in 2007 he was "elected" to the inner sanctum of Chinese politics, the seven-member (then nine-member) Politburo Standing Committee. No one knows exactly how or why Xi or his colleagues were chosen, since the Party carefully keeps the deliberations secret.

Members are not actually "elected." Instead the outgoing Standing Committee helps select them, and retired senior leaders have enormous influence. For example, Deng Xiaoping personally chose Jiang Zemin to take over the position of party general secretary in 1989, and according to scholars, Jiang played a major role in shaping the current Standing Committee before it was chosen in 2012.

Much of the last-minute haggling for these coveted spots happens at the Communist Party "summer camp" at Beidaihe. Several decades ago, most senior Party leaders lived in the same elite compounds in Beijing in neighboring apartments, as Xi's family did, and so the leadership and their families interacted all the time. This is less the case now. As the children of senior leaders made money, they moved into better apartments.

One Mao-era tradition that remains, however, is that each summer the current Politburo members descend on Beidaihe, a seaside town of gravelly beaches and cypress groves about 180 miles from Beijing. Each Politburo member has his own villa facing the sea. In the old days, Mao (who loved to swim) and Zhou Enlai were often seen in the sea, or eating at restaurants in town. These days leaders remain secluded. Their personal gardeners and cleaners travel with them so they don't mingle with the locals. Leaders use the beach time to debate important policies in private ahead of the formal Party Plenum in the fall. Most observers assume that Party leaders discussed Xi's elevation to the Standing Committee there in 2007, and the decision to make him general secretary in 2012.

The secret debate about who will join the Standing Committee or become China's president often reveals the divisions between China's various political factions.

As an authoritarian, one-party state, China of course has no formal political parties. Yet China scholars such as Cheng Li at the Brookings Institution and Alice Miller at Stanford University, who have studied generations of Chinese leaders, draw distinctions between various factions. Alice Miller argues that in the 1950s and '60s, Mao so dominated China that any dissenters were immediately purged (as happened to Xi's father for liking a contentious book). During the Cultural Revolution, there was a clear division between hard-line Maoists and moderate reformers like Deng Xiaoping. In the 1990s, the first generation of heavyweight revolutionary veterans, who had dominated politics until then, retired from politics. More nuanced factional politics began to evolve.

Rather than being distinct "parties" with differing policies, it is easier to understand them as a series of patron-client chains, which are the key building blocks of Chinese politics. In a system with no elections or parties, loyalty and trust come from doing reciprocal favors over long periods of time. These chains of loyal bureaucrats and Party members eventually form a faction with similar views. Xi's anticorruption campaign is now straining this system as some people within almost every patronage group—and some entire chains—are being investigated.

The most prominent alliance is the "Shanghai gang," led by Jiang Zemin and his followers. Confusingly, some members of it—and others not from Shanghai—are also sometimes referred to as the "princeling" faction, because several of its members are children of former high-ranking officials. Xi Jinping leads this faction, and five other current Standing Committee members are also considered princelings.

Xi and many other princelings think of themselves as the true heirs of the Communist Party, who must save and reform it before it loses its legitimacy. Xi's crackdown on corruption and fancy banquets is designed to purify the Party and improve its image for ordinary Chinese. The astonishingly broad national security law Xi endorsed, which took effect in July 2015, also shows his desire to shore up the Party. It defines "security" as everything from military security to oddly broad things like protecting China from internal protests; ecological, cultural, and religious security; and "financial risk prevention." One Chinese dissident told me that the law reflects the Party's desire to aggregate as much power as possible at the center, because the "princelings are paranoid that the Party's time is ending."

The "Communist Youth League" or "populist" faction is the other prominent force in politics. It is associated with Hu Jintao, who led China from 2002 through 2012. Unlike Xi, Hu did not come from a prominent revolutionary family. His father ran a tea shop and he worked his way up by his technocratic skills. Hu's premier, Wen Jiabao, was the son of a teacher. Hu relied on and promoted his network of loyalists from his time leading the Communist Youth League in the 1980s. Li Keqiang, China's current premier (and the country's number two), is the only Hu protégé currently on the Standing Committee.

Scholar Cheng Li argues that the "princeling" coalition tends to represent the interests of China's entrepreneurs and emerging middle class. The "populists" often voice the concerns of vulnerable social groups, such as farmers, migrant workers, and the urban poor. Osnos reports that in private, some princelings refer to former President Hu Jintao and Premier Wen Jiabao disparagingly as *huoji,* or "hired hands." In other words, not true stewards of the Communist Party's legacy. When they see Xi, by contrast, Chinese observers are apt to mention his *guizuqi*, or "air of nobility."

Despite these labels, it is sometimes difficult to determine which faction will promote which policies (unlike in the United States, where you could generalize that Republicans are usually more pro–national security and Democrats more pro–social policies). Factions are more useful for determining the balance of power in the top leadership and, as a result, which lower-level "client" of the top Party bosses is sufficiently in favor to get things done.

With his flawless revolutionary pedigree and a talent for courting the right people, dodging controversy, and making good policy choices, Xi Jinping rose to the top of China's leadership structure. By most accounts he is the most powerful leader since Deng Xiaoping in the 1980s.

Yet Xi is not quite as powerful as he sometimes appears from the outside. The seven-member Standing Committee—while less a "rule by committee" than it was during Hu Jintao's years in power—constrains Xi's authority somewhat. According to one source, Xi has a healthy ego, and once told his Standing Committee colleagues "you all work for me."

The Standing Committee's operating procedures are shrouded in mystery. Insiders say that its members meet several times a week. Xi comes to meetings well prepared. Senior leaders speak first. Consensus is the goal, but if that is not possible, the majority decides. Normally, serious differences in opinion are worked out behind the scenes before the meeting, to avoid anyone losing face. Disagreements stay private.

Most Chinese jaws dropped when, after the 1989 Tiananmen Square crackdown, policy differences broke into the open. It became public that a general who defied the order to place Beijing under martial law was sent to prison for five years. Communist Party General Secretary Zhao Ziyang openly pushed for leniency and government reform in response to the massive student protests. He was placed under house arrest. Hard-liners argued that permitting free expression could result in chaos like the Cultural Revolution. China's leaders are careful not to repeat any such public disagreement today.

China watchers assume that Xi is a dominant influence in the Standing

Committee, but even he has to compromise on some policies. To make this point, a Chinese government official whispered to me: "If Xi were so all powerful, he wouldn't have had to visit all the PLA regiments and ask them to declare their loyalty to the Communist Party—they would already be loyal." Others speculate that political rivals have tried to kill Xi and that he wears a bulletproof vest because his anticorruption campaign has created so many enemies among the Party's elite. No one knows the truth.

To enable the government bureaucracy and the Party leaders to work together in a cohesive way, China has since the late 1950s used "Leading Groups." While not listed in the government's organizational chart, these groups are the key way the Chinese government creates new policies. Some groups are permanent (like the current ones on foreign policy or on the economy) and others are used for specific issues and then disbanded. The most infamous of these was the "Cultural Revolution Small Group," which led to the insanity of the Cultural Revolution and from 1966 to 1967 nearly displaced the Standing Committee itself in importance.

Leading Groups have been less exciting, and less divisive, since then. They usually consist of several Standing Committee members to give general oversight, other vice premiers, and the relevant government ministers for that issue. Xi is particularly fond of Leading Groups and has created one for everything under the sun, from economic policy to the Internet to foreign policy. To keep a tight rein on his fellow politicians, he personally chairs all the most important groups himself. A small general office, generally led by an excellent thinker who is a close personal ally of President Xi, does the background policy work and presents it to the Leading Group for decision.

Using these groups, Xi has amassed unprecedented power over China's national security and foreign policy in particular. Unlike the United States or India, where a national security council brings ideas from the foreign ministry, military, and others to the head of state, who then decides a course of action, China has several groups that deal with foreign policy matters. The National Security Commission, led by Xi, oversees China's foreign and domestic security. The Leading Group on Foreign Affairs deals with diplomacy, and several others handle economic diplomacy and trade. Xi chairs all of them, so he is the only central power that ultimately makes these decisions. He is a princeling with a broad mandate.

The recent pension reform is a perfect example of how policies are made in this autocratic, Leading Group–based system. While Xi is quite powerful, and there is no division of powers in the American sense, Chinese leaders have to take into account many opinions when they craft new policies. The government announced that as of October 2015, China's 40 million government workers have to pay into their own pensions, or else they will eventually bankrupt the system. This difficult reform took more than a year of preparation to achieve.

Liu He, a childhood friend of Xi Jinping who has become his closest economic advisor, leads the general office of the Leading Group for Financial and Economic Affairs. His team, or the general office of whichever Leading Group is in charge, sketches an idea of the policy change they want. The general office then asks many people for input: business leaders, other ministries, and prestigious academics. The general office then comes up with a proposal. The Leading Group discusses the proposal, tweaks it, and then decides by consensus whether it should move forward. At its annual spring meeting, the National People's Congress (NPC) then signs off on it.

Although there is no formal "lobbying" in the American sense, many people with a stake in the outcome are able to have their say, as long as they do so in a way the government approves. Recently the government has begun to publish proposed legislation on the Internet, so anyone can comment on it—although this may be more a way to pulse public views rather than take them into account.

Sometimes, when one faction of government wants a particular reform, it plants comments in the media or at key business forums to make its argument. The Yabuli Forum (or China Entrepreneurs Forum) was one such event. The forum is China's answer to the World Economic Forum in Davos, Switzerland. Here Chinese billionaires and economists mingle with government officials at a chic ski resort in northern China.

At the 2013 forum, something strange happened. Instead of the typical colorless speeches, entrepreneur after entrepreneur argued that China needs better rule of law and property protection. They spoke out force-fully, with some comments blunt enough to make one fear for the speak-er's safety. One prominent economist said: "We all remember how during the Cultural Revolution there were no laws and this led to great suffering. Yet in China today laws are devised for the benefit of monopolies and go contrary to nature. And that makes them bad laws." As the billionaires spoke, the audience tapped their mobile phones and rolled the comments out to the rest of the country over China's ubiquitous Sina Weibo social media service.

As a result some rule of law and property protections were enshrined in Fourth Plenum reforms a year later.* Was Premier Li Keqiang, who strongly believes in these reforms, behind these comments? Did the gov-ernment plant them? No one knows for sure. The comments were helpful to what Li and his faction wanted to do—and they helped them make the internal case for reform.

Of course this type of outspokenness is only possible if powerful Party leaders sanction it. Other criticisms are firmly stamped out. Soon after the Yabuli event, several prominent entrepreneurs used their blogs to urge other reforms the government is also pushing—such as environmental protection and anticorruption. They were made to regret it. Pan Shiyi, a real estate mogul, had to publicly praise new rules prohibiting spreading rumors online, entrepreneur Wang Gongquan disappeared for more than a year, and angel investor Charles Xue was detained for seven months after criticizing the government on his blog. This is a government that wants to firmly control its narrative.

The chorus for more "rule of law" is not coming just from comments planted at a big business event. Across China, people are demanding more rules: rules that apply to everyone, regardless of their personal power. As one Chinese diplomat told me, "In Beijing you can park anywhere, how-ever you want. No clear rules tell you what to do—everything is based on informal systems. This means some people get away with too much."

---

* It is important to remember that rule of law—*fazhi* in Chinese—has a different meaning in China than in the United States. Instead of creating free speech and other individual liberties, these rule-of-law reforms are intended to strengthen control over the Party and state so that the same rules apply to all, and individual officials cannot run amok.

Ordinary Chinese are clamoring for transparent laws that determine who owns the land, who has to pay for environmental cleanups, and who is entitled to social benefits. Most of my Chinese friends aren't looking for democracy, just fair and transparent governance. Xi Jinping and his fellow princelings have much work to do.

★　★　★

Narendra Modi, India's powerful prime minister, is no princeling. In contrast to Xi Jinping, he had modest beginnings, which he loves to emphasize. He also has not had a "typical" rise to the top of the Indian political ladder. In a country of political dynasties like the Nehru-Gandhi clan, where the left-leaning Indian National Congress Party largely dominated national politics for seven decades, the business-friendly son of a tea seller from the center-right BJP was an unlikely choice for prime minister. Yet his story helps us understand how India's unruly 1.3-billion-person democracy works.

As in America's democracy, it is sometimes difficult for Indian leaders to push through difficult reforms. Infighting between political parties, politicians focused on short-term election wins instead of long-term solutions, and the fact that many key policies, such as education, policing, and some economic issues, are determined by India's states, all make the Indian government a slow-moving beast. Modi has navigated most aspects of this complex Indian political system in his career.

Like Xi in China, Narendra Modi is the first Indian leader who was born after the founding of the country. Born in 1950 to a family of grocers from one of India's lower castes, as a child he helped his father sell tea in a railway station.

Modi was born just as India's new, democratic constitution went into effect, after three years of riots, food shortages, and massive refugee resettlement. The new government of Prime Minister Nehru, naturally concerned with stability, put in place a system of checks and balances that has lasted nearly seven decades, an impressive feat in a country with six major religions and hundreds of different languages.

After considering the American, Swiss, and other models of democratic government, India's constitutional assembly decided largely to follow the British model. They created a powerful lower house of parliament, the Lok Sabha, whose members are directly elected. All Indian adults can vote, including women and India's "untouchables"—the lowest caste, which was traditionally discriminated against. India's upper house of Parliament, the Rajya Sabha, is modeled on the House of Lords. But members are not appointed; rather India's state legislatures elect them. The Rajya Sabha is designed to check the lower house and sometimes stops legislation that is unfavorable for India's states. It has recently done just that with two of Modi's signature reforms, the Land Acquisition Bill and the Goods and Services Tax. To add further checks and balances, India's founders also ensured that the country's courts would be fiercely independent (if sometimes painfully slow) and that the army would remain under strong civilian control.

As in the United Kingdom, India's prime minister is not directly elected. Instead, the leader of the largest party in the Lok Sabha becomes the prime minister and creates a coalition if his party alone does not have a majority. For the first two decades of Modi's life, from 1947 to 1964, Jawaharlal Nehru served as India's prime minister.

While India has a raucous, lively democracy, at the national level the Congress Party of Gandhi and Nehru has dominated politics. Nehru provided much-needed stability after the violence of independence and partition from Pakistan. His Congress Party's moderate socialism appealed to most Indians. Congress won five overwhelming election victories in a row before 1977. Nehru also cultivated state officials and India's big business families. Two years after Nehru's death, in 1966, his daughter, Indira Gandhi, became Congress Party leader and prime minister. After Indira was assassinated in 1984, first her son Rajiv Gandhi and then her daughter-in-law Sonia Gandhi have run the Congress Party empire. Rajiv and Sonia's son Rahul led the party in the 2014 elections. Politics is a family business.

Some critics argue that the sole remaining organizing principle of the Congress Party is to be sycophants to the Nehru-Gandhi dynasty. Party officials often vie for "Madam Sonia's" approval for even the most mundane projects. In my own meetings with Prime Minister Singh, his top economic advisor, Montek Singh Ahluwalia, and others in the last few years of Congress rule, it seemed that these trained technocrats were pushing business-friendly economic reforms that were somewhat out of step with the Gandhi party hierarchy. Sonia Gandhi was focused mainly on her responsibility to protect her base of rural and poor citizens, both out of conviction and to win the next election. Internal party infighting stalled many of India's much-needed reforms.

If the Congress Party is populist and secular, the Bharatiya Janata Party (the "Indian People's Party," or BJP), India's other major national party, is free-market leaning and Hindu. The BJP has its roots in the Hindu nationalist movement going back to the 1950s. Officially established in 1980, the party has shifted to the right over time, sometimes supporting Hindu nationalist causes. Today's BJP, however, wants to be known for being business friendly and advocating good governance. The BJP proudly announced recently that it has surpassed the Communist Party of China and is the world's largest political organization, with a whopping 88 million members.

Narendra Modi was drawn to the BJP's Hindu nationalist message when he was only eight years old. He joined the RSS, a volunteer, right-wing Hindu organization, and began attending its local training sessions. There he met several older politicians who helped found the BJP Party in Gujarat and served as political mentors to the ambitious Modi.

Engaged while still a child to a local girl, Modi rejected the arranged marriage when he graduated from high school in 1967. His family was mortified at this decision, so he left home to wander across northern India for two years, visiting the ashrams established by one of India's foremost Hindu gurus, Swami Vivekananda, whose philosophy influences Modi to this day. Modi was rejected from various ashrams for not having a college degree, which was a standard requirement at the time, and so in 1970 he returned home to Ahmedabad, the capital of Gujarat, and worked in his uncle's canteen. At the same time he completed a distance-learning degree from Delhi University in political science, which contributed to his strong later advocacy for online learning.

Modi's hardscrabble beginnings are a world away from those of the patrician Rajiv Gandhi, Modi's contemporary in the Nehru-Gandhi clan. During Rajiv's youth in a leafy Delhi mansion, his grandfather and then mother were prime ministers. He attended the best private schools in India and then studied at Cambridge.

In the 1970s, Modi left his uncle's canteen and became a full-time organizer for the RSS. In 1975 there was a political crisis in India when the Supreme Court ruled that Prime Minister Indira Gandhi should lose her parliamentary seat (and her prime ministership) due to election fraud. Gandhi suspended the constitution and ruled by emergency decree until 1977, nearly undermining India's democracy. She banned opposition groups like the RSS and jailed many political opponents, including Arun Jaitley and Rajnath Singh, who now serve as senior ministers in Modi's government.

Modi went into hiding but continued organizing for the RSS.

A decade later, he entered elected politics as organizing secretary of the BJP in Gujarat. He later helped organize BJP leader L. K. Advani's ill-fated march on the Ayodhya mosque in 1990. This cynical anti-Muslim move helped the BJP score some electoral successes, so that by 1991 they had more than one hundred seats in the Lok Sabha and took power in four states. The party had broad support among members of the higher Hindu castes and in northern India. In 1998, Modi helped his party win its first national election.

As a reward for his loyal and impressive service, the BJP made Modi its candidate for chief minister (similar to a governor in the United States) of Gujarat state in late 2001. A chief minister of a fast-growing state in India is a powerful man. Unlike in China, where provincial officials report directly to the Communist Party apparatus in Beijing, in democratic India a politician becomes chief minister when his or her party wins a majority of the state's legislative assembly seats. So even if the Congress Party controls the central government in Delhi, powerful regional political parties and individual leaders call the shots in many of India's twenty-nine states.

India's constitution also reserves many important powers for the states. While the central government handles defense, foreign affairs, the currency, and hundreds of lesser items, the states are responsible for administering justice, the police, public health and sanitation, education, the distribution of electricity, and many other functions. Key policies such as economic and social planning are shared responsibilities of the center and the states. This independence allows India's states to manage their own economies and try independently to attract foreign investment.

Some states—including Modi's Gujarat, Andhra Pradesh under Chief Minister Naidu, and Tamil Nadu under Chief Minister Jayalalithaa—were spectacularly successful at this. They created business-friendly regulations, worked hard to attract global investment in information technology and manufacturing, and improved their infrastructure and educational systems. (They also started with a better baseline than some of the populous, agrarian, desperately poor states in India's north.) These star performers averaged over 10 percent annual growth between 2005 and 2012. Others, such as Chief Minister Nitish Kumar in Bihar, made important reforms in some of India's most desperately poor areas.

As chief minister, Modi proudly told visiting reporters and international businessmen that Gujarat was "open for business." He pushed militantly to get steady water, electricity, and Internet connectivity to all businesses in the state, and then courted Indian and foreign companies for investment. His annual "Vibrant Gujarat" business confab became a cultlike event—part political rally, part business meeting, and part Modi fan club. CEO after CEO took the stage to praise Modi's policies, while committing to invest even more in the state.

While Modi stole much of the limelight, other chief ministers also led valiant experiments to improve the lot of their people. In 2006, former chief minister Naidu of Andhra Pradesh told us proudly that he prioritized roads, airports, biotech, governance, and above all, excellent education. While Andhra Pradesh had only eight thousand yearly engineering graduates in the mid-1990s, now there were a hundred thousand.

More than a decade after unleashing the states to experiment, India is a patchwork of economic and policy contradictions: some areas are painfully bureaucratic and poor, with no infrastructure or good education, while others are vibrantly capitalist and fast growing. When I advise American companies on investing in India, I often recommend they go directly to one of these pro-reform states rather than navigate the bureaucratic webs of Delhi.

The breakneck economic growth in states like Gujarat has had downsides. Modi's single-minded focus on growth left some of Gujarat's poorest behind. Rates of child hunger and malnutrition are still sky-high and the number of families under the poverty line has increased. Some of Modi's critics also find his role in the Gujarat riots of 2002, mentioned in chapter 1, unforgivable. More than a thousand Muslims died. Whether it was, as Modi insists, a rookie political error, or a willful policy of Hindu retribution the world will never know. The incident stains both Modi himself, his BJP party, and India's otherwise impressive record at keeping interreligious violence to a minimum.

In May 2014 Modi rode a tidal wave of anger at the Congress Party's ineptitude to a landslide victory in India's national elections. After years of lackluster economic growth and some serious corruption scandals, the Indian voters had had enough. Despite the best intentions of Prime Minister Singh and his team, in ten years the Congress Party failed to unshackle the economy, such as by permitting foreign companies to invest in many sectors, like retail and insurance, and making it easier for manufacturers to buy land, to hire and fire workers, and to get environmental and other licenses efficiently. Most voters were tired of ideology and simply interested in competent governance. Young, urban Indians voted for Modi because they wanted jobs and more livable cities. With one eye on Pakistan and another on China's assertiveness, others liked Modi for his tough stance on national security. A core group of Hindu nationalists, including his old friends at the RSS, were the "ground troops" who helped get out the vote.

Two years after the vote, Modi still has a clear mandate for change. Yet India's complex democratic politics make it difficult for even the most committed reformer to push through changes.

How are policies actually made? Modi's attempt to pass his labor market reform package—made up of four bills aimed at making it easier to hire and fire workers and expand the minimum wage—provides a glimpse into the byzantine policy-making process. As is the case in most democracies, the relevant ministry comes up with proposals for change. India's entire cabinet must then approve each bill. Once a law is drafted, it then has to pass both the Lok Sabha (lower house) and the Rajya Sabha (upper house). With a BJP majority in the lower house Modi and his team thought labor reform would be easy. But he has been facing intense opposition even at this level because many parliamentarians, looking ahead to the next election, are worried they will be voted out of office if they roll back the generous protections that Indian workers enjoy. (China's Standing Committee has no such worries.) In the Rajya Sabha, the BJP does not have a majority and has not done enough to bring its political opponents on board. Finally, even if the reform passes at the central government level, India's states have much leeway in how to implement it. Some states have already passed more business-friendly labor reforms, but in true Indian style, others lag behind, creating a patchwork of regulations.

Even if a particular reform passes these hurdles, its implementation depends on the willingness of India's notoriously slow bureaucracy, the Indian Administrative Service. Many Indians think their bureaucrats are coddled and overpaid. Stories abound about their fabulous benefits and first-class travel. It is no wonder that entering India's Administrative Service or Foreign Service is even more competitive than in China. More than four hundred thousand aspirants take the exam each year, and far fewer than 1 percent are chosen.

The bureaucracy, in the form of the Indian Foreign Service, also has much leeway in creating India's foreign policy. The tiny Foreign Service is, in my experience, filled with dedicated and smart diplomats. However, it is so overwhelmed with day-to-day issues that it has little time for long-term planning. This sometimes makes the country seem hesitant to embrace its status as a rising power, and shy about trying to create its own vision for the world. Prime Minister Modi is trying to change this culture, and the prime minister's office has been more active than ever in trying to shape India's role in the world.

★ ★ ★

When Xi and Modi appear onstage representing their countries, we tend to see India and China as monoliths. Statesmanship hides the internal constraints in their very different political systems. These systems will impact both how fast each country can reform internally and how it will act on the world stage. China's "fragmented authoritarian" system makes internal reform easier than India's raucous, decentralized democracy.

As we will see in later chapters, the Chinese system is coming under so much strain that several scholars have predicted it will crack up. (Since no one accurately foretold the collapse of the Soviet Union, I will not try to predict here how long China's system can last.) The Chinese Communist Party is increasingly worried about its own legitimacy, and this makes it see domestic and foreign security threats around every corner. To shore up the Party's control, Xi is trying to make the Party less corrupt and more responsive to Chinese citizens, and is centralizing control over everything from the media to China's external and internal security. Unlike in India, citizens can't "turf out" politicians they don't like and give others a turn at the steering wheel. This makes the Chinese system inherently brittle, capable of shattering with one unexpected shock. Wealthy Chinese are worried enough to move a large amount of wealth outside the country. The anticorruption campaign is breaking up traditional patronage chains. Since most Chinese are looking for transparent, competent governance rather than true democracy, a challenge to Xi is more likely to come from his enemies within the Party, rather than from a Tiananmen Square–style mass unrest.

From the United States' perspective, a Communist Party that gradually adopts real rule of law, including property rights and independent courts, would be very helpful, even if China does not move all the way to democracy. This would make the whole system more stable and its leaders less anxious, and thus less likely to make mistakes of bravado on the international stage.

In India, Modi entered office like a bulldozer, promising economic reform, better governance, and a more assertive foreign policy. But the checks and balances India's founders put in the constitution, and the inevitable emphasis on short-term results by elected politicians, are making it more difficult to push through unpalatable, long-term reforms. The United States should want these reforms to succeed. Although its democracy gives India resilience, it needs to improve governance and basic services for all its citizens to be a strong, confident world player, and a democratic counterweight to China.

3 | ECONOMIC TAKEOFF

ODI, MODI, MODI! The chants of nineteen thousand spectators were deafening. They were enthralled at a rock-star-like
rally for India's new prime minister, Narendra Modi, at New
York City's Madison Square Garden in September 2014. Not even the
Rolling Stones and U2 get such a reception. Responding to the crowd,
the prime minister promised to "form the India of your dreams." After a
frustrating few years of economic slowdown and gridlock in Delhi, Indians had "had" high hopes the Modi government could complete long-
overdue economic reforms.

★　★　★

"What is your plan for benefits? Can we do a rotation in the United States?
Why don't we get more say in the technical development of the products
we build?" Five hundred young, Chinese employees of an American semi-
conductor company looked intently at us as I toured their research facility
in Xi'an with some American executives. No browbeaten, passive communists here: the highly educated, twenty-something Chinese peppered
their CEO with questions and sounded exactly like any bright, assertive
audience in Silicon Valley would. Most young Chinese have expectations
well beyond a steady job—they want to travel, enjoy first-world health
care, and be taken care of in their old age. The Chinese government is
struggling to provide for these ever-increasing aspirations.

★   ★   ★

The trajectory of India's and China's twentieth-century economic revolutions provides a baseline for understanding the future of these giant economies. Their recent blistering economic growth means that both populations now have very high expectations for a prosperous future. But there are tall hurdles both economies need to overcome.

"Socialism with Chinese characteristics," the phenomenally successful system that Deng Xiaoping and his heirs established in the 1980s, is still the lodestar of China's current economic policies. The limits of that system are now becoming clear—overinvestment, inefficient state-owned enterprises, slowing demand for exports, mounting government debt, and growing inequality. So the Chinese leadership hopes to press ahead with a second round of reforms, further opening the capital markets, breaking the power of state-owned enterprises, and creating a modern health-care and pension system. Many in the Chinese leadership support this new round of reforms, but important constituencies like some state-owned enterprises are lobbying against it, and the reform momentum has slowed. While they debate behind closed doors the pace of reforms, Chinese leaders repeat endlessly that slower growth of 6 to 7 percent a year is the "new normal."

Some journalists and economists have recently had a heyday predicting China's economic collapse. While growth will slow, possibly even to 4 percent or lower in the short term, in the long term these predictions are likely too negative. The long-term trend will depend on whether President Xi and his advisers are willing to push forward with needed reforms to the pension, health-care, and tax system, as well as the banking sector and SOEs, or whether they prioritize short-term stimulus and thus undermine market-friendly reforms. Understanding the trajectory of the Chinese economy is key to determining how confident the Chinese government—having shored up economic growth—will be on the international stage.

India was slower to pursue economic reform. Former Finance Minister (and later Prime Minister) Manmohan Singh's impressive opening of the Indian economy in the 1990s was incomplete and resulted in a hybrid economy that produced somewhat lopsided results. While the IT and telecom sectors have been able to modernize, largely due to lack of control by the government, much of the manufacturing, agriculture, and infrastructure sectors are hobbled by overregulation. This incomplete transformation set the stage for the reforms Prime Minister Modi and his team are trying to enact now to keep the economy on course.

Chinese and Indian economic growth is entirely in the United States' own interest. If we want an expanding world economy, we need its two largest, most dynamic engines to prosper. Chinese and Indian growth means that American companies will be able to export more, which supports jobs at home. As these economies rely less on heavy, dirty manufacturing and become more sophisticated, they will gradually pollute less. The increasing economic ties between China, India, and the United States also help raise the costs of potential military conflict, and so the more the world's three giants interact economically, the better.

★   ★   ★

How did the Chinese economy become the juggernaut that American commentators love to fear today? As recently as 1979, the Chinese economy was entirely state planned.

Before 1800, the Qing dynasty was a major power, accounting for roughly one-third of the world's economy, with high living standards. From the nineteenth century on, however, China's economy stagnated as it struggled with a rapidly growing population and a shortage of jobs and usable agricultural land.

The "unequal treaties" China was forced to sign with industrializing European nations, America, and Japan opened China's ports to predatory trade practices. This forced opening to the world brought industrial technologies and free trade to China, but continuous civil wars and political instability prevented real industrialization until the 1950s.

When the communists came to power in 1949, China was primarily an agricultural economy that only accounted for about 5 percent of the world's total economic output. Hyperinflation and decades of incessant war had left the economy in shambles. Mao Zedong and his colleagues focused on rebuilding and industrializing a devastated China to benefit even the poorest Chinese.

Between 1949 and 1956 the country rapidly built steel, chemical, and textile industries, and gross domestic product (GDP) briefly grew at more than 20 percent per year. Yet Mao's aggressive efforts to collectivize agriculture during the "Great Leap Forward" led to painful famine and economic disaster. The economic dislocation caused by the Cultural Revolution again stalled growth.

By the end of the Cultural Revolution in 1976, centrally controlled, state-owned enterprises manufactured more than three-fourths of all Chinese products. The government generally forbade foreign companies and private enterprises from operating in China. China traded mostly with Soviet bloc countries. Competition was virtually nonexistent, and the government's strict controls on how much should be produced at what price caused widespread distortions. Farmers and workers had no profit incentives, and the economy stagnated.

Then China had a great stroke of good luck: Deng Xiaoping. The Chinese revere Deng Xiaoping almost as much as China's founding father, Mao. They are right to. More than any other Chinese leader, he made the tough decisions that moved China toward a modern, prosperous market economy.

Born to prosperous landowners in 1904, Deng studied in France before he joined the Red Army's Long March and helped lead the Communist Party to victory in the civil war. He rose quickly through the Party ranks, becoming general secretary in 1955. Deng's ideas for economic development often put him at odds with Mao. After proposing reforms to the Great Leap Forward, he was placed under house arrest, "paraded in a dunce cap through the streets of Beijing, and forced to wait tables at a Communist Party school." During the Cultural Revolution, Deng and his family were exiled to Jiangxi Province. After Mao died in 1976, a dangerous power struggle ensued between the Gang of Four and other hard-liners on one side, and Deng Xiaoping and his reformist allies on the other. By 1980, Deng had won.

He and his team strove to create a partial market economy without the upheavals the Soviet Union and other postcommunist states experienced. The secret lay in Deng's careful approach. He did not take down Mao's "central plan," which set targets for how much each farm and factory had to produce each year, all at once. Instead he used a "dual track" approach: many farmers were allowed to sell their surplus on the open market. Others stayed strictly on the plan, and could not interact with the free market. In this way Deng's team kick-started enormous growth without creating too much pain for those still within the communist economy.*

Deng dismantled China's immense agricultural communes. People could continue to farm collectively if they wished. But he allowed peasants to also farm small family plots, and sell or keep the surplus, a revolutionary shift in incentives. Yen Jingchang, a farmer in Xiaogang in 1978, described farmers' desperation in 1978 before the reforms started: not enough food, hungry children, and no means to improve a family's fortunes. "Work hard, don't work hard—everyone gets the same, so people don't want to work," he said. Before the reforms, farmers dragged themselves to the field only when the village whistle blew at 8 a.m. Once they could keep their surplus, families went out before dawn. At the end of the season, they had harvested more than in the previous five years combined. Rural per capita income more than doubled between 1978 and 1984.

The Chinese government also created a strict separation of the domestic and foreign sectors so it could allow foreign investment without impacting the internal economy. Starting in 1980, China allowed foreigners to build factories in "Special Economic Zones," similar to free trade zones in other countries, largely along the Pearl River delta near Hong Kong. However, the foreigners had to import all materials, such as fabric and sewing machines, from abroad, and had to export everything they made. The only thing they could "purchase" from China was its inexpensive, abundant labor. There were two prices and two markets for every good, such as a pair of jeans. This ensured that internal prices didn't suddenly spike.

After these initial reforms jump-started growth, the government grad-

---

*I am indebted to economist Larry Lau for sharing his thoughtful and well-researched insights on the Chinese economy with me. I also received valuable assistance from Chong En Bai, chairman of the Department of Economics, Tsinghua University; Professor Fan Gang from the Graduate School of the Chinese Academy of Social Sciences and Beijing University;and many others.

ually took bolder steps. In 1984, China's planners agreed to keep the overall size of the central economic plan fixed. If firms produced more, they could sell their goods at market prices. As the economy grew, it slowly outgrew the central plan.

At the same time, the government allowed entrepreneurs and smaller "township and village enterprises" to thrive. These small private sector firms could produce what they liked (bricks, fertilizer, and clothing, for example). A number of start-up firms rushed in to take advantage of these opportunities.

Many of these early entrepreneurs were the "sent-down youth"— educated young people sent to the countryside to work during the Cultural Revolution. In the early 1970s many young Chinese were unemployed. By sending them away, Mao saw a dual benefit: they had a "true" revolutionary experience to reinvigorate the party, and it prevented hordes of unemployed from creating instability in the cities. When these youths returned to their cities in the late 1970s, many still had no jobs. As Deng gradually opened the economy, they became China's first entrepreneurs, opening tiny teahouses and restaurants, and later larger companies.

Huawei, the telecommunications juggernaut, was one of these early start-ups. A former military signals intelligence officer founded it in 1987. Huawei is now one of China's largest and best-known companies, competing globally with Cisco and other top-tier technology firms. In just fifteen years, through the efforts of many small entrepreneurs, the state-owned sector shrank from 75 percent to about 40 percent of the economy, and the township enterprise sector grew from 9 percent to over one-third of total GDP.

As a result of these reforms, from 1978 to 2013 the Chinese economy grew at a blistering rate of almost 10 percent per year. This upswing continued for an astonishing twenty-five years, with only small interruptions after the Tiananmen Square uprising and again during the economic crisis in 2008. Trade with the world skyrocketed.

Within China, the bulldozer of market capitalism arrived by boat on its shores and then rolled slowly inland. Coastal provinces like Guangdong, Shanghai, and Zhejiang industrialized first, and many coastal cities became an aesthetic wasteland of miles and miles of assembly plants.

Modern apartment blocks followed the factories, and soon perfect roads, malls, and eventually western luxuries from KFC to Louis Vuitton followed. Industrialization then spread to the inner provinces. As the coastal economies matured and their growth slowed, central and western Chinese cities like Chongqing, Henan, Shaanxi, and Sichuan took their turns as the country's fastest-growing areas and thus kept the overall growth rate high.

China's economic boom was so dramatic partly because it finally harnessed China's underutilized strengths: cheap, plentiful labor and a high savings rate that provided massive capital for investments. Thus China's sparkling airports, railways, roads, and hundreds of townships rose from the dust. Like many business travelers, I regularly buy a new map every time I am in a Chinese city. Invariably, since the last time I visited a few months before, a whole neighborhood has disappeared. One warm fall afternoon, I walked around central Beijing looking for the lovely bed-and-breakfast in a traditional *hutong* courtyard where I had stayed in late 2008. The whole neighborhood had been razed, and instead a dozen matching, soaring apartment blocks were rising in its place.

Yet there are dark storm clouds on the horizon for the Chinese economy. Since about 2012, the economy has begun to slow down closer to 7 percent annual growth, and some economists believe that it is currently growing much less than that.

Chinese local governments and companies overinvested in factories, machines, housing, "technology parks," and roads. Economist Larry Lau and other scholars argue that this happened because, in the early 2000s, local government officials discovered that the land they controlled could be very lucrative. For example, a local mayor could declare formerly agricultural land as suitable only for manufacturing. He could then enter into an agreement with a steel company (which not infrequently gave him a percentage of their profits as a kickback) and help that steel company get cheap loans from local banks. To protect his "investment," the mayor could then declare that anyone building apartment blocks in the city must use only steel manufactured by the local plant.

One example of this is the East Hope Group. In the early 2000s East Hope cut a deal with the local Party Secretary of Sanmenxia, a midsize city, to purchase the province's plentiful bauxite, a key mineral for making aluminum. With local government support, the East Hope Group started to produce aluminum in 2005. Its founder, Liu Yongxing, became one of the wealthiest people in China. When asked what helped him succeed in this cutthroat industry, Liu said: "Pardon me for being frank, but local officials, even corrupt ones, all need to have political achievements." Many of these local plants now stand idle, great hulking sores that, government sources say, will have to lay off 5 to 6 million workers. Others operate at very low capacities, and often don't make enough money to cover their debts. Overcapacity in steel, aluminum, coal, and cement plants is a particular problem, and will not be resolved quickly.

There is also a glut of housing. Some of China's much-touted new townships are ghost cities. Wenjiang, near the epicenter of Sichuan's terrible earthquake, for example, is filled with dozens of modern, clean, if boring skyscrapers surrounded by mature trees. Looking closer as I drove through in a taxi, however, I could see that no one actually lives there. There are no stores, and not a single person walking down the street, like a sanitized postapocalyptic world. My taxi driver explained that many people bought apartments purely for financial speculation, not to live there. This overcapacity means that the central government cannot invest more in this type of infrastructure to crank up economic growth.

Local governments have enormous debts—much of it from opaque sources such as shadow banks—that they took on to fund grandiose infrastructure projects and loans to businesses like East Hope. The government is working hard to fix this teetering system. China's central bank has taken on billions of dollars of this dodgy local debt. Since 2015, local governments are now able to issue bonds (at lower interest rates than they paid to borrow from state banks) to finance public infrastructure projects like roads, just as they would in the United States. In contrast to the past, provincial governments can now collect and keep some taxes to pay off these bonds, and they can no longer give special preference to certain land developers or companies. China has also announced that it will set "reasonable" limits on new local government debt in 2016.

Some American scholars argue that this local government debt is unsustainable. Chinese economists I speak to are much more sanguine. They point out that central and provincial government debt together is only approximately 60 percent of GDP, a much lower percentage than in the United States, whose debt is estimated by McKinsey to make up about 90 percent of GDP. This debt is all in local currency, so in a worst-case scenario, the government can print more renminbi to get rid of it (unlike the Greek government, which has no control over the euro money supply). Although some localities will suffer, this problem will gradually be worked out without substantial harm to economic growth.

Overcapacity in some sectors and massive local debt are the largest problems. However, three other factors—growing income inequality, a rapidly aging population, and environmental degradation, which we will explore in later chapters—also negatively affect growth.

Due to decades of rapid growth, some Chinese "got rich first," in Deng Xiaoping's famous words. From a relatively egalitarian society, China became one of the most unequal countries in the world. There are huge inequalities in education, social mobility, and government services, especially between China's urban coastal residents and those living in the rural hinterlands. To address this, President Xi has promised to expand state spending on social welfare, education, and health care, and has already introduced reforms to make the health-care system more egalitarian.

China is aging. The size of China's elderly population is set to double by 2030, and the working-age population will decline. This means that by 2030, less than half the population will be working age but will need to support the rapidly growing number of retirees. China is reforming its pension system and recently relaxed its controversial one-child policy. It must urgently complete pension and health-care reforms before the working-age population begins to shrink. Young working couples now save with the expectation that they may have to support their parents and possibly grandparents in old age. If these citizens could save less and consume more, it would help China's economy grow.

China's rotting rivers and smog-filled air are also having an effect on growth. In addition to shortening the lives of its citizens by more than five years in some parts of the country, according to the Paulson Institute, China's environmental degradation and resource depletion has cost nearly 10 percent of GDP over the last decade.

Finally, the tough anticorruption campaign Xi and his allies launched in 2012 has also slowed growth, as government officials and managers at state-owned enterprises in particular are hesitant to sign off on any new projects.

★   ★   ★

With all these headwinds, will China continue to grow? Recently western journalists have become fond of predicting China's imminent economic collapse. Headlines call China the "Doomed Dragon," predict that "China Will Implode," explain "Five Signs of the Chinese Economic Apocalypse," or ask "Will China Crash?" Anne Stevenson Yang, a noted China "pessimist," and other economists argue that China's government debts and the massive overcapacity in the steel, aluminum, and housing sectors mean that soon Chinese banks will buckle under bad debt, and economic growth will come crashing to a halt. Some independent outlets such as the Conference Board believe the economy is only growing at 4 percent, not 7 percent as the government claims.

These predictions are likely too negative. China is a large economy, with plenty of natural resources, labor, and capital. Annual growth may slow to 6 or even 5 or 4 percent for a time, but these are still numbers that Americans could only dream of. The concern about slowing growth is more political: by saying repeatedly that growth between 6 and 7 percent is "the new normal," Chinese leaders are signaling that this is the lowest growth rate they will accept. Senior government economists have said in private, however, that they are disappointed at the slow pace of reforms. Before the reforms are complete, growth could slow to 4 percent before ramping up again to still reach an average of 7 percent over the next five years. If Chinese leaders persist with the key reforms they have announced, instead of getting spooked into another short-term stimulus, growth should recover.

Economist Larry Lau argues convincingly that several factors weigh in China's favor. Its high savings rate (nearly half of people's incomes) means that China is not reliant on fickle external capital to finance investments. Even as consumption gradually increases, Chinese culture will keep people saving at fairly substantial rates and thus supply plenty of internal capital for investment. Lau also argues that in spite of its rapidly aging population, China still has surplus labor, and will have it for at least the next few decades. Retirement ages are currently artificially low (as low as fifty-five for some sectors) and the government is raising them. Nearly a third of Chinese still work in agriculture, and will slowly move to cities where they can earn higher wages. Finally, the country recently relaxed its one-child policy so that young couples now will be able to have two children, although the effect of this won't be felt for several decades. Chinese growth is not constrained by lack of labor. With more than 1.3 billion consumers, China also has a large internal market, and so is less affected by external economic shocks than small economies. As a result, its economic growth has been more stable than that of Taiwan and Singapore, for example, which can fluctuate substantially.

If China's reformers are able to move the economy closer to a true market system, a big internal market, growing consumption, abundant natural resources, and high savings will help the country overcome many long-term economic difficulties.

China does have a temporary, large oversupply in manufacturing, infrastructure, and housing, described above, which may hurt its growth in the short run. Investment in these areas has slowed dramatically, which is a good thing in this overheated environment. Since the second quarter of 2014, and accelerating through the beginning of 2016, firms in all of China's regions, in every sector and size, have been cutting their capital expenditures. In inland cities it has virtually stopped, because many smaller state-owned enterprises are no longer able to borrow from banks or local governments. Manufacturing is slowing.

To keep economic growth at the "new normal" of between 6 and 7 percent, the government *must* make a few key reforms to keep domestic demand high.

The Communist Party knows it needs to build a larger consuming class, but this will take time. Most Chinese still save instead of shopping wildly, because they have no real social safety net. Allowing Chinese to have more children will quickly help boost demand: according to one scholar, Chinese households with one child saved over 20 percent of their incomes in 2009 while two-child families saved only about 12 percent.

Another way to keep China growing now is to invest in public services, for example by building schools, health facilities, and environment and clean energy infrastructure. The government understands this. It is growing health-care spending by well over 10 percent a year, and it will likely rise to $1 trillion (more than in the United States) by 2020. Western and Chinese companies are pouring in to build new hospitals and retirement homes. The government is shoring up the pension system so that families will be less burdened by caring for elderly parents. Providing these public goods will allow people gradually to save less and consume more, and thus keep the Chinese economy growing.

Finally, the thirteenth Five Year Plan, announced in spring of 2016, will place an even bigger emphasis on much-needed environmental stewardship. By building mass transit systems and investing in clean technologies, the government can create jobs and gently stimulate the economy, much the way its road and airport building did after 2008. Another benefit of these investments in public goods is that they will improve China's painful income inequalities: the poor will benefit disproportionately from better health care and more generous pensions, and cleaner air benefits everyone equally. As the anticorruption campaign slows, that should also boost economic growth.

There are some signs that these efforts are beginning to pay off: household consumption in China is already growing at one and a half times the rate of real GDP growth. The services industry (such as nursing, law, retail, etc.) is hard to measure, but most scholars believe it is growing at over 10 percent, much faster than manufacturing. It is now China's largest sector.

Even as market jitters sent the Chinese stock market reeling in the fall of 2015, and predictions of Chinese economic collapse dominated American newspapers, Apple's CEO, Tim Cook, had a different view. He emailed a CNBC financial journalist to say that iPhone activations in China had accelerated over the past few weeks and the App Store was performing better than ever, with iPhone sales up 87 percent in China over the previous year. Chinese consumers are starting to spend.

The government also recently announced financial reforms that will make capital flows and the exchange rate freer. This is a good thing: the colossal stock market rally and then correction in 2015 and early 2016 shows that a partially free stock market is unsustainable. China's stock exchange is dominated by small Chinese individual investors instead of more sophisticated institutional investors, who have more information and more patience. Chinese retail investors have few other options—they are not allowed to invest in international stocks and the housing market is slowing down. They rush for the exits at the first sign of trouble. Until the government stops interfering in the market (by keeping international investors out, telling state-owned enterprises not to sell their shares, and otherwise "blocking the exits"), the market will stay immature and more volatile than a larger, more established market would be. The government is planning to make it easier for foreigners to invest in Chinese company shares, and to allow some of the many companies waiting to list shares in Shanghai to do so. These reforms would bring more buyers and sellers into the market and make it more mature and robust. Unfortunately, concerns over public panic and abrupt market slumps slowed down these reforms. The 2015 stock crash made headlines in the United States, and the Chinese government mishandled the response. But as Tim Cook recognizes, it will not really affect China's underlying economic growth.

The government is also eager to make the renminbi more accepted internationally.* To do so it will have to let the market determine the value of the renminbi, and it is beginning to do that. American politicians who

---

*Mostly due to pride, China pushed hard to have the renminbi accepted as one of the world's reserve currencies in the International Monetary Fund's Special Drawing Rights (SDR) basket, which the IMF recently did. The SDR supplements reserves of member countries to provide liquidity in a crisis. To be included, the currency must be freely usable and play a central role in the global economy. The latter is beginning to happen. Five years ago, almost no trade with Chinese companies was settled in renminbi, which created some of the huge dollar-currency reserves the Chinese government holds. Now almost one-third of trade with China settles in renminbi, which will slowly fix this imbalance.

criticize China for keeping its currency artificially low have largely gotten what they wished for. The renminbi has appreciated almost 25 percent over the past decade against the U.S. dollar, even taking into account the well-publicized devaluation in fall of 2015. China took steps recently to make the value of its currency based more on the market than on government fiat. This is hurting China's manufacturing sector because Chinese exports are now relatively more expensive. At the same time it helps Chinese consumers spend more and Chinese companies buy assets overseas, and thus supports the shift to more consumption and away from manufacturing, which China desperately needs.

The government is also trying to make state-owned enterprises more accountable to the market by feeding them less free capital and forcing them to diversify their ownership.

At the local level, there is some progress. Local governments are privatizing small state-owned enterprises (those factories producing far more steel and aluminum than anyone needs) so they can pay back their massive debts.

It has been much harder for the central government to restructure some of the state-owned behemoths, the "SOEs." SOE bosses report to the Party, not to shareholders, and are paid very little, so the best talent often goes elsewhere. They have also been among the most vocal opponents of change, so their restructuring has been timid at best. Many SOEs have natural monopolies in the oil, electricity, aluminum, or part of the banking sectors. CITIC, Shanghai Electric, and other giants are moving some assets into publicly listed subsidiaries or merging with each other, hoping that this will force them to be more efficient, which seems unlikely. For example, Sinopec sold many of its gas stations to investors including Tencent, a successful, private Chinese Internet firm. However, the government retains majority control in most of these companies, and in the recent stock market slump, it prevented the companies from selling shares. In March 2016, anonymous government officials said 5–6 million employees of "zombie" firms will be laid off in a long-overdue step, and that the government would provide some unemployment insurance. It will take many years for SOEs to be reformed and free from political interference. As the private sector grows, however, this will matter less and less.

Finally, everyone from President Xi to university leaders and high school professors have been pushing the mantra of the innovative economy. "Entrepreneurship" programs are springing up everywhere. When I speak to elite Chinese students at Beida and Tsinghua universities, their hero is Alibaba founder Jack Ma, and they want to start successful companies like him. (Almost none want to join the government.) Innovation fever is gripping the nation. At a conference in Wuzhen, China, in December 2015, I was pushed aside by hundreds of young Chinese wielding their phone cameras at midnight in my hotel lobby. I thought they were waiting for a rock star to arrive, but who walked in the door to loud cheers and flashbulbs: Jack Ma and his fellow entrepreneur, Lei Jun, the founder of Xiaomi phones.

So far the results of innovation fever have been mixed. China files more domestic patents than any other country, but many are low quality and not recognized internationally. Chinese technology companies like Alibaba and Tencent are booming, and do genuinely innovate. They also benefit from a protected market that keeps many American and European competitors out (by forcing them to provide user data and decrypt user messages upon request, or to adopt content restrictions that are hard for our companies to defend in the United States). Others, like cell phone maker Xiaomi, have invented novel marketing and inexpensive production techniques. True technological innovation, however, is still not the norm. We should want the Chinese economy to become more innovative. As Chinese companies file their own patents, they will naturally become a constituency for better protection of everyone's intellectual property and will have less interest in keeping the Chinese market closed to foreign firms. More competition will help everyone. It is too early to tell whether that will happen.

China's leaders are experienced technocrats with one big advantage: with no elections to contest, they can focus on long-term strategy. Their primary goal is to keep the economy growing steadily while managing a transition to higher wages, more social services for their people, and higher domestic consumption: the "Chinese dream." Despite U.S. newspaper articles to the contrary, it will likely keep growing at between 5 and 7 percent. China needs economic development to underpin its political stability. One cannot exist without the other, and both depend good relations with their trading partners, including India, the United States, and Europe. Helping Beijing to "realize the Chinese dream" ultimately benefits us all.

★   ★   ★

Indians tire of economic comparisons between their country and China, and for good reason: India's reforms began twenty years after China's, and even with continued high growth rates, its economy will be far behind China and the United States in 2030. This "horse race" is beside the point. India will have the world's third-largest economy, an enormous internal market our companies will want to sell to, and will be the largest democratic power other than the United States to help influence China's rise. India's growth is constrained by the noisy collection of special interest groups that oppose reform in the country's decentralized, democratic system. Unlike in China, where the central government can push through tough compromises, government gridlock stalls many key economic reforms, as Prime Minister Modi and his team are discovering.

India's economic history strangely parallels that of the China. In the sixteenth and seventeenth centuries, India's economy was the envy of the world. The Mughal kings drew ten times as much revenue as Louis XIV did in France. India's living standards were the same or higher than Europe's. In the eighteenth century, India was one of the world's leading manufacturing countries—it produced a quarter of the world's trade in textiles. India's fabulous wealth set the Europeans on their quest to discover and trade with it.

In the nineteenth century, the fortunes of India, Europe, and the United States diverged. England led the industrial revolution, and its new manufacturing processes were quickly adopted throughout Europe and the United States. India fell behind. Economist Angus Maddison has calculated that India had one-quarter of the world's economic output in 1700, but only 4 percent right after it gained independence.

Why did this occur? After Independence, a generation of Indian economists argued that Britain willfully deindustrialized India. The Brits, the argument goes, forced India to export raw materials like cotton, jute, and indigo, and encouraged it to import the manufactured textiles and other products that British factories created. The English did not bring their technological advances to India and treated Indian hand weavers as near slave labor. They taxed the Indian farmers so heavily that agriculture stagnated, and they also benefited from taxing opium sales. There is evidence to support this view.

More recently, however, economists have converged on a more moderate view, which argues that Britain didn't intend to impoverish India. India's decline was caused by technological advancement in the industrial revolution. As Britain became more efficient at weaving cloth in factories, world textile prices plummeted, making the "by hand" cottage production in India too expensive for the market, and thus stagnating its growth.

When the Indian flag rose above Delhi in August 1947, India had a chance, in its view, to rectify the damage the British had done. Unlike China, independent India did not ban private ownership. However, India's first Prime Minister Jawaharlal Nehru and his advisors believed the nationalist argument: that foreign trade and investment were responsible for India's terrible poverty. Nehru was pessimistic about Indian businesses' ability to compete in the world. So he gradually closed the economy. India became the classic model of "import substitution." The government protected local industries through high tariffs and government loans to develop domestic manufacturing (especially in heavy industries such as steel) and to decrease India's dependence on trade.

In 1954, Nehru declared he would create a "socialist pattern of society" and began drafting Five Year Plans based on the Soviet and Chinese model, although without mandatory production quotas. The government directly owned key economic sectors, including airlines and railroads, postal and telephone companies, radio and television broadcasting, and many others. India barred large companies from competing in eight hundred "small-scale industries" by decreeing that only tiny domestic companies could make pencils, shoes, clothing, and toys. Strict labor laws deterred entrepreneurs from hiring workers because it was and still is nearly impossible to fire them in a downturn. The government hamstrung industry with countless regulations, which became known as the "license raj."

Indian leaders learned the wrong lesson from history. As a result, India's economic growth rate after independence never rose much above 4 percent a year. Cynics called this the "Hindu rate of growth."

By the late 1980s, India's economy was faltering. Its share of world trade had declined from 2.4 percent at independence in 1947, to a minuscule half a percent in 1990. To add to the crisis, oil prices rose due to the collapse of the Soviet Union and the 1991 Persian Gulf War—a serious problem since India imports almost all its oil. The many Indian laborers who had been working in the Gulf and sending money back had to return home, so the country lost this large source of foreign exchange. By mid-1991, India was close to defaulting on its international debts.

In the midst of this crisis, Finance Minister Manmohan Singh decided to take drastic action. Singh is an Oxford-educated economist, a gentle, understated man with an impeccable turban and a soft voice. He proposed sharp cuts in government spending and devalued the rupee to make Indian exports more competitive. The International Monetary Fund (IMF) and World Bank pledged billions in new loans. He threw open the doors of the Indian economy by courting foreign investment (Ford and IBM were two of the first to open joint ventures), slashing import duties, and encouraging Indian companies to export. He also began the difficult process of trimming the license raj.

It was a spectacular success. In less than five years, India's economy grew as much as it had during the previous forty. The stock market boomed. From 1991 to 2011, India's GDP quadrupled and exports surged fourteenfold. This opening— along with the development of broadband infrastructure that made it easy to send data across the oceans—jump-started India's technology boom. Starting in the late 1990s, India's talented university graduates began developing much of the world's software, reading and analyzing its spreadsheets, and manning its IT help desks. Manmohan Singh was the hero of the hour.

Unfortunately heroes have a short shelf life in India. Singh and his colleagues were (deservedly) lionized for unshackling the economy. When Singh became prime minister in 2004, many assumed that he would push through a second wave of reforms. But a decade went by without much action. In spite of the valiant efforts of some officials, the government barely improved on India's decrepit infrastructure. It only marginally enhanced the investment climate, and did not cut down India's notorious license raj, make it easier to hire and fire employees, get environmental clearances, and get title to land for commercial projects. Trade negotiations with the West stalled. The dire state of Indian education did not much improve.

A combination of complex domestic politics and populism explains this failure. As we saw earlier, many important reforms can only happen at the state level in India. States such as Maharashtra, Andhra Pradesh, and Gujarat raced ahead and unleashed foreign investment and economic booms, while others stagnated. The more populist wings of the Congress Party, including reputedly its leader, Sonia Gandhi, were opposed to policy changes that might hurt the poor. The political base for the left-leaning Congress Party is blue-collar labor and the rural poor, so the party had limited incentives to help big business. Finally, Prime Minister Singh and his smart, thoughtful, reformist economic advisor, Montek Singh Ahluwalia, just seemed exhausted when I last met them in office in 2013.

In May 2014, India's voters were fed up. In a landslide, they kicked out Congress and elected the brash, pro-business Narendra Modi as prime minister. Expectations could not have been higher—thus the nineteen thousand Indian-Americans shouting their hero's name in Madison Square Garden.

Prime Minister Modi had some lucky breaks in his first year in office and was able to deliver stellar growth: in 2015, India's GDP growth rate was over 7 percent, higher than China's for the first time in decades. Due mostly to lower international oil prices, Indian inflation nearly halved. The rupee is firm. The stock market boomed as investors poured a record $42 billion into Indian stocks and bonds, expecting that reforms would finally start.

Prime Minister Modi, Finance Minister Arun Jaitley, and their teams have a herculean task ahead. While the economy is growing well for now, and India's large, young population will be an advantage as the workforce expands in the coming decades, the government must implement major reforms in order to take advantage of this youth bulge. We will examine this in more detail later in the book.

These reforms are made more difficult by the same factors that slowed down Prime Minister Singh's administration: India's competing political factions, the fact that Modi's BJP does not have a majority in the upper house of Parliament, and that many key issues, such as energy, infrastructure, and even many labor policies, are reserved for the states and cannot be changed easily from the center.

India's economy is in certain ways the mirror image of China's. China grew through massive investment in infrastructure and manufacturing (with some outside capital, but also by using its large domestic savings), and by sending its many young people to work in factories. According to Indian scholar Gurcharan Das, India has higher domestic consumption, which insulates it from global downturns as long as Indians keep shopping. More than a third of GDP growth is due to rising productivity, a good sign—rather than to big capital investments, which helped China's recent growth. That is the end of the good news.

India, in contrast to China, lags far behind in both the manufacturing sector and in infrastructure. It needs huge foreign investments in both sectors so that new factories can absorb the massive wave of young, low-skilled workers who are about to become adults. It also needs better education and training programs to help this generation, if its "youth bulge" is going to pay off.

India's dreadful infrastructure is legendary. Even in large cities, buses careen around potholes the size of small cars, bridges collapse in the monsoons, and it took eight years to build a paved road to the new Hyderabad airport—and another four to complete all the ramps leading onto the expressway, as the state's Chief Minister Naidu once told us in an exasperated tone. Unlike Beijing's gleaming Olympic stadiums, a key pedestrian bridge and a portion of roof collapsed on the brand-new stadium for the Commonwealth Games in Delhi less than two weeks before the games were to start. Many new projects are delayed due to bureaucratic holdups.

The government is rightly focused on this. Since Modi came into power, he has committed an additional $52 billion to infrastructure spending in 2014–16. This is a good start but a drop in the bucket compared to the estimated $1 trillion India needs: fifty times the amount it is spending. Half of this is expected to come from private capital. Finance Minister Arun Jaitley also set up an off-budget National Infrastructure Investment Fund with a seed grant of $3.3 billion. This is small start, but significant. As state-owned companies are privatized, proceeds are supposed to go into this fund so important infrastructure projects will no longer be scrapped when budgets get tight. The fund will raise additional money from private investors by issuing tax-free bonds—similar to American municipal bonds.

In addition to infrastructure, Modi needs to actively court foreign direct investment in manufacturing to absorb the many unskilled young Indians entering the job market. A legacy of Nehru's statist economic approach to the economy was that foreigners are not allowed to invest in many industries. Modi is trying to change this. So far his government has opened the railway infrastructure, telecommunications, insurance and pensions, retail, food marketing, and defense manufacturing to outside investors to help create jobs or bring key technologies to India.

To make India attractive for investors, Modi has actively tried to move India up the "ease of doing business index," where it still ranks an abysmal 130th out of 189 in 2016 (but up an impressive twelve places from 2014). Companies can now apply for industrial licenses and obtain environmental clearances online—a huge improvement from the opaque, often corrupt, and painfully bureaucratic former process. India's power minister told me proudly that in the BJP's first six months in office, it had cleared a backlog of 650 proposals. Distorting and expensive fuel subsidies have been cut.

In December 2014, the government issued an executive order to make it easier for companies to buy land to build factories for six months, but Parliament must agree to more permanent reforms. Famously, India's most renowned businessman, Ratan Tata, had to give up on building a car factory that could have created ten thousand jobs near Calcutta in Bengal state. The Bengal government botched the land purchase by forcibly removing farmers from land instead of compensating them. The farmers protested. Sensing a win, Modi, who was then chief minister of Gujarat, sent Tata a text saying only, "Welcome to Gujarat." He made the land acquisition transparent and simple, and fourteen months later Tata began producing his Nano cars there. Now the important central government land reform bill is stalled in Parliament.

The Labor Ministry is negotiating with trade unions to make it easier to hire and fire workers—a major obstacle to companies hiring in India. More comprehensive labor market reforms are stuck in gridlock. Finally, the government is working to simplify the tax system and create one national tax on goods and services (the GST) to replace many layers of competing state, local, and national taxes. The complex system invites confusion, corruption, and tax evasion. As of March 2016, this legislation was still stalled.

These are all well-meaning, important reforms. Largely through faith in Modi's single-minded focus on growth, overall foreign direct investment flows did rise impressively, doubling in the first half of 2015 compared to the previous year. Samsung is considering building a third manufacturing plant in the country, although nothing final has been decided. Airbus reportedly will aim to increase its sourcing of parts from Indian companies to $2 billion in the next five years. A Chinese commercial property developer plans to invest $10 billion to build industrial parks. Yet recent surveys of German, Chinese, and other businesses in India find that many companies still find bureaucracy to be a major obstacle.

Unfortunately, India's hard-fought parliamentary and decentralized politics means that no matter how well-meaning, the Modi government can't achieve change nearly as quickly as the Chinese. State bureaucracies can frustrate foreign investors: one recent study revealed that forty of India's top fifty stalled projects were being held up by red tape at the state level. As we saw earlier, some states are pushing forward, while many more are making no efforts to change.

Despite Modi's speeches around the globe to promote growth and create jobs through his "Make in India" campaign, India is still far behind countries like China in the push for manufacturing might. Even with a slowing economy, China created more than 13 million jobs in 2014, while India struggled to achieve even a million. In light of competition from other cheap-labor countries such as Bangladesh and Vietnam, India will need a miracle to turn itself into a manufacturing powerhouse. Its democratic institutional stickiness means that the "Make in India" campaign is almost certainly doomed to end with a whimper.

*   *   *

The economic weight of the world has already shifted, quietly but relentlessly, in China and India's direction. It will continue to do so. Tuning out the noise in economic estimates, it is reasonable to assume that the Chinese economy will keep growing at between 5 and 7 percent for the next several years—likely with a slowdown first, followed by a rally when China's economic reforms bear fruit—and then growth rates will slowly decline toward western levels as the economy matures. China's internal market is so large, and the private sector is becoming so dominant, that even if the government does not complete some of its most ambitious reforms (such as privatizing SOEs, which likely won't happen quickly), growth will remain fairly high. At these rates, China will surpass the United States as the largest economy by 2030, although the United States and Europe will still have an advantage in living standards, and in many technical, high-value sectors.

India has a larger task ahead. Its population is still much poorer. As a democracy, reforms will be harder to push through. Many foreign companies are waiting to see if it truly does become easier to do business in India before they invest. If Modi's zealous reforms continue, India can unlock some of its latent potential and grow faster than China. It is more likely that the current trajectory of 5–8 percent growth continues in India as well. This would make it the world's third-largest economy in 2030, with the largest or second-largest middle class, and Asia's key economic engine outside China.

What does that mean for the world? I am often asked if it wouldn't be good for the United States if these two giants—especially China—stumbled. If that happened, the argument goes, American companies could again manufacture at home, the United States would dominate world trade, and the financial institutions that made the rules of the economic game for nearly seven decades would not have to change. Perhaps, some argue, a drastic economic slowdown in China would even cause the regime to fall, and democracy would take its place.

Unfortunately, history has no reverse gear. We want China to grow, even if it means that the Communist Party, with all its downsides, will remain in power for the foreseeable future. We want India to grow for its own sake, and as another strong, democratic state to help shape China's rise.

Chinese and Indian economic growth is entirely in our interest. If we want a growing world economy, we need its two largest, most dynamic engines to prosper. As former U.S. Treasury secretary Hank Paulson has explained, China is America's fastest-growing export market, so problems in China will hurt our companies, and cost us jobs. Since China's entry into the WTO in 2001, U.S. exports to China more than quintupled. In general we export sophisticated products such as electronics and chemicals to China, which support well-paying jobs here at home. Chinese companies invested an astounding $42 billion in the United States in 2013–end 2015 alone—still a small amount compared to what is possible. Many are afraid of Chinese investment, and it is right that we rigorously review investments (including from China) in strategic sectors like national security, energy, and some infrastructure. Nevertheless, these investments can also save or create jobs and be another unifying force between the two countries. Chinese investment has directly created more than eighty thousand jobs in America, and U.S. exports to China indirectly support hundreds of thousands more.

It is also very much in our interest for the Chinese economy to move from exporting goods made with cheap labor to one that is more consumer and services oriented. As China's overinvestment in infrastructure and manufacturing slows down, commodities prices will fall. This will hurt raw materials exporters like Australia but will help the United States, Europe, and India, who all import these products and will benefit from lower prices. As Chinese domestic consumption and incomes rise, American companies will be able to export more, and more sophisticated, products. An added benefit is that as China stops relying on heavy, dirty manufacturing, its contribution to the world's pollution will decline.

A growing Indian economy also helps the United States. As India grows, its wealthier, fast-growing population means that U.S. companies will be selling to hundreds of millions of additional consumers. By 2030, based on current trends, India will be adding more people than China to the world's middle class. While trade between India and the United States is small compared to American trade with China, it is growing steadily, and we should want that to continue.* India and the United States are also increasingly investing in each other's economies, which supports good jobs both here and in India. Indian foreign direct investment (FDI) is thought to have created at least ninety thousand direct jobs, with other reports estimating the Indian tech industry alone was responsible for supporting more than four hundred thousand U.S. jobs in 2015.**

Completing the triangle, India will benefit from China's growth, and vice versa. As wages in China rise and it moves to a service economy, India's growing manufacturing sector will hopefully become more competitive. Trade between the two giants has grown to more than $70 billion in 2014, up from less than $3 billion in 2000. This trade is imbalanced and mostly based on affordable Chinese exports to India. The Indian government is well aware of this and working to correct it. The relationship may also naturally rebalance: as China's wages rise, it will export fewer manufactured goods to India. China will need more services, including the IT and mobile services that India is so good at providing.

Finally, if these two countries do not grow, it will have a major impact on emerging economies. China is already the largest export or import partner of at least ninety-six countries around the world, more than the United States.

As both China and India grow and their economies become more

---

* The Congressional Research Service reports that total U.S.-China trade in 2014 was nearly $550 billion. According to a 2015 report by the National Association of Software and Services Companies (NASSCOM), U.S.-India bilateral trade in 2014 was $103 billion.

** It is of course true that American investment in China and India has created many more direct jobs in those countries than they have so far created here. The point here is not to ignore that fact, but merely to point out that cross-border investment increasingly helps the United States as well.

sophisticated, they will also have a stake in international governance. If they want to export more technologically advanced products, they will naturally want to protect intellectual property and keep the trading system open.

The United States has excelled in the face of economic competition for three centuries. Doomsday newspaper articles about the rise of India and China in particular may make us insecure, but American companies are excellent innovators and benefit disproportionately from open, growing international markets—including those in China and India. We must work hard for the rules of the game to be fair and take care of those Americans displaced by a more open, high-skill economy, but we should not be afraid to compete. Finally, economic interdependence also helps raise the costs of potential military conflict, so the more the world's three giants interact economically, the better.

PART II

★ ★ ★

BUILDING A
BRAVE NEW
WORLD

4 | SHARING THE WEALTH

T HE FIRST thing that struck me was that the streets were spotless, polished clean with the swing of hundreds of broom strokes a day. Women squatted in front of their corrugated iron homes, wearing ragged sweaters and hats to ward off the January Delhi chill. They chatted while they ripped the feathers off scrawny, recently butchered chickens. Preschool-age children played with sticks in the dirt, and one three-year-old girl in a dusty pink hoodie with bunny ears confidently grabbed my hand.

The waste-picker slum community that I visited in east Delhi in January 2015 works off the landfill. Every day parents and children hike a one-thousand-foot tall mountain of rubbish and hunt for plastic bottles, metal cans, and other goods, which they then sell to recyclers, earning about eight dollars per family each day. In India the 1.5 million waste pickers reside near the bottom of the social and economic ladder.

Mohammad Asif and his family are among the more affluent in the community. In addition to the one-room hut he shares with his wife and children, he has a small, covered storage area where his extended family works at separating small mountains of plastic water bottles from Tetra Pak juice packs and aluminum cans. The poorer slum residents (who have no storage area) sell their daily finds to Mohammad, who sorts and stores them to sell to larger, more professional recyclers. He pays significant rent for his hut to a slum landlord. His family has enough food to eat, but barely.

Mohammad's lanky, elegant daughter Farida is in first grade at a government school and also studies at the special learning center for children in the slum that a nonprofit organization that helps waste pickers, called Chintan, has set up. The learning center helps her catch up with the other kids in her formal school, and additionally serves as day care: it keeps her and other children off the toxic waste dump where her parents work, and where she would be exposed to chemicals and disease.

Supriya Bhardwaj, the energetic, young director of Chintan's children's programs, walked me around the learning center and the slum community, and explained much about the life of Delhi's urban poor. We stepped gingerly around several cows feeding on trash and over an open sewer, and then climbed rickety stairs to a collection of four tiny, windowless rooms on the second floor of a listing concrete structure. In each room fifteen or so children sat happily on the floor in front of a teacher, learning basic writing and math, and spontaneously sang a welcome song for me.

Cows grazing near a 300-meter-tall trash heap in Delhi.
photo credit: *Anja Manuel*

Supriya explained that it is an enormous challenge to get the local families to trust Chintan enough to send their kids to the school. "You must understand, each child that is in our learning center is not out on the landfill trash picking, and that takes several hundred rupees a day away from the family income. Our teachers walk through the slum every morning to bring the children here. It is positive peer pressure, and they love to come, and beg their parents to let them go."

Waste-picker children living in Delhi's slums.
photo credit: *Anja Manuel*

★   ★   ★

In total, almost 65 million Indians live in urban slums, and 300 million live under the World Bank poverty line, which is a depressingly low $1.25 each day. Almost a third of the rural Indians and a quarter of its city dwellers are this destitute. This seemingly incurable poverty—despite decades of effort—is *the* most fundamental problem India faces on its way to becoming a true world power. It is the issue that keeps Indian politicians up at night, determines whether they are reelected, and has until recently kept Indian leaders—who were preoccupied with solving these domestic issues—from engaging more deeply in international affairs.

By contrast, China's economic juggernaut has lifted many millions out of poverty, so fewer Chinese live in extreme deprivation. According to the latest World Bank data, in 2011 approximately 84 million Chinese lived on less than $1.25 per day, many of those in the rural interior of the country.

The massive efforts the Chinese government has made to build housing in the country's interior means there are far fewer Chinese urban slums like the one I visited in eastern Delhi. However, vast income disparities remain. While the GDP per person in Shanghai and Beijing is close to that of Portugal or the Czech Republic, the per capita GDP of interior provinces like Xinjiang resembles that of Congo. As a result, hundreds of millions of migrant workers left their farms in the interior over the past three decades in search of higher incomes in the giant metropolises near the coast. Until recently the government attempted to ignore this enormous migrant community of nearly 220 million people. Instead it tried to push them back to their villages by refusing to provide them with any services at all in the cities.

Xian and her younger sister Qian are two tiny, energetic women in this mass of migrant humanity.* Xian, the quieter, older sister, dropped out of high school at age sixteen, married a man her parents found for her, and moved with him to Guangzhou, where they worked in separate gar-

*I am indebted to Sungmin Rho (PhD, Stanford), assistant professor at the Graduate Institute of International and Development Studies in Geneva, and one of the world's foremost experts on Chinese migrant workers, for sharing these stories with me, as well as some records and pictures of her more than three hundred interviews of migrant workers. To protect them I have changed the names of the two sisters and not disclosed the name of their employer, a well-known electronics manufacturer. Chinese migrant workers are very sensitive about speaking to foreigners and several refused to be interviewed by me, worried that the Chinese government would somehow penalize them for talking about their difficult circumstances.

ment factories—twelve-hour shifts, six days a week. After two years, the garment factory reduced the number of overtime hours Xian was able to work, so they moved to Shenzen, where she and her sister were lucky enough to land a job in one of the enormous, city-like electronics factories that assemble our cell phones and tablets.

Xian and Qian do not live in a slum, but their life is at times more reminiscent of Upton Sinclair's *The Jungle* than Mohammad's life in Delhi. Their dorm room, for which they each pay 100 yuan (sixteen dollars) in rent a month, has eight bunk beds covered in polyester blankets. Suitcases under the beds hold the women's few possessions. It smells of Chinese noodles and inexpensive room freshener. A blanket covers the one filthy window at all times, because five of the roommates work at night, and the others during the day, so someone is always sleeping.

Xian last saw her husband three months ago because he lives in a similar men's dorm attached to a different factory across town. "That's fine," she comments; "it's better than fighting all the time when he is around." It is harder for Xian to talk about her one-year-old daughter, who lives with her husband's parents in their home village in Hunan. She sees the little girl only once a year, during the spring festival, and says "she hardly recognizes me." Xian talks about her family as if she is describing someone else's life—with no real feeling. She acts a decade older than her twenty-two years and is quite pessimistic about her future. Young factory workers are more often single, but being married, like Xian, is not unheard-of. Migrant workers endure long separations from their partners and children in order to make enough money to send home. The *Economist* estimates that 61 million Chinese children are left with relatives in villages while their parents work in big-city factories. Factory life is all-consuming, and there is not much room for personal lives.

Xian and Qian's parents were also migrant workers, who eventually saved enough to open a small shop and returned to their village. They came of age a few decades ago, before the Chinese economy took off. This first generation of migrants was grateful to work in factories, send every extra yuan home, and return home after several years. They never made much money, certainly not enough to send either daughter to university. This older generation does not complain much about the conditions they endured. Their daughters have higher aspirations than their parents. Xian in particular seems frustrated that she can't achieve them.

Qian is only two years younger than her sister Xian, but more energetic and outgoing. She wears makeup and the latest knockoff fashions, as many migrant workers her age do. "I was happy to drop out of high school," she says. "Even with two more years of school, I would have gotten the same job I have now, and at least now I'm away from home and earning money. Twenty-six hundred yuan ($400) last month!" she adds proudly. Dorm life bothers Qian less than it does her sister, and she says she doesn't yet mind the grueling hours. On her day off, she and other young workers go into Shenzhen to window-shop, rather than using the ping-pong tables and other bare-bones recreation facilities that the factory provides. Qian hasn't thought much about her future, but she is saving some of the money she doesn't send home to buy one of the shiny smartphones that she spends her days making.

Unlike their parents, Xian, Qian, and their young colleagues at the factories are bombarded with information from advertising and social media that shows other Chinese making more money, buying houses, building families, and creating what President Xi calls the "Chinese dream." This goal of basic prosperity resonates with Chinese. It is unattainable for most migrant workers. Yet young, recent factory hires don't tend to know much about labor laws or the benefits they should be receiving, so they often don't protest about their difficult working conditions. Instead, just as Xian and Qian did, they simply leave a factory where pay is too low and move to another city in search of better wages. Their older colleagues have had more time to learn about labor rights. These older workers are causing the stirrings of a labor unrest movement in China that has the government very worried.

★   ★   ★

Workers like Xian and Qian (who did not want to be
photographed) at an electronics factory in China.
photo credit: *STR/AFP/Getty Images*

Income disparity is a serious concern in both India and China. Yet urban
poverty feels very different in the slums of Delhi and in the *Blade Runner*
landscape of a Shenzhen factory town. Indian slums are more desperately
poor. They also function as complete communities, with families of the
same caste or religious group shopping from the same street vendors and
going to the same schools, and at times living in the same slum for generations. A manufacturing industrial revolution has so far skipped India, so
93 percent of India's workforce is in the "informal sector." That includes
virtually all of the urban unskilled poor, who recycle trash from landfills,
drive rickshaws, or clean toilets in wealthy houses.

China's manufacturing boom has raised the incomes of millions of former peasants, who now get meager paychecks from factories each month.
Unfortunately, the factory towns tend to be lonely places, without much
community: Xian and Qian say they don't have many friends because
workers come from different regions and often speak different dialects,
and because the turnover at the factories is so high that it is hard to form
lasting bonds.

That India's poor work mostly in the informal sector while their Chinese counterparts often work for formal corporations creates a key difference in how each government is able to help its poorest citizens. India cannot even begin to create a western-style social safety net—most of its poor don't have paychecks or even bank accounts. As a result, most assistance comes in the form of subsidized food and fuel and, in some lucky cases, free health care and housing. India has established enormous wealth transfer schemes, but they are highly inefficient and often corrupt. The schemes also sometimes leave out portions of the population that are not helpful voting blocs for local politicians, such as the Muslim community of Mohammad and Farida. The government is trying to fix this by signing up the poor for bank accounts and biometric identification, and by moving to direct cash transfers for many assistance programs.

In China, most workers have formal jobs with paychecks. That makes it easier for the government to send assistance in the form of social security, unemployment insurance, and other benefits, if it chooses to. China was until a few years ago reluctant to create any social safety net at all for the migrant poor at the bottom of the scale, like Xian and Qian, because they wanted them to move back to the countryside. Even for the middle class, the Chinese government is just beginning to improve the social services that would allow families to spend more rather than save every yuan for emergencies or retirement. Through social media, the poor and lower middle classes increasingly see that China's boom times are leaving them behind. There are stirrings of discontent.

Though the United States cannot solve these problems for China and India (as we struggle with getting our own welfare system right), we can and should help in a limited, often nongovernmental way. The United States has an interest in helping China's poor because the feeling that some are being left behind could create unrest and end in a messy power transition, instead of a gradual movement toward more inclusive government. India has a much larger task than China's and we should want it to succeed. It will be strong enough to take a more prominent diplomatic role in the world—including perhaps pushing back against some of China's more aggressive international behavior—if it resolves this most basic domestic concern. Private companies can help here more effectively than the U.S. government just by encouraging their suppliers in China (and to a lesser extent in India) to offer reasonable working conditions, salaries, and benefits. American shareholders are beginning to demand this kind of oversight, and it is making a real impact for factory workers on the ground. They can also earn the gratitude of the Chinese and Indian governments, and likely get useful tax incentives, by investing in the less developed provinces of both countries. How well both giants deal with their growing income disparities will have important implications for the stability of their governments, which in turn will affect whether together we can achieve the positive vision of 2030.

★　★　★

Why does such poverty exist? In spite of well-meaning efforts to end it, India's caste system has kept some groups poor for generations, and it persists into the twenty-first century. The caste system is essentially an ancient Hindu division of people into "pure" and less pure groups that assigns one's line of work at birth. According to some experts, it became entrenched around two thousand years ago. It was rigidly enforced during the British colonial period, but has loosened considerably in the decades since India's independence, especially among the elite and middle castes. Intermingling and intermarriage, even among the highest Brahmin and the relatively lower Baniya (business) castes, are now common, especially in cities. Many of India's wealthy new entrepreneurs come from the "middle" or trading castes. As one Indian journalist explained to me, some of India's most famous Internet entrepreneurs came from the "moonshine" caste: their ancestors brewed gin for the British colonial masters. Eventually they learned English and their children became clerks for the British, then bankers, and now many in that caste are technology entrepreneurs. The most famous of these is Shiv Nadar, the founder of HCL, a giant IT conglomerate. Cooks in wealthy households are often Brahmins—the highest caste—so that the more conservative older people in the family can feel comfortable about who touched their food.

Still, the worst jobs, such as scrubbing toilets or sorting garbage, continue to be performed mostly by Dalits, the lowest caste. Indian columnist Shikha Dalmia explained why many Dalits continue to work such unappealing jobs although they may have other options. She says a woman named Maya has worked in her family for thirty-five years because the job offers her a small financial safety net. Since only Dalits are willing to take out garbage and clean toilets, many have created small multigenerational cartels for themselves. When Maya married at age sixteen, one of her wedding presents was the "right" to service ten houses in Dalmia's neighborhood. Although this right could never be enforced in court, Maya's fellow Dalits, who own the "rights" to other houses, do not try to work in her territory, just as she doesn't work in theirs. Employers cannot "fire" her, because no other Dalit would do her work. She earns about a hundred dollars a month with this arrangement.

This income comes at a price: while other castes mingle somewhat freely now, no one is willing to socialize with Dalits doing this kind of work. The families she works for give Maya lunch every day on separate plates reserved for her low caste. The Dalmia family driver, who is poorer than Maya but belongs to a high caste, would not accept a glass of water from her. Maya's son, who is by birth a Dalit, has given up cleaning work and is a sales representative for a large company. He is embarrassed about his mother and often lies about her work. Maya refuses to give up her work even though her son could support her: her tiny cartel is her safety.

In spite of a "reservation" system that sets aside almost half of university places and central government jobs for India's lowest castes and tribes, Muslims, Dalits, and India's remaining tribal people are persistently the poorest economic classes in India. According to a government report, around a third of Muslims and "scheduled castes" (essentially, Dalits) were under the poverty line in 2012, the most recent year such data was gathered. While this is an improvement from the approximately half of both groups that were poor just six years before, they are still much poorer than higher-caste Hindus, who have a poverty rate of only 12 percent.

India has numerous wealth transfer schemes to help Mohammad, Farida, Maya, and the hundreds of millions of others like them. The previous Congress Party government budgeted nearly $41 billion a year for food, fuel, and fertilizer subsidies alone—almost 15 percent of the total government budget. While Prime Minister Modi is trying to streamline these programs, and has already scrapped diesel subsidies that were perceived as mostly helping the wealthy, the overall subsidy budget is now only slightly lower. In 2016 the Modi government announced it would cover catastrophic healthcare for the poorest Indians for up to $1,500 per family. It is working on basic social security and pensions as well. In addition, the National Rural Employment Guarantee Act (NREGA) provides at least 100 days of guaranteed wage employment per year to every rural household whose adult members volunteer to do unskilled manual work, at a cost of $5 billion annually to the government.

In spite of these large investments, India's public social spending is only between 3 and 4 percent of GDP, compared to China's more impressive 7 percent, and has gone down slightly under Modi. The poorest segment of Indian society has not benefited as much as other groups from the recent economic boom. "Quality of life is improving for everyone," Supriya from Chintan assures me, as we survey Mohammad Asif's neighborhood, a landscape of recycled plastic bottles, scavenging cows, a mad tangle of pirated electricity lines, and, surprisingly, a number of white satellite dishes hanging like Mickey Mouse ears off the corrugated plastic roofs. "There are just fewer improvements at the bottom of the scale."

Mohammad and his family have access to basic health care at a rundown government clinic a ten-minute rickshaw drive from the landfill. The Indian government has for a decade or more emphasized building basic primary health centers and community clinics, but they are often severely understaffed. To reduce infant mortality, the clinics encourage women to give birth there—and, surprisingly, close to 75 percent of all Indian mothers now give birth in a medical facility, and almost two-thirds of children receive their immunizations. It is a big success, but there is much work to be done. Currently, Indian public spending on health care is a little over 1 percent of GDP, as compared to 3 percent in China and a whopping 8.1 percent in the United States. The Modi government wants to double down on this investment and proposed rolling out a universal health-care system between April 2015 and 2019. Under it the government would provide many basic drugs and diagnostic treatments for free and insurance for serious illnesses. Due to costs, the program is unfortunately on hold.

Along with a staggering 820 million other Indians, Mohammad's family receives subsidized rice, wheat, and other staple foods, although he and his neighbors often receive only a fraction of what they are entitled to. "Many people administering these programs cheat to line their own pockets," Supriya explains. The Indian government agrees with her and is trying to fix this.

The new National Food Security Act, passed in 2013, was another gigantic effort to feed India's poor. It covers three-fourths of rural and half of urban Indians and costs a whopping $21 billion a year, twenty-five times more than when the program started in the 1990s. Yet according to its own data, less than 60 percent of the grain the government purchased for the subsidy program reaches the people the government is aiming to help. Because of corruption, the government has been able to reduce hunger only marginally. Thirty percent of Indian children are still underweight.

Mohammad's family is entitled to other government aid, such as subsidized fuel and housing, but he does not receive any of it. This is a common experience. In spite of well-meaning government aid schemes, many of India's poor, especially in urban slums, don't get the help they are entitled to.

Why is it so difficult to help India's poorest residents? It is a failure both of getting the word out, and of governance. "Often they don't know that they qualify for subsidized food, fuel, and housing," says Supriya. "Even when they do, government officials refuse to give them identity cards." Many urban slum residents are migrants without formal government ID cards so they are unable to take advantage of most government assistance.

Sometimes banks won't give slum residents bank accounts—which they need to get cash aid from the government—because bank officers are often prejudiced. Muslim migrants like Mohammad are at the bottom of the social order, along with the lowest Hindu castes. Government officials argue—without basis—that they are Bangladeshi refugees and so not entitled to subsidy programs. Mohammad and others often don't have birth certificates, so they can't prove they are entitled to benefits. "To make matters worse," Supriya adds, "they don't have voter cards, so they are not useful as a vote bank for any politician. As a result there is no reason for local politicians to help them."

A biometric identification program, called Aadhaar, founded by Indian billionaire technology entrepreneur Nandan Nilekani, could help both to identify those at the bottom of the ladder who need assistance, and to help stem the massive "leakages" from these programs. The program is taking the fingerprints and iris scans of every Indian who wants to participate. Almost a billion have done so to date. As we will see later, with their new biometric ID, India's poorest residents can then prove they are who they say they are and get the subsidies they are entitled to without having to pay off corrupt officials at every step.

In 2014, Prime Minister Modi announced a plan to phase out some subsidy programs by providing a bank account for every household to which cash transfers could be deposited. Currently two out of five people in India do not have access to bank accounts. At the lowest end of the income scale, for example among rural laborers who take part in the guaranteed employment scheme, only 2 percent (!) had bank accounts in 2007. The Modi government has pushed hard to fix this and by the fall 2015 had vastly exceeded its own goals: 200 million Indians had opened new bank accounts. The government launched a cash transfer plan to replace the hugely inefficient kerosene cooking gas subsidy. Instead of having state energy firms distribute gas canisters to the poor (with the inevitable bribery and disappearance of many canisters), they have begun to pay $6.50 a month directly to household bank accounts. Some wages from the rural employment scheme are also being paid in this way to stop corruption. The government has also begun rolling out cash transfers ($19 a month per family) to replace food subsidy programs. While direct transfers alone will not solve the problems of corruption and inefficiency, they are a big step in the right direction.

China's history of poverty is different. Unlike India, China has no painful legacy of a caste system to battle. Until the early 1980s, the Communist Party emphasized egalitarianism and development above all else. Massive income disparities existed when Mao came to power in 1949. This improved in the first three decades of communist rule but became much more pronounced again as a result of the economic boom that started in the early 1980s. Deng Xiaoping famously said it would be all right for "some to get rich first," and some did, leaving millions of others behind.

While there are no castes, in China inequality is heavily reinforced by the system of *hukou,* or household registration, which assigns people to be "rural" or "urban" at birth, and thus intentionally makes migrating to the cities very difficult. Xian, Qian and their 200 million fellow migrants generally have a rural *hukou,* so they are not entitled to receive any real social services in the cities where they work the world's assembly lines.

The *hukou* system, now more than fifty years old, is only now being gradually relaxed. When the Chinese Communist Party rose to power in 1949, its goal was to develop and industrialize China as quickly as possible. The government prioritized the industrial sector, so the 15 percent of Chinese working in urban factories received basic welfare and pensions. There was not enough money for the remaining 85 percent of the population, the peasants, to receive any real assistance from the state. They were collectivized into enormous communes to provide cheap food and raw material for the industrial class in a system reminiscent of Aldous Huxley's dystopian *Brave New World,* where an underclass happily provides basic goods for the small percentage of "alphas" who direct the system.

Not surprisingly, many peasants fled to the cities. To help stem these massive migrations, Mao introduced the *hukou* system, where legal residences were fixed for life. With few exceptions, peasants were not permitted to move their *hukou* to the cities.

This system continued largely unchanged even after 1978, when Deng Xiaoping disbanded many rural communes. However, because of poor administration, most households received little more than an acre of land, hardly sufficient to feed an average household of more than four people. One scholar has argued that as a result, "half of China's 400 million rural working people became unable to sustain themselves." Although the *hukou* system did not permit them to move, hundreds of millions of farmers illegally migrated to the cities in search of better-paid work. Xian and Qian's parents were part of this first tidal wave of migrants.

Very few of those who migrated to the cities in the past three decades were able to obtain an urban *hukou.* This created a second, lower, class of citizens, who are routinely discriminated against. Most Chinese say that they would not want to live next door to a migrant. A person's *hukou* also determines the level of welfare benefits he is entitled to. Migrants without urban *hukou* often receive no pensions. Their children are often denied access to urban state-run schools. They have to clear higher hurdles to get into universities, and in some cities, like Beijing, are not allowed to buy cars or houses unless they meet impossibly exacting conditions.

Of the more than 200 million migrant workers in China, remarkably few live in slums like those in India, due to the government's tough controls on building shantytowns. Instead, many like Xian and Qian live in cramped factory dormitories. Migrants who do not work in factories but clean offices or work as beauticians, for example, have to find their own housing. In Beijing, a photographer touchingly documented the lives of the "rat tribe"—the Chinese name for migrant workers who live in cramped, sixty-square-foot basement rooms under Beijing's skyscrapers, with no ventilation or windows, in order to make ends meet. Scholars estimate that there are more than *one million* people living in such basements in Beijing alone. Housing is a major source of inequality in China: it accounts for almost two-thirds of the wealth of most households, according to a Chinese State Council report. While nearly all rural residents (those still in the villages) and 90 percent of urbanites own their homes, fewer than 10 percent of migrant workers do. Xian says that with her factory salary, she will never be able to afford her own apartment.

In 2011, the government pledged to construct and renovate 36 million apartments for urban low-income families, and officials say the government has done this. The catch is that, like many government pledges to help the poor, this housing is available only to those residents who have the right *hukou*, so even this massive building effort has not helped Xian or Qian and their peers.

The situation is a bit better when it comes to health care. Chinese health minister Li Bin optimistically proclaimed in late 2014 that China had "achieved over 95 percent health coverage." Most migrant workers know that this is a vast exaggeration in practice, and Beijing implicitly agreed when it pledged recently to provide universal healthcare by 2020. There is government-subsidized rural medical insurance. Yet the rural insurance is generally not valid in the cities where migrants live and work.

Xian and Qian say that when they get sick, they go to the local pharmacy and buy a traditional remedy with their own money. The electronics factory where they work, one of the most progressive in China, has a health clinic for employees, but it is only for minor illnesses. In theory, Xian and Qian's employer takes a small percentage of their wages each month to cover health care, and another amount to cover care for personal injury on the job, but neither knows whether they would get such help if they needed it. They have never been to a hospital themselves, but know that other migrant workers who get seriously ill end up paying for most of the hospital costs. "It would be a disaster to get sick," says Xian. "I would lose many days of work to go home to the village and see a doctor, and then probably lose my job."

Many migrant workers, including Xian and Qian, have never heard of unemployment insurance, maternity benefits, or pensions, although their factory is one of the few that offer modest benefits. When Xian had her baby, she worked until the last day she could, gave birth, took a week off to bring her daughter home to her in-laws' house, and then returned to her assembly line. She did not seem upset about this—it is just the way life is.

Xian and Qian represent the views of most young migrant workers: they expect very little from their employers or their government. At the same time, their grievance against the unfairness of the entire system is growing stronger.

Belatedly, the Chinese government is making a sincere effort to reform the *hukou* system. It is worried that migrants and their children from what the *Economist* calls "an increasingly angry urban underclass, unable to live the 'Chinese Dream' being touted by China's president, Xi Jinping." A new plan published in March 2014 calls for 100 million migrants to be given urban *hukou* by 2020, with all the benefits that entails, but there will still be conditions: at a minimum, applicants will need a stable job and a legal place of residence. In late 2015 the government announced that it will merge China's urban and rural medical insurance schemes, so that the services Chinese city dwellers receive are no longer so much better than rural ones. It also said it would grant *hukou* to 13 million undocumented Chinese citizens, many of whom were born in violation of the one-child policy. The pace of reform is slow. Urbanites in big cities do not want to give up their privileged access to schools and health care. Local governments, which will be stuck with most of the bill for providing a basic social safety net, are reluctant, since many migrants move on in a year or so in search of higher wages elsewhere. Critics of the proposed reforms note that they focus on cities with fewer than 5 million people, whereas the big cities such as Beijing, Shanghai, Chongqing, and Guangzhou are exempt. The government argues, not unreasonably, that it is easier to start in smaller towns because fewer people want to migrate there.

Some cities have created a point system based on how educated a migrant is, how much money he invests in a city, and even how often he gives blood. One father donated blood almost once a week just to get his son into a school that required an urban *hukou*—and he still didn't make it. In a strange irony, many migrant workers are surprisingly suspicious of the move to give them urban status. They fear they may lose their one special privilege: the right to a small patch of land in their home village.

The Chinese government is also working hard to tackle the problem of rural poverty. Xi pledged in November 2015 to eradicate poverty by 2020, which means helping 70 million poor, mostly rural people, and in 2016 started rating regional officials on their success at eradicating poverty. The government will increase support for education, employment, health, and public services for villagers. The 20 million poorest Chinese will have their incomes topped and "receive subsidized health insurance, public housing, subsidized utilities and free schooling." As a result, they are sometimes better off than households just above the poverty threshold.

The United States and Europe should care about this domestic concern in the world's rising giants. Poverty and perceived unfairness create discontent, and discontent can breed internal turmoil, extreme nationalism, or both. This is a concern particularly for China, where the government has in the past played up the threat of foreign enemies to distract citizens from internal problems.

While India's democracy offers it more valves to vent discontent, the United States should want India's economy to grow strong, and that requires helping its poor. Only a strong, confident India can take a more prominent diplomatic and, if necessary, military role in the world. A strong India can help moderate China's more extreme international behavior, for example, by pushing back on China's encroachment into the Indian Ocean and over the two countries' Himalayan border.

Of course, China and India will have to do almost all the heavy lifting on this issue without outside help, by making good decisions about how to allocate their own resources. They will not get large-scale assistance from the United States or other governments, since much of the West is struggling with income inequality in their own countries. At the State Department, we actively considered whether, in light of their booming economies, the United States should stop giving aid to these countries altogether. The United States continues to give a small amount to each country (most recently $13 million to China and $84 million to India), mostly for environment, education, and social programs. The United States should continue these limited donations to help the hundreds of millions still struggling in both countries.

Income disparity, however, is one important issue where American companies, organizations, and individual citizens may be more helpful than governments—especially in China. As Sungmin Rho, a Stanford scholar who has interviewed hundreds of Chinese factory workers, explained, "Many of the workers asked me to write letters to headquarters to help improve worker conditions." By "headquarters" the workers mean the foreign corporations whose products are manufactured in China's factories, even though these corporations often don't own the factories directly: Apple, Hewlett-Packard, Samsung, and others for electronics, and Nike, the Gap, Puma, Adidas, and Levi's in apparel. And these corporations—after some pressure from shareholders—often do improve working conditions. The factory where Xian and Qian works still has difficult conditions, but they pay 60 percent more than the garment factory where both women started their careers, for only ten hours a day of work. They also pay into the government-mandated pension, unemployment, and health schemes, and don't allow workers to do more than thirty-two hours a week of overtime. None of this would have happened without pressure and scrutiny from their American customers.*

In India, U.S. corporations can be similarly helpful, although a manufacturing boom has not yet taken off there and so there are fewer suppliers the United States can influence. Instead, some multinationals that sell into India have created effective programs to help India's poor generate their own income. PepsiCo pioneered a program that provides twenty-four thousand farmers with superior potato or other seeds and fertilizer and then buys back the crops at a fixed price. This helps increase productivity and insulates farmers from price fluctuations. Potato farmers in the PepsiCo program doubled their crop output and increased their revenue between two and four times, to up to six hundred dollars an acre. A California company, D.Light, manufactures and distributes solar lanterns and small personal solar grids throughout the developing world, including India. Many of D.Light's customers use the lantern to generate income: they charge others in their community a small amount to charge their mobile phones and other devices on the D.Light system. The Indian nonprofit Chintan is actively looking for partners, including American recycling firms, to teach India's waste pickers how to do their job directly at large offices and factories, and how to do it safely without being exposed to toxins on the landfill. This would enable India's poorest citizens to be part of the environmental cleanup and give them additional income by cutting out middlemen. These efforts leverage U.S. ingenuity and ethical corporate standards, not our scarce government aid dollars, to help both China and India.

A longer-term solution would involve the trade policies of all three countries, as we will see in chapter 11. Most economists agree that lowering trade barriers benefits the poor in the long term. In particular, research

---

* Sungmin Rho serves on an advisory board at Apple that monitors worker conditions at their supplier factories. Her research finds that western firms face significantly higher numbers of protests for better working conditions than Chinese-owned firms because workers actually believe their demands will be met, and they know the government is much less likely to clamp down on their protests (as they are often framed in an anti-foreign light).

has shown that when a country lowers its agricultural subsidies, it ultimately helps its own farmers, although it can have negative effects on the poor in the short run. This is particularly contentious in India, which has a long history of fixing prices for agricultural goods. More open agricultural trade would also require India in particular to teach many of its small farmers other skills and move them into more efficient employment, an enormously tricky task. Whenever the United States brings up this issue in trade talks, according to U.S. trade negotiators, the Indian delegation stonewalls.

More trade, ethical corporate policies, and some dedicated nonprofit work can help China and India build a prosperous society for all its citizens, for everyone's benefit. The staggering corruption that plagues both societies is a more intractable problem.

5 | BANISHING BRIBES

O NE OF China's best boutique hotels has a sleek modern bar and perfect cocktails. Successful Chinese entrepreneurs mingle seamlessly there with foreign investors and well-heeled tourists. It is always crowded, so I was surprised to hear that the western owner—whom we'll call John—recently sold it. A mutual friend told me "John was happy to get that monkey off his back."*

He elaborated that as a successful businessman with hotels in many countries, John was careful about new ventures. At first he was enthusiastic about how smoothly the project was going. The municipality seemed eager to help, the land was easy to obtain, and construction was proceeding ahead of schedule. But then the problems started.

His story was familiar: to get the sixteen permits required to operate the hotel, John and his partners had dinner after dinner with local officials to establish the right *guanxi,* or relationships. When John followed up to ask when the permits would be issued, he was not given a date. Instead he was told that he should hire a specific consultant for the fire permit, another for the building inspection, a third to get the alcohol license, and so on. The "consultants" cost at least four times the price of the permits themselves, and John was not naïve about where the additional money was going.

---

* "John" has authorized me to use this story. To protect the individuals described here, I have changed his name and key identifying details of the place and situation.

At first he pushed back. To finish work ethically, he installed the lobby security cameras exactly where and how the *anquan ju* (the State Security Bureau) had told him to do so. When the inspector came out, he told John "this is all wrong, you need to move the cameras to the other side of the lobby." Once that was accomplished, the inspector had another complaint. After several more rejections, John caved and called the "consultant" the inspector had recommended. Once John paid the exorbitant fee, the security cameras magically passed inspection.

Trees were similarly problematic. John was told that the lovely trees in the hotel courtyard weren't getting enough airflow and he would have to modify the building plans substantially, at great cost and delay. The tree bureau suggested he hire a helpful, if expensive, construction company. That company made tiny adjustments to the courtyard facade, and surprise (!), the trees suddenly had enough airflow and the permit was issued.

John persisted for several years, but finally the constant low-level corruption was too much. It wasn't just the initial "consultants," he told my friend. After the initial shakedown for the permits, there were opaque, recurring "service fees," not to mention that some officials expected to come by the hotel once a week for free steak and wine.

Aware that he was jeopardizing his ethics, John finally had enough, and sold the hotel. He believes, and I agree, that the Chinese bureaucrats saw nothing wrong with their behavior. Before the dramatic recent anticorruption crackdown, the long-standing mentality was that this is the way business is done.

Corruption is also endemic throughout Indian business and government, though it has a different character. I discovered just how blatant it can be when I traveled to India as an official for the U.S. State Department in 2007.

The U.S. government enforces stringent anticorruption rules. No U.S. government employee can receive any item valued at more than twenty dollars. This leads to awkward moments in countries where giving substantial presents to dignitaries is customary. I have been given carpets, gold bracelets, a solid lapis lazuli jewel box, and a hilarious pink plastic alarm clock in the shape of a mosque, which wakes me to the loud wail of the Islamic call for prayer. As government officials we smile apologetically when we receive these gifts and either return them or accept them on behalf of the U.S. government, which means they are turned over to an embassy vault. (Full disclosure: I kept the mosque alarm clock.) In return we offer a gift of "minimal value." My personal favorite was a coffee table book about uninspired American embassy architecture, which I am sure thrilled all who received it.

Because our rules are so strictly enforced, foreign governments generally accept that no shady dealings with U.S. officials are possible. To my surprise, a midlevel official in the Indian Science and Technology Ministry had different ideas.

I met with him briefly in 2007 in his dilapidated office to discuss Indian-U.S. cooperation on scientific research. After a few minutes of conversation about ways to collaborate, his face lit up with an idea. "The ministry has a large budget to host a conference for U.S. and Indian entrepreneurs working in the sciences," he said. "Why don't you organize the conference for us. I will pay you to do it, and you can give me one hundred thousand dollars of the fee back."

I stared at him in silence for a moment. He was proposing a kickback that would have nearly doubled my government salary. He clearly felt not the slightest embarrassment and waited calmly for my response. I mumbled something about not being the right person for this, and got out of his office as fast as I could.

★   ★   ★

The rampant corruption in China and India functions as a substantial tax on their economies, draining funds from public services. A scheme uncovered in India in 2008, in which broadband licenses were sold at below-market prices in return for bribes, cost the government $39 billion in missing revenue. That was roughly the size of India's defense budget at the time. In China, one estimate concluded that a full 10 percent of government spending is either misused as bribes or is simply stolen. Poorly equipped schools, dangerous counterfeit medicine, and buildings that crumple in earthquakes are just some of the consequences. The risk of being ensnared in illegal practices holds back some companies from investing in both countries, despite their enormous potential.

To achieve strong economic and political ties with the United States, both must make clean government a priority. It is the linchpin to address the problems of growing income inequality, environmental problems, creaking education and pension systems, and growing public anger in both countries. Anticorruption efforts will also make it easier for businesses in the United States, China, and India to invest in each other, and thus to strengthen relations. An additional danger is that as Indian and Chinese companies become the dominant investors in the emerging economies of Africa, Central Asia, and Latin America, corrupt business practices might become even more entrenched in those regions as well.

The encouraging news is that anti-graft movements are under way in both countries, though of very different natures and uncertain prospects. The nature of China's and India's political systems mean they will follow very different paths. China's authoritarian approach has been entirely top-down. No one doubts that courts will convict any official accused of corruption if China's central anticorruption czar believes they should. A number of Chinese thus wonder quietly if the crackdown isn't also a purge of Xi's enemies. India's solid institutions and dispersed political power means that anticorruption efforts have been entirely bottom up—fueled by citizens' protests, a free press, an independent court system, and some innovative technical solutions to tackle some of the worst problems.

In China, President Xi Jinping has made rooting out corruption in the Communist Party a signature initiative of his regime. Often referred to as the "tigers and flies" campaign—because it has gone after both powerful, high-level officials and many lesser players—the crackdown is astounding in its vigor and in the public way it is being conducted. Xi appointed one of his most trusted allies, Wang Qishan, to run the operation, naming him head of the dreaded Central Commission for Discipline Inspection (CCDI). The CCDI is housed in a nondescript, beige concrete block in Beijing that was historically known for using torture to extract confessions. At least seventy detainees are rumored to have died in CCDI custody as late as 2014, a number of them by suicide.

Wang Qishan is an unlikely boss of such a fearsome entity. He is known as smart and honest, with a dry sense of humor. A former mayor of Beijing, he has an impressive resume, which includes setting up the first investment bank in China, handling the SARS crisis, and preparing Beijing for the 2008 Olympics. Former U.S. Treasury Secretary Henry Paulson, who worked closely with Wang during the 2008 financial crisis, believes that he is an experienced and battle-tested crisis manager as well as a skillful politician, so he is often called in as the fire brigade whenever an important problem needs solving. Corruption is Wang's biggest challenge yet, and well-informed sources describe him as a true believer. He has a friendly demeanor but hardens visibly in his traditional Chinese jacket when he begins to talk about ethics. His goal is to hold Communist Party members to the highest ethical standards; to renew the Party so it can rule for another century.

Under Wang Qishan's leadership, the government's crackdown has led to the punishment of over 280,000 officials in 2015 alone, and China plans to sustain this rate in 2016. Senior Chinese officials say in private that Xi will not slow down and that the crackdown is required "for social stability." In fall 2015 the Party also updated ethics regulations to apply to all 87 million Communist Party members. In addition to theft, abuse of power, and graft, the new rules specifically prohibit gluttony, adultery, and—more bizarrely—playing golf. China's leaders are serious about purifying the Party.

Wang has targeted some of the most powerful figures in the country. In October 2014, the official Chinese news agency Xinhua reported, "Xu Caihou, former vice chairman of China's Central Military Commission, has confessed to taking 'extremely large' bribes." Xu was the second most senior leader of the People's Liberation Army, with which even China's highest-level politicians are usually afraid to interfere. The transgressions he was accused of exemplify one common style of bribe taking: he sought and received large payments from lower-level military employees in exchange for promoting them.

Chinese friends and even government officials were surprisingly eager to talk openly about the case. "This arrest is great news," one diplomat told me. "I have heard that if a colonel in the PLA wanted to become a major general, he had to pay a lot of money" (up to $4.8 million, according to news reports). "The PLA was always immune from everything, but this guy [Xu] was skimming off everyone who wanted to get promoted. People are glad he has been arrested." Xu died of bladder cancer in 2015, before his trial ended.

Perhaps the most powerful tiger taken down so far is Zhou Yongkang. With a stern look and pockmarked face, he was the powerful chief of China's fearsome internal security apparatus—the shadowy network that runs everything from the police to the infamous secret detention camps for political prisoners. He was seen as untouchable. When he was arrested in the summer of 2014, his case was unprecedented. No corruption investigation had ever been initiated against a member of the Standing Committee, the seven-member top leadership group of the Party. The last Standing Committee members to be put on trial were the infamous Gang of Four, who controlled the powerful organs of state during the Cultural Revolution. They were later blamed for the worst societal excesses of that painful period and put to death.

Zhou was one among the small group of elite government officials who have run Chinese government and businesses for decades. The families utilize the officials' power and protection and often manage vast empires of crooked family-controlled businesses.

During Zhou's years in public service, his family and associates amassed an estimated $14 billion fortune through sweetheart deals on construction and other government projects. Zhou's eldest son allegedly made more than $1.6 billion from public works in the city of Chongqing alone. He also allegedly used his father's prominence to extort millions of dollars in protection fees, mafia-style, from businesses and organizations. In June 2015 a court sentenced Zhou to life in prison.

The anticorruption drive is extremely popular with the Chinese public. Media outlets, such as the financial media company Caixin, have reported on it with glee. Caixin ran lengthy articles on Zhou's biography, published colorful charts of the corrupt businesses run by his family members, and cheerfully color-coded what had happened to each of Zhou's associates: gray for under investigation, blue for under arrest, and red for death sentence. Yet even a relatively independent media outlet like Caixin follows the bidding of the regime. Caixin reports in depth on officials who no longer have the backing of the CCP but stays carefully away from reporting on the suspicious wealth of President Xi Jinping's allies, for example. (The *New York Times* was not so careful. Its reporters were denied visas after the paper reported on the ostentatious lifestyles of Wen Jiabao's family.) Some bloggers are even more daring, publishing pictures of local officials with Rolex watches in an effort to show they are taking bribes. This puts the Communist Party leadership in a complicated bind. On one hand they want to use the anticorruption drive as an outlet for discontent and want it to be popular. For example, after the 2015 stock market tumble, corruption investigations against leaders of state-owned banks suddenly increased. On the other hand, they do not want social media to run wild with allegations, because ethics problems go much deeper than the current crackdown can solve. Some "Rolex wearers" have been prosecuted, but the corruption bloggers expose only leads to government action if the Communist Party leadership determines that it is in its interest.

The Chinese public's individual gratification at seeing the most corrupt get their comeuppance should not be mistaken as a broad-based movement for change. There is no widespread citizen activism about corruption, and there is no *independent* legal authority empowered to lead the charge, or to continue the fight should the current leadership abandon it, or be forced from power. China has only a nominal legal system that runs at the discretion of the Party leadership. So the future of the anticorruption effort is subject to the prevailing political winds. The motivations of the campaign may also not be as pure as the regime promotes.

Some analysts argue that the government's main intent is to direct public anger at a few big offenders, rather than engage in system-wide reform, and to shore up Communist Party power. The theory is that President Xi believes that if the most egregious offenders take the fall, growing public frustration about the wildly unequal rewards of the economic boom will be tamped down.

This makes sense since the Party leadership is determined to avoid the fate of the Soviet communists who fell from power after former Soviet president Mikhail Gorbachev's opening of the domestic economy and political system. Many Chinese leaders, especially those arguing for reforms, like Xi Jinping and his top advisors, believe the Soviet Union fell because its Communist Party was ossified, corrupt, and mismanaged the country's economy, so that ultimately it lost credibility. The Chinese communists made a six-part documentary about the Soviet Union's collapse and showed it recently at dozens of Party meetings. It begins with the ominous warning, "On the eve of the twentieth anniversary of the death of the Soviet Union and its party, we are walking on the same ground." An article in the Party-run journal *Seeking Truth* expressed the concern this way: "If corruption cannot be effectively controlled, the people will eventually no longer recognize [the validity] of the ruling Party."

As a top-down mandate, China's crackdown has benefited from the remarkable efficiency and concerted power that the Party leadership can bring to bear. Whether it will move beyond the pursuit of trophy targets and bring about institutional reform is very much in question.

★　　★　　★

In India, the situation is largely the reverse. Forceful grassroots leaders, and at least one entrepreneurial technology billionaire, are waging a ground-up battle, but high-level officials have so far mostly limited themselves to decrying corruption in speeches, rather than fully embracing the fight. The Indian political system is so factionalized that even if some political and business leaders throw their weight behind reform, progress is likely to be painfully slow, with rearguard resistance from those who benefit from graft.

In contrast to China, India's rule of law is highly developed. Its legal system is based on the British model and includes strong anticorruption laws. These laws are often not enforced, however, because the notoriously inefficient court system is overwhelmed with cases. It is not uncommon for an Indian legal dispute to drag on for a decade or more.

India's byzantine bureaucracy creates a fertile environment for bribery. Several Indian companies I work with freely admit to making payments to speed up approval of the innumerable business permits they need. Foreigners are also frequently embroiled in scandal. In 2013, the CEO of the mining conglomerate Group DF, Dmytro Firtash, was ordered to pay a staggering $174 million in bail while corruption charges are pending against him in both Austria and the United States. The U.S. government alleges that Firtash oversaw the payment of $18 million in bribes to Indian local officials to obtain titanium mining licenses.

In a case I investigated as a private sector lawyer, a large western pharmaceutical company found that its local subsidiary consistently paid off health inspectors to overlook severe hygiene lapses at a medicine factory. The climate of the facility was supposed to be strictly controlled to preserve the medicine, but the refrigeration system only worked two hours a day. When I toured the factory in 2009, it was sweltering, not to mention hopelessly rat infested. Headquarters shut the facility down immediately.

The lavish government programs that offer income subsidies and social services to the poor are also plagued by graft. An enterprising local official, for example, is supposed to distribute ten pounds of rice to a poor farmer, but gives out only seven pounds and sells the remaining three for a profit. Indians trying to collect their pensions or subsidies must routinely hand over a significant "commission" to government officials just to get the money they are owed. Another style of graft involves hiring "ghost employees," such as fictional schoolteachers or train conductors. Corrupt officials collect paychecks made out to the ghosts. Jagdish Bhagwati, a renowned Indian economist, contrasts India's corruption, which carves out a cash portion of every government transaction for cronies, to China's, where officials tend to take a share of profits in the corrupt company, and so are incentivized to see a particular business deal succeed. He argues that India's graft "undermines growth in our institutions. It's a very expensive way to be corrupt."

Public anger over corruption has been building. While the vibrant Indian press has always reported on corruption scandals, the scale of recent outrages has riled the normally complacent public. Indians reacted angrily to allegations that $1.8 billion of the Commonwealth Games budget was misappropriated, and that broadband licenses were sold at below-market rates, costing the government $39 billion. In the "coalgate" scandal, the government sold coal mining rights without open bidding, costing the country an estimated $34 billion in lost fees. Prime Minister

Modi's government canceled all these licenses and rebid them in early 2015 in a more transparent process. A court recently summoned former Prime Minister Singh to question him, and accused him of criminal conspiracy related to the deal. This is a tragic comedown for the nonpolitical, respected father of India's economic opening in the 1990s. Most Indians believe that he is personally innocent, and just permitted a culture of corruption to flourish around him. Indian politicians have long thrown corruption allegations at each other for political gain, and it is unlikely that any political party is completely innocent.

In April 2011, the widely admired Indian activist Kisan "Anna" Hazare drew attention to the problem by going on a hunger strike, which developed into a massive grassroots anticorruption campaign. Hazare comes from a relatively poor village family. He sold flowers in Mumbai's railway station as a young man. After fifteen years of distinguished service in the Indian army, he became an activist. Starting in the 1980s, he led a number of protest movements to promote rural development, end alcoholism, increase government transparency, and punish corruption. He describes himself as a disciple of Gandhi. Although Hazare has been campaigning against corruption since 1991, it was his latest campaign that caught fire.

In 2011, Hazare called for the government to create a national ombudsman's office, a "Jan Lokpal," that would quickly investigate and prosecute corruption—and include everyone, even the prime minister, within its jurisdiction. He engaged in repeated fasts and protests for more than two years, inspiring hundreds of thousands of Indians to join him and demonstrate in support throughout the country. Two years later, after initially passing a weak bill that Hazare and his followers rejected, the government could no longer ignore him and sent legislation to Parliament to establish the Lokpal office, with divisions in each state to which citizens can report instances of corruption. The ombudsman in charge would be required to investigate all such accusations, and to fully prosecute cases within a year—warp speed by Indian judicial standards. As of early 2016, while such a bill passed in the Delhi state parliament, the legislation was still frustratingly stalled in the central government legislature due to government redrafting and infighting.

Supporters of anticorruption activist Anna Hazare.

photo credit: *Deepak Malik/Pacific Press/LightRocket via Getty Images*

Hazare's movement has had considerable effect on the government. His exposure of high-level sleaze contributed to the resounding defeat in 2014 of the moribund Congress Party. Narendra Modi and his BJP party campaigned hard on fighting corruption as well as economic development and were swept into office. The brand-new Aam Aadmi ("Common Man") Party won local elections in Delhi in 2013 and 2015 by campaigning on an anticorruption platform, and other parties also embraced the good governance message. BJ Panda, a well-respected, centrist member of Parliament, told me that he believes a real movement for change is building. "Political parties used to pay lip service to anticorruption concerns but then campaign by focusing on empowering certain groups and appealing to caste. That has changed recently. The most successful parties focused their message mostly on good, clean governance and delivering services to citizens. Now we will see if they can deliver."

Prime Minister Modi's government has taken small steps in the right direction: rebidding the infamous coal licenses, and passing a bill to unearth assets by Indians stored abroad. In April 2015, Modi's cabinet proposed tougher anti-corruption laws that would increase prison time for offenders and hold corporations—not just individuals—responsible for bribery. The law has not yet passed Parliament. Senior government officials also say that Modi has quietly changed the culture in Delhi, making it much harder for tycoons to get special favors from the government. Modi's government has held transparent auctions for private sector permits and contracts, a big change from the former culture of allocating permits to favored businesses. These are good starts, but Delhi still has work to do.

The most effective solution so far has come from outside the government, led by Internet entrepreneur and self-made billionaire Nandan Nilekani.

Nilekani is nothing like Hazare. He is no neo-Gandhian folk hero. A tall, dashing man with graying Rhett Butler mustache, dressed impeccably in western suits, he is a strong believer in clean capitalism. Although his father was a socialist, Nilekani went to a prestigious private boys' school in Bangalore, and then to India's legendary, competitive IIT Bombay engineering school. He is a regular fixture at Davos.

Along with four other partners, Nilekani founded Infosys in 1981, which grew into one of India's premier technology companies. It had a $30 billion market capitalization when Nilekani stepped down as CEO in 2007. When Nilekani and his business partners founded Infosys, they put in place western accounting practices and strict no-bribery policies. This was highly unusual at the time and remains depressingly rare at Indian companies.

When I met with him with a small group of former American government officials in 2013, Nilekani was bursting with enthusiasm about the project he had designed and was managing for the Indian government. With Prime Minister Singh's support, in 2009–10 Nilekani and his collaborators created a program called Aadhaar, to generate a national identity number for every Indian, much like a Social Security number in the United States. Nilekani told Prime Minister Singh that he would do this, and volunteer his time, only if Indian bureaucrats kept their fingers off the project. He brought in one hundred of his brightest engineers and they built the most advanced biometric identification system in the world today, at the staggeringly low cost of three dollars per Indian. To enroll, Indians go to small kiosks scattered around the country to have their irises scanned and fingerprints taken, and receive a number and card. Their identity can then be verified by just touching their hands to any biometric application on any smartphone.

Although many had signed up for the program by the time of our trip in 2013, our group was skeptical. "Wasn't this an invasion of privacy? Why would Indians want this? Would it really prevent corruption?"

"This is India, not Europe or the U.S.," Nilekani responded patiently. "There are no real IDs here—you have to understand that most Indians have no documents at all to prove that they exist. This means it is hard for them to collect pensions or any of subsidies India's poor are supposed to receive. They are less worried about privacy—there isn't any privacy in the slums in any event—and more interested in receiving anything that will help their families survive."

The program has been an enormous success. As of late 2015, and as mentioned earlier, more than 920 million Indians had voluntarily signed up. Those with numbers can now use a simple application on any smartphone to collect government pensions or scholarships, or receive banking services—all bribe free.

But opposition to the program persists, despite or perhaps because of its impressive results. By eliminating duplicate identities and ghost employees, Aadhaar has become a powerful tool for preventing graft. Many who benefited from the opaque former system don't want it to succeed.

I reached out to Aadhaar's chief engineer, Srikanth Nadhamuni, who now works for an American venture capital firm. He explained how the program worked and told me a number of moving stories about how Aadhaar had helped people, such as that of a man named Ram, who is a farmer in Tikkamgarh district in central India, famous for its lovely white and red Mughal palace. Ram is entitled to a number of government assistance subsidies. He works for the National Rural Employment Guarantee Scheme, which guarantees the poor a minimum of 100 days a year of paid work building roads, upgrading irrigation systems, and other infrastructure projects. Before he got his identity card, to collect his meager wages of eight hundred rupees (twelve dollars) a week, he had to take a day off work (and thus lose over 100 rupees in wages) and pay twenty rupees for a bus ticket to central Attariya town, where the bank is located. Ram then stood in line in the dusty heat for three hours to pay a bribe to the local bureaucrat in order to receive his money. This reduced his actual pay by more than one-third. A study conducted by the Indian government found that, on average, those receiving funds through the Rural Employment Scheme received only 61 percent of the wages they were owed—the rest of the money just disappeared.

Ram was one of the early adopters of Aadhaar. Now he proudly shows off his Aadhaar ID card, and to get his pay, he simply stops by the a new Micro ATM at the local *kirana*—the ubiquitous corner grocery stores in India that sell everything from one-use toothpaste packets to cell phone minutes. The owner scans Ram's fingerprints on a phone app and then pays Ram, keeping only a ten-rupee (sixteen-cent) commission.

Those who have benefited from India's opaque systems for years are naturally opposed to Aadhaar. Some politicians argued that the Aadhaar system was a waste of money, or infringed on people's privacy. The more conspiracy theory inclined said it was a plot by the Congress-led government, who approved it, to give government handouts only to its supporters. That is untrue.

The privacy argument is the only one that has made some headway. The Indian Supreme Court ruled in August 2015 that no government agency could mandate that citizens sign up for Aadhaar in order to receive services, and that the program must be voluntary. The program was indeed designed to be voluntary, but over the last year, more and more states and government agencies were making its use mandatory for services ranging from buying cooking gas to registering marriages.

Nilekani met with new Prime Minister Modi, who was initially a skeptic, and convinced him of the value of the system. Modi's support gave Nilekani momentum to put the program beyond the reach of its detractors.

Aadhaar was a big investment and that was one of the initial objections. The World Bank said in January 2016 that the program is already saving the Indian government an impressive one billion dollars a year! Tackling corruption pays, both for the many ordinary Indians who no longer have to pay bribes to get basic services, and for the government coffers. The success of the program offers hope, but the rearguard battle demonstrates what a herculean task real reform will be.

★   ★   ★

Both India and China will have to make more comprehensive reforms to get into the league of Hong Kong, Singapore, or South Korea, who have successfully tackled graft. It is worth their while to do so because corruption has significant negative effects on investment, entrepreneurship, and government efficiency, and takes points off economic growth. Corruption also harms human development in other ways—by degrading the environment (as corrupt officials look the other way when companies pollute), human health and safety, and the equality of the society. Most important, it erodes trust in government, as India's Congress Party discovered when it was turfed out of office in 2014, in large part because many ministers were seen as inept and corrupt. Rumblings about corruption on Chinese social media have the Chinese Communist Party worried that it may meet a similar fate—through revolution or an internal power struggle, not elections.

The best anticorruption methods are not a secret—they have been implemented successfully in many countries, including in Asia. Hong Kong provides an excellent case study, in part because it is culturally so similar to mainland China.

Four decades ago, according to Transparency International, an international nonprofit dedicated to fighting corruption, Hong Kong was one of the most corrupt cities in the world. Much of the local government was a mafia-style kleptocracy. Change came only after Peter Godber, the police superintendent, fled the territory while being investigated for his suspicious luxury cars and lavish mansion. Mass street protests—similar to the recent ones in Delhi—forced the government to take action.

In response to the public outcry, the Hong Kong government established an independent commission to battle corruption, called "ICAC," in February 1974. The commission is not political, has wide investigative powers, and is able to dole out tough punishments. It is similar to the Jan Lokpal that Hazare has campaigned for in India, but which has not yet been fully set up. Wang Qishan and his team have vast powers similar to ICAC. However, in spite of his courageous prosecutions, Wang cannot shake the perception that as a close ally of President Xi and an arm of the Communist Party, his bureaucracy is tainted by politics, and that the prosecutions are a convenient way to take down enemies of President Xi.

The ICAC commission in Hong Kong created a comprehensive education program. According to news reports, "this process starts at local kindergartens, where characters created by ICAC present children with ethical dilemmas and stories, and where the honest person always wins." The program has helped change the cultural norms around corruption from "this is just the way we do business."

Hong Kong declared an amnesty for anyone but the worst offenders in return for disclosing their assets. All officials were required to disclose their assets and were restricted from dealing with companies they had authority over while in government, similar to the requirements for government officials in the United States. Wang Qishan has advocated similar disclosures in China but has not yet been willing to grant an amnesty to government workers, which means that compliance is slow. For the past several years, Indian politicians have also been required to disclose their assets.

As a carrot to comply with all these new restrictions, Hong Kong added substantial pay increases for public officials. While most anticorruption scholars agree this is a good idea, a minority has found that pay increases have no impact on corruption. China is experimenting with the same idea and recently gave many public officials a whopping 60 percent pay increase.

Hong Kong also benefited from its policies of free speech and expression. Mass protests against the government in the 1970s caused it to take action on bribery, and the press freely reports on investigations today. India's commitment to free expression permitted Hazare to gather tens of thousands of followers and demand that the government set up the independent commission. Similar protests would be unthinkable in China, where censors walk a fine line: allowing people to report on corruption on social media on the one hand, but cracking down if that leads to any criticism of (not to mention public protests against) the government. Various studies have found a strong correlation between freedom of expression and rooting out corruption, which creates a real dilemma for China.

Hong Kong was an early adopter of making government contracts more transparent and putting government services—such as obtaining land records—online. China has taken some steps in this direction. Prime Minister Modi and many state-level leaders in India have made this a signature initiative. The efforts to move to direct cash transfers to the poor through the Aadhaar system, and the government's new initiatives to allow companies to obtain business licenses and environmental clearances online, should help to reduce graft.

These reforms worked in Hong Kong and in many other countries that adopted versions of them. From one of the most corrupt cities in the world, Hong Kong moved up to now rank eighteenth in Transparency International's Corruption Index—directly behind United States.

Can the United States do anything to support these types of reforms in India and China? This is a sensitive issue. I was reminded of this when I undiplomatically raised the issue of corruption at a meeting of high-level former U.S. and Indian government officials in Delhi in 2011. While two young Indian parliamentarians actively supported my view that India should get serious about this, the older Indian officials told me in no uncertain terms that the United States should keep its nose out of such things and that, in any event, there was no corruption problem in India.

Somewhat surprisingly, China has asked the United States and other governments to help with its anticorruption drive. It has given the United States a list of more than 100 people suspected of corruption who are believed to be hiding here and promised to share up to 80 percent of the fugitives' seized assets with the U.S. government. So far the United States has been reluctant, because it doesn't trust that suspects will receive fair trials in the Chinese judicial system, and worries about its use of the death penalty for corruption. Sending Chinese fugitives back is also difficult. U.S. law requires that assets must be traced directly to unlawful activity before they are seized—a virtually impossible task given China's opaque system. Although both countries signed an agreement on repatriation in

April 2015, the Obama administration has only returned about a dozen individuals wanted for corruption, including wealthy businessman Yang Jinjun who was sent back to China just days before President Xi Jinping's first state visit to the United States in September 2015. The United States has thus far refused to hand over Ling Wancheng, another wealthy businessman wanted on corruption charges, who may possess embarrassing information about officials loyal to President Xi.

Despite the potential traps, the United States should find a way to support China on this issue—even if it means asking the FBI or local police to undertake complex investigations into the origins of funds. American officials are quietly trying to find ways to help the Chinese government by expelling the Chinese fugitives based on immigration or money laundering charges. These efforts will be seen by China as a mark of friendship and respect and gives the United States leverage to nudge China to make other anticorruption reforms.

The American government can also assist by contributing the technology behind online platforms that provide government services, or by sharing their best practices. (This is more difficult with China because of the two countries' mutual distrust over cybersecurity.) Although the effort is in its infancy, the United States and India have agreed to collaborate to implement India's ambitious Digital India initiative, including by helping India deploy the e-governance initiatives that will make interactions with the government more transparent. This is already showing some success. It is unlikely that China would welcome similar assistance.

The most important thing the United States can do is continue to enforce its own anticorruption laws. The United States and Great Britain are the world leaders in this space. They have set an example by prosecuting their companies for bribery violations if they—or, increasingly, the company's foreign joint venture partners, distributors, or sales agents—pay bribes. This means that American corporations are careful to only work with reputable local partners in India, China, and elsewhere. They also force local partners to disclose any past bribery, often audit their books, and ask them to sign documents promising not to pay off any local official. This forces Chinese or Indian companies that want to partner with foreign multinationals to adopt western standards. U.S. laws have already set a good example that many modern, global Indian and Chinese companies, including Wipro, Infosys, and Tencent, follow.

American corporations and the government can and should support the nascent efforts by the giants to become more transparent. As China and India expand their own companies' and government influence abroad, it is in our interest that everyone plays by the same rules. I often hear complaints from American clients that they were underbid for a government contract in a third country—such as in Africa and Latin America—by a Chinese (or in more rare cases) Indian company that appeared to be offering handouts to officials as part of its sales strategy. If we want China and India to "come onto the governing board of the world," and to develop the positive vision of 2030 together, this is one of the major cultural factors on which we will have to become more aligned.

6 | THE YOUNG AND THE OLD

I N 2008, President Hu Jintao told U.S. Secretary of State Condoleezza Rice that his biggest concern was to find jobs for the 20 million young Chinese coming in from the countryside or entering the workforce each year. Only six years later, in the summer of 2014, President Xi's chief economic advisor, Liu He, said that his most pressing concern is now with an entirely different group: the elderly.

Almost 200 million Chinese are over sixty years old (compared to just 60 million Americans), and that number will nearly double by 2030. China's working-age population will peak within the next several years, and decline thereafter. By 2030, only about 47 percent of Chinese people are expected to be of working age. In an attempt to avoid a crisis, the Chinese government recently ended its one-child policy. Liu He and his team have begun a number of reforms. He expects that people are going to have to pay more into their pensions.

This prospect has already set off a heated debate. It turns the expectations of China's Mao generation on its head. Rural retirees expected very little. Urban Chinese who worked in state-owned companies or for the government implicitly relied on the "iron rice bowl": the idea that workers stayed at one place throughout life and that the enterprise would take care of them in old age. The iron rice bowl has become untenable as China moves toward a market economy—in fact, the bowl is nearly empty and many retirees have to rely on their children to survive. Each young working couple saves with the expectation that they may have to support their parents and possibly grandparents in old age. If these young workers could save less and consume more, it would help China's economy grow. At the end of 2014, the Chinese government announced an important pension reform. Without more drastic steps, however, even this reform is unlikely to be sufficient. The graying of China may be the most important obstacle to China becoming a stable, relatively affluent, middle-income country.

While China scrambles to address the challenges of an aging population, India is growing younger. Indian Prime Minister Modi likes to talk about the coming "demographic dividend": the idea that India's growing workforce could raise its economic growth. Indians are proud of their young population. In 2030, almost 70 percent of Indians will be of working age, giving India the world's largest labor force and a growth advantage that could add up to two percentage points to India's GDP annually.

The challenge of making this demographic dividend a reality weighs heavily on India's Finance Minister Arun Jaitley. After he spoke to our small group of former U.S. government officials in Delhi in January 2015, he leaned in to reveal his biggest worry: to make sure all those young Indians are an asset, his government must help provide quality education and jobs and close the gender gap for the 12 million youngsters entering the workforce every year.

India is far behind in this epic challenge. Its education system needs an overhaul. Nearly 300 million Indians are illiterate. Indian kids still only attend school an average of about five years, compared to China's eight years. Only one-tenth of working-age Indians have received any vocational training. The government is pushing hard to fix these problems, but the task is enormous. To compete internationally, it must also be able to place Indian students into growing industries in the country, hence Prime Minister Modi's emphasis on building a large manufacturing sector.

★   ★   ★

David Zhou is one of the young Chinese whom the Chinese government would like to help. David is charming and smart. With dark-rimmed glasses and designer jeans, he has a PhD from a famous university in Shanghai and is now a star professor of energy studies at Zhejiang University. His English is excellent, and he frequently participates in U.S.-China "young leaders" initiatives. He is not much different from an upper-middle-class, well educated American, yet he carries a very significant burden: in addition to taking care of his wife and young son, he sends a substantial part of his salary back home to his parents, although he is hesitant to say how much. When I ask why, he tells me his background.

"I am not like other successful city kids," he explains. "I grew up in a small fishing village near the East China Sea. It's lovely there—filled with orange groves that my parents farmed. Our house is right by the fields. My parents built it around the time I was born. My parents had three children, and I am the youngest, so of course they had to pay a big fine to have me."

In a nod to Confucian filial piety, he doesn't expect the government to bail him out: "My parents worked day and night, and really gave up everything for us. Now they are old and we must take care of them. Luckily they are healthy, and still work a bit, although they are over sixty," he adds.

David and his older brother both went to university, which was very expensive for their parents. His brother founded a successful IT start-up in Shanghai. His sister is married, works at a local company, and lives near her parents' village to help take care of them. When I marvel at how successful each of the children have been, David gently chides me. "This is the new China," he said. "We get a pretty good education, even if we are just smart farmers. There weren't many village kids who got PhDs like I did, but the story is not unheard-of. Now there are more and more."

David is touchingly concerned about his parents. He regrets that he can only travel home about twice a year. Instead, his parents stay with him and his wife for several months a year. Although the Confucian tradition of caring for elderly relatives remains strong, this tradition presumed that many siblings would share the burden and the entire family would live in the same house or in close proximity. David is lucky to have siblings to help.

His wife is an only child, far more common for this generation, so they may have to take care of her aging parents as well. Only-children support up to four aging parents and, in some cases, up to eight grandparents. In modern China, most working couples also live in tiny city apartments, often far from their hometowns, and this makes it hard to house and care for aging parents. These young couples will need help from the government.

Luckily, elderly citizens don't yet expect much from the government. Most are happy to receive anything at all. David gratefully describes the new rural pension system China's government recently implemented for people like his parents. Before 2009, Chinese living in the countryside had no pensions. Now they can make modest, voluntary contributions to individual accounts that the government subsidizes. Without having paid in, David's parents now receive about one thousand yuan each per year, and this could go up somewhat if they work longer and contribute.

"That's less than two hundred dollars a year!" I exclaimed.

"It's better than nothing," David responded with a smile. "Their farming income and this pension is not enough to live on well," he added. "So my brother and I send money to help with the rest. Later, if my parents get sick or too old to take care of themselves, we will have to do much more. It's not like the United States or Europe, where you expect the government to take care of your old people."

China's nascent pension system is small, and similar to the United States' first Social Security system, in 1935. When Social Security expanded after World War II, the relatively poor Depression-era generation received benefits without ever having contributed. Similarly, a now-booming China has to bail out the unlucky generation, like David's parents, who began work during the Cultural Revolution and had no opportunity to pay in to a pension or save. This generation is extremely poor: a Chinese starting a job in 2000 will earn six times as much in his life (in constant terms) as his father who started work in 1970. As in the United States, Chinese who are working now think they are paying into their own pensions, but this money is actually being paid out to their parents and grandparents. The crucial difference is that when the United States was ramping up its Social Security system in the 1940s, a smaller portion of the population was old. The task China is attempting now is comparable to the United States creating Social Security virtually from scratch in the 1990s, with the baby boomers retiring without having paid anything in.

The Chinese retirement edifice is shaky. It is a patchwork of thousands of state and local pension funds with no real central oversight. The rural pension scheme that covers David's parents is not very generous. Since 2009, when China created the system, some 325 million Chinese have been promised retirement benefits—almost as many as the entire population of the United States. David's parents are lucky enough to receive about $200 a year now, with the hope that it could rise as high as $350 a year in the future. The plan is to expand it to cover the unemployed as well.

Chinese government workers are the only ones who receive a relatively generous retirement, a fact that many private sector workers resent. In 2011, government workers received about 40 percent of their working pay (about $4,000 a year), even though they never had to pay into the system. By contrast, workers in large private sector companies have to contribute eight percent of their wages. After they have contributed for fifteen years, they are entitled to approximately $2,900 a year. The employees' individual accounts are supposed to be reserved specifically for them, similar to a 401(k), but many local governments have had to "borrow" from these accounts to pay the pensions of the people retiring now, just like in the United States. Accurate numbers are hard to come by, but this has left a gap of an estimated hundreds of billions of dollars in unfunded pensions. This gap will rise to $128 trillion (yes, trillion) by 2050, according to the Chinese Academy of Social Sciences. It sounds very much like the problems we have in the United States, only, like most things in China, on an even more epic scale.

Without massive investment, the tidal wave of elderly Chinese who will retire in the next decades will bring the fledgling pension system to its knees. Almost 400 million Chinese will be over sixty years old in 2030—more than the population of the United States. The Chinese government now permits each couple to have two children instead of just one, but this will not alleviate the current demographic crisis.

As China scholar Mark Frazier has argued in a thoughtful book, there are obstacles to pension reform. Wealthy cities like Shanghai and Beijing would rather operate their own pension systems than see them centralized with poorer parts of the country. State-owned enterprises are reluctant to pay into pension systems, arguing (paradoxically, for a government-owned entity) that profits should go to shareholders. The government made the unpopular but necessary decision in February 2016 to raise the retirement ages from the currently low age of fifty-five for women and sixty for men. Many Chinese argue that early retirement helps make room for young workers, although it adds to the demographic burden.

The man in charge of preventing a coming pensions meltdown is Liu He. Tall, slim, and bookish, with a Harvard economics degree, he doesn't look the part of a Chinese Communist Party apparatchik. Yet he is one of President Xi Jinping's closest confidants. Liu and his team have the unenviable job of keeping Chinese growth on track, and of fixing China's enormous pension gap.

Under Liu's stewardship, at the end of 2014, the government introduced reforms to reduce inequality between public and private sector pensions, and unify pensions under one nationwide scheme—similar to Social Security in the United States. The government has promised to implement a universal old-age pension by 2020, along with big changes to provide medical insurance to all, as we saw in the previous chapter. Until now, the government was paying public sector pensions out of the general budget. There was no dedicated revenue source. Beginning in October 2015, 40 million Chinese public servants must now contribute 8 percent of their income to their retirement to address the shortfall in funds, just as private sector workers do. This was of course unpopular with public employees, so the Ministry of Human Resources and Social Security agreed to give all public servants a pay raise that same year. However, this risks undermining the reform.

Even with these substantial gaps, the Chinese pension system is the envy of many Indians. Only about 12 percent of India's working population is covered by any social security. About 90 percent of Indian workers are in the unorganized sector—everything from small shops that don't pay taxes, to day-wage construction workers, and the waste pickers I met in eastern Delhi. As a result, even if India wanted to build a comprehensive pension scheme, it would be nearly impossible for people to contribute some of their paychecks to this effort. There are no paychecks. Under a new reform any worker—even those in the informal sector—can invest a small amount every month in a fund they choose and get a lump sum payout when they retire, similar to a 401(k). Few Indians have any cash to save, so the plan is not very popular yet. In this way, India's youth bulge is a double blessing: relatively few Indians are currently of retirement age, and almost none expect their government to provide for them. If the government can take advantage of a large and productive working class, it can avoid a pension crisis similar to China's.

China's retirees will soon need a slew of other services, most important, decent health care and senior housing. Until recently, the thought of shuttling grandparents off to nursing homes seemed almost offensive to most. David explains that his grandparents lived with his family until their deaths. It is harder for David and his wife to live up to this Confucian ideal. They live in a tiny apartment in the city of Hangzhou, both work at universities, and they don't plan to move back to their home village. It would be almost impossible to house his parents, or hers. He is reluctant to think that far ahead, and says only that he is happy that his parents are healthy so far, and that his sister lives nearby.

China's health-care system is more developed than the concept of elder care. Since 2003, China has expanded public spending on health care and the health insurance system at a breakneck pace. Many poor people, especially migrant workers like Xian and Qian, do not know they are covered by basic health insurance. Even if they are aware, the new insurance schemes only cover between 4 and 50 percent of health costs (compared to 88 percent in the United States) and there are annual caps, which means the family must pay if someone has a serious illness. Beijing has ambitious plans to expand these schemes to effectively cover all Chinese by 2020. While David is grateful that the government pays some of his parents' health-care costs, he is worried he won't be able to afford to pay if they fall seriously ill.

The Chinese health-care sector remains inefficient and fragmented (as in the United States). On average, households, including David's, spend more than 8 percent of their incomes on health care, similar to the United States, although the care is far more basic. Patients rely on hospital care

instead of prevention, many don't know how to manage diseases of afflu-
ence that are becoming more common, like heart disease and diabetes,
and China has a painful lack of doctors. It needs to nearly double the
number of well-qualified doctors in the country to deal with the bulge of
elderly patients, which means training nearly one million new physicians.

This litany of aging-related problems keeps Chinese officials up at night
because it is holding back their country's growth. As we saw earlier, the
Chinese economy is slowing to a more moderate pace. The economic
boom driven by massive infrastructure investment and easy credit cannot
continue indefinitely. So the government must find a way to encourage
people to save less and consume more to stimulate the economy.

The Communist Party, and in particular its economics guru, Liu He,
believe a new lever for growth is to invest more in public goods, in part
by building the health facilities, pension systems, public transit, and other
goods the aging population needs. This transition has started, as Chinese
learn to rely more on professional health, pension, and elder care services,
rather than shouldering these burdens one family at a time. By building
out its safety net for the elderly, China will permit its working families
to save less for their parents' care, and spend more on themselves, thus
growing the economy.

American companies are well placed to help China make this vital
transition. Doing so is in their economic interest and in the political interest of the U.S. government. Politically, the United States should want
to see a China that emphasizes the well-being of its people through social
spending on pensions and health care rather than investing more in its
enormous internal security and military apparatus. Additionally, if China
does not successfully address these domestic problems, the government
will face unrest, which might lead it to be more aggressive internationally
as a way to distract from internal discontent.

Economically this is a new, potentially enormous market for American and European insurers, retirement money managers, health-care pro-
viders, pharmaceutical companies, and real estate companies investing in
housing for the elderly.

The insurance industry in China was until recently largely off-limits to foreign investors, but since 2012, foreign companies can own 100 percent of a Chinese insurance operation. China does not yet have much of a private health insurance industry, and only very few private hospital chains. This may all be changing as the government encourages the private sector to help meet the growing demand for health care.

American companies such as Methodist Healthcare and Swedish Medical Center are partnering with Chinese companies to build hospitals. Columbia Pacific and Merrill Gardens are creating senior housing. The New York hedge fund Fortress is working with China's Fosun Group to invest $1 billion in senior care in China. They opened their first senior living facility in Shanghai several years ago. A variety of senior care product companies have begun to work in China, including Direct Supply, the largest U.S. company providing elder-friendly beds, rehabilitation, and transportation equipment to nursing homes. The private pension market is in its infancy, but Australian company AMP was the first foreign company to buy a stake in a Chinese pension company in October 2014. This is likely the beginning of a much larger wave.

By helping its companies gain market access to this opportunity, the United States can help China gain the skills and technical know-how to meet its retirement challenge. Only the Chinese government, however, can figure out how to pay for the critical economic transition it must undertake.

★　★　★

As China grays, India faces the opposite problem. It is struggling to create sufficient education and job opportunities to keep its young adults gainfully occupied. The Modi government knows that if it misses this demographic dividend, the Indian economic juggernaut may stall and a new generation of hundreds of millions of Indians will be trapped well below the middle-class life they aspire to. To take advantage of a youth bulge, India will need decent schools. It will also need to create labor-intensive jobs in manufacturing and bring in more foreign direct investment. India must slow population growth in some states so that its youths are not working solely to feed their own many children. As the population gets wealthier, the "bulge" will also increase demand for electricity and water and put more strain on India's creaking infrastructure. The prime minister and his team are urgently pressing many reforms precisely to help India catch the wave of its youth boom.

Looking around the room of well-heeled CEOs at an annual conference celebrating the "the Indus Entrepreneurs" in Silicon Valley, one could imagine that India has the best education system in the world. Graduates of India's elite engineering schools, the Indian Institutes of Technology (or IITs), helped found dozens of America's most successful technology companies. Indian-born executives run some of our best-known companies, such as Google, PepsiCo, Microsoft, and MasterCard.

After independence, Prime Minister Nehru dedicated enormous resources to creating some of the world's premier engineering universities, sometimes at the expense of basic education for all. Without exaggeration, Indian students describe getting into an IIT as a "ticket to another life."

The first generation of this technical elite often emigrated to make their fortunes in the United States or Europe, an unfortunate brain drain that is now being reversed. The star Indian students of today are much more likely to stay in India, or to attend universities abroad and then return to India to build their careers there because they see bigger opportunities at home.

Unfortunately, educated Indians are an exception. From elementary schools to graduate degrees, the education system is underresourced and creaking. The Delhi slum school I visited crammed twenty kids into each twelve-by-twelve -foot, furniture-less classroom. Children sat on the brown floor and wrote with stubs of donated pencils. They created an art project for me out of trash they had found. Fittingly, it looked like a red phoenix rising from the ashes of the waste heap. To contrast with the glittering world of Indian engineering stars, India has by far the most illiterate adults in the world. Nearly 300 million adult Indians cannot read, more than a third of the total illiterate population on earth.

Nevertheless, the country has made some real progress. In the 1980s, only 60 percent of Indian youths could read; now the number is over 90 percent. But Indian children still receive far fewer years of schooling than Chinese or American children—only a bit over five years on average. If they make it through high school, very few Indians receive any vocational training. Stories like those of David Zhou, the Chinese farmer's son who got his PhD, are far more common in China than they are in India. The reason is straightforward: India until recently concentrated its scarce resources on creating first-rate universities, rather than basic education for all. India spent 11.3 percent of the total government budget on education in 2012, compared to more than 16 percent in China, and 13.8 percent in the United States.

At the youngest grades, India has recently made progress. After long battles, in 2010, India's energetic human resources (education) minister, Kapil Sibal from the Congress Party, passed the Right to Education Act, which made eight years of education a fundamental right for every child. The act guarantees free and compulsory education for children from six to fourteen years old and forces private schools to reserve a quarter of their seats for low-income students. Children from the poorest neighborhoods are now attending some of India's most prestigious private schools.

According to UNICEF, since the law took effect, 11 million more children have enrolled in schools, which means an impressive 96.7 percent of children between ages six and fourteen are now in school. Farida, the young girl I met in the east Delhi slum, has benefited from these programs. Her family initially did not want to send her to school; they were reluctant to lose the few rupees she could earn by sorting plastic bottles from the landfill. A combination of coaxing by teachers from the Chintan nonprofit, and outreach by the Indian government encouraging everyone to enter school, helped convince Mohammad that this was right for his daughter. The state governments have experimented with giving children free lunches, uniforms, and stationery and have made real efforts to build usable toilets and add running water in schools—all as incentives for poor parents to let their kids go.

Although it has improved enrollment, India faces chronic problems because there are not enough teachers, some existing teachers are unskilled, and others chronically miss work. India needs a sobering 1–2 million (!) new teachers for the bulge of children who are entering its creaking school system. Minister Sibal told me in 2012 that India has to train *several hundred thousand teachers* a year to teach the 200 million Indian schoolchildren. He added that in the United States, there are about

3,000 teachers per million people, but in India there are only 456. The government is racing to establish teachers' colleges to overcome this painful gap.

Even when there are teachers in a school, they are often absent. Farida comes to the Chintan nonprofit school partly because her government teacher is very often not there. Indian teachers are not lazy. Their wages are meager and often paid late, and so many take a second job to pay their bills. Teacher absenteeism is one of the many problems the Aadhaar biometric identification scheme is helping to fix. Increasingly, teachers are asked to swipe in using their Aadhaar ID, and then get paid electronically if they have taught the required number of hours. Some states now monitor teachers with cameras to police whether they come to school. This improved attendance and drove test scores up. Others have tried paying bonuses to teachers for good test scores.

Unfortunately, the problems don't end in elementary school. Dropout rates are high. Only about a third of Indian teens finish high school, compared to about 85 percent in China. Dalits and Muslims at the bottom of the social ladder are particularly unlikely to complete their schooling. As a Muslim girl, Farida is 63 percent less likely than a non-Muslim to graduate from high school. Muslim and lower-caste Hindu boys have similarly low graduation rates. This discrepancy is one of the main reasons that inequality in India persists.

For the lucky Indian teens who manage to finish high school, their prospects are not rosy. A vast majority of them cannot get jobs even if they finish university. This was brought home to me in striking fashion in Delhi last January. As I strolled around Connaught Circle, the old business center of town, with multiple ringed streets of hip bars, elegant clothing in somewhat shabby shop windows, and a warren of run-down offices, a young man followed me. I felt out of place in my American business suit and tried to avoid him by crossing the street—a death-defying stunt of dodging buses, new Toyotas, and ancient black Ambassador taxies. He was undeterred. "Madam—please stop!" he insisted, and when I did, he put a grimy resume into my hand. "I am a university graduate. In business. Excellent marks. Can I work for you?"

"You don't know who I am or where I work," I responded, incredulous.

He seemed not at all perturbed by this, and launched into his dream of working for a western company, and naturally assumed that an American woman wandering the streets of Delhi was working for one and might be able to help him with his bizarre job search strategy. I finally agreed to take the resume (I am ashamed to say mostly as a way to get rid of him) and explained that I worked across the world in San Francisco. How can a university graduate in one of the world's fastest-growing economies be reduced to this?

Even for the lucky few who attend, Indian high schools and universities don't teach the skills that modern companies need. While an ambitious, young graduate searches for a job on the street, the Indian economy is creating millions of jobs. According to the government, the IT sector alone is expected to create 20 million new jobs in the next six years, and health care 40 million. Yet industry executives complain that they can't find skilled labor to fill these jobs. Large companies such as Tata and Wipro run their own training institutes to get recruits up to speed. Hundreds of Indian companies retrain workers who have higher education but who studied an outdated curriculum on inadequate equipment. As many as 83 percent of engineers graduating from Indian universities in 2013 could not find jobs, due to poor English language and other skills. The call center company 24/7 Customer Pvt. Ltd. hires only three out of every one hundred Indian applicants and now recruits in the Philippines and Nicaragua, where the qualifications are better.

I asked Ajay Kela, the CEO of the Wadhwani Foundation, one of the most innovative foundations in India working on education issues, what creates this paradox. "India's education system has a long way to go—I would rate it a three out of ten," he explained. "Outside of the Indian Institutes of Technology [IITs, the elite engineering schools that take only about 2 percent of applicants], Indian Institutes of Management, and a few others, the quality of universities has fallen dramatically. Less than half of the yearly high school graduates in India go to university. For the rest, there is almost no option, and they are left behind." Kela himself is a graduate of the illustrious IIT Bombay, and ran several technology companies in Silicon Valley and Bangalore before dedicating himself full time to the foundation.

"So many Indian companies hire university graduates to do jobs that someone with a twelfth-grade education and a good six-month training program could do better. Banking sales agents, call center workers, nursing assistants and paramedics—today most of these are university graduates in India.

"What's the outcome? More than half leave their jobs within a few years because job skills do not match their aspirations. In the meantime, those with no university education have essentially no good job options. It's a colossal waste."

To help fix this and prepare India's workforce for the twenty-first century, Romesh Wadhwani set up his foundation in 2000. Wadhwani himself is one of the success stories of Indian higher education. He was among the speakers at the glittering "Indus Entrepreneurs" event in Silicon Valley. A graduate of IIT Bombay and Carnegie Mellon, he settled in Northern California and started many technology companies, one of which he sold for several billion dollars. He now lives in a vast Italianate mansion in an exclusive Silicon Valley neighborhood. Guests are asked to leave their high heels at the door and put on slippers as they enter—in the style of a European chateau tour—to avoid damaging the antique mosaic floors. From his cozy library, Wadhwani keeps a firm grip on the reins of his for-profit and nonprofit empire. We met several times over the years to discuss his substantial charity work and vision for improving Indian higher education. Wadhwani and Kela are working with India's central and state governments, corporations, and like-minded foundations to expand the skills of India's future workforce.

"We don't want to go back to the old brick-and-mortar model of education when technology can help deliver high-quality learning on-demand," Kela explained. "The Indian government has funded a pilot for four hundred skills colleges. Instead of building more physical schools, our foundation can best help by helping to create up-to-date educational content that can then be delivered online to millions of students, anytime, anywhere."

The foundation has researched which jobs will have high demand in the future—such as nursing, cybersecurity, sales representatives, and others. For dozens of such job roles it has funded creating online courses that are updated as knowledge in each area evolves. Large Indian corporations like Narayan Health, Future Group, and others worked with them to develop the content.

"The corporations are willing to help," Kela explained, "because hiring someone who can only do the job after six to twelve months of training is hugely expensive and wasteful. So they are sharing their content and helping to build multimedia courses delivered through the cloud."

Now that the initial five skills courses are up and running, the government has agreed to fund almost all of the cost of creating forty-five more up-to-date course curricula that will be taught partly online, and partly to high school graduates who go to the new vocational colleges in the evenings.

Suman Singh is one of the first graduates of this new skilling initiative in Haryana State—northeast of Delhi. She is diminutive, but when I spoke to her by phone, she was surprisingly forceful, determined to achieve her goals, and grateful to the program. "My father is a laborer who only made sixty thousand rupees [approximately $950] a year," she began. "I wanted to support my family after finishing twelfth grade, and I was lucky to enroll in one of the new IT courses. It has changed my life. My teacher was like a friend, philosopher, and guide to me," she adds poetically. "I used to be shy, and from a government school in a rural area, so I had not experienced anything. Now I know Word, Excel, and even the Internet. Our teacher took us to a real mall on our industry visit. Being there for three hours was a dream come true—after that, all I could think of was to work in such a beautiful and posh office."

Suman has realized her dream. In an on-campus interview, Dish TV hired her, and she does data entry for another firm in her spare time to earn more money, in total about four thousand dollars a year. Suman says the figures proudly, repeating each number twice for emphasis. "I earn five times more than my father! It is a golden opportunity for me," she adds. "I am thankful for all who have helped, and I will do more online courses." The Wadhwani Foundation skills initiative could not have a more fervent spokesperson.

Prime Minister Modi wholeheartedly embraced this and similar projects—although many were started under the previous government.

He calls the new Skill Development Ministry his "favorite ministry." With new ideas like these, the Indian government plans to increase the workforce with formal vocational training from 12 to 25 percent in five years. This means training 70 million people, greater than the entire population of France.

The 2015 and 2016 Indian government budgets focus on these "skilling" initiatives but leave the allocation for primary and secondary education basically flat. The government has announced its first massive online courses—some created in cooperation with the Wadhwani Foundation and others. In addition, it is consolidating student loan schemes into one financial aid authority that will administer loans by sending digital vouchers directly into a student's bank account. In February 2016, the government announced that it would build 1,500 new skills training institutes across the county—specificially to help students like Farida and Suman.

It is too early to predict whether these well-meaning initiatives will succeed. My visits to mostly decrepit Indian schools and their more impressive Chinese counterparts make me skeptical that India will turn its education system around in time to reap fully its "demographic dividend." It will be hard for India's unruly democracy, with permanent budget shortfalls, to sustain the effort and funding needed to truly upgrade the education system, rather than just making marginal fixes. India's federalist system means that much of education policy is decided at the state level. This leads to serious differences between India's various states.

The United States should promote collaboration on education as one way to expand our strategic partnership with India. A strong, economically healthy India is in our long-term interest. If India's demographic dividend pays off, a more educated, wealthy generation of Indians will increasingly buy American products, thus expanding our own economy. A more educated workforce is also likely to promote environmental stewardship, as we are already seeing in China, and an economically strong India will have the resources to project its power abroad in a constructive way.

As with China's pensions conundrum, the United States cannot fix the budget crunch that makes it difficult for India to upgrade its education system, but we can help make that system more efficient and effective. The U.S. government is already implementing an assortment of small initiatives to this effect, including establishing a new IIT and bringing three hundred Indian Fulbright scholars and 110 teachers to the United States for training last year. This makes for nice lines in diplomatic speeches but is a tiny drop in the bucket. A more ambitious approach might take the budding collaboration between U.S. community colleges and their Indian counterparts and ramp these up substantially. While U.S. community colleges also need some reform, many already have workforce programs that are aligned to the needs of local industry. The students who finish those programs have high employment rates. As economies globalize, the skills people need for modern jobs converge. Ajay Kela points out that car engines are now so similar in India and in the United States that a mechanic in both countries will need nearly the same skills, as will a software developer, or a nurse's aide. Improving these vocational courses and putting them online, which the United States can help do, will open vast areas for collaboration with India, at very low cost to the U.S. government.

Traditional American universities are eager to help fill India's education gap, but this will take longer. While foreign universities are legally allowed to partner with local universities, and a few have done so, in practice India's license raj deters most American institutions from working there. Indian officials insist that they want to change this, but so far have not had success.

Private companies can also play a role. Indian students are already adopting the new "MOOCs"—U.S. companies that offer "massive open online courses"—at impressive rates. Sebastian Thrun, the founder of U.S. online university Udacity, told me that even without doing any advertising in India or tailoring his curriculum, a full 7 percent of Udacity's 160,000 weekly students are from India. This is by far the largest group from any country outside the United States. The Khan Academy, a U.S.-based non-profit e-learning website founded by MIT graduate Salman Khan, also launched free online tutorials in Hindi in India in December 2015. If multinational corporations focus less on which degrees students received from which colleges, and instead hire based on the student's skills, this move to online education could benefit underprivileged students like Suman.

★   ★   ★

Educating its "youth bulge" is a major obstacle on India's path to becoming a middle-income country. Finding a reasonable retirement for its growing number of retirees challenges China in a similar way. These are also noncontentious topics where there are many positive ways for the United States, China, and India to collaborate, and thus to strengthen the budding partnership between both giants and the United States.

7 | HALF THE SKY

*C*HAL KAPDE UTAAR!' 'Come on—take your clothes off!' my rapist barked at me. He was a high-caste man and had followed me into the field. I shouldn't have headed to the pastures alone, but I really had to relieve myself.

"I tried to run on the mud path, but the man caught up with me and slammed my head against a tree. . . . After he was finished, he spat on me. I was only eighteen. I went to the police, the politicians. Everyone said I had asked for it, going into the fields by myself. I wept a lot. My husband finally left me and he took our boys. I was left with nothing at a young age. Now in my fifties I go around beating men who attack village girls. You asked me why I joined the Gulabi Gang. . . . So that women after me can walk through fields with long, fearless strides."

Banwari Devi was defiant and proud as she told her story to Dr. Atreyee Sen.* Banwari is one of the senior members of the Gulabi Gang, a group of village women from northern India founded in 2006 to combat violence against women.

Banwari herself was fifty-two when Dr. Sen shadowed her and the Gulabi Gang for a month in 2009, but she looked much older—with shriv-

---

*I am indebted to Dr. Atreyee Sen, assistant professor of anthropology at the University of Copenhagen, for sharing with me her extensive research on vigilante feminism and the Gulabi Gang, and in particular her quotes from her interviews with Banwari Devi.

eled brown skin and a crooked back from a lifetime of hard labor in the fields. Like many women in rural India, she was married at fifteen. Her husband left her because it was shameful to be married to a woman who had been raped. For a woman with no husband, life is very difficult— she often cannot get consistent work and is dependent on odd day jobs. Getting financial support from an ex-husband is nearly impossible, particularly for poorer women who can't afford the lawyers and years of wrangling to force their husbands to pay. It is also seen as inappropriate for single women to live alone, so most have to move back in with relatives where they are seen as a burden. Banwari experienced this excruciating injustice. Yet she and her fellow gang members are not victims. They are strong and unbowed.

While India has a fairly modern penal code prohibiting rape and domestic violence, in rural areas, and especially for low-caste women, these laws are rarely enforced. Police routinely refuse to get involved.

The Gulabi Gang finally had enough. The women wear pink saris and carry bamboo sticks to confront abusive husbands, protest against child marriage, and force recalcitrant policemen to take action on rape cases. The pink Gulabi ladies are now such a powerful presence that they rarely have to resort to violence. Just appearing in a village is often enough to get domestic disputes resolved. Gang members mediate disputes about whom a daughter is permitted to marry, or how much her family must pay in dowry money. Other times they sit silently in a family's courtyard— a mass of hot pink fabric and black hair—to shame physically abusive husbands or fathers-in-law into treating women with respect.

Ten years into its existence, the gang has an impressive four hundred thousand members across India. Their fame has spread around the world, with chapters in France and Berlin and many foreign financial supporters.

In India, traditional values have often held women back, both at work and at home. Just like the caste system, the subjugation of women has been difficult to root out, despite well-meaning government attempts to do so. During the colonial period, the British outlawed some of the most egregious practices—such as burning wives on the funeral pyres of their

Banwari Devi and her "Gulabi Gang" dressed in pink saris
and protecting women's rights in Indian villages.
photo credit: *Jonas Gratzer/LightRocket via Getty Images*

husbands. India's 1949 constitution proudly prohibits discrimination on the basis of sex. Today women inherit property equally, there are good laws against sexual harassment in the workplace, women are entitled to paid maternity leave, and violence against women can be punished with long jail terms. India has had several powerful female politicians, including one female prime minister and the current head of the Congress Party. There are of course enormous differences between wealthy, educated women—who fare relatively well—and their poor or rural counterparts. Unfortunately, good laws (and senior female leaders) have done little yet to improve life for India's women, especially the poor or low caste.

Domestic violence and rape are just some of the problems India's women face. The country ranks an appalling 127th out of 187 countries on the UN Development Program's 2013 gender-equality index (this compares to China's impressive 37th place, followed by the United States'

47th). * Wealthy and high-caste women do much better than their poorer sisters. Yet fewer Indian women of all social classes work outside the home than in other Asian countries. When they do it is often in agriculture and as servants, so they are paid poorly and get no benefits. At home, girls are valued less than boys, partly because of the large dowries their families must pay to marry them off. As a result, parents invest less in girls' education, and many female fetuses are aborted (as in China). Violence against women is common. Indians' demands for change recently made international headlines when nationwide protests erupted over the 2012 rape of a woman on a Delhi bus.

The treatment of women in India is a tragedy for human reasons. In cold economic calculus, it also retards India's growth. The Organization for Economic Co-operation and Development (OECD) estimates that enlarging opportunities for women could raise India's GDP growth by around two percentage points per year, putting it well ahead of China's current growth rate. The Indian government thus has an incentive to promote the betterment of women to help its economy, as a way to prevent more citizens' protests, and because the injustice done to many of its women reflects poorly on the entire country.

★   ★   ★

A tragic story of violence such as Banwari Devi's is far less common in China. When her interviewer asked about sexual violence at the factory, the migrant worker sisters Xian and Qian, whom we met in chapter 4, seemed nonplussed. China's massive factories have separate dorms for men and women, and they employ security guards. Xian explained that while cell phones and other items are sometimes stolen from the dorms, rape is very rare. There are cases of sexual harassment and violence, of course, but both women and men are outraged when they occur. One male manager at a factory near Xian's was caught checking the women's bathrooms often, ostensibly to make sure workers weren't hiding there to

---

* The United States ranks relatively low on the gender-equality index for a variety of reasons, such as the relative low percentage of women in high-powered political positions, lack of paid maternity leave, the wage gap, many teenage births, and the high proportion of young AIDS patients who are women, among others.

take extra breaks. The entire factory, women and men, went on strike to protest this behavior and he was forced to apologize.

The Chinese Communist Party deserves credit for promoting Chinese women's equality, especially for encouraging work outside the home. Historically, China was a patriarchal society, starting with Confucius's influential views. Confucius taught that women were subordinate first to their father, and then to their husband. A woman's duty was to bear a son, and then look after her husband and children.

Mao Zedong's Communist Party was less patriarchal. Some Chinese women fought alongside men in the civil war as the communists battled their way out of the wilderness. The communists believed that women working outside the home would help build a robust economy and thus strengthen the communist system. Beginning with Mao's famous declaration in the 1950s that "women hold up half the sky," the communists outlawed forced marriages, prostitution, and foot binding, and allowed women to divorce. In general, the government emphasized that women were to be considered equal to men.

With China's recent swing to market capitalism, however, the communist insistence on gender equality is less prominent and patriarchy is creeping back into the system. While there are some powerful female entrepreneurs and business leaders, Chinese women's incomes have fallen in the last decade compared to those of men. Abortion of female fetuses and violence within the home continue. Women also haven't pushed to the top of the political ladder—only two of twenty-five members of China's Politburo are women. The system is far from perfect, and again there are large differences between educated urban women and their poorer counterparts, but in general, Chinese women face problems more akin to those in the United States.

Chinese women work. Overall, almost 70 percent of Chinese women are employed outside the home, compared to 25 percent of Indian women, and 58 percent and declining in the United States. The difference is most pronounced among more highly educated women, meaning that Chinese women contribute more to their country's "human capital" stock—and to the country's economic growth—than Indian women.

China also has 29 million female entrepreneurs—a quarter of the nation's total—and more self-made female billionaires than any other country. Chinese women own and run everything from small restaurants or beauty shops, to some the country's largest film studios, most successful dating websites, paper mills, investment funds, pharmaceutical companies, and real estate empires.

A wave of Chinese women like Xian and Qian have left the countryside and piled into the electronics factories near China's coasts. They lead dreary lives of twelve-hours shifts and cramped dormitory living, but earn more money than their parents ever dreamed of. Others enter universities at the same rate as men.

Chinese women are also far more likely to work for a full-time employer than Indian women, and thus on paper have benefits like health care, pensions, and maternity leave. Maternity leave is quite generous in China compared to India: since 2012 Chinese women have been able to take fourteen weeks of leave after having a child. The state pays their salaries during this time. Men also have paid leave, but usually not more than two weeks. This is impressive compared to India, which mandates twelve weeks of paid leave—of course only for those few lucky women with formal paychecks. China also compares well to the United States with its twelve weeks of only *unpaid* leave, which puts us in a class with Papua New Guinea and Oman.

In spite of these generous benefits, many Chinese women, especially in blue-collar jobs, say that they do not take time off. Xian's story, mentioned earlier, is typical. When her baby daughter was born, she worked her normal factory shifts until a few days before the birth, when she could no longer stand for long hours. She took a crowded train home to her village, gave birth, left the baby with her in-laws, and was back at her assembly line, manufacturing the world's cell phones, about a week later.

For working women in China, the controversial one-child policy, which was enacted nationwide in 1980, reduced the burden of housework significantly. Most Chinese women over thirty still take almost full responsibility for the home, children, and family elders, regardless of the hours that they work or the income they earn. There is less such work with one child. The one-child policy also created a generation of doting, hands-on grandparents with very few grandchildren. Babies frequently live with their grandparents for the first few years of their lives, or the grandparents move in to look after young children. For wealthier families, nannies are affordable. For Chinese urban millennials, even this culture is changing rapidly. As only children themselves, both girls and boys are used to being "baby-royals," as one friend put it to me. So neither young spouse tends to do much housework. They order takeout and hire cleaning services, like young professionals in New York or London.

Despite the millions of female entrepreneurs, Chinese women are underrepresented at the tops of traditional corporations. Many highly educated Chinese women prefer to work for foreign companies, where the culture tends to be more egalitarian. In addition, due to unofficial (and unacknowledged) university quotas that favor men, Chinese women must also increasingly score higher on university entrance exams than men to be admitted.

In contrast to China, only about a quarter of India's women work outside the home, mostly in the informal sector. They help their husbands in small shops, cleaning the homes of wealthier families, trash picking, or growing crops. There is a "U-shaped" relationship between education and how much Indian women work. Low-caste, poor, and rural women work in high numbers just so their families can eat. When I met Mohammed and his family of trash pickers (see chapter 4), about ten female relatives were sitting in his storage area sorting plastic bottles from cardboard boxes and aluminum cans. Middle-class women with a high school degree or some college face the most cultural pressure not to work. In these families, social status is often considered higher if the woman "can afford" to stay at home. While Indian law requires paid maternity leave, only a small number have formal jobs, so a minuscule 2.5 percent or so of Indian women take advantage of these benefits. Many women in India are also illegally fired when they get pregnant.

Only highly educated women have decent job opportunities as lawyers, accountants, or executives at multinational corporations. Some of these elite women have serious responsibility, especially in banking and the tech sector. Women currently run many of India's public and private sector banks, as well as the local subsidiaries of Morgan Stanley, J.P. Morgan, Intel and Hewlett-Packard.

Even for this educated group, cultural norms and family pressure force many to drop out of good careers early, so the examples above are outliers. I am always surprised how many of my Indian friends were educated at elite U.S. universities but gave up their high-flying jobs as soon as their first baby was born, by choice or as a result of family pressure. My Chinese friends with similar backgrounds are more likely to make big sacrifices to stay at work. In some cases both husband and wife work in the United States and only see their young children, who live with the grandparents back in China, on holidays two to three times a year.

In contrast to China's 29 million female entrepreneurs, in India just 3 million women own (or partially own) small enterprises across the country, such as tea stalls, laundries, and corner stores. Most of these women cannot get formal loans from banks, so they have to turn to family members, friends, and loan sharks to get the capital they need to start and expand. In November 2013, India opened its first bank exclusively to provide loans and financial services to women. The government provided modest initial funding of $161 million. Chinese Internet giant Alibaba has its own loan scheme for the female shop owners who sell on its site, which lends out an impressive $80 million a year. One Chinese company alone is doing half of what the entire government of India can muster. Other than small initiatives such as these, though, the Indian government is not doing much to encourage women to work—at its peril. So far, women's empowerment hasn't featured prominently in Modi's program for economic revival, although he did mention to a Facebook audience in September 2015, somewhat bizarrely, Hinduism is the only religion with female goddesses and that India treats its women well. The country is missing out on the untapped economic potential of half its population.

Chinese women also fare better in their own homes than Indian women, although problems persist. The very first law passed by the communists after they seized power in 1949 outlawed arranged marriages and concubines, and enabled women to divorce. To this day it remains a symbol of the communists' commitment to women's rights.

When the Chinese government implemented the one-child policy in 1980 to slow its population growth, it did not anticipate that this would result in a massive gender imbalance. The one-child policy laid bare the continued Chinese cultural preference for boys. Families prefer boys because of their higher earning potential, so having just one daughter could be an economic disaster. When the policy was implemented, there was a surge in killing of infant girls and aborting female fetuses. Today only about 893 girls are born in China for every 1,000 Chinese boys.

Chinese girls are now so scarce that men have to compete more aggressively to get a wife. By 2030, studies suggest that a full quarter of Chinese men in their late thirties will never have married. The government is beginning to worry about large groups of unmarried men leading to social unrest, and thus has launched campaigns to encourage parents to value and raise daughters, and as of January 2016 it ended the controversial one-child policy. In the meantime, trafficking of women from Vietnam, the Philippines, North Korea, and Cambodia has started to fill some of the demand for brides.

Large companies are getting into the act of encouraging marriage, since there is not much time for flirting on the assembly lines. Xian and Qian report that their giant electronics factory has regular "date night" mixers. These are awkward affairs in fluorescent-lit recreation rooms on the factory campus, where the company provides food and drinks and the young workers are encouraged to mingle. Young men also prefer to work in factories where there is a higher ratio of women workers, so some companies advertise this as a lure to recruit more skilled male workers.

The Chinese government acknowledges the problem of missing girls and introduced laws to deal with it: female infanticide has been forbidden since 1995, and clinics are not allowed to use ultrasound to tell parents the sex of the child. This is almost impossible to enforce, however, and in practice most doctors still tell parents whether they will have a boy or a girl.

Even without a one-child policy to spur them on, Indian families abort girl fetuses at similarly alarming rates as the Chinese. Studies estimate the figure is around 600,000 per year, although the real number is likely much higher. India's child sex ratio is almost as bad as China's and has deterio-rated over the years. In 2014, there were 900 girls born for every 1,000 boys (compared to 893 in China and 1,030 in the United States). Al-though abortions have been legal in India since 1971, most rural women can't reach the clinics, so an estimated two-thirds of abortions performed are unsafe, done at home or by quacks in dirty back-alley sheds. The pink ladies like Banwari tell many stories of young women who come to them feverish and ill after having seen the village midwife, or *daai*, for an abor-tion, which is usually done by giving women an abdominal massage with oils designed to kill the fetus. As in China, Indians prefer boys for eco-nomic reasons: girls are a financial burden to their parents, who must pay expensive dowries to marry them off—especially in rural areas. In addi-tion to having a better chance at finding a good job themselves, boys will get married and thus bring dowry money into the family. Many families are understandably terrified of having more than one daughter. Wealthier and better-educated Indian families are even more likely to abort female fetuses, because they can afford the prenatal tests and medical interven-tion they want. This practice persists even though it has been illegal since 1996 to have an ultrasound scan that identifies the sex of a fetus. As is the case in China, the law is hard to enforce, so doctors continue to do what their patients ask.

China's rush into a market economy coincided with some patriarchy creeping back into marriage as well. Beginning about 2007, the Chinese government began a concerted effort to get its "A" quality women—those with a university education and good jobs—to marry younger. While China doesn't officially acknowledge it, scholar Leta Hong Fincher has argued convincingly that China has an unstated eugenics policy: it wants its most intelligent, educated women to marry and have children. Like many of their peers in the United States, however, these women often marry late or not at all because they are busy working on their careers.

To remedy this perceived problem, for the past few years the media and, perhaps most troublingly of all, the All-China Women's Federation (a government organization founded in 1949 supposedly to defend wom-en's rights) have aggressively pushed the idea that unmarried women over twenty-seven are "leftover women." One particularly sexist television drama was called, not so creatively, "Old Women Should Get Married." It features a thirty-three-year-old woman who watched her younger sister's wedding, went on a terrible blind date with a drug dealer, and put up with her family telling her to stop being so choosy and just settle down. Sungmin Rho, a scholar who lived in China for many years, says that the cultural pressure to marry is extreme. As an unmarried thirty-year-old, she was often called a "dinosaur," or "third-gender."

Yet not all young, educated Chinese women are buying the brainwashing. Gong Ting, a graduate of prestigious Beijing University, who wears bright red lipstick and fashionable curly hair to her waist, tells me that while the pressure to marry is there, many of her elite friends are ignoring it. They tend to settle down later to get their careers established first. Many of her girlfriends want to start their own technology companies, and they know that will be harder with a husband and kids in tow.

Divorce has been legal in China for decades. Slightly less than a quarter of marriages end in divorce (compared to about half in the United States). Just in the past few years, however, Chinese courts have slowly rolled back some progressive divorce laws. In August 2011, for example, the Chinese Supreme Court—which has only one woman among its thirteen judges—ruled that an apartment or house bought before marriage goes back to the buyer on divorce, while the remaining assets such as furniture and bank accounts are split equally. Previously, the family home was common property, split equally. This hurts women, since men or their families traditionally buy an apartment before the wedding as an enticement for the young woman to get married. The wife's family pays for all its furnishings, which are often just as expensive. With the new rule the money the woman brought in is split between the two spouses while the man gets his share back in full. Rural women fare particularly badly under this new rule, because they also lose the right to farm the couple's land after a divorce.

In India divorce is still rare, estimated to be only around 1 percent, and difficult to obtain. Despite several well-meaning attempts by India's Supreme Court to liberalize the law, divorces are granted in India only if both spouses agree, or if the husband or wife can prove adultery, cruelty, or insanity—all hard to establish. As a result, many Indian couples separate but don't legally divorce. At lower income levels or castes, men often abandon wives they no longer want to live with—as Banwari's husband did after she was raped.

An astounding 240 million Indian women were also married off as children, according to the UN Children's Fund (UNICEF). More than two-fifths of Indian women are married before they are eighteen, and for uneducated women that number is much, much higher. Banwari was married at age fifteen. She now fights with village elders and parents to let their girls finish basic schooling before sending them off to the altar.

Even powerful Prime Minister Modi was married as a teenager to a woman (then seventeen) whom his parents had found for him. He abandoned his wife almost immediately to join the Hindu nationalist RSS, which discourages its members from having family ties. Modi kept the marriage secret for years but now acknowledges his wife, a retired teacher who lives with her brother. He has not spoken to her in decades. In interviews with the press, she modestly says that she hopes Modi will return to her one day. In a bizarre twist of Indian bureaucracy, the Indian government recently provided the estranged Mrs. Modi with a large security entourage. She has sued to get rid of them because they are a burden—she and her family are expected to feed them and treat them as guests despite her meager income.

Although divorce rates are low, domestic violence in India is depressingly high. According to a government survey, 40 percent of women have experienced it, but experts believe the figure is over 84 percent (!) of women.[*]

Dowries cause much violent suffering for Indian women. The practice has been illegal in India since 1961, but the centuries-old tradition is hard to stamp out. Especially in rural areas, the bride's parents usually give cash and gifts to the groom's family as part of the wedding festivities.

---

[*] This compares to between 25 and 40 percent in China, and about a quarter of women in the United States.

The amounts can be oppressive: up to several years' salary in cash as well as farm animals, jewelry, motorcycles, or air conditioners. If a woman's family fails to pay their daughter's dowry to the satisfaction of her new in-laws, she might be beaten, raped by her husband or his relatives, have acid thrown on her, have her clothes and food taken away, or burn to death in an "accidental" household fire. When I walked around the Delhi slums to meet Mohammad's family, the nonprofit worker I was with pointed out a charred one-room hut and whispered that a young bride had died there in just such an "accident" the previous week.

These are not isolated incidents. The Indian government estimates that nearly *one woman an hour* is killed in dowry-related violence, and that incidents that don't result in death are chronically underreported. Even wealthy and well-educated women are not immune to such violence. In 2012, Akansha Rathi, a glamorous thirty-two-year-old, was found hanged days after she complained to police against her in-laws for dowry harassment. Her in-laws had objected to her marrying their higher-caste son and the lack of dowry she brought in, although Akansha later became a successful businesswoman and helped her husband run their steel company. After her husband's death, Akansha's in-laws confiscated all of her property. When she complained to the police, she was found murdered.

Again, the Indian government has reasonable laws in place, which allow the police to immediately arrest and jail the accused husband and his family, but they are rarely enforced.

Indian families discourage women from reporting domestic abuse. Well-meaning American-funded organizations have set up shelters, but they have not been a big success. Most Indian women consider it prestigious to be a wife and mother. Even if she could leave her abusive husband to then live alone in a battered women's shelter or with her relatives, her life would be tragic. Women who leave their husbands or are left by them—like Banwari—are called "half widows" and can't marry again until their former husband dies. Mrs. Modi, for one, has been waiting for her husband to return for almost fifty years.

This is not limited to the poor. A 2014 study reported that Indian women who are more educated than their husbands are at higher risk of domestic violence, since men see in it a way to reassert their power over their wives. Elite women are also less likely to report such crimes, possibly because divorce would mean losing social status or a comfortable lifestyle.

Even when women do report domestic violence, policemen are more likely to jeer or attempt to take a bribe than assist. Dowry-related violence is difficult to prove in court and conviction rates are abysmally low: only 24 percent for rape cases and 33 percent for those accused of killing women while trying to extort more dowry from their families. With these statistics, it is understandable that the pink sari ladies of the Gulabi Gang have taken the law into their own hands.

The violent mistreatment of women may be reaching a boiling point in India. In December 2012 the issue exploded into the national consciousness when a twenty-three-year-old college student was returning with a male friend from a movie on a New Delhi bus. Four young men beat her friend unconscious and then took turns brutally raping the woman. She died a few weeks later in a hospital in Singapore. In response, thousands protested in Delhi and across Indian cities. The authorities at first responded in exactly the wrong way. Instead of sympathizing with the protesters, they invoked emergency policing laws, closed off the center of Delhi, blockaded roads, and even shut down subway stations.

The news coverage and chauvinist comments by some male government officials fueled the firestorm, and finally forced the government to take action. The four rapists, one of whom still unapologetically blames his victim for "asking for trouble" by riding a bus at night, were convicted and sentenced to death. My Indian friends say cynically that the verdict might have been different if the victim had been a rural lower-caste girl, like Banwari, instead of an urban college student.

As a result of these vocal citizen protests, India's Parliament passed a sweeping new law in 2013 to protect women against sexual violence. It makes stalking, voyeurism, and sexual harassment a crime. It provides the death penalty for repeat offenders and for rapes that lead to the victim's death. The law also makes it a crime for police officers to refuse to open cases when they receive complaints of sexual attacks. Marital rape, however, remains legal.

In a typical Indian pattern, citizen activism forced the government to act. Tough laws are now on the books. It remains to be seen whether the police will enforce them.

Chinese society has also begun to debate domestic violence publicly and demand change, although the debate is hampered by free speech restrictions. Kim Lee, an American teacher married to a Chinese man, made headlines a few years ago when she posted photos of her battered face on the Internet. Her multimillionaire husband, Li Yang, the founder of a well-known English teaching company, repeatedly beat her and slammed her head into the floor.

Studies estimate that between 25 and 40 percent of women in China suffer domestic violence, although activists believe it is closer to 40 percent. Beating is illegal in China, but many Chinese see abuse of a spouse or child as a private concern. Families often tell the victims to save face and solve household conflicts themselves, and *quietly*.

Kim Lee wasn't quiet. She posted pictures of her bruises on Weibo with the tagline "I love losing face = I love hitting my wife's face?" The pictures went viral. Kim spent hours and hours waiting at police stations, only to be told, among other excuses, that she hadn't submitted her evidence to the right hospital and that she needed voice recordings of her husband's threats. Kim persisted to set an example for her daughters and for the many women who supported her. A Beijing court finally granted her a divorce and full custody of her children.

But her story is unusual. Even for those who do reach out for help, police are reluctant to intervene and the men are rarely prosecuted. Yet China has seen a rise of women speaking out. In early 2015, a small group of young feminist activists marched through Beijing's tourist district wearing red-splattered wedding gowns chanting, "Yes to love, no to violence." Even the All-China Women's Federation, the official Communist Party group that was so unhelpful with the "leftover women" issue, is organizing anti-sexual-violence seminars on college campuses. Although Ms. Li and Ms. Wei were advocating for an issue that the Chinese government supports, China's authoritarian streak won out. Li, Wei, and their friends were arrested and detained for over a month.

Despite some setbacks and a push by the government for "Confucian" values, there is progress. In 2015 China passed a domestic violence law that allows social organizations and individuals to report violence and obliges police to investigate claims. It also requires local governments to set up shelters. Those convicted could face up to seven years in prison if the abuse led to serious injury or death. Human Rights Watch critiqued the law for applying only to married couples and protecting women only if they complain within thirty days. The government has tried to be responsive, but it simultaneously cracks down on activists who dare to challenge its "harmonious society."

Like the United States, in both India and China women are not fully represented in politics. India has some prominent women politicians. China has the better record of supporting women's rights, even though there are almost no senior female Chinese politicians to advocate for them.

Women in both China and India have had the right to vote and run for office since each country's foundation in the late 1940s. India is one of the few countries in the world to have been ruled by a woman. The powerful Indira Gandhi, daughter of India's founding father, Jawaharlal Nehru, served as prime minister from 1966 to 1977. Indira's Italian-born daughter-in-law, Sonia Gandhi, has been the leader of the Congress Party and the undisputed power behind the prime minister since 1998. Several of India's powerful chief ministers (equivalent to governors of U.S. states) are women.

Indian women vote as much as men, and there are some prominent women politicians, yet India's political parties remain mostly male dominated. Women are often discriminated against when they try to run for office. Only 12 percent of India's parliamentarians are women, while the world average is 20 percent. There has been dramatic debate for almost two decades about creating a quota for women legislators at the national level. Studies from the United States show that women legislators tend to advance family-friendly policies, education, and health care, and other studies suggest that when female political representation reaches 30 percent, policies become much more equitable.

While some of India's have adopted quotas for local government, such a quota is unlikely to pass at the national level. Margaret Alva, a prominent Indian parliamentarian, told me that when she helped introduce the quota bill, "the male Lok Sabha members ran onto the floor of Parliament and tore up the bill. They felt so threatened by anything that would help women." The upper house of Parliament finally passed the bill in 2015, but the lower house has yet to do so and likely will not.

Despite China's relatively progressive stance on women, Chinese women are all but absent from high-level politics. The highest-ranked woman politician in China's recent history was the infamous Jiang Qing, Mao Zedong's wife, one of the "Gang of Four" Politburo members who terrorized the population during the Cultural Revolution. Since Madame Mao's time, no woman has risen to the country's most senior decision-making body, the Politburo Standing Committee, and as mentioned earlier, only two women serve on the twenty-five-member Politburo. Only one-fifth of all party members and about a quarter of national-level civil servants are women. As of 2015, China has had only one female provincial governor, Li Bin, and only one female party secretary of a province or city, Sun Chunlan. While nearly a quarter of China's parliament was composed of women in 2014, this group in reality only serves as a rubber stamp for the party's decisions.

Confucian gender stereotypes remain. Many Chinese (including women) would argue that women "lack self-confidence" or "lack quality" (*suzhi di*) and so are not suited to politics. Politicians attend nightly banquets and are expected to smoke and drink heavily, behavior not very compatible with family life. The male-dominated Chinese political system will be difficult to change.

★   ★   ★

Unequal economic opportunities, violence against women, and underrepresentation in politics continue to be serious problems in India, and it is one of the worst democracies in which to be a woman. Chinese women face serious obstacles, yet these are more similar to those of women in developed societies.

Additional gains for women will help China move toward a more pluralistic, open society in general, and thus in the long run help its values converge with those of the United States. Similarly, to achieve a strong, prosperous, resilient India, which is in America's interest, India must include its women more completely in the country's economic and political development. Global research has found that countries with more gender equality also have higher levels of competitiveness, GDP per capita, and human development.

This is one issue that is not at all contentious *between* these countries. Instead it creates an opportunity for joint problem solving, and for exchanges between Chinese, American, European, and Indian female politicians, journalists, military, and business leaders. Such exchanges specifically for women are rare now. The Asia Society, a New York–based nonprofit, used to host excellent events for senior Asian female politicians and business leaders. Many of us alumnae of these exchanges are still in touch and work on occasional projects together. In May 2015, Alibaba started another such initiative by launching a "Global Conference on Women and Entrepreneurship," which founder Jack Ma hopes will evolve into a "women's Davos." By increasing such relatively inexpensive exchanges, India, China, and the United States can create a generation of female leaders who know and trust each other, and have learned to understand each other's viewpoints.

American corporations play an important and mostly positive role to include women more effectively in the economy. Most major U.S. technology firms have operations in India. They employ women in higher numbers than Indian firms and many are pushing to retain them and move them into management roles. The country leaders of Intel and HP India are both women. Both firms have leadership programs to help keep talented women in the workforce longer. Several years ago, Google was surprised that every year many of the women it hired to work on Google Maps in Bangalore quit very quickly. After some research, Google learned that the women felt unsafe taking taxis or public transport home after dark, so it set up a safe shuttle service for them and substantially improved its retention. Ernst & Young started a similar program. These commendable steps unfortunately impact only a tiny percentage of well-educated, elite women. American companies are underrepresented in manufacturing, so it is harder to set a good example by hiring women at the lower end of the economic spectrum, but these steps are an important start.

In China, American businesses can and are helping women both at the elite and blue-collar level. Many well-educated Chinese women work for American accounting, law, and technology firms, because they tend to be somewhat more egalitarian than state-owned enterprises. Chinese tech firms, however, do better than American ones: Alibaba, for example, employs 40 percent women. For female blue-collar workers, working for western-owned firms is also often advantageous. Rho has found that Chinese workers at western firms are significantly more likely to protest for rights and benefits —and to get them—than are workers at Chinese companies.

Helping more women on both sides of the Pacific engage in politics may also have another positive side effect. Political science research shows that female legislators are often more collaborative, willing to compromise, and interested in achieving outcomes that benefit everyone, than men. No such studies exist for senior female diplomats because the sample size is disappointingly small. However, encouraging more women political leaders to step up in China, India, and the United States just might lower the level of international grandstanding around difficult issues like the South China Sea.

8 | ENERGY VS. THE
ENVIRONMENT

Y ou *must* come see the horticultural exhibit," Communist Party
secretary Sun Qingyun told our jet-lagged delegation. It was October 2011, and Condoleezza Rice and I were with the CEO of
an American technology company visiting the city of Xi'an, one of China's
four ancient capitals. Founded six thousand years ago, Xi'an is now a booming modern metropolis with a population of 8.4 million. We were there to
discuss high-tech cooperation, not flowers. After the typical long lunch of
toasts, a horticultural exhibit was the last thing we were expecting, or interested in. Condi protested politely that time was short, but Secretary Sun
insisted.

He enthusiastically explained that the exhibit was on the shore of the
Chan-He River, which had once been horribly polluted by nearby industries. Under Sun's leadership, the city had cleaned it up in record time, and
the exhibit was the centerpiece of the newly created "Chan-Ba Ecological
District." We expected to see a bucolic lake and some native flowers, and
be on our way.

We were wrong. This was environmentalism Chinese-style. No peaceful nature walk awaited us. The "Ecological District" encompasses an
enormous area of manicured landscaping and ritzy high-rise buildings.
The horticultural exhibit was Disneyland-esque, featuring ornate flower
gardens overshadowed somewhat by colorful replicas of the Eiffel Tower

and Taj Mahal, and a zoo housing several of China's beloved giant pandas. Twelve million visitors had come through in eight months, 150,000
of them on that day alone. The pandas were designed to be the premier
attraction, but to her embarrassment, Condi soon eclipsed their popu-
larity. Our group was surrounded by a crowd snapping photos on their
smartphones as the party secretary beamed, apparently delighted that his
environmental spectacle had attracted a celebrity of equal "wow factor."

★   ★   ★

Chan-Ba is spectacular. It also illustrates the sometimes schizophrenic
approach China uses to combat its environmental problems. To cynics,
Chan-Ba is just a Chinese-scale version of a Potemkin village: one section
of one river has been cleaned up, but the larger story in the country is of
widespread environmental devastation.

Anyone who has watched news coverage from Beijing has witnessed
the horrendous smog enveloping the capital and almost all of the country's major cities. Dinner party guests in China regularly strip off white
surgical face masks along with their coats as they walk into a private home.
In January 2013, Beijing experienced a prolonged bout of smog so severe
that the citizens dubbed it "airpocalypse." The government shut down all
factories outside Beijing in the days before a major military parade in fall
2015 to clear the air, only to run them at 120 percent capacity later.

The problem doesn't stop at China's borders. The governments of
Japan and South Korea have complained vociferously about the impact
of China's air pollution on smog levels in their countries. The United
States is being affected as well. Winds traveling across the Pacific Ocean
can carry pollutants from China to the West Coast in just a few days. And
recent research has found that the runaway air pollution in Asia is contributing to strengthening storms above the Pacific.

The severity of such a glaringly obvious problem seems to belie claims
by the Chinese government that it is working hard to solve its environmental crisis. Skeptics argue that the government is focused on economic
growth and—when the cameras are not rolling—largely turns a blind eye
to environmental concerns.

The truth is more complicated. Both the Chinese people and their government are deeply concerned about these problems. Some wealthy Chinese and expatriates are leaving the country to avoid exposing their children to the constant smog. My Chinese friends in Beijing check a U.S. Embassy Twitter feed with the day's air quality ratings. Although the government demanded that Washington cease issuing the feed in 2012, later that year Chinese authorities began publishing their own hourly data in seventy-four cities.

Public patience with pollution is running out, and frequent protests have erupted. In 2014 in the southern city of Maoming, at least one thousand people (those present insist there were twenty times that many) protested the government's plan to build a petrochemical factory in their city. Pictures of protesters bloodied by police circulated briefly on the Internet, until censors quashed them. A government report acknowledged that hundreds such protests happen every year, and increase yearly. A March 2015 documentary on China's environmental woes racked up more than 175 million online views in two days. Again, censors stepped in to take it down.

The Chinese government is taking the issue seriously because, despite attempts at censorship, complaints about the environment increasingly unite all Chinese. It is now making sincere efforts to clean up the environment across the board—from air, to land, to its seriously challenged water system.

In India the story is also more complicated than the media coverage tends to suggest. The problems are urgent. Air quality is worse in India's large cities than in China. The World Health Organization recently revealed that thirteen of the world's twenty most polluted cities are in India. Even so, many Indians—especially those who grew up in the painfully poor decades after independence—are more concerned about lifting people out of poverty and see environmental stewardship as incompatible with that.

Yet there are glimmers of hope. The younger generation of Indian officials and business leaders takes environmental concerns seriously, and is willing to work with Americans on creative solutions.

The U.S.-India civilian nuclear deal is a good example. In 2006–07, I served as one of the U.S. negotiators of this agreement. The "civ-nuke deal," as we in the delegation affectionately called it, broke India's decades-long ban on collaborating with any other country on civilian nuclear energy. The United States agreed to remove sanctions and permit foreign companies to help India construct nuclear power plants, subject to regular international inspections. India ambitiously plans to build enough new carbon-free nuclear reactors to power four cities the size of New York. Although the primary purpose for the deal was strategic—to forge a closer political relationship between the United States and India—some of the Indian and American negotiators, particularly the younger ones, saw it as a way to generate the electricity India needs while weaning the country from its heavy reliance on polluting coal.

I naïvely expected that because the United States was making a major concession to India, our negotiations would be fairly straightforward. Instead, the talks were grueling, and consistently obstructed by the older members of India's nuclear establishment, who were not motivated by environmental concerns.

At one particularly memorable session in the summer of 2006, Subrahmanyam Jaishankar, the foreign secretary of India, who at the time was the lead Indian negotiator, looked dejected. After four hours of heated discussions in an aging, grand conference room in Delhi's lovely colonial-era Foreign Ministry building, we had gotten nowhere. The complex text lay in front of me covered with red scribbles. All morning, our five-person U.S. team had suggested creative workarounds to various disagreements. Brilliant, young, and energetic, Jaishankar and his Foreign Ministry colleagues had the same "can-do" style. But their energy was stymied by the éminences grises in the room: two senior leaders of India's cloistered nuclear establishment. Their role seemed to be to take each creative idea and say "no." Jaishankar seemed as exasperated as we were. He stopped the negotiations and recommended that the U.S. delegation see some museums in Delhi: *not a good sign.*

As we wandered around the stifling city, Jaishankar pushed hard on his own side. He told me later that he had to get Prime Minister Singh involved to break the logjam. Finally, in the early evening we reconvened and continued negotiating into the night. We finally concluded the agreement a year later.

I have seen essentially the same drama play out repeatedly in India. The "old guard" of Indian diplomats grew up after India's independence and was ideologically formed by former Prime Minister Nehru's insistence on state intervention in the economy, a "nonaligned" stance to world affairs, and a distrust of close relations with the United States. They have personal experience with India's crushing poverty, which leads them to focus intensely on growth and social justice above all other concerns. The new guard grew up with a more open worldview. They trust the United States more and want India to play a larger role in world affairs, including by solving environmental challenges.

★   ★   ★

India's and China's galloping economic growth has left behind a filthy mess of unbreathable air, undrinkable water, and carbon emissions that threaten the world. The stories of the Chan-Ba Ecological Park and the Indian civilian nuclear deal offer snapshots of how both are beginning to tackle these problems within the constraints of their culture and political system. Propelled by its citizens' rising anger about pollution, China is rapidly becoming greener. In India there has been less public demand for change. The central government is also less able to impose reforms on reluctant states.

The Chinese government can move quickly on these issues when there is both a top-down decision to do so *and* a willing local government. This was the case with the Chan-Ba cleanup, which Beijing supported with funding. There are many similar examples. With central government encouragement and cheap loans, China invests almost twice as much in renewable energy as the United States. These are significant improvements. Unfortunately, the lack of enforceable regulations and an independent court system means that environmental initiatives still too often happen at the whim of Party officials.

India's solutions are more democratic and bottom up, but also less rigorous. Some Indian states, like Gujarat, have developed clean energy sources such as solar, while others have made no real progress. The central government seems genuinely enthusiastic about environmental efforts but lacks the detailed plans and regional clout to push them through.

In 2015, the new Indian Environment Minister Prakash Javadekar spoke poetically to our small group of former U.S. officials about the ambitious new national solar standards, but didn't have many details about how these would be implemented.

The environmental problems of both countries are massive. A full accounting would require a library, but highlighting a few key challenges illuminates why the United States shouldn't expect that simply cajoling or applying more pressure will bend their behavior to our will.

Let's begin with air quality. The public health toll of air pollution in each country is devastating. Life expectancy in China's north is estimated to have decreased by five and a half years due to air pollution, and a 2015 study at the University of California, Berkeley estimates air pollution prematurely kills 1.6 million Chinese a year (or 4,400 a day). A different study estimates that in India some 620,000 premature deaths were due to poor air quality in 2010, largely from respiratory infections and lung cancer.

The problem in both countries is coal. China is the world's largest coal producer and consumer, accounting for almost half of global consumption. In recent years, the country added a new coal-fired power plant about every week, although this has recently improved somewhat. India is the world's third-largest coal producer and consumer. This is particularly frightening because government inefficiency has so far held production down. India's new energy minister, Piyush Goyal, implemented reforms that led to coal production growing at its fastest pace ever in 2015. As India learns to fully exploit its massive reserves, the problem will be more severe.

The best way to appreciate both countries' insatiable hunger for coal is to see one of their many massive strip mines. On a recent trip to China, my husband, Greg, visited a mine about two and a half hours from the city of Kunming, in China's far south. The experience was like traveling to another planet.

As he and his business partners approached the mine, terraced fields gave way to a landscape of gray on gray. On the road, they took photos of miners with deeply wrinkled faces sitting on their haunches on the doorsteps and spitting into the street, a life reminiscent of Zola's *Germinal*. Then the mine lurched into view, a behemoth amphitheater cut into the dull gray ground—thirty football fields in size. Rough-cut roads crawled with monster-sized orange dump trucks loaded with coal. The roar of vast machines shaving away layer after layer of earth was deafening. The United States too has devastated landscapes. To see the work in progress in China today, though, on such a staggering scale, is to feel in one's gut the inexorable drive of China to do all that is necessary to maintain growth.

Monster dump trucks look tiny as they cart loads
from a massive coal mine in China.
photo credit: *Greg Manuel*

Dirty, carbon-emitting coal is unfortunately still the least expensive way to connect Indians and Chinese and their growing industries to electricity. Both countries will balance any measures to rein in deadly CO2 emissions against this hard fact. In the near future, coal production will continue to soar.

When it comes to water supplies and the degradation of farmland the story is comparably dire. Many experts believe that the pollution and depletion of water supplies is the biggest environmental threat each giant faces, and the most likely to lead to conflict, both between them and with other countries. Severe shortages grip both countries. Experts usually define "severe water stress" as access to less than 1,000 cubic meters of water per person per year. In India the supply is a bit higher than that and declining quickly, while China is suffering with just 450 cubic meters. The supply per person in the United States is nearly 8,000.

India has sufficient overall water supplies. Its problem stems almost entirely from poor management. The country's legion of small farmers is digging ever-deeper wells instead of using modern irrigation methods, severely depleting the groundwater. Several of the largest cities, including Hyderabad, Delhi, Mumbai, and Chennai, may run out of groundwater within the next several years.

India failed to build adequate water treatment plants as its population surged, leading to filthy rivers and lakes. I had a dispiriting experience of this on a visit to Varanasi, one of the oldest continuously inhabited cities in the world. Its location on the banks of the Ganges River, one of the most revered spiritual destinations for Hindus, has been both a blessing and a curse. Each year millions of Hindu pilgrims come to Varanasi. They believe that bathing in the Ganges will absolve their sins and release them from the cycle of reincarnation. Many go there to die and have their cremated remains cast into the waters. The relatives of those who can't afford cremation release the cadavers of their loved ones into the river directly.

Traveling with friends, I experienced the pathos of Varanasi firsthand. The narrow lanes of the old city are largely impassable, crowded with thousands of pilgrims. Elderly men and women, dressed in their shabby best clothes, lie in doorways along the tiny streets, waiting for death. Holy men called *sadhus* chant in their saffron loincloths. Cows, which are considered sacred, roam the streets eating trash and defecating.

Eager to escape the stench, we followed one of the more persistent "tour guides" to his small boat to view the city from the relative peace of the Ganges. The one-hour boat trip did not faze our guide in the least, but it shocked us. He cheerily showed us many lovely temples lining the banks and the platforms used for cremating bodies over open fires, called *ghats*. He pointed out the macabre sight of dozens of burning human bodies, as well as several cow carcasses in the water. I recoiled at a ghastly vision of a vulture feasting on a floating human corpse. Nearby a crowd of pilgrims bathed, some of them crouching down to defecate in the river. Our guide exclaimed, "You must take pictures! Holy Varanasi!" This was not the India we wanted to capture memories of, however, and we kept our cameras tucked away.

Pilgrims bathing next to a burning corpse
on the Ganges River in Varanasi.
photo credit: *Tim Graham/Getty Images News/Getty Images*

India has a plethora of schemes to clean up its rivers, but so far, none has been particularly effective. Since the 1980s, India has had Ganges cleanup plans that would require building sewage plants and stop the dumping of industrial waste. These plans were not implemented because no region had any incentive to spend money on more advanced technology, since their waste would just be washed downriver. The Modi government's current plan, which pledged $8 billion over eighteen years for Ganges cleanup, has been criticized by environmentalists and India's Supreme Court as "more of the same" and unlikely to yield results. Plans to force industry to first monitor and then stop dumping pollutants have met with stiff resistance. As of late 2015, they are finally, slowly moving forward. This is the conundrum that India faces with other environmental challenges: the central government is not dominant enough to force local towns and private industry to implement expensive regulations, so it must create incentives. So far, the new Ganges action plan is short on these.

In China, water shortages stem not only from its immense population, but also from geography. Much of its water is in the wrong place. While four-fifths of the supply comes from rivers that originate in the Himalayas (often in Tibet), in the south of the country, half of the population and two-thirds of the farmland are in the north. In rural areas, some 300–500 million people lack access to piped water, and some rivers dry up before they reach the sea.

Even where water is plentiful, it is often polluted. In March 2013, Shanghai citizens were disgusted to find the carcasses of sixteen thousand dead pigs floating in the Huangpu River, which is the city's tap water supply. The pigs most likely died of disease due to overcrowding on farms lining the river. Almost 90 percent of underground water in the cities and 70 percent in the rivers and lakes is polluted.

Chinese citizens are increasingly worried about this problem, and the government is struggling to fix it. The 12th Five Year Plan, issued in 2012, was the first to include a section on water and impressive sections on environmental cleanup, espousing policies often more progressive than those in the United States. It set out detailed directives, including that 80 percent of Chinese should have access to clean, piped water by 2015, and has since met these goals.

The shortage of clean water in both India and China could even cause violent conflict between the two. China has dammed every major river on the Tibetan plateau to use the water from China's high southern mountains to help its parched north. Proposed dams on the upper reaches of rivers with sources in Tibet, such as the Brahmaputra and Mekong, may alleviate China's crisis, but they could leave downstream countries like India increasingly parched.

The giant and placid Brahmaputra River seems an unlikely cause for war. It flows east along the Tibetan plateau, and then makes a dramatic U-turn south and enters India's far eastern states of Arunachal Pradesh and Assam at a place called the "Great Bend." Unfortunately, this U-turn happens right near territory that China and India dispute, and over which they fought a brief war in 1962, which left India humiliated.

Feelings over the Brahmaputra run hot in Delhi. When a former Chinese military officer wrote a report that recommended diverting the Brahmaputra into China, bloggers, newspapers, and politicians in India exploded with anger. A former Indian military officer argued to me in private that if the Chinese did this, it would mean war. To damp down the outrage, Prime Minister Singh was forced to publish a statement saying that the Chinese had personally assured him that they would not divert the river.

Thankfully, the technical feat required for this looks impossible, even by ingenious Chinese standards. Engineers would need to use nuclear explosions to make tunnels through a series of mountains ridges to divert water east from the Great Bend. At least for now, this is very improbable, but one should never underestimate the Chinese.

The Great Bend of the Brahmaputra. China is considering diverting its flow, which has caused ire in India.

photo credit: *Imgur*

★   ★   ★

Why have Delhi and Beijing not done more to clean up this mess? The thick blanket of smog in Delhi and Beijing, the squalor of the Ganges, and sixteen thousand dead pigs floating near cosmopolitan Shanghai seem unfathomable, especially for countries that both have booming economies, world-class tech sectors, and first-class scientific communities. China's and India's particular political systems limit how each country can tackle these concerns.

In India, casting human remains into the Ganges is a long-rooted Hindu tradition, and even hard-nosed government efforts to change this have met with stubborn refusal. Powerful state chief ministers control issues such as water treatment, water usage, agriculture, electricity distribution, and the use of renewable energy. The central government can raise the alarm, and has done so, and provide funds. Yet little is achieved without impetus from a local chief minister.

Following the tradition of Gandhi and Nehru, older leaders are laser focused on alleviating poverty and social inequality, and often see environmental protection as in conflict with these goals. Well-meaning Nehruvian social policies exacerbated some environmental problems. His land reforms, for example, created many small farm plots and allowed farmers to drill for water for free and with no restrictions. Artificially subsidized diesel fuel often doesn't benefit the poor, as intended, and at the same time makes renewables like solar relatively expensive. Gandhi's powerful example has led Indians to embrace citizens' initiatives and bottom-up approaches. Swami Nigamananda, a Hindu priest, died in 2011 after fasting for four months as a protest against the pollution of the Ganges by unauthorized mines. Such grassroots efforts and some vocal environmental activists are raising awareness, but most Indians seem surprisingly unperturbed about the filth. Solving these problems has not yet become a major national concern in the way it has in China.

Mao's centralization of power would seem to give today's Chinese leaders a firm grip on environmental initiatives. The Party's penchant for big, showy projects, such as Three Gorges Dam, which was an enormous win for hydropower (though creating other environmental problems), certainly seems to indicate this.

Implementation is another story. The Party leadership can announce policies, and regularly does, but until a promising legal reform in 2015, it lacked real control to enforce compliance. Because local officials are accountable to the Party, rather than to local citizens, they have an incentive to cover up environmental problems.

The Songhua chemical spill is a perfect example. In 2005, an explosion at a chemical plant in China's northeast released 100 tons of toxins into the Songhua River. The toxic slick flowed downriver past the large city of Harbin into Russia. For five days, chemical factory bosses and local officials attempted to manage it themselves, not notifying Beijing, terrified of being blamed for the incident. They ineptly released drinking water to make the toxins less visible in the river, and shut down the municipal water supply in Harbin without telling anyone why. After rumors began circulating on Chinese Internet sites, the central government stepped in and effectively aided the cleanup.

In a tragic but not unprecedented outcome, the local mayor later committed suicide, and the leader of the central government environmental agency SEPA—who had inherited the problem and fixed it, rather than causing it—resigned in disgrace.

Local leaders were terrified of the central government but did not follow its directives. The disconnect exists because environmental protection bureaus report to local party bosses, rather than to SEPA, the national environmental protection agency in Beijing. Local party bosses prioritize economic development and have an incentive to hide problems.

China's central government recently moved to fix this with a far-reaching series of reforms. Since January 2014, it has required fifteen thousand factories to publicly report real-time figures on their air emissions and water discharges.

In January 2015, a new Environmental Protection Law went into effect, the most promising step yet to fix problems exposed by the Songhua spill. Local party officials are now scored on their environmental stewardship—not just economic growth—and may be fined, lose their jobs, or be criminally prosecuted if they do not deliver. For the first time the law permits citizens and environmental organizations to file public interest suits, and substantially raises the fines for polluters. This is a real win for the rule of law in China and a rare example of the government empowering civil society. The new law is a significant step toward more robust environmental protection in China. Some lawsuits have actually been filed under the new law, although activists report that local governments often pressure plaintiffs to drop out. So far fines have been higher against foreign company polluters than domestic ones. For example, ConocoPhillips paid a total of $432 million and the China National Offshore Oil Corporation (CNOOC) only $75 million to resolve a suit arising from the same oil spill where the companies were partners.

★   ★   ★

Severe as the giants' air, land, and water pollution are, they will have only limited impact on the United States. Their impact on the climate, however, is unique and potentially disastrous for the world. With surging numbers of cars and trucks on the road, China will soon overtake the United States as the world's largest oil consumer. While China will lead rising energy demand this decade, India, with its fast-growing population, will surpass it in the years before 2030.

As their energy demand increases, China and India will spew ever-larger amounts of greenhouse gases into the atmosphere. China is currently the world's largest carbon emitter. As of 2014, the last year for which data is available, its millions of cars and smokestacks gush more than 10 billion tons of CO_2 into the atmosphere each year, followed by the United States at 5.3 billion, and India's 2.3 billion. We are the top three countries on a depressing scoreboard of pollution.

It is promising that China's CO_2 emissions are increasing much more slowly now than over the last decade, and even slower than India's, yet both still have some of the fastest emissions growth rates of any country. Both U.S. and European emissions, by contrast, are declining modestly from year to year.

This has frightening implications for the world in 2030. On current pace, and even after the recent commitments made in Paris, the International Energy Agency (IEA) warns that China and India alone will blow through the entire world's "quota" of CO2 and thus, according to these estimates, *climate change will be irreversible*. Even if the industrial countries meet their very ambitious pledges to cut emissions by more than 80 percent in the next three decades, China would still need to cut its current emissions by *half*, and India would have to *not grow its emissions at all*, to make the world's climate math work out.

Not long ago, we believed that if only the United States and Europe could reach a binding agreement on climate change, the world could be saved. It is clear now that China and India have a veto position in any such negotiations.

Since their per capita emissions are still much lower than those in the United States and Europe, senior diplomats in China and India are understandably suspicious of large international negotiations led by the West. Both countries perceive these as an unfair attempt by the developed world to foist its responsibilities on still-impoverished countries.

Xie Zhenhua, China's chief climate negotiator, has said that developed countries should bear the brunt of addressing climate change, and provide financing for developing countries to invest in low-carbon solutions. India argues, not without reason, that when adjusted for population, its carbon emissions are four times lower than the average in China and eleven times lower than the average in America. Senior Indian policy makers have therefore argued for decades that India should not take substantial steps on climate change until the developed economies first drastically slash their own emissions output.

The argument of India's "old guard" is slowly changing. Indians now see the direct effects of climate change: changing weather patterns have led to a 10 percent reduction in annual monsoons, melting Himalayan glaciers threaten India's water supply, and rising sea levels put millions of Indians in low-lying cities at risk. Prime Minister Modi strongly supported clean technology in Gujarat and wrote a book on climate change that his ministers proudly give to visitors. While India has not agreed to an overall emissions cap since this would restrict its growth, for the Paris climate talks in December 2015, Modi agreed to slow the growth of India's greenhouse emissions and boost its energy production from renewable sources to 40 percent of the total by 2030 in exchange for help with new technologies and inexpensive loans from wealthier nations.

These commitments give one reason to hope, but implementation will be difficult. India's initial steps on clean technology are not nearly as impressive as China's. Promisingly, India recently removed a subsidy on diesel consumption—which effectively subsidized carbon—and encouraged people to waste less gas by replacing subsidized gas with a cash payment for the poor. In 2016 the government also doubled the tax on each tonne of coal and will use the proceeds to fund renewable energy. Modi vastly expanded India's solar mission and wants to deploy up to 100 gigawatts of solar power in the next few years. This is a great idea, because India has such an atrocious electricity grid that the quickest way to give many Indians access to electricity is through solar panels on houses or micro-grids for a village.

Unfortunately, for all the pronouncements, in my conversations with Indian ministers, they were short on details for how to implement the ambitious targets. Solar entrepreneurs complain that the feed-in tariff (the price at which solar companies sell electricity into the grid) is too low, so reputable companies can't compete. There is no appropriate financing for solar installations, and entrepreneurs are expected to build—without government assistance—both the roads to their installations and the power lines to feed solar power into the grid. Indian Energy Minister Piyush Goyal was quite clear that coal will have to remain the largest source of power for India's electricity grid, and make up between 60 and 65 percent of the total mix. In fact, even as India committed to increase its renewable energy capacity by fivefold in the five years following the December 2015 Paris climate talks, the country also set higher production targets for coal, planning to double its annual output by 2022. The renewables strategy is starting to take off, but it has a long way to go.

Chinese officials are more progressive. They frequently describe how China will suffer with climate change: already its deserts are spreading, crop yields are plateauing, and at least 80 million people who live at sea level are vulnerable to higher storm surges. Temperatures are rising much faster on the high-altitude Tibetan plateau than elsewhere in China. As a result, glacier melting and flooding has become a major problem.

Long before the landmark agreement reached in December 2014 between China and the United States, Beijing embraced clean energy solutions and mapped out ambitious climate change initiatives. The 2012 Five Year Plan was the first to mention "climate change" and included binding targets to reduce energy consumption. The government has pledged to spend $275 billion over the next five years to clean up the air and announced that it will launch a nationwide cap-and-trade system for CO_2 in 2017, as well as an environmental tax.

China funds impressive initiatives to increase the use of solar, wind, biomass, and hydropower. Coal still generates approximately two-thirds of all the electricity in China, but its energy mix is rapidly changing.

China claims that 60 percent of *new* power plants China installed in 2013 and 2014 use renewable carbon-free sources, though this statistic does not tell the whole story: China added the equivalent of a staggering sixty-three large plants in the first ten months of 2013. This means it added one coal-fired plant about every two weeks, and one carbon-free power plant about every ten days. Beijing will close its last four coal plants this year to improve air quality, and overall, coal consumption fell nearly 4 percent in 2015. Many environmentalists also worry about China's large reliance on hydro dams to generate carbon-free power, since they create other problems, such as blocking fish migrations and changing the ecology with the result that local plants and animals can no longer survive.

China is the undisputed world leader in renewable energy investment, surpassing all other countries since 2009. In 2015 alone, it invested $110.5 billion in all renewable technologies. The United States was a distant second at $56 billion, and India managed only a paltry $10.9 billion.

The solar industry provides a perfect example. Unlike India, China has built an impressive solar industry in barely a decade, transforming the country quietly and very quickly from a producer of panels to "dump" on the rest of the world at low prices to a consumer of solar energy.

One fascinating character in this story is the mysterious Chinese entrepreneur Zheng Jianming. Until recently, even experts in the renewable energy community had never heard of him. Then, at a fall 2014 dinner in California, the soft-spoken, round-faced man in a gray tracksuit announced to American investors that in two short years he had amassed the world's largest empire of solar companies. He bought into solar as the industry slumped due to a global oversupply of panels, and now owns an impressive $20 billion in Chinese solar manufacturing assets. In 2015 he also invested in American solar firm Suniva, in Boston Power, and in Philips's LED division. Through a translator, he told the stunned crowd:

> My goal is to deploy more than fifty gigawatts of installed clean energy capacity in the next ten years—*the equivalent of fifty nuclear power plants* and enough to power over thirty-seven million homes.

The gathering was too wowed by this announcement to ask tough questions. Even by Chinese standards this is an audacious plan—one entrepreneur alone is planning to install half the solar energy that the entire Indian government has committed to.

Zheng's success is an outgrowth of the often opaque Chinese business structures that developed as China was moving from a command economy to capitalism. Speculation abounds that someone high up in China's Politburo has anointed Zheng's company as a national champion on renewable energy, which means that cheap debt and many lucrative contracts (like powering billions of square feet of residences and office space) are being funneled in his direction. Opaque or not, the fact that the government is encouraging Zheng and many others like him to bet big on renewables is a sign of its commitment to sustainable development.

★   ★   ★

China is moving at a breakneck gallop and India at a more moderate canter to fix its environmental problems. It is solidly in the United States' interest to support these efforts if it wants to avoid irreversible climate change. To move China and India to a less carbon-intensive economy, Europe and the United States should lure them with incentives. Shaming or bullying them into action has been unsuccessful since the Kyoto negotiations twenty-five years ago.

One such incentive-based approach was the civilian nuclear deal we negotiated with India from 2005 to 2008 and which I described earlier. If coal is not the answer to India's need for electricity—although it will stay an important part of the mix—added power must come from renewables or nuclear power. The renewables sector in India is still in its relative infancy. The civilian nuclear deal is not yet implemented due to a dispute over nuclear liability law. When it does go into effect, India plans to build new nuclear reactors with 25 gigawatts (GW) of capacity. By increasing the production of clean nuclear energy to that amount, a Stanford scientist estimated, India would reduce its carbon emissions by more than 130 million tons each year. (For comparison, the full range of emission cuts planned by the European Union under the Kyoto Protocol will total 200 million tons per year.) If new nuclear power reactors can be constructed with the latest safety features, and international monitoring ensures that accidents are unlikely to occur, the U.S.-India civilian nuclear deal will be a real win for climate change. This type of large-impact, bilateral initiative may help India get around the multilateral bickering of the UN climate change negotiations and have a positive impact on the environment.

Similarly, the United States is learning that bilateral cooperation—not lecturing—is the way to make progress with China on combatting climate change. The breakthrough agreement announced by Presidents Obama and Xi in late 2014 is a case in point and should serve as a model for future bilateral and international climate negotiations. Under the agreement, the United States committed to emit 26 percent less greenhouse gases in 2025 than it did in 2005. China agreed, for the first time ever, to reach peak carbon emissions by 2030. China also announced that clean energy will account for 20 percent of the country's total energy production by 2030. To reach this goal China will have to build between 800 and 1,000 large, carbon-free power plants. This is a move well beyond the status quo for both countries.

Chinese officials have told me repeatedly that the U.S. decision unilaterally to reduce its carbon emissions was a great example that made it easier for them to push their own government to do the same.

These unilateral, coordinated steps, announced a year before the 2015 United Nations Climate Change Conference, established the United States and China as leaders on this issue and created valuable momentum going into multilateral negotiations. President Obama personally called Modi several times to bring him into a deal, and also enlisted Microsoft founder Bill Gates, who helped create what is being called the largest public-private coalition for funding renewable energy. These creative steps and intense personal lobbying by the president also helped push Prime Minister Modi to come up with his more ambitious target, which he announced in October 2015. Several other developing countries followed suit. These examples of successful U.S. climate diplomacy with India and China offer useful lessons for future bilateral and multilateral climate negotiations.

Environmental degradation in India and China has a direct impact on the United States: from the Chinese smog cloud that at times reaches all the way to California, to the Pacific garbage patch, to the painful fact that the world cannot slow global warming without significant concessions from its largest carbon emitter (China), and the fastest growing (India). Each country will find its own solutions to environmental problems. Climate change is one area where China and the United States can usefully cooperate to convince others to act. This both benefits the environment and serves as a positive agenda item for China and the United States to practice cooperation. Incentive-based schemes, such as the U.S.-India civilian nuclear deal, the recent U.S.-Chinese agreement to combat climate change, and private sector cooperation on clean energy technologies, will help all three countries make the right choices, for everyone's benefit.

9 | MANAGING DISCONTENT

Two days after the Tiananmen Square massacre on June 4, 1989, Xiao Qiang, a brilliant, idealistic astrophysics PhD student, boarded a plane. He left the comfort of his dorm room at the University of Notre Dame and returned to his native China to "help in any way [he] could." The son of a prestigious, politically connected family, he had lived for several years with his aunt in Beijing in one of the elite compounds set aside for high-level politicians, just downstairs from the family of Xi Jinping. In 1986 he left China to pursue a PhD in the United States.

Unlike his countrymen, who were completely cut off from news about the fateful student protests in Tiananmen Square, he saw the events unfold live on CNN along with millions around the world: the sea of Chinese protesters, including many of his friends and his brother; the "goddess of democracy" statue erected right in front of the iconic portrait of Mao Zedong; the banners demanding "democracy or death." Like many watching in the United States, Xiao believed that this was the beginning of a new era in China. Then, on June 3 and 4, the People's Liberation Army brought in tanks and turned its guns on its own people.

Watching his fellow students shot by Chinese soldiers "was the turning point in my life," Xiao says. "Hundreds died, and many more went into hiding, or were picked up by Chinese internal security."

"I had no real plan for what to do in Beijing," he told me in 2015 in Berkeley, California, where he has lived in exile for more than a decade.

"I just had to go home. I had to do something." Xiao at first didn't tell his parents he was in Beijing, and instead lived in hiding at friends' houses. Many of the hopeful student protesters were part of China's intelligentsia. Even the children of prominent politicians were involved. At night Xiao snuck into his aunt's elite compound and secretly gave donations from concerned Americans to the families of the elite young people who had died or disappeared.

★   ★   ★

What led to Tiananmen? Xiao explains that the 1980s was a "hopeful" time, when people were politically engaged. Starting in the late 1970s, along with his economic reforms, Deng Xiaoping presided over a gradual political opening. The government amended China's laws to protect freedom of speech, correspondence, the press, and the freedom to demonstrate and strike. People were allowed to post complaints on Beijing's so called Democracy Wall—which Deng Xiaoping personally described as "a good thing." By the late 1980s, China's young elite had watched the gradual political opening in the Soviet Union. Students were gathering at Beijing University for weekly salon discussions and public debates about democracy. They felt emboldened to criticize the party. Naïvely, many believed it was China's time for political reform.

The idealists were proven painfully wrong in 1989. Xiao says while some of his friends demonstrated, others—many now part of China's elite—fully supported the bloody crackdown on protesters. This hardline political faction is still dominant today. Chinese leaders are now more obsessed than ever with avoiding the fate of the Soviet Union, where gradual economic and political opening in the 1980s quickly led to the collapse of the Communist Party.

Since 1989, China's leaders accelerated economic reforms while slamming the door on political liberalization. They argue that if people are increasingly prosperous, their complaints against government will be few. This trend is extreme under President Xi.

The government has done its best to wipe clean any historical references to Tiananmen Square. The protests and massacre do not appear in Chinese history books. The government went to great lengths to ensure that there was no mention of the event in any news source—paper, broadcast, or online—on its twenty-fifth anniversary in 2014.

Scholar Louisa Lim argues convincingly in a book about Tiananmen that after 1989, the Party reinvented itself as defender of Chinese interests against "western values" and what it believes are western attempts to contain a rising China. Lim describes the patriotic education campaigns waged in schools, newspapers, and on television to deemphasize individual freedoms and democracy.

My Chinese friends who became adults after 1989 epitomize the generation that learned the Communist Party's narrative in this way. In exchange for greater economic prosperity and small personal freedoms (such as the ability to dress in fashionable clothes, listen to the latest music, travel freely, eat in restaurants, and generally lead a "normal" life), they are willing to forgo political reform. "Our government has delivered the world's highest growth rates. Our airports and roads are better than yours in the United States. My children go to a good school, and my company is doing well," said one highly educated, forty-two year-old Chinese friend who runs a fashion company and did not want to be identified. "I know the government monitors my WeChat account, so I don't say anything stupid. Why should I worry about abstract freedoms?"

Her attitude is understandable. The Chinese system has lifted hundreds of millions out of poverty in the past twenty-five years. For its beneficiaries, it seemed reasonable to trade abstract democracy for competent governance.

This implicit deal between the Chinese government and its citizens is fraying today. Unlike the 1980s, when protests came in large part from elites wanting democratic reform, discontent in China currently takes three forms.

The loudest complaints come from those who are left behind by China's economic boom and are protesting about pocketbook issues: labor reform, local government land grabs, and, increasingly, pollution. The Party often allows these protests, as long as they are not directed specifically against the government. A second group are disgruntled Chinese who feel discriminated against by the Han-ethnic majority culture: Muslim

Uighurs and East Turkmen, Tibetans, the Falun Gong, and an increasingly large number of Christians who are still required to worship mostly underground. Layered on top of that are the grumblings from millennial netizens who have never experienced a violent crackdown, are more reckless than older Chinese, and increasingly ask uncomfortable questions online about their authoritarian government.

While the Internet has permitted some dissent at the margins, the regime has actively discouraged real civil society from flourishing. When China's massive security apparatus gets involved, it can be brutal and often ham-handed. The Party even controls protests about popular issues that are in line with government policy—such as the anticorruption campaign we saw earlier—obsessively from the top, instead of by encouraging freer media, more independent courts, and watchdog groups to expose and check corruption.

By 2030, these tensions within the system will likely have reached a breaking point. Of the various scenarios one can envision, a gradual, nonviolent move toward democracy—on the model of Singapore or Indonesia—is much preferable to violent revolution, but seems unlikely. Political scientists argue that creating a sustainable democracy after a violent revolution is more difficult than when the transition is peaceful.[*] We should of course speak up about China's human rights violations and repression but understand this will have little real impact. The United States (and ideally India) can best help by gently nudging China toward greater openness; for example by encouraging one, open world Internet, by helping western companies do business and share best practices in China, and most important, by demonstrating that the United States' own liberal civil society and institutions remain strong. This will help all three countries build the positive vision of 2030: a violent government overthrow or bloody crackdown in China is in no one's interest.

★   ★   ★

---

[*] While these scholars accurately find that many prodemocracy revolutions fail, of course in the real world no one can choose when or how people are fed up with authoritarian regimes, and whether they have any interest in a negotiated transition with the old guard.

In contrast to China, India's citizens are empowered to protest openly and vent their frustration at the ballot box—it is a functioning democracy. Protests happen because they are part of the essence of India. In China, discontent alarms the regime because it cannot be accommodated through peaceful political change. In India, change often starts at the bottom, as recent massive demonstrations against corruption and rape demonstrate. Yet many Indians feel that change isn't coming fast enough. They are demanding better governance. In 2012, the Singh government demonstrated the danger of weak governance: instead of implementing the economic reforms people were clamoring for, the government abruptly ordered Facebook and Google to take down satirical cartoons making fun of the prime minister. It can be tempting even for a strong democracy like India to try to suppress dissent if it feels cornered. A well-governed, strong, open India is very much in the United States' interest. It can take a larger role on the world stage and thus defend our common values much more than a weak one.

★   ★   ★

A staggering 180,000 physical protests take place in China every year, according to estimates by Tsinghua University professor Sun Liping. His most recent data is from 2010, so the number may be even higher now.

Most of these protests are by those who have been left behind economically—migrant workers, ethnic minorities, peasants, and factory workers. Research by the Chinese Academy of Social Sciences shows that the protests tend to be over concrete "pocketbook" issues, rather than broad political ideals. Factory workers want better conditions and fair salaries. Farmers want local officials to stop confiscating their land or to compensate them fairly for land grabs. Homeowners want to stop demolitions. People want safer food and cleaner air and water. Citizens want to stop corruption and abuses of power by local government officials. For example, anger exploded when a general's teenage son hit another car with his BMW in Beijing and then harassed the victim car's occupants. Some want to worship freely. Even tensions in China's Muslim minority are not always about freedom of religion. Just as frequently, Chinese minorities are concerned about their crushing poverty and about being displaced by Han Chinese. As an ethnic Uighur student from Xinjiang bravely explained to Condoleezza Rice after a speech she gave at Beijing University in 2014, "Everyone thinks my people are terrorists, but we are not. We are just poor."

Even the most brazen of Chinese protesters are careful not to step over the line, since if they do they pay a heavy price. Scholar Sungmin Rho, who has interviewed hundreds of Chinese migrant workers and labor strike leaders, told me that Chinese authorities generally permit protests about conditions in specific factories. They crack down fiercely, however, when protesters question the authority of the government. Strikes happen far more frequently, and are more successful, at foreign-owned factories.

In one factory of a U.S. paper products manufacturer, Sungmin explains, three hundred workers protested their relatively low year-end bonuses. The local government refused to intervene, and the U.S. company caved to strikers' demands almost immediately.

By contrast, a few years ago, Chinese police harassed and then pushed a pregnant migrant worker to the ground in Guangdong. Tired of police brutality and general mistreatment, more than a thousand migrant workers protested. Chinese police immediately surrounded them and shut down the city. The young workers Rho interviewed were shocked at the hard-line response—born after 1989, they had never experienced such repression.

There are of course more fundamental reasons for protests, like freedom of religion, as well. The government's crackdown on the Uighurs' home province of Xinjiang stepped up in late 2015. Officials banned mosques from broadcasting the call to prayer, prohibited parents from choosing names for their children that sound too Muslim, and are arbitrarily stopping people at highway checkpoints to search the content of their cellphones for jihadist videos and messaging apps such as Skype and WhatsApp, all in the name of preventing threats to public security.

A third form of dissent is the irreverence of China's generation of "only children." Born in the late 1980s and 1990s, they grew up in a far more prosperous society than their parents and have correspondingly higher aspirations. They have no memory of violent crackdown. While they do not form a coherent political group and generally do not advocate for specific political reform, they spend a lot of time online and ask uncomfortable questions.

I am always struck by the combination of their audacity and lack of real political engagement. On a trip to Chengdu in December 2014, I spoke to many twenty-something graduates of China's most elite universities. They are exactly the demographic that would likely have been in Tiananmen Square in 1989. Yet they had heard only vaguely of Tiananmen and were hesitant to discuss it. They do express their opinions, however, about their favorite American movies and shows (*Black Hawk Down, Pearl Harbor, House of Cards,* and *Fifty Shades of Grey* made the list), say they envy American environmental regulations that hold companies accountable for pollution, and argue that the Chinese anticorruption campaign had better move quickly before people lose faith in the party entirely (!). A young translator—a Chinese government employee I assumed would be more circumspect—told me on an earlier trip to Xian that she and her friends switch frequently to the newest chat and social media services "because the government hasn't yet figured out how to censor them."

Apparently, she is not alone in trying this trick. Martin Lau, president of the Chinese Internet company Tencent, commented to me on the sidelines of a Stanford conference in late 2013 that he believes one of the reasons hundreds of millions of users so quickly adopted Tencent's famous WeChat service is that the government didn't monitor the one-on-one WeChat conversations as intensely as Sina Weibo's microblogs, where one user can broadcast to large numbers of people at once. I thought of his comment when the Chinese censors cracked down on WeChat just six months later. The Chinese government is playing—and gradually losing—a cat-and-mouse game of censorship with its young citizens.

Xiao Qiang, who was forced to flee back to the United States, has dedicated his life to promoting democracy in China. He launched a powerful online platform called *China Digital Times.* It scans through traffic on the Chinese Internet and social media and captures the terms that suddenly disappear because they are censored. He thus has a front-row view of the collective complaints of the Chinese people, and says they include, not surprisingly, pollution, corruption, and pocketbook issues.

Less written about, but more important, in Xiao's view, is the fact that more people now openly question the legitimacy of the Communist Party online. He saw countless comments (quickly censored) around the March 2015 National People's Congress meetings in Beijing asking, "Who elected these people? I didn't! They don't represent me!" Direct comments like these are of course deleted immediately, but they are becoming increasingly common. He adds: "The Communist Party won't be able to hold back this tide forever."

Xiao believes that the Party's efforts at "purifying" itself may ultimately backfire. The anticorruption campaign is the prime example. Although the campaign continues to be popular, it is exposing corruption by Party members on such an immense scale that "it is becoming counterproductive. It has shown everyone how rotten the system is at its core. The unintended effect is that it confirmed what people suspected but didn't know, and thus is making people lose confidence in the Party." The Communist Party is trying to quell dissent by taking populist actions, like the anticorruption campaign. Ironically, this offers further evidence that it is worried about staying in control.

Speaking to Chinese about reform in their own country is a bit like criticizing someone's family: while they can be critical, they do not want to hear the same points from outsiders. My guide at the Dujiangyan irrigation system in Sichuan Province—the famous canal system hewn into the cliffs by hand more than two thousand years ago—demonstrated this. Dressed impeccably in high-heeled boots and a fashionable gray coat, she worked as a "VIP" government tour guide when I met her in December 2014. While visiting the site, I asked about her experience during the Sichuan earthquake—still a taboo subject because of the government's clumsy response and reluctance to acknowledge how poorly constructed many schools and apartment buildings were.

She was forthcoming. "My entire apartment building collapsed," she said. "Luckily, I was at work. My neighbors and twenty other people in my building were crushed by the rubble and killed. We all helped dig them out." When I asked about the Chinese government response, she said openly: "The government didn't help much, but we don't expect them to.

Corrupt companies cut corners when they built the buildings that collapsed. I lost all my possessions, so I had to move back in with my parents for a bit, and then start over." Like most Chinese I meet, she does not expect much from her government.

I asked her view of artist Ai Weiwei's public advocacy on behalf of the Sichuan earthquake victims like her, and his criticism of the government's response, which landed him in jail. Her face turned suddenly stony. "Ai Weiwei should not be talking about such things—especially to foreigners," she insisted. "He made China lose face."

Chinese millennials may grumble on social media, some ethnic and religious minorities protest openly, and citizens increasingly speak out about quality-of-life issues. At bottom, however, fiercely nationalist attitudes like my tour guide's suggest the Communist Party's propaganda works on most Chinese. Public shaming of the government, especially by outsiders, is clearly a sore spot.

How is the Chinese government responding to its disgruntled citizens? Chinese can't show their displeasure by voting out the government. There is no democratic escape valve. So, to stay in power, the government engages in a perpetual race.

On one hand, it strives to fix the problems its citizens are concerned about—income inequality, corruption, pollution. Surprisingly, the government has even begun to solicit public input on proposed laws. For example, it placed drafts of a new food safety law online and invited public comments four times over the past two years. The law passed in April 2015 and is the toughest food safety law in China's history. Rather than a real way to get input on proposed laws, several scholars believe that the Communist Party is using this more as a tool to understand what people are thinking, which is common in authoritarian regimes.

More ominously, the government ruthlessly preserves "stability" through its vast censorship apparatus and by jailing and often brutally beating protest leaders.

On the "light" end of this repression, it intimidates those who speak out and tries to frighten citizens into silence. In March 2015, police detained five young women for leading small groups in Beijing, Guangzhou, and Hangzhou that walked around in wedding dresses splattered with red paint to protest widespread domestic violence; although the Chinese government claims to support this issue. As journalist Eric Fish explained in an in-depth profile, the Party's "stability maintenance" apparatus had already tried several other tactics to silence the group's leader, Li Tingting.

After she led a small protest advocating for more women's toilets in 2012 (a nonthreatening issue if ever there was one), plainclothes policemen bundled her into an unmarked car. To her surprise, they took her to a fancy dinner, where they warned her to stop her protests. They later encouraged Li's father to pressure her to accept a job in the Chinese government. When that didn't stop her, they began to tap her phone and hack her email. Li's college professor was forced to tell her not to leave campus for any reason. Since threats, cajoling, and bribery didn't work, in 2015 the Party arrested Li and her friends.

There was a predictable outcry. John Kerry, Hillary Clinton, and other western politicians advocated for the women's release. Many young Chinese supported the women's cause by starting petitions on social media. A generation ago, the state could have dealt with Li and her friends by dispatching them to a labor camp. As Fish remarked, "in today's information age, Li's network gave her a measure of security."

When China's censors tried to silence the students supporting Li by having university officials reprimand anyone who signed the petition, many weren't cowed. One student insists that the government's overreach helped publicize Li's cause, saying that its response was "ridiculous and frightening. . . . We have our own independent personalities and ideas. Please respect us." The Communist Party will have a hard time reining in its young, self-confident, only children. The more millennials learn how repressive their government is, the more likely they are to challenge it.

Public protests like those by Li Tingting and her friends are rare. No strong, overt advocacy organizations exist in China. Even leaders of small, loosely organized networks advocating for rule of law, transparency, and human rights routinely get long prison sentences. Dissidents routinely "disappear" into the vast network of the internal security apparatus without formal trial, and strike leaders are detained without charge if they step over the line.

Nobel Prize winner Liu Xiabao is serving an eleven-year prison sentence for coauthoring a prodemocracy manifesto in 2008. Dissident Chen Guancheng famously fled to the U.S. Embassy after living under house arrest for eighteen months just for advocating on behalf of peasants and people with disabilities. Human rights lawyer Gao Zhisheng served five years in solitary confinement for defending Falun Gong members. Another human rights lawyer, Pu Zhiqiang, was convicted in December 2015 on charges of "picking quarrels and provoking trouble" in Weibo posts that seem very benign to a western reader. (One post about China's legislature read "If you want to live like a fish in water, either you play the fool or be a real fool.") He was held for eighteen months in detention and will no longer be able to practice law. In the past two years, the Chinese government removed 1,300 crosses from churches in Zhejiang Province and arrested nearly twenty pastors and their lawyers who protested these actions. Political artist Ai Weiwei was jailed in 2011 and held for eighty-one days on trumped-up charges of tax evasion. His arrest was part of a roundup of artists, bloggers, and human rights activists the government thought could foment a "jasmine revolution" similar to the uprisings sweeping the Middle East.

Freedom House, an American nonprofit organization, reports that "tens of thousands of grassroots activists . . . are believed to be in prison or extrajudicial detention for their political or religious views." These draconian sentences explain why several leaders of nonprofit organizations in China were adamant that they did not want to be interviewed for this book. A new draft law will prevent Chinese nonprofits from receiving foreign funding and will require foreign nonprofits, or those that receive money from foreign donors, to register with the Chinese public security apparatus.

For years, China has spent more on internal security than on its military, $130 billion in 2013. Domestic security spending covers everything from monitoring dissidents online and eavesdropping on journalists to stopping terrorist attacks. Since China's high internal security budget has drawn unfavorable headlines even within the country, in 2014 the Chinese government stopped publishing the overall figures.

At times of crisis the Communist Party plays on nationalist sentiment to create an escape valve. In August and September 2012, thousands of Chinese protested in cities across China against the Japanese government's decision to purchase the disputed Diaoyu islands in the East China Sea from a private owner. Japanese-owned factories and restaurants were vandalized. It is unclear whether the protests were spontaneous or encouraged by Party officials. But the Chinese government likely had a hand in redirecting public opinion away from domestic troubles just before the change in Party leadership in November 2012. According to one account, Chinese police showed protesters to the best possible location to demonstrate. Chinese propaganda officials also encouraged journalists to cover the pro-China nationalistic element of the protests—and warned them not to mention the violence.

This nationalism directly impacts China's foreign relations. Japanese firms are hesitant to invest in China when their factories may be vandalized as a convenient way for Chinese to "let off steam." Japanese foreign direct investment (FDI) into China declined by almost 50 percent in 2014 compared to earlier years and by another 16 percent in the first half of 2015. Japanese companies are focusing on Southeast Asia instead.

The Communist Party also employs an army of censors. Chinese censorship swings wildly between the sophisticated and the clumsy. When my husband, Greg, arrived in Beijing in fall 2012 after a sixteen-hour flight, he tried to open the taxi window to get some fresh air. "Absolutely not," insisted his driver. "This week, no open windows in taxis. At all." Greg laughed when he learned that the propaganda department had issued this directive to ensure that no dissident would throw leaflets out of car windows during Xi Jinping's public ascent to power. With hundreds of millions of Chinese on the Internet, the regime oddly took time to worry about photocopied leaflets.

In traditional media, such as television and print, the Party controls the message almost completely. President Xi poignantly reminded Chinese media in February 2016 that their job is not to report the news but to make the Party look good. CCTV, China's ubiquitous television station, shapes the opinions of China's older generation (millennials don't really watch). CCTV can reach 1 billion people within China. It is available in seven languages and more than one hundred countries, so it expands Beijing's propaganda reach into the developing world. Even foreign journalists must stay within Party-designed boundaries, as the *New York Times* found out when it was blocked after writing about Wen Jiabao's family's suspicious wealth. Evan Osnos wrote in *Age of Ambition* about his experience as a China-based journalist of getting the "ping" of texts from the Chinese propaganda bureau telling him which topics were taboo that week.

Censorship is more difficult online. China has set up a sophisticated filtering scheme, dubbed the "Great Firewall," to give Chinese citizens the feeling that they can communicate freely, while the Party strives to "curate" the conversations of millions to stay away from sensitive topics.

In 2004 there were just 96 million Chinese Internet users. By 2016 this had ballooned to 724 million (about as many Internet users as in the United States and Europe combined). The number of physical protests also increases each year in large part because of social media. When Sungmin Rho interviewed uneducated migrant workers, she was struck at how adeptly they use messaging platforms such as Weibo and WeChat to organize strikes. They are also public relations savvy—posting pictures and videos of their unfair treatment online. Social media is a censor's worst nightmare.

The Communist Party apparatus walks a tightrope. On the one hand, in a one-party system the online grumblings of Chinese citizens help the government understand which issues to fix, and social media is so popular that it would be impractical to shut it down. On the other hand, the government is racing to censor these platforms, and to push back with its own propaganda. The Chinese government has reportedly hired some *two million people* to monitor the Internet. It also pays individual Internet users to post pro-government content in comment sections of newspapers and on blogs.

China has one of the largest and most sophisticated content filtering systems in the world. All Internet companies must scan for "unpatriotic" content up front. Five years ago, Sina Weibo alone employed more than one thousand people to censor its microblogs. I have never seen such a content deletion factory but can only imagine hundreds of neat desks and laptops lined up in a drab warehouse, just to expunge the free expression of others. The Central Propaganda Department routinely calls Internet executives into closed-door meetings to "encourage" them to self-censor. It also issues keywords that are automatically erased. These range from what you would expect—"anticommunist" or "prodemocracy" and "tyranny"—to things like "oral sex" and "electric chicken." Yes, you read that correctly. Chinese bloggers often use plays on Chinese characters like "electric chicken" to get around censors. I have not puzzled out the hidden meaning of that particular term.

According to Xiao Qiang and other scholars, China's propagandists usually let citizens gripe about government policies such as corruption, pollution, and land grabs. They instantly delete, however, any information that could lead to collective action or demonstrations. Xiao says his algorithm also finds that China deletes unflattering information about China's top leaders and their families, controversial historical events like Tiananmen and the Great Leap Forward, and even information about China's censorship system itself. These days Chinese citizens are very aware of these restrictions, where the red lines are that they shouldn't cross, and what the consequences can be if they do.*

Smaller dictatorships like North Korea and Turkmenistan have shut down much of the Internet entirely. Only the Chinese would tackle the monumental task of sifting through the world's information fire hose to give their citizens the entertainment content they crave, but not the "harmful" political free expression that often comes with it.

★ ★ ★

---

*Just recently, China added the offensive "Great Cannon" to its defensive "Great Firewall." It blitzed websites outside of China that were giving Chinese users access to content that is illegal in China. San Francisco–based site GitHub, which hosts links to content restricted in China, such as the Chinese-language version of the *New York Times*, suddenly found itself bombarded with requests from Chinese Baidu users (a "dedicated denial-of-service" attack) that shut it down. The Great Cannon has been mysteriously silent since then but could be brought out again at any time.

In contrast to China's authoritarianism, India is accurately described as a "raucous democracy." Its constitution grants citizens the fundamental right to freedom of speech and expression, and Indians use it. Since independence in 1947, elections have been held regularly and—with minor exceptions—they have been free and fair. Political parties argue in public and the media is diverse and very vocal. Indians, who famously invented nonviolent protest and used it to gain their independence from Britain, still exercise these freedoms, often in dramatic ways. Public protests are common, vociferous, and largely peaceful. Civil society is strong.

I often visit public protests when in India. No matter how serious the issue, they always have an air of a street festival, and renew my faith in the power of citizens to improve their own government. In December 2011, a rickshaw driver took me to the edges of one of the anticorruption protests of Anna Hazare, India's fierce but gentle clean-government crusader, whom we met earlier. At the time, he had riveted his country's imagination. Hazare chose Jantar Mahar as his backdrop. It is large open space dotted with astronomical instruments built in the eighteenth century: from pillars arranged in circles, to staircases leading to nowhere. It seemed an unusual place for an anticorruption protest, one of those Indian idiosyncrasies that a foreigner like me never quite understands. Hundreds of people surrounded a dais where Hazare sat cross-legged and silent. Politicians made impassioned speeches in Hindi, people chanted in support, and vendors did a brisk business selling street food. Saffron, white, and green Indian flags waved. A few policemen lingered around the edges of the gathering, but they seemed more interested in the samosas than in a crackdown. This was no Tiananmen.

When I asked an elderly man in dust-colored trousers and shirt why he was there, he responded in an articulate and pithy way: "Our government is failing us. We must help it get better! It is our job as Indians." He couldn't quite believe that I was there as a "protest tourist" and found the idea hilarious. I liked his attitude, which I have heard from many other Indians. While there is significant cynicism about the government, many Indians feel it is their duty to speak up and advocate for change. If change doesn't come fast enough, the government is turned out of office, as happened in the landslide defeat of the ruling Congress Party in May 2014.

After dozens of demonstrations and several hunger strikes, Anna Hazare forced the government to push through real anticorruption reform (which is not yet implemented). Similarly, thousands of people took to the streets after the horrific December 2012 rape of a woman on a Delhi bus, described in chapter 7. India passed tough, new anti-rape laws several months later. This is Indian citizen activism at its best.

Yet a darker trend clashes with this hopeful one. Just one day after touring the anticorruption protest, I sat in the office of Kapil Sibal, India's powerful minister of communications, information technology, and human resources, as part of a small delegation of former U.S. government officials and business leaders, debating the right of Indian citizens to post bad-taste cartoons of local politicians on the Internet.

Sibal, one of the prime minister's most trusted advisers, had a broad portfolio that included supervising the country's information technology industry. The *New York Times* had caused a minor uproar a week earlier by exposing the Indian government's quiet policy of pressing many IT companies—Facebook, Google, Yahoo, and Microsoft among them—to monitor and proactively remove content that disparages public figures or religious symbols.

When our delegation raised the issue, Minister Sibal protested that he was misunderstood. He explained that the Indian government was concerned only about "lascivious" content that could incite violence between the different religious groups, such as "pictures of Muhammad fornicating with a pig." This is a reasonable concern in India, where interreligious violence is still too tragically common. When we asked him to clarify whether any political content was covered by the new rules, he answered that it wouldn't be unless it is "indecent," such as for example a picture showing the prime minister with the body of a dog. (While in poor taste, in the United States and in India this is legally considered core, protected political speech.)

I have rarely seen an Indian politician as defensive as Minister Sibal that day. His government was under fire for doing too little to improve the stagnant economy, and at some point he seemed to realize that this bout of censorship would not end the criticisms. Perhaps he also sensed that the episode violated India's view of itself as a country that protects freedom of speech.

India, the country of Gandhi, with thousands of annual protests and countless nonprofits and citizen advocates, is sometimes surprisingly repressive. It ranks a low 80 out of 199 countries in press freedom (China ranks 186). As Minister Sibal demonstrated to us, the government sometimes blocks political content online. Some bloggers have been arrested. Freedom House found in 2015 that India's Internet was only "partly free," with a score of 40 out of 100. (China scored an abysmal 88 out of 100—the worst score of any country.) In 2015, Indian authorities banned the domestic broadcast of a documentary film about the infamous Delhi rape, and said they were also trying to prevent it from being shown worldwide.

The Indian government is suspicious of nonprofit organizations, especially those receiving foreign funding. In a move more typical of China or Russia, in April 2015 the government canceled the licenses of almost nine thousand charities. Among them it blocked the bank accounts of Greenpeace India, which has led campaigns against coal mining and nuclear power projects. The accounts have been unfrozen but the organization is no longer allowed to raise money from overseas. Big donors like the U.S.-based Ford Foundation are also being investigated. Modi's government has done little to explain the sudden crackdown. It is likely that the Hindu xenophobic wings of his BJP party advocated for it—for years they have been concerned about U.S. nonprofits spreading Christianity in India. So far, Modi's government has not completely relented, despite a stern warning from the U.S. ambassador to India and an appeal by almost two hundred Indian charities, who called the crackdown "arbitrary" and "nontransparent." We must be clear, however. While India is making it difficult for some charities to operate, it has not thrown their leaders in jail, as China would likely do.

India ranks lower than one might expect on press freedom in part because there is violence against journalists—particularly in Kashmir and Chhattisgarh states, where there are low-level violent insurgencies against central government rule. In June 2015, a journalist was killed in Uttar Pradesh after posting allegations of political corruption online. Police opened a case against the politician, who denies the charges. In 2014 in Srinagar, Indian police reportedly threw rocks at journalists covering political demonstrations. These are isolated incidents, but they can make India a dangerous country for journalists. Again, this is different and much less concerning than in China, where the government censors all content and targets journalists for political reasons.

India's notoriously independent courts serve as a real check on government overreach and sometimes declare such conduct unconstitutional. Minister Sibal had the authority under a broadly worded Indian IT law to censor the Internet content he found so outrageous. The law criminalizes "grossly offensive" or "menacing" online speech and writing false information that causes "annoyance, inconvenience, danger, insult, injury, . . . hatred or ill will," so it is broad enough to cover almost any speech that another person finds "annoying" or "insulting."

Indians arrested under the law include a university professor who emailed his friends a comic strip showing West Bengal Chief Minister Mamata Banerjee wielding magical powers to force the local railway minister out of office, and a woman who asked on her Facebook page why Mumbai shut down for the funeral of a controversial Hindu nationalist leader. The police also arrested a friend of the woman's who simply "liked" the original comment. Unlike Chinese dissidents serving long jail terms, all three were quickly released.

Upset over these and other incidents, a courageous twenty-four-year-old law student named Shreya Singhal sued the government. With her round face and long curls, she looked closer to sixteen, and got lots of press attention for taking such a courageous stand. In March 2015, India's Supreme Court agreed with Singhal. It struck down the law as unconstitutional. In an interview after the verdict came out, Singhal explained that she was compelled to act because "anyone who uses the Internet could have been arrested for doing anything."

Singhal's experience is a world away from the young Chinese women who were detained and threatened for walking down the street in paint-splattered wedding gowns. Like other democracies, India at times struggles to balance freedom of speech against other interests, and occasionally the government overreaches. Unlike in China, however, India's democracy and strong rule of law means that courts are empowered to correct such pendulum swings (although it often takes years for a case to be heard).

★ ★ ★

Some of my Indian friends ponder whether too much protest and citizen activism is crippling India. It is difficult for the government to pass any legislation, as it is in the United States, because irate activists argue different sides of each issue. Farmers stalled a long-pending bill to make it easier to buy land to build manufacturing plants. One hundred fifty million workers protested against Prime Minister Modi's proposed labor reform in September 2015. Different protestors shut down much of the Delhi water supply in February 2016. With no such civil society to answer to, the Chinese government appears more decisive and efficient. China has demonstrated the value of top-down control to build infrastructure and quickly change government policies. India has a good chance of demonstrating how millions of individuals, free to express their views, will in the long term create a more stable, resilient, and happy society.

Despite its massive efforts, the Chinese Communist Party is gradually losing its battle against free expression. It is virtually impossible to rein in more than 700 million Internet users. As long as the gripes of Chinese citizens are about marginal issues—factory working conditions, food safety, or environmental issues—the regime can stay in power, but a serious economic downturn could quickly turn into a political crisis.

No one can predict how this will end. It is easy to picture negative scenarios. By 2030, the Chinese government could have become more authoritarian. Some whisper that an internal Party coup could topple President Xi. If a crackdown is too draconian, however, China's self-confident millennial generation may have their own Tiananmen Square moment, similar to the Arab Spring. If revolutionary fervor spreads in China, it likely will end in violent crackdown, as in Syria, or in a new authoritarian regime, as in Egypt, rather than in a peaceful transition to democracy.

Revolution is not the best route to democracy. Scholars Michael

Albertus and Victor Menaldo have found that since the end of World War II, there have been roughly fifty revolutions that toppled autocratic regimes or led to significant political reform in "flawed" democracies. Only about a third have resulted in transitions to democracy. After a violent change in government, the Chinese (and thus world) economy would suffer. China is too large for the United States to support with massive aid while it develops democratic institutions.

So we must tread carefully. Western activists often argue that we should be "tougher" on China for its abysmal record on human rights and freedom of speech. In my experience, U.S. leaders in both political parties rightly admonish China on these issues, and the issue is near the top of our talking points. The Chinese generally listen stone-faced and do nothing, however, and there are no good ways for foreigners to impose consequences for China's inaction.

Drawing attention to isolated egregious incidents—such as the detentions of Chen and Li—can be effective and shame the government into releasing specific individuals. We should continue to apply pressure in this way. However, no amount of lecturing will move China into dismantling its "stability" apparatus. Economic sanctions or withdrawing from our engagement won't improve China's behavior because the Chinese see censorship as fundamental to regime survival. International punishment will only empower the hard-liners who argue that the United States is nefariously pushing for regime change in China.

Engagement with China will be more effective than hectoring. The U.S. (and ideally Indian and European) governments should gently nudge China toward greater openness. Both can also help by encouraging an open world Internet, and helping western companies work in China. This will help build the positive vision of 2030: a gradual movement by China toward greater political openness. Such an evolution would allow better rule of law and civil society institutions to develop before permitting all 1.3 billion Chinese to vote.

More engagement at all levels would help. If our companies trade with each other and students attend each other's universities, China is more likely gradually to absorb the West's values, including free expression. Americans should engage Chinese students, millennials, and the urban middle class. These groups are most likely to share our values. Opening this dam will make it increasingly difficult for the government to silence dissenters, as we see with millennials and their social networks.

Within reason, we should also support our Internet companies' desire to do business in China, aware that they will have to follow Chinese law: they will censor content and will have to turn over data about activists to China's security apparatus, just as their Chinese counterparts do. This is a difficult pill to swallow. American companies should not be playing integral roles in China's brutal political repression. However, the companies did not create the problem of censorship—China's government did. If these companies warn Chinese users, in clear terms, that all posts will be censored, they will raise Chinese awareness of this issue as well as contribute in general to the free expression of ideas and to the ability of Chinese to engage with others around the world. More trade and interaction is good, and each tiny wedge in the Chinese firewall will be helpful. Only openness and truth can beat back China's misinformation offensive.

It is also in the United States' interest to support Indian civil society. We want India to be an open, free counterexample to China's repression. U.S. Internet companies have made impressive inroads in the country. Facebook has 125 million users, and Google nearly 200 million. As a friend, the United States can encourage India to curb its negative impulses—as our delegation did when we openly debated with Minister Sibal about restrictions on social media, and as U.S. ambassador Rich Verma has done by calling on the Modi government to stop restricting the work of nonprofit organizations. India occasionally needs a nudge in the right direction (as the United States does), but it is a living example that even in a very diverse society, people can air their grievances peacefully and push their government to reform.

PART III

★ ★ ★

STEPPING ONTO THE WORLD STAGE

10 | THE NEW MERCANTILISTS

GRIZZLED AFGHAN warlord, now a member of Parliament, wiped away a tear. Not far from him, a young woman parliamentarian, typing on her iPad, did the same. Indian Prime Minister Manmohan Singh's speech to the Afghan Parliament in 2011 left few eyes dry. India had spent millions to build a new Parliament building in Kabul—part of the nearly $2 billion in aid it has pledged to Afghanistan over the past decade. When Prime Minister Singh spoke to the assembled legislators, he talked about the two countries' shared history and civilization, and India's commitment to helping Afghans build a democracy. The Kabul Parliament building is partly a way for India to ensure that Pakistan doesn't dominate Afghanistan in future, but it is also a powerful symbol of India's altruistic approach to foreign aid.

Despite India's generous aid, Afghanistan's day-to-day economy is more closely tied to China. Walking around Kabul's lively bazaar, one sees that much of the clothing, toys and electronics on offer are made in China, not India. Only the DVDs are Indian: Bollywood is a huge hit.

Down the road from Kabul, Chinese workers began large works on a copper mine several years ago. They didn't hire many local Afghans, except to provide security. While China has given relatively little aid to Afghanistan (it has committed just $320 million to reconstruction aid since 2001), it is responsible for the country's single largest foreign investment: in 2007, amid rumors that the Chinese paid off an Afghan minister to get the deal, China paid $2.8 billion for the rights to mine copper in the Aynak mine. Due to security concerns and the fact that ancient archaeological ruins were uncovered on the site, all work at the mine has temporarily stopped. Across the border in Pakistan, China has committed to build an avalanche of infrastructure, from hydropower plants and coal mines to upgrading pipelines, ports, roads, and rails.

★   ★   ★

China and India's influence on its poorer neighbors is a microcosm of how they conduct their economic diplomacy on the world stage.

China has become a twenty-first-century mercantilist. It coordinates aid, government loans, foreign direct investment, and to some extent trade to help its own companies and keep its economy growing. Chinese diplomats and businessmen work hand in hand in an unprecedented way: they build roads and ports in exchange for lucrative oil contracts, and promise to lay railroad tracks across the Andes and Africa, thus challenging U.S. influence on these continents. In China, investment is part of a government-encouraged industrial strategy to secure natural resources, create opportunities for state-owned enterprises as China's internal boom slows, invest China's massive currency reserves, and expand its political influence all at once. Its huge infrastructure investments are also upending the clubby world of international economic institutions like the World Bank and IMF. China is making its economic presence felt around the world in spectacular fashion. As scholar Steve Levine put it, China is "quickly growing into history's most extensive global commercial empire. . . . It views almost no place as uncontested."

India has no such comprehensive strategy. While it is gaining on China in many other areas discussed in this book, its economic sway beyond its borders is still relatively minor. China's rapidly expanding influence in India's region, however, is slowly spurring it into action. In the past year, India has made a renewed effort to negotiate regional trade agreements (although it is too soon to tell if its notoriously difficult trade bureaucrats will agree to anything). It is also working harder to influence its neighbors with aid and political pressure as a way to push back on what it sees as

China's encroachment in its neighborhood. Even with these new initiatives, India is punching under its economic weight.

★   ★   ★

India likes to emphasize that is it a gentle power. "We don't like to throw our weight around," is how Ronen Sen, India's longtime ambassador to the United States, explained it to me. Since independence, no unified policy has determined the aid India gives, how it trades with other countries, and how the foreign direct investment of its companies can help India prosper.

In many ways it is stunning to talk about India's economic influence on the rest of the world at all. For decades after independence, painfully poor India was the world's largest recipient of development aid. The government had no extra funds to give away. Nehru and his successors kept trade barriers high to support India's fledgling industries, so trade was minimal, and partly as a result, few Indian companies grew large or powerful enough to invest directly in other countries.

This has all changed drastically in the last decade or so. India now gives more development aid to other countries than it receives. In 2015, it gave an impressive $1.6 billion in aid grants, almost the same as China with its much larger economy. The vast majority of this money goes to help India's immediate neighborhood, to build the Parliament building in Afghanistan, give humanitarian aid to Nepal after the recent earthquake, and give health and education funds to Bhutan and Sri Lanka. In addition to direct grants, India gives nearly $12 billion in soft loans to countries in need—largely in Africa, Asia, and Latin America. India was one of the first countries to give to the United Nations Democracy Fund in 2006. It has also trained thousands of civil servants in 161 different developing countries. While India gives mostly out of altruism, its close connection with other developing countries means they often support India's initiatives in the United Nations.

The tsunami that rocked Asia in December 2004 demonstrated India's unselfish approach to aid. India's coastline was badly beat up. Eighteen thousand Indians died, tens of thousands of fishing boats were destroyed, and whole cities were underwater or flattened. The price of fish dropped suddenly due to local concerns that the fish were eating the dead bodies of those killed in the disaster. The Indian government quickly put together a $600 million reconstruction package for its own tsunami-affected regions.

India could be forgiven if during this terrible crisis it had only focused on itself. Yet it also helped others. More than sixteen thousand Indian troops used navy ships and aircraft to deliver thousands of tons of relief supplies to Sri Lanka, the Maldives, and Indonesia, and donated an additional $23 million in aid.

Why would India—which still houses one-fourth of all the world's poorest people—give to other countries at all? Humanitarian giving lies at the heart of India's cultural values. Hinduism, Buddhism, Islam, and Sikhism all encourage the devout to empathize with those in need and to give without expecting a return. The Indian government stresses over and over again that its aid is not linked to political objectives. In addition, India feels a strong connection to other countries that were subjugated under colonial systems. Its assistance promotes development and democracy in these countries, and shows India's solidarity with them.

India's foreign direct investment is still quite small. Even its best companies still invest relatively little abroad, just $10 billion in total in 2014. China, by contrast, is the second-largest investor in the world (China and Hong Kong together invested $249 billion in 2014), after the United States with $337 billion.*

In China, investment is part of a government-encouraged strategy and often comes from its mammoth state-owned enterprises. India has no such industrial strategy. Most Indian investment, by contrast, comes from private companies who want to improve shareholder value, not please the government. Tata is a perfect example. As one of India's biggest private companies, run by the legendary Ratan Tata, it has sprawling

---

* These numbers are notoriously hard to collect and report accurately. The figures for India and China are all from the United Nation's 2015 World Investment Report. The Reserve Bank of India reports India's outbound investment was higher for 2014, $38 billion.

interests in automobiles, hotels, steel, and consulting, among other industries. In 2008, Tata bought Jaguar Land Rover from Ford for $2.3 billion.
Jaguar had been operating at a loss for several years. Tata patiently gave
the struggling company capital until it could turn itself around, and gave
the English managers free rein. Now Jaguar Land Rover's sales are growing rapidly and profit is substantial. The company has created thousands
of jobs and is the United Kingdom's largest automotive employer. It was a
purely commercial transaction.

As the Tata case shows, Indian companies are buying more assets in
developed countries like the United States, the United Kingdom, and the
Netherlands. Some Indian companies invest in South Asia, or in countries where there is a large Indian diaspora, such as Kenya and the United
Arab Emirates, yet only 38 percent of Indian investments are in the developing world.

China and India have so far invested very little in each other, although
Chinese investment has begun to flow in just in the past few months. The
war the two fought in the 1960s, China's massive aid to India's archrival
Pakistan, and niggling border disputes all undermine the trust needed to
feed cross-border investment. China has invested just $20.1 billion total
in India in the decade since 2005, and does not even make the list of top
ten investors in India.

To help his "Make in India" campaign, Prime Minister Modi is actively
courting Chinese investment. He announced proudly that Chinese companies and the government agreed to spend $20 billion in India over the
next five years. The initiative is off to a good start. In January 2016, China's
Dalian Wanda Group revealed plans to invest a whopping $10 billion to
build industrial parks in the Indian state of Haryana. If it goes through,
this will be India's largest investment by a single foreign company to date.
However, as we'll see below, it is still small compared to China's spending
elsewhere. Changing this would go far to improve relations between the
two giants and create a powerful business constituency in each country
for them to get along.

If India's aid is altruistic and its foreign investment is ad hoc, its trade policy is obstinately protectionist. Prime Minister Modi talks a lot about free

trade, but so far, American trade negotiators tell me, the BJP government is just as protectionist as its predecessors. To make India a manufacturing powerhouse and employ its youth bulge, India will have to find a way to export all those manufactured goods. So Modi talks about doubling India's exports to reach almost $900 billion within the next five years, a nearly impossible task even for committed free traders. Unfortunately, so far, India's free trade rhetoric does not really match reality.

More than its other diplomats, Indian trade negotiators tend to be stuck in the nonaligned movement and protectionist rhetoric of the Nehru era. Many Indian officials still don't see the benefit of free trade for their country. The biggest concern is around opening up India's heavily subsidized agricultural sector. India's rural poor are a powerful voting bloc, especially for India's Congress Party, and many believe that farmers and small shopkeepers will be harmed by free trade. Domestic politics plays a big role in India's protectionism, as it does in the United States and elsewhere.

The trade bureaucracy is at times more protectionist than Delhi's political leadership. A senior White House official told me that one recent trade negotiation was a thriller by mild-mannered diplomatic standards. In July 2014, India unexpectedly blocked the passage of a World Trade Organization (WTO) deal that would have been the first multilateral trade deal in two decades—and according to some calculations would increase global GDP by 1 trillion dollars. India's controversial food subsidies program was on the line. Indian negotiators had already agreed to a compromise, but after Modi took office, the trade bureaucracy suddenly balked at its commitment. It took intense midnight negotiations in Washington, Geneva, and Delhi between the Obama administration and a few trusted people in the Indian prime minister's office—all kept completely secret from India's trade bureaucrats—to turn the issue around. This was a good but insufficient start.

India continues to sit on the sidelines of almost all the big new regional trade agreements. Even modest trade initiatives, like a bilateral investment treaty with the United States and a free trade agreement with Europe, have been largely stalled for years.

India also still trades mostly with other Asian countries, rather than with the rest of the world. In 2014 its trade with Asia was $246 billion (including China), compared to $98 billion with the European Union and $64 billion with the United States.

China has become India's largest trading partner. The two traded more than $72 billion in 2014, up from almost nothing in 2000. This is good news, but unfortunately the relationship is lopsided. China exports almost six times as much to India as the other way around. Where India sends mostly raw materials such as cotton yarn, copper, and petroleum to China, the Chinese export clothes, computer hardware, industrial machinery, and other manufactured goods to India. This is a constant source of friction. India's bazaars are filled with inexpensive Chinese-made toys and clothes, and its offices are filled with Lenovo computers and Xiaomi phones, just like in many places in the United States. When I tried to buy one of India's famed pashmina shawls on a recent trip there, I was surprised to see the ubiquitous "Made in China" tag on the back.

So far, economic relations between India and China are similar to those between the United States and China. The two economies depend on each other but have not developed the trust that should come from so much economic activity. To help avoid political and military tensions, it is in America's interest to encourage better economic relations between all three countries.

As India takes tentative steps into foreign investment, aid, and trade diplomacy, China is already the eight-hundred-pound gorilla on the world economic stage. Seventy Chinese supertankers ply the oceans. It is the largest consumer of the world's natural resources, from steel and iron ore to copper, zinc, and aluminum. It imports more oil than any other country on earth and consumes almost half the world's coal.

The Chinese government claims that it was the largest trading partner of 130 countries around the world in 2013. The CIA *World Factbook* believes the number is lower, and that ninety-six countries counted China as their largest exports or imports partner. Even using the conservative CIA numbers, more countries trade more with China than the United States.

It is most astounding that in recent years, China *alone* loaned more to developing countries than the World Bank, according to research by the *Financial Times*.

China's authoritarian, more centralized government also means that it can be strategic about spreading its economic influence. Unlike in India and the United States, China uses aid, trade, and foreign direct investment strategically to build goodwill, expand its political sway, and secure the natural resources it needs to grow. All are part of one, mostly coherent, national industrial policy.

China's One Belt, One Road initiative (OBOR) is the latest and by far the most spectacular example of this. In the next three decades China plans to build a dizzying mesh of infrastructure around Asia and, through similar initiatives, around the world. It also has plans for greater financial integration, trade liberalization, and strengthening of people-to-people ties between China and its neighbors.

The maritime "road" will include perhaps a dozen ports from Asia to East Africa and the Mediterranean. A planned rail network will connect China with Laos and Cambodia, Malaysia, Myanmar, Singapore, Thailand, and Vietnam. To the west, new rails and roads travel through Kazakhstan, Iran, Turkey, and Russia to Europe. Because of these initiatives, you can already ship a container from China's coast through Chengdu and Xinjiang all the way to Germany by rail. Shipping time from China to Germany has been reduced by almost half, to just sixteen days.

No one knows quite how much this will cost. One Belt, One Road will be implemented over the next several decades and will be funded through a number of vehicles, most importantly through the new Asian Infrastructure Investment Bank (AIIB), with its $100 billion in initial capital, and through a separate $40 billion New Silk Road Fund. The New Development Bank, launched by China, India, Russia, and South Africa, will kick in $10 billion. The China Development Bank reportedly said it will invest a staggering $890 billion in loans over time to finance projects in sixty countries. It is impossible to predict just how much money the initiative will bring to developing economies in total, because this capital is only the beginning: as we will see below, the One Belt, One Road initiative will give mostly loans, not grants, and in addition Chinese state-owned enterprises will be encouraged to invest.

Why is China undertaking these hugely expensive projects? Many American commentators see a dangerous scheme to dominate the rest of the world economically. China reiterates over and over that its motives are benign, done "in the spirit of open regional cooperation" and to create an "economic cooperation architecture that benefits all." The policies are certainly designed to benefit China, but seen from China's perspective, they are not necessarily menacing.

First, while China's own infrastructure is gleaming, many of its neighbors and economic partners are hard to reach. If China's companies want to get natural resources from Central Asia and export their goods to Europe, having a faster, more reliable road and rail system is helpful. Second, more than 80 percent of Beijing's oil and many of its other natural resources pass through a narrow, five-hundred-mile stretch of sea between Malaysia and Indonesia, the Malacca Strait. China worries that if relations become hostile, the United States and its allies could blockade the strait and starve the country of its lifeblood resources.

Third, China has such large foreign currency reserves that it is hard to convert these into renminbi, because so much money flooding into China would force prices to rise rapidly there. China has been investing this money mostly in U.S. Treasury bonds, but these pay very low interest, so China thinks it may make a better return investing them in infrastructure projects abroad. This buys goodwill with its neighbors and helps connect western and rural China to the world.

Now that China's infrastructure has been built (or overbuilt), many state-owned enterprises also have extra capacity. So the government helps them stay afloat, and saves lots of Chinese jobs, by giving Chinese companies low-interest loans to build foreign mega-projects. Finally, cultural factors are important. Chinese companies are new to overseas investment and so often act just like they would at home: in China there is no real sanctity of contract, so companies often buy the land, the transportation links, and whatever else is necessary to get the oil out of the ground or the project completed. When they go abroad, they do the same.

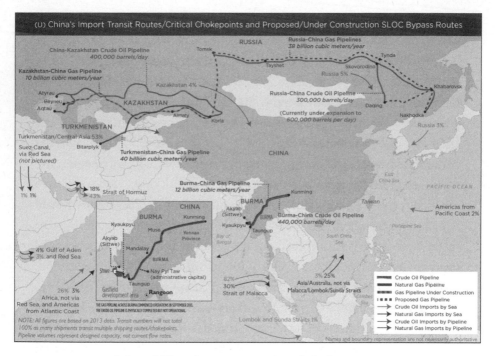

Map of China's transit routes and chokepoints.

photo credit: *Courtesy of the United States Department of Defense*

An important side effect is that many developing countries feel grateful and beholden to China for its generosity and are thus more likely to side with China in international disputes. The Communist Party's economic diplomacy is not meant to be malicious, but it certainly is China-centric.

The current centerpiece of China's One Belt, One Road initiative is its tidal wave of projects with Pakistan. They perfectly illustrate how and why China is expanding its economic influence and how it combines aid, trade, and direct investment for maximum effect.

Amid sentimental pronouncements that Chinese-Pakistani friendship is "higher than mountains," "deeper than oceans," "sweeter than honey," and "stronger than steel," Beijing announced in 2014 that it would finance a 1,800-mile-long superhighway, a high-speed railway, an oil pipeline route to the inland Chinese city of Kashgar, and the expansion of a deep-sea port in the once-tiny village of Gwadar.

Gwadar, filled with dust-colored cinder-block houses and trash-strewn streets and ringed by cliffs, desert, and the Arabian Sea, was formerly at the forgotten edge of the earth. It is about to experience a storm of Chinese construction. A new 114-room "Pearl Continental" hotel stands mostly empty, its landscaping perfect, ready to receive an onslaught of Chinese engineers who will upgrade its port.

In total, China agreed to lavish $46 billion on Pakistan alone—much more than America's yearly aid budget for the entire world.* Chinese engineers have already begun digging tunnels and building bridges to improve safety along the legendary Karakoram highway, one of the highest paved roads on earth, which links Pakistan to China. China also gives Pakistan trade preferences through a free trade agreement signed in 2006 and is Pakistan's largest trading partner, although the volume of trade with Pakistan is a drop in the bucket for Beijing.

Pakistan desperately needs the friends. It attracts few foreign visitors or businessmen these days due to safety fears. When I went to see the famous Wagah border crossing in mid-2013—where Indian and Pakistani troops show off their stomping and drills each night to great cheering—on the Indian side there was a healthy mix of Indian families, western businessmen, and tourists from around the world. On the Pakistani side, by contrast, among several thousand spectators, the only foreigners were thirty Chinese businessmen and myself. Chinese guests also fill the five-star Serena hotel in Islamabad, which was formerly the haunt of western diplomats and aid workers.

With such Chinese largesse, it is no wonder that Pakistanis are ecstatic about the China-Pakistan Economic Corridor, as the project is called. Shiny new billboards proclaiming their enduring partnership can be seen along every highway. Chinese contractors reportedly say they shouldn't have to pay to enter some of Pakistan's beloved tourist sites since they built the roads leading to them. Almost four-fifths of Pakistanis have a positive opinion of China, while only 14 percent feel warmly toward the

---

* The $46 billion certainly grabbed headlines, but only $28 billion was agreed to during Xi's visit. Andrew Small from the German Marshall Fund, who has written a book on the China-Pakistan axis, thinks the whole amount may not materialize.

United States, despite our own substantial aid to Pakistan. In recent years, the United States has given Pakistan more than $1 billion a year in aid, much of that to their security services, to help them fight militants in the border region. Pakistanis see China's engagement emotionally, as friendly assistance by a brotherly neighbor. In fact, much of this assistance is coming on commercial terms. China has been known to walk away from projects if there are safety concerns or loans are not repaid.

Helping Pakistan in such dramatic fashion fits well into China's economic strategy. If it can create a deep-sea port in the Arabian Sea and a land route to western China, much Middle Eastern oil could travel the short route through Pakistan, instead of six thousand miles through the Malacca Straits to Shanghai. Chinese companies are happy to have work to do. And the initiative has the convenient side effect of annoying India, Pakistan's archenemy and China's potential strategic rival.

How can China afford all this? Looking behind the impressive headline numbers, very little is actual aid. Neither side usually makes the details of the investments public. From what I could glean speaking to local officials and U.S. scholars about the $46 billion committed to Pakistan, almost all of the money is in the form of loans, often to Chinese companies that will build the projects. This is not a great act of Chinese generosity.

China has a very different definition of aid than the United States and India, which distinguish clearly between grants that will not be paid back—aid—and other financial flows related to commerce. China has a broader definition that includes some grants, government loans, export credits, and preferential trade relationships. More than 80 percent of China's "aid" is actually in the form of projects to develop natural resources or build infrastructure. Looking at the endless list of contracts signed for the Pakistan projects, it fits this pattern. Other than some small grants for feasibility studies, the Chinese government is contributing very little cash. Instead its development banks loaned money to various *Chinese* firms to build a hydropower plant, develop several coal mines, and complete a pipeline to Iran, and to various Pakistani entities to build all the roads and rails to connect the projects within Pakistan and to China.*

Many of the Chinese government loans have real collateral behind them. For example, the Chinese have the rights to operate the Gwadar port for forty years. If Pakistan can't repay the loans, China could own many of Pakistan's coal mines, oil pipelines, and power plants. While American journalists tend to see a nefarious desire to control the world economy in all this, scholar Parag Khanna points out that Chinese have been generous in the past about loan repayments. He believes China would likely soften repayment terms rather than use "gunboat diplomacy" to extract concessions.

In dusty Gwadar, there is an air of expectation. Former fishermen are jockeying to be employed in port and road construction. The government is looking forward to the "transformative impact" it hopes the port will have on Pakistan, and Gwadar is bracing to eventually to house half a million people. As the projects begin, Chinese overseers will rush in to oversee an army of Pakistani manual laborers, who will dig, flatten, and pave their way from the Arabian Sea, over the Himalayas, to the Chinese border.

Pakistan is the spectacular recent example of Chinese economic diplomacy. But it is only one of many. China is lavishing concessionary loans and infrastructure projects on the entire world—lending more to developing countries than the World Bank in recent years.

When I met with Chilean foreign minister Heraldo Muñoz in July

---

* The Chinese Railways Ministry is paying a small amount to do a feasibility study to build the rail line in Pakistan. After that, the free money mostly ends. The China Development Bank is loaning some money to Chinese enterprises. The "Silk Road Fund" made its first signature investment in Pakistan. It is loaning almost $2 billion to finance a hydropower plant, at close to market-rate returns. In one controversial project, the Chinese have agreed to fund a natural gas pipeline from Iran to energy-starved Pakistan, in anticipation that sanctions on Iran will soon be lifted. Chinese state-owned enterprises have been encouraged to invest in Pakistan, so the Chinese government can announce this investment as part of an overall "aid" package. Shanghai Electric, for example, will develop several coal mines.

2014, he only wanted to talk about China: the generous grants and loans from China to Latin America, the booming trade between the two, and the unbelievable infrastructure projects the Chinese planned to build, starting with a 3,300-mile railway across the Andes. "China is courting us," he said. He was too diplomatic to add the point that hung in the room: many Latin American countries feel that, by contrast, the United States either lectures or ignores them.

Tiny Kyrgyzstan also illustrates China's immense sway. Every road appears to be built by Chinese contractors and many signs are in Chinese. When an American in our group asked a Kyrgyz prodemocracy advocate whether Russia or the United States would win the "great game" for influence in Central Asia, he laughingly responded: "China has already won."

The *New York Times* published a telling analysis of how China wields its new financial clout. It argues that often "China is going where the West is reluctant to tread." It is the largest investor in many countries that others ostracize—because they are run by dictators, don't respect human rights, are corrupt, or otherwise make it unpalatable for American companies or the World Bank to go in. The countries that rely most on Chinese investment read like a list of the world's outcasts: Zimbabwe, North Korea, Niger, Angola, Myanmar, and other unsavories. Of course China doesn't just invest in pariah states. More than a third of China's investments actually go to developed countries. But Zimbabwe and other outcasts get so little foreign investment, even smallish Chinese loans make it the dominant economic partner there.

When James Kynge from the *Financial Times* recently interviewed Ugandan President Yoweri Museveni, the latter explained unabashedly why Chinese investment is so attractive to questionable regimes. The Chinese don't ask too many questions, Museveni said, and they "come with a sense of solidarity and . . . big money, not small money." In addition, with Chinese money for infrastructure, the Ugandans don't have to listen to endless pedantic lectures from the World Bank or western donors about structural economic reform or Uganda's domestic politics, such as its laws that discriminate against gays. "They are jokers," Museveni says of western critics. "You can't impose middle-class values [like gay rights] on a pre-industrial society." "The Chinese," he adds by way of contrast, "are more practical."

As Museveni implied, as part of its march onto the world economic stage, China is rewriting the rules of doing business. China's white papers on aid emphasize over and over again that it will not "impose any political conditions" and won't "interfere in the internal affairs of the recipient countries." Chinese money comes with its own conditions, however, and this worries the United States and European nations.

First, China usually requires donee countries to use Chinese firms for infrastructure projects, as we saw in Pakistan. A research firm recently found that 70 percent of China's loans were linked to involvement of a Chinese company. Over the past two years, China has provided its companies with $670 billion in export financing, while America's Export-Import Bank has given American exporters only about $590 billion in financing—over its entire eighty-one-year history. China is flooding the world with cheap money that mostly helps its own enterprises. These companies hire many more Chinese than local workers, so these loans are less effective than traditional aid at promoting economic growth for the recipient country.

Second, while these loans used to have low interest rates, around 2.5 percent, more recently they are creeping up to near 5 percent as China gets more savvy about assessing the political risk. This will make them harder to repay. China is taking on real financial risks by exposing its government and companies to authoritarian and shaky political regimes. A large scale default by these countries on Chinese loans, or a third-world dictator nationalizing the assets the Chinese built, would be bad for China's economy and ultimately for the world. Scholar Parag Khanna believes that Ecuador, Zambia, and some other countries already owe more to China than they can afford.

Finally, reports keep surfacing about China's troublesome records regarding worker safety, corruption, and environmental standards. Especially a decade ago, when China first ventured abroad, these standards were often abysmal, and in some areas Chinese firms still leave behind a mess of underpaid miners, devastated forests, and ruined rivers. China is slowly improving on all these measures. The Chinese government has developed new guidelines for outbound investors, the new AIIB also wants to use world-class standards, and many Chinese companies are improving as they become more international, and as nonprofits and local governments push them to do so.

Many of the large, more professionally run state-owned enterprises are aware of all these risks. A decade ago they rushed into resource-rich, difficult countries. Now they also worry about bad governance and low standards there and are increasingly trying to invest in countries with good rules. One businessman explained to me that his Chinese colleagues in the mining business even see Russia, China's supposed friend and ally, as "riskier than Congo," because the government is "too strong." They are trying to limit his exposure to Russian President Vladimir Putin's "unpredictable" regime. In spite of China's largess toward others and its constant declarations of friendship with Moscow, it has invested relatively little in Russia. In another example, China's state-owned oil company, CNOOC, has its largest investment in the world in Canada's tar sands. Direct investment from China into the West was tiny before 2008 but has been increasing exponentially since then.

Chinese businessmen also recently started talking about "high standards." Li Fanrong, CEO of CNOOC, proudly wrote his shareholders in 2014 that "health, safety and environmental protection work" are a "top priority," and noted that his company's investment in Canada's tar sands achieved "record high" safety ratings.

Ideally, China's rush into infrastructure investments in difficult places will create a net positive effect even though it will make many small countries beholden to China. If the One Belt, One Road initiative is a success, asphalt will be smoother, logistics will run faster, and countries that were cut off from world markets will be able to trade more. Chinese companies are likely to face some setbacks such as nationalizations and unpaid loans along the way. As long as these are manageable, they may have a salutary effect: both the government and state-owned enterprises could be more inclined to follow western standards, and Chinese foreign investment could be a real positive for the world.

★   ★   ★

So how does India feel about its assertive neighbor? Chinese investments in every corner of the world worry the United States because this activity means we will no longer be able to dictate the rules of the road for economic reform, transparency, and environmental issues. Delhi is alarmed for a different reason: it sees China's sudden wooing of India's neighbors as evidence that it wants to replace India as the region's hegemon.

South Asia is one of the least economically integrated regions in the world. Many South Asian countries, following India's model, still have protectionist trade policies. Desperately poor, South Asian governments could not afford to build the road, rail, and sea links that would make trade easy. The many wars between India and Pakistan mean the flow of goods from India to Pakistan (and potentially beyond to Afghanistan) is a mere trickle.

Although there was not much trade, due to its size and location, India was for decades a natural top trading partner for South Asian countries. It also gives almost all of its aid to its neighbors.

China recently entered this sleepy scene in spectacular fashion. Formerly, China traded only with Pakistan. Now it has begun to build an economic ring around India by stepping up its relations with each of India's neighbors. China replaced India as Bangladesh's top trading partner and has increased its economic ties to Nepal, Sri Lanka, Bhutan, and others as well. Inexpensive Chinese goods are replacing Indian-made ones at every turn. Add to this that China has invested $1.4 billion in a gigantic port in Sri Lanka, which is much bigger than Gwadar in Pakistan. It is giving $128 million in aid to Nepal and considering building a new railway across the Himalayas, not to mention the whopping $46 billion in infrastructure promised to Pakistan. One can see why Delhi worries about this. If the China-Pakistan Economic Corridor is actually built, India could find itself excluded from the biggest new supply chain in the region.

India feels surrounded. Recently, its aid programs have become more ambitious and sometimes directly aimed at countering China's influence in its neighborhood. To compete, India is building some infrastructure, training government officials, and funding education and health initiatives. India is investing in a port in Iran that will allow it to access Afghanistan without going through Pakistan, and is prioritizing Bhutan—which does not have diplomatic relations with China—in its foreign aid budget.

Chinese and Indian efforts in South Asia should be complementary since the region's infrastructure needs are so great and will require trillions of dollars in capital. A more connected region will benefit both India and China as all countries trade and invest more in each other. Unfortunately, India worries—probably correctly—that China will provide most of the cheap products these markets need and that it has a hidden agenda to use its influence over some of India's neighbors to gain a military foothold in the Indian Ocean.

★   ★   ★

Afghanistan's copper mines, Gwadar's futuristic port, and the rapidly growing web of rails and roads across Asia, Africa, and Latin America demonstrate that globalization has firmly taken root in today's world. China's immense infrastructure investments abroad are turning our traditional notions of what is aid and what is foreign investment on their head. Very rapidly, China has become the world's dominant player in outside investment. This is not likely to change, even if the Chinese economy slows down somewhat over the next few years. In 2014, mainland China and Hong Kong together invested $249 billion abroad. This does not yet match the United States' $337 billion but it is much more than India's $10 billion. It is a reminder how far India still lags behind China in global economic clout.

Try as we might, the United States and India will never have an industrial policy as coordinated as that of China. Indian and American companies will continue to invest to benefit their bottom line, not the government's political objectives. Foreign aid will continue to be mostly humanitarian and altruistic, and the budgets for such aid will always be smaller than some of us would like. It is certainly a drop in the bucket compared to China's game-changing spending. To counterbalance our worries about China's new economic clout, and create real domestic constituencies for good relations, China, the United States, and India should do their best to increase each country's investments in, and trade with, the others. In the conclusion, I make some suggestions for how we might collectively achieve this.

While China has been largely mercantilist to date, two important trends are beginning to develop that are worth watching, and we will see them in more detail in the next chapter. First, instead of investing only on a bilateral basis, as China could easily do, it is beginning to create and voluntarily tie itself into some institutions, such as the Asian Infrastructure Investment Bank, the AIIB. By investing abroad together with other countries, who all have a say in the governance of the AIIB, China ties itself more closely to high international labor, environmental, and lending standards.

Second, China may feel a bit stung by the mercantilist label, and so it is becoming slightly more altruistic about its giving. At United Nations meetings in September 2015, President Xi announced substantial aid to support the UN's sustainable development goals. Both of these initiatives are important positive developments. For years the United States has pushed China to become a "responsible stakeholder" in the international system. By this we meant that as it becomes more powerful on the international stage, it should begin to uphold international norms. The initial Chinese rush into Africa a decade ago, with payoffs to corrupt ministers and gifts of grandiose football stadiums while local laborers suffered terrible conditions, was not a promising start. There is reason to hope that as the Chinese government and its companies have some setbacks (such as dictators refusing to pay back loans), they will be inclined to follow and promote higher standards. If that is the case, Chinese investment will make rails faster, roads smoother, and trade more efficient—a real positive for the world.

11 | THE WORLD THEY
WILL MAKE

T
RAFFIC ON Park Avenue in New York was at a complete standstill. Sirens whined in the distance as motorcade after motorcade screeched around the city for the seventieth anniversary of the United Nations in the fall of 2015. More than 150 heads of state attended the summit. Xi Jinping and his delegation commandeered much of the Waldorf-Astoria, the grande dame of New York hotels, which is now owned by a Chinese insurance company. Prime Minister Modi and his team had a decampment nearly as large on a different floor.

★ ★ ★

Governments and scholars like to complain about international institutions such as the United Nations: they are bureaucratic, ponderous, ineffective, and reflect the power of their member states rather than altering these states' behavior. For decades, international relations scholars have argued about whether such institutions forge close enough bonds to make war less likely. Without engaging in this debate, let me make some observations.

Most governments believe that institutions from the United Nations to the World Bank and smaller regional clubs have some utility, or else they would withdraw from membership. If they were useless, 150 heads of state would not travel around the world to meet at the UN General Assembly meetings in New York, or at similar gatherings.

It is impossible to generalize about how effective "all" international institutions are. At a basic level, they are the grease that keeps many aspects of global interactions running: a UN agency determines what standards we use to make phone calls seamlessly between countries, another recommends aviation regulations to keep a hundred thousand global daily flights safely in the air, yet another coordinates the world's response to health crises such Ebola. The World Trade Organization has gradually lowered trade barriers and its existence allows countries to adjudicate trade disputes without gunboat diplomacy. Even the much-maligned UN Security Council does good work by consensus on global development or by establishing peacekeeping missions in African conflicts, the Balkans, and Afghanistan. It can't magically resolve difficult issues over which big powers disagree, such as what to do about Syria, but this is not a surprise.

Partly thanks to this good work in opening trade, setting standards, and in some cases resolving conflicts, globalization has firmly taken root. This is demonstrated by the rapidly growing web of rails and roads across Asia, Africa, and Latin America, and by the container ships laden with goods from all over the world. Unfortunately, our economic, political, and security institutions are stuck in the past. We haven't yet found a way to modernize global governance or to integrate China, India, and other rising powers effectively into the system.

Most of the world's large institutions were set up in the decade after World War II, including the United Nations, the World Bank, the International Monetary Fund, and the General Agreement on Tariffs and Trade, which would ultimately become the World Trade Organization. In the late 1940s, when these institutions were formed, America produced a whopping 25 percent of world GDP. Despite their large populations, China and India each had only around 4 percent. Both were desperately poor countries with no real clout in world politics. Now China and India are the second- and eighth-largest economies on earth.

For the past decade, American policy makers have encouraged India and China to be "responsible stakeholders" in the international system and "come onto the governing board of the world." The unstated hope was that in return for this generous gesture, both giants would accept and help enforce the international norms the United States and Europe have established. We also wanted China and India to accept, without real change, the international institutions the West created after World War II. This is exceedingly unlikely. China, and to a lesser extent India, understandably have worldviews that differ from ours. India is still less influential than it should be in many world institutions, partly because it is at a different stage of economic development, but it is making a real push to get a better seat at the table. China emphasizes that it does not intend to undermine the existing institutional order, but wants to amend it. President Xi argued in Seattle in 2015 that developing countries want "to see a more just and equitable international system, but it doesn't mean they want to unravel the entire system and start over."

There is no one prescription for integrating China, India, and other growing nations more effectively into the world's key institutions. Below I outline some of the thorniest of these problems.

* ⋆ ⋆ ⋆

As both India and China gain confidence, they are upending the rules of the game for international trade talks.

For several decades, the West dominated trade negotiations. It created the General Agreement on Tariffs and Trade in 1948 to have consistent rules for trade negotiations and gradually open the world's markets. Through seven negotiating rounds, tariffs were lowered. In 1995, the eighth round (the Uruguay Round) formally created the WTO and expanded trade rules to cover services, intellectual property, environmental, food safety, and other standards. India joined the WTO in 1995. After long and difficult negotiations, China joined in 2001. Both China and India felt that they had made many difficult concessions to open their markets, even though as developing countries they had to meet lower standards than the industrialized nations.

This global, WTO-centric approach to trade broke down somewhat about a decade ago. Just as the United States protected its nascent industries when it was industrializing in the nineteenth century, India and China try to shelter key domestic industries and politically sensitive sectors.

As a result, China is flagrantly violating many of its WTO obligations. At a recent dinner I attended in Beijing with fifteen China CEOs of western corporations, executive after executive shared stories of how he was being gradually pushed out of the Chinese market. Long-promised licenses were held up for years, antitrust actions appeared out of nowhere just as the foreign company was gaining traction, and stringent new security criteria will make it difficult for western banks and technology firms to do business in China.

India isn't violating its existing trade commitments, but it has refused to open its markets further. More problematic is that it plays a spoiler role in multilateral trade talks. By refusing to take on its key domestic agricultural constituency, it helped kill the latest Doha round of trade negotiations for the entire world. America's former chief trade negotiator Susan Schwab described some of the stonewalling to me. For months, she said, Indian trade minister Kamal Nath refused to set a date for a difficult conversation about India's agricultural and other protections. Frustrated, the United States, European Union, and Brazilian trade ministers, who were jointly working on a compromise, finally flew around the world to Delhi. When they walked into the conference room, however, they were in for a surprise. Without telling anyone else, Nath had invited the Japanese to join the talks, because he could rely on them to be just as obstinate as India on these issues. Schwab put it bluntly: "It was one more round of negotiations down the drain."

"Negotiating with the Chinese can be just as frustrating," she adds, "but in a different way." Where every trade minister in the world has some flexibility to close a deal, the Chinese often show up to talks with only "red lines." To make any compromise at all, they have to phone home to Beijing for instructions. Getting an answer from authoritarian Beijing can take weeks, so the whole negotiation with dozens of countries stalls out.

Due to this obstruction by India, China, and other countries with growing industries they want to shelter, trade talks have splintered. Instead of getting nowhere at the WTO, the United States is pushing for bilateral or regional trade agreements in part to counter the more mercantilist Chinese approach. India so far has sided with the lower-standard, Chinese goals. This risks creating two parallel trade regimes—one led by the United States and Europe and tied to strong labor and environmental standards, and intellectual property protection. (Of course some of these "high standards" hide our own protectionism. Americans have legitimate worries about their jobs, and our corporations want to save their patents more than they care about sea turtles.) The other is led by China and is more focused on market access and economic growth, and some continued protection for domestic companies.

America and China are pursuing three separate trade pacts that "could define the future of trans-Pacific commerce," as the *Economist* described it in a thoughtful article. One of the three does not include China or India, another includes the two rising giants but excludes the United States. The third is still a distant dream. All three involve an alphabet soup of acronyms, so bear with me.

The furthest along is the American-led Trans-Pacific Partnership (TPP), which was concluded in October 2015. It is dominated by America and Japan and includes most other smaller Asian powers,* although *not* India or China. Together these countries account for about 40 percent of the global economy, making it America's biggest regional free-trade agreement, even compared to NAFTA. The agreement manages its members' trade and investment relations and contains many giveaways to powerful business lobbies, so we shouldn't be overly critical when China and India do the same.

Washington says the TPP is open to China, India, and anyone else who wants to join after it is concluded and approved by Congress. The Obama administration hopes the U.S. Congress will have agreed to TPP by the time you read this book, but this is unlikely since some U.S. industries and presidential candidates on the left and right have disavowed the deal. Strategically, TPP is the economic linchpin of the Obama administration's pivot to Asia. Unfortunately, it has unintentionally taken on an air of excluding China (and India), when we should be doing the opposite.

TPP's emphasis on high standards, and on reducing nontariff barriers

---

*The other members are Australia, Brunei, Canada, Chile, Malaysia, Mexico, New Zealand, Peru, Singapore, and Vietnam. South Korea is supposedly thinking of joining.

such as complex regulations and lengthy custom procedures, has so far made it unattractive to India and China. To join the WTO, China had to meet many new, difficult standards and change its domestic regulations. Joining the TPP would require more such changes. The Chinese and Indian governments aren't ready to push their countries this far, and some U.S. officials were worried that including them early would delay the negotiations. Yet their failure to join could negatively impact both: If TPP is implemented, and India does not join, the Peterson Institute estimates it will divert $5 billion worth of trade away from India each year by 2030, and China could lose $18 billion a year. These costs will go up as more of India's and China's trading partners, like Korea, join the agreement, and will be terrible for India in particular if China eventually joins but India stays out. In addition, the TPP and other agreements will incentivize Chinese, Indian, and other companies to invest in TPP countries, to get the benefits of exporting to any country within the free trade zone without tariffs. For example, the *New York Times* reported that a Chinese bra manufacturer said he would start scouting for factory locations in Vietnam if TPP is concluded. Ultimately, we will have to find a way to integrate Asia's two giants into a freer trade regime that benefits all.

On a parallel track, though further behind, is the Regional Comprehensive Economic Partnership (RCEP), which includes China and India, plus several countries that are also negotiating the TPP.* Some read this deal as an effort to oppose and create an alternative to the TPP. Together the RCEP countries represent 30 percent of global GDP. The RCEP has lower labor and environmental standards, allows countries to protect sensitive industries, and is more focused on market access. This makes it more attractive than TPP to some developing countries. RCEP would help China export even more goods at lower tariffs to its region. RCEP helps India because it already trades a lot with the countries in this group, and it does not want to be left out of a vast regional market stretching from Japan to Australia. It could also help India become

---

* The following countries are part of the RCEP negotiations: China, India, Japan, South Korea, Australia, and New Zealand, as well as all the ASEAN members—Brunei, Cambodia, Indonesia, Laos, Malaysia, Myanmar, the Philippines, Singapore, Thailand, and Vietnam.

Asia's hub for services, and is an important piece of Modi's "Act East Policy." Despite these potential benefits, senior U.S. trade negotiators think RCEP may never actually happen. To get a comprehensive agreement some of Asia's archrivals—China and Japan, Japan and Korea, as well as China and India—will all have to agree. This is not likely to happen very quickly.

The distant dream is the Free-Trade Area of the Asia-Pacific (FTAAP), which would include America, China, and India, and possibly cobble together elements of both TPP and RCEP. China has been careful to say FTAAP is not a China-led initiative, even though it pushed hard for it before an economic summit in Beijing in November 2014. China insists it could be a complement to the TPP. To date there is not much hope that FTAAP will swallow the other two trade initiatives. But this does not mean that two competing trade blocks, one led by China and one by the United States, will emerge.

Trade is a tricky institutional issue, but also the one that could yield the most long-term benefits for the people of India, China, and the United States. Research has shown that freer trade increases overall GDP, and ultimately helps even a country's poorest citizens, although the gains can be distributed unevenly. Other economic surveys conclude that protectionism, while intended to shield local businesses and jobs from foreign competition, hurts job growth in developing economies in the long run.

Ideally China, India, and the United States would work together to fix the WTO process and go back to negotiating freer trade for the whole world. So far, neither China nor India seems willing to do this. To achieve the positive vision of 2030 despite these constraints, the United States should work hard to bring others, especially reluctant China and India, on board with future high-standards regional trade deals. Even small steps in this direction can create big gains, because, as Susan Schwab explains, trade deals don't really stop at the border anymore. Often they involve changing a country's internal laws, from how much a country can subsidize domestic industries, to overhauling intellectual property laws. So if any country joins a high-standards regime it benefits the entire world, not just the other countries in the trade pact. If FTAAP can eventually be a "hinge" that creates a free trade area stretching from New York through

Shanghai and Xinjiang to Mumbai, or if the United States can persuade more of Asia to join TPP, it will be a great gain for the world.

★   ★   ★

China's and India's refusal to agree to western-led trade initiatives gives our trade ministers headaches. The recent penchant China has shown for creating its own economic institutions when it doesn't like the existing ones creates migraines.

In 1944, the United States and United Kingdom created the World Bank and International Monetary Fund to drive postwar recovery in Europe and prevent future economic crises such as the Great Depression, which had fueled the rise of Nazi Germany. The Allies believed economic cooperation would drive global stability. Over time, the World Bank focused more on poverty alleviation in the developing world. The IMF promotes global cooperation on monetary policy and financial stability. Both were created at a time when the United States and Europe together dominated the international economic scene. In many ways, they are not well suited to today's environment.

In recent years, China, India, and other large developing countries have wanted more say in the running of the World Bank and IMF to reflect their growing importance in the world economy. In 2010, the World Bank increased the voting power of developing countries to over 47 percent to help fix this imbalance.

IMF reform has been harder. The so-called BRICS—Brazil, Russia, India, China, and South Africa—represent more than 20 percent of global output but have only 11 percent of IMF votes. The International Monetary Fund proposed reforms in 2010 to increase the voting power of developing countries including India and China, and decrease the power of the European countries. IMF officials were frustrated that the White House waited more than a year to send these reforms to Congress and Christine Lagarde, the IMF's chief, says that if the U.S. Congress refused to make this more equitable, it risked losing its influence in world economic institutions. In late 2015, Congress finally approved the reforms. China will now become the fund's third largest shareholder, and Brazil and India will join the top ten, and thus all will have more voting rights.

Additionally, many developing countries feel that IMF and World Bank conditions for loans are unnecessarily harsh. The organizations often impose painful austerity measures on countries that are already suffering. Rebecca Liao and other scholars agree that these conditions often lowered long-term economic growth for loan recipients, and that countries allied with the United States often received more lenient conditions. Both the World Bank and IMF are changing the way they do business, but very slowly.

Not surprisingly, the slow pace of voting annoyed key emerging economies. Both China and India have complained vociferously. Influential Chinese bloggers have called the IMF a "puppet" of the United States and say resistance to reform "illustrates the parochialism and rascality of the U.S."

Acting on their frustration, in July 2015, China, India, Brazil, Russia, and South Africa launched the "New Development Bank" with initial capital of $50 billion to finance infrastructure projects in developing countries. This bank strengthens already important South–South economic ties. As a finger in the eye to the stubborn U.S. Congress, it will have an equal-share voting system.

Even bolder was China's launch of the Asian Infrastructure Investment Bank (AIIB), which opened its doors in January 2016. So far fifty-eight countries, including the United Kingdom, Germany, and India, as well as most of the developing economies along the "One Belt," have joined. China invested almost a third of the bank's initial capital of $100 billion. It will thus have veto power over some decisions, but all founding members have substantial votes and will be able to check China's influence. India's government has largely supported the creation of the AIIB. It hopes the AIIB can help with India's infrastructure needs, for example, by financing the building of new coal power plants. The World Bank's environmental standards limit World Bank lending for such projects.

Washington looks like the odd man out here: it has so far refused to join, worried that the AIIB will undermine the World Bank and Asian Development Bank (which is dominated by Japan), and that China will use the AIIB to create its own rules, with lower expectations for transparency, governance, and the environment. Skeptics also argue that, instead of spreading liberal democracy, as the institutions the West set up after World War II hoped to do, the AIIB will give China and its values undue influence in the countries benefiting from the AIIB's generosity. Beijing will be able to direct money toward investments (such as the Pakistan corridor) that benefit China directly, both economically and politically, all under the guise of "development." Some Indians share this concern. They question whether the AIIB is in India's long-term interest, since it is seen as China's initiative and will finance projects in India's neighborhood that may move these countries into China's orbit.

In January 2015, the AIIB announced it would denominate loans in U.S. dollars rather than renminbi, reassuring some observers who feared China would use the bank to help its currency become more frequently used internationally as a reserve currency. The United States worries that if the renminbi ultimately replaces the dollar as the world's reserve currency, our borrowing costs would increase and it would become harder to sanction difficult regimes like Iran.* This is a legitimate concern, but not something we likely need to worry about for several decades. China pushed hard to get the renminbi included in the IMF's basket of several reserve currencies (which also include the euro and yen), as a symbol of the country's growing power. The IMF decided to add the yuan to its basket, effective 2016, representing the strides China has made integrating into the global economic system, increasingly moving toward market valuation of its currency, reduction of capital controls, and other financial reforms that the United States would welcome.

American worries about the AIIB are likely too pessimistic. The positive way to read the AIIB is that, first, it is fixing a big western market failure, and second, it is the first example of China willingly tying itself into a multilateral institution when it could just "go it alone." After more than six decades, the World Bank and others have not been able to provide the infrastructure that a modern, connected world needs. China's flood

---

*Western financial sanctions are currently so powerful partly because if a country like Iran can't settle its accounts in dollars, it does not have many other options to finance its trade. If the renminbi becomes more widely accepted, the United States would lose this leverage.

of cash is helping to fix this. It will help all the economies in the region, and yes, also make them somewhat beholden to China. But just as beneficiaries of western aid and loans don't always do our bidding, this won't automatically make them client states of China, or export China's political system around the region.

China realizes that its unilateral approach to aid and investment worries many around the world, and it wants to work more closely with others. That is a good thing: even if the AIIB had never been founded, Chinese infrastructure investment would continue, without any international input. Jin Liqun, the AIIB's new chief, is working hard to implement good standards, saying in a speech I attended in December 2015 that the AIIB's goals are to be "clean, lean, and green." The AIIB has announced that it will conduct environmental impact assessments and promote clean technology, for example. Jin has traveled the world to learn best practices (and avoid the worst) of other development banks. The AIIB is cooperating with the Asian Development Bank, its closest "rival," and has signed agreements with the World Bank to finance some projects together. Jin says the AIIB will help the "shared aspirations of all Asian countries, not just China." With eyes open to the potential problems, the United States should view this as an opportunity to engage constructively with China, India, and other Asian powers. We can't influence their actions if we petulantly refuse to sit at the table. The new AIIB and BRICS development banks are warning shots: unless we reshape outdated postwar institutions, India and China will ignore or leave them.

★ ★ ★

The United Nations is the biggest and most complex organization to restructure. When it was founded in October 1945, China obtained one of the coveted five spots on the UN Security Council because it had been a crucial Allied power in World War II. The United States has openly supported only two additional countries of Security Council membership: Japan and, since 2010, India. Surprisingly, after years of taking a backseat at the UN, China recently stepped up its involvement dramatically and can now be described as a "responsible stakeholder." India is pushing hard

for a permanent seat on the Security Council, but most American diplomats find India one of the most frustrating nations to deal with at the
United Nations.

For years China has been very quiet on the Security Council. Its diplomats abstain on many key votes and defer to the Russians on others. The
Chinese permanent representative to the UN is not a senior advisor to
the president, as in the United States. He is also not a senior player in the
Chinese Communist Party, so he often doesn't have the authority to bind
his government. China voted with the United States in the General Assembly only a bit more than one-third of the time in 2014 (compared to
93 percent agreement between the United States and Israel, for example).

In the past few years, however, China has made a stunning reversal
and dramatically stepped up its engagement. The *Economist* reports that
in 2015 China paid 5 percent of the total UN budget, almost tripling the
contribution it made in 2010. It dispatched its first combat troops to a
UN mission, in South Sudan. President Xi committed to increase Chinese
peacekeepers to eight thousand and agreed to give the African Union
$100 million for its own standing force. For more than a decade, China
ignored the UN's sustainable development goals. In 2015 it reversed
course, signed up to the new goals, and committed serious resources to
meet them: $2 billion for the poorest countries to spend on health and
education, $1 billion for a China-UN "peace and development fund," sev-
eral billion (not through the UN) to ameliorate climate change, and so
on. China could do this all alone or bilaterally, so it is significant that it is
funneling much of this largesse through the United Nations. The trend is
very much in the right direction even as China continues to act militarily
in some ways we don't like, as the next chapter will explore.

India is a different story. While our diplomats in Washington and
Delhi agree on many issues, at the United Nations, India continues to act
as the lead in the "nonaligned movement" of developing states. In 2014,
India voted with the United States in the UN General Assembly only 27
percent of the time. It contributes a paltry 0.6 percent annually to the UN
budget.

When India served as a nonpermanent member of the UN Security
Council from 2011 to 2012, American officials tell me, they nearly tore

their hair in frustration. For example, India's representative tried to obstruct the vote to establish a no-fly zone that allowed for military intervention in Libya's civil war in 2011, even after the permanent five council members supported it. India is one of the top three countries contributing soldiers to UN peacekeeping missions. Cynics say, however, that this actually helps India: the UN pays India's military more for peacekeeping than the Indian army pays in salaries, so it is making money while gaining valuable training. UN diplomats say with irritation that Indian peacekeepers (as well as those from other countries) have been known to stay idle in their camps while the civilians they are sworn to protect are killed.

As a reflection of India's growing partnership with the United States in other areas, President Obama said in 2010 that he "look[s] forward to a reformed United Nations Security Council that includes India as a permanent member." This is the right approach, and a shrewd diplomatic move. In the short run, it is also an empty gesture. A bewildering number of proposals have been put forward to reform the Security Council. All inevitably require the United States, France, and the United Kingdom (who currently have three of five vetoes, and often agree with each other) to relinquish some power to allow India and other developing countries a larger role. So far, no one can agree on one reform plan. China opposes a permanent seat for India. The United States and Russia, who both support India for a seat, clarified in 2015 that they oppose any reform right now that would give any additional countries a veto. The UN has created an "Open Ended Working Group" on reform. Its title itself implies a lack of urgency. As long as we keep involving key countries on issues that matter to them (such as Japan and South Korea in six-party talks over North Korea, or Germany in P5+1 [permanent five members plus one] talks on Iran sanctions), the status quo on the UN Security Council may hold for another decade.

In addition to the UN, World Bank, and other global institutions, numerous regional organizations are active in Asia. Unlike the European Union and the North Atlantic Treaty Organization (NATO), which despite their flaws are strong enough to have helped keep the peace in Europe for seventy years, Asian institutions are still nascent. Asia is becoming the fulcrum of the global economy, with China at its core. There is real economic integration, as we saw from the various regional and bilateral trade agreements above. But the Association of South East Asian Nations (ASEAN), the Shanghai Cooperation Organisation, Asia-Pacific Economic Cooperation (APEC), and others remain mostly talk shops. China, India and the United States have all recently stepped up their engagements with some or all of these institutions, which should help diffuse disagreements and misunderstandings. Yet, no strong security organizations exist to temper the military rise of China, as NATO did for postwar Germany. As we explore in the next chapter, while many Asian countries are integrating economically with China, they are increasingly wary of its military power and intentions. They are seeking closer security relations with the United States and each other as a hedge against their giant neighbor.

★   ★   ★

The world's institutions are outdated. They have been terrible at accommodating ascending powers, especially the largest ones: China and India. There is no easy, one-size-fits-all solution.

Some argue that the United States and other western countries should change the UN, World Bank, IMF, and other organizations to make real room for new players like China and India. If it is a simple matter of changing voting powers at the World Bank and IMF, we should certainly do so. We should also encourage the giants to join regional trade agreements that will benefit all. But we should not lower the environmental, labor, lending, and other standards of these organizations. Nor should we feel threatened by China's interest in building its own group, like the AIIB. So far, the AIIB seeks to cooperate with others and build on their best practices. This is the best example yet of China becoming a "responsible stakeholder." India has already joined the AIIB and is said to be playing a constructive role. We should join as well, to be both an advocate for high standards and an internal critic if things go awry. Since the World Bank, IMF, and others are far from perfect, and have been slow to change, a little friendly "institutional coopetition" might improve the way we all invest in, and give aid to, developing economies.

The UN Security Council will take longer to reform. India has been strangely obstinate at the UN, and this makes some wary of supporting it for a larger role. Outside the UN, India and the United States cooperate frequently and well. For example, India (eventually) supported sanctions on Iran to curb its nuclear ambitions even though it is highly dependent on Iranian natural gas. Although it means ceding some influence to India and other countries that will not always agree with us, we must ultimately support a more equitable power distribution at the United Nations as well.

While the Chinese don't like to admit it, India occasionally moderates Beijing's behavior on the world stage. During recent BRICS summits, India helped temper proposed Chinese statements on Syria and Iran. According to press reports, while China initially wanted a dominant role in the New Development Bank, Modi successfully pushed President Xi to share the initial capital and influence equally. This moderating influence is one reason we should want India to have more clout on the international scene.

China and India are rightfully pushing us to rethink the outdated, post–World War II global order. They will not agree with the United States on all issues. As both show an increasing willingness to shoulder global burdens, however, we should welcome them as partners rather than obstinately refuse to acknowledge that the world is changing.

12 | THE NEXT MASTER AND COMMANDER

O N A craggy, treeless Himalayan ridge, hundreds of Chinese and Indian soldiers shove each other, shout insults, and throw punches. A video posted on YouTube shows two Chinese soldiers rushing past the Indian guards and breaking into Indian territory. To calm the tension, an Indian commander shouts "Take it easy!" while his Chinese counterpart offers a cigarette to the Indians that no one accepts. Both sides keep their guns tucked safely away, but their video cameras out, to record any infraction by the other.

Thousands of miles to the south, an Indian fisherman in a tiny village near Chennai recently received an electronic tracking device. It will make him part of the eyes and ears of the Indian coast guard and navy. India is worried about terrorism from Pakistan and China's increasing assertiveness in the Indian Ocean, so it is issuing these devices to two hundred thousand fishing boats. From a central command center, the Indian coast guard will use these censors to distinguish Indian vessels from intruders, such as the boats that carried terrorists to Mumbai in 2009. Although they do not acknowledge it publicly, Indian naval officers also hope it will help them find the brand-new Chinese submarines and naval ships that increasingly creep past India's shores on their way to Sri Lanka or Pakistan. Military tensions between India and China are high.

Chinese fishing boats are also getting into the act in a way that worries the United States and others. In March 2009, two Chinese trawlers nearly rammed a U.S. Navy surveillance ship, the *Impeccable,* south of China's Hainan Island. They waved Chinese flags and yelled at the U.S. sailors to leave. When the Americans sprayed water at the ship, the Chinese bizarrely stripped down to their underwear and got even closer. Even as the Americans tried to leave the area, the trawlers dropped pieces of wood in the *Impeccable*'s path to stop it and tried to grab its sonar instruments. These types of incidents are becoming disturbingly common.

★   ★   ★

How will the two giants project military might? In spite of their mostly cooperative economic relations, the United States, India, and China are engaged in a gradual, great power military escalation that no one really wants. India is nervous about China's moves into its traditional spheres of influence. China's new submarines cruise the Indian Ocean, new border fortifications encroach on land India claims as its own in the Himalayas, and a series of new ports in South Asia will allow Chinese ships to rest and to push even closer to India's shores.

In response, India is dramatically increasing its defense budget and stepping up military cooperation with Japan, Australia, the United States, and others. The Chinese interpret this as encirclement. It is a classic security dilemma.

China is legitimately worried about protecting both its sprawling economic interests around the world and the maritime economic supply lines it needs. The United States' military "rebalancing"—shoring up Asian military alliances and adding troops in Australia, Singapore, and the Philippines—makes the Chinese nervous. China sees this as effort to contain and diminish China, in part due to its historical memory as a victim of western imperialism.

In an attempt to avoid military escalation between the powers, the United States has started a few important confidence-building measures. For example, former U.S. Navy Chief of Operations Gary Roughead told me that he recently convinced the Chinese navy for the first time to allow its sailors to make radio contact with the American navy. This is a small but important move to remind everyone there are human beings inside the other side's ships, and to help deescalate the situation if an accident occurs.

While China does not want a direct military conflict with India or the United States, the increased jostling of ships, planes, and submarines for position in the Pacific and Indian Oceans could easily lead to an accident that could in turn spiral into a conflict.

★　★　★

With its emphasis on "soft power," India has not historically stepped on many toes around the world, and has not made many enemies. India's politicians were for decades concerned mostly with a potential threat from Pakistan. Since their painful partition in 1947, the two countries have fought four wars, and smaller incursions are common. For seven decades a border dispute over Kashmir has festered, and the two militaries exchange fire over the disputed border almost weekly. India also accuses Pakistan (accurately) of sending terrorists into India. These terrorists launched dozens of attacks over the years, including on India's Parliament and packed commuter trains, killing thousands of Indians. In late 2008, the world watched as Pakistani-funded terrorists shot their way into Mumbai's elegant Taj Mahal Palace hotel, killed dozens there and around the city, and held hundreds hostage for three days. Not surprisingly, India's politicians are fixated on solving the terrorism problem.

Yet for the past few years, Indian military officers and diplomats, including their chief of naval staff and national security advisor, have implied to me that their major worry is China, which is encroaching into India's region from every direction.

For centuries, the two Asian giants lived mostly in peace along their 2,500-mile Himalayan border. More recently, these high-altitude ridges have become a source of contention, for no real reason other than both countries' pride.

The dispute originated when Britain ruled India, and the British moved bit by bit into the Tibetan high plateau. When India gained its independence in 1947, it inherited all of the British territorial agreements, including the disputed "McMahon Line" as the border between it and China. When the Chinese occupied Tibet in 1950, they began pushing into what India considered its land. To complicate matters, India granted asylum to the Dalai Lama after Tibetans rose up against Chinese rule in 1959. China accused India of undermining its rule in Tibet, and there were a series of violent border incidents. Both began to build some roads and place guards along the deserted mountain peaks at the top of the world. In 1962, the People's Liberation Army launched a surprise attack on India's unprepared and ill-equipped border force. The Chinese killed several thousand Indians and quickly forced the rest into an embarrassing retreat deep into northeastern India, before declaring a unilateral cease-fire. Humiliated, the Indians never really trusted China again. The brief war helped lead to India's decision to start a nuclear weapons program a few years later.

Never completely resolved, in the past five years, this quarrel has heated up again.

During President Xi's first summit with Prime Minister Modi in September 2014, the two stood beaming at the podium, eager to portray a united front. But beneath the handshakes and smiles, relations were tense. During the summit, Chinese troops had forcibly entered the disputed border area between India and China. Modi cautioned the Chinese leader: "Even such small incidents can impact the biggest of relationships, just as a little toothache can paralyze the entire body." India claims the PLA has illegally transgressed beyond the "line of actual control" hundreds of times in the past few years.

China's tidal wave of infrastructure projects has reached into Tibet and close to the border with India, making the border issue more "live" than it has been for decades. High-speed rail now connects Lhasa to China's population centers. In 2014 things got worse. Indian soldiers discovered that China has built airstrips, roads, and observation towers near, and in some cases within, parts of the Ladakh region that India considers its own. To counter China, India now plans to build fifty-four new outposts along the border and invest tens of millions of dollars in roads. Yet it will be nearly impossible for India to catch up to Chinese building. Under Modi, India is taking a much tougher line with China on this issue. When I asked Indian Home Minister Rajnath Singh about these border incursions in early

2015, he responded that India will not permit such invasions in future. So far both sides have strict orders not to shoot first.

The border issue is far from the only thorn in the side of the relationship. India feels encroached on by China at every turn.

The two countries are also feuding over shared water supplies. India has water-sharing treaties with all of its neighbors except China. China controls the upper reaches of several rivers that flow into India, most important the Brahmaputra, which flows into India from Tibet. China says publicly and loudly that it has absolute control over these rivers. It recently finished a major hydropower dam on the Brahmaputra, and will finish five other generating units of the project in 2015. So far these are just "run of the river" power projects that don't affect the water flow, but India worries that China could cut off Indian water supplies if it wanted to. A recent Chinese military paper suggested that it might divert the flow of the entire river north to irrigate China's thirsty central regions, as we saw in chapter 8, but luckily this seems to be an engineering feat too difficult even for the Chinese.

Most dangerous to India is what China, as we saw earlier, serenely calls the "One Belt, One Road" initiative. In China's view this magnanimous aid project will help infrastructure-starved developing nations. India prefers to call it a Chinese "string of pearls," a plot Indian military planners believe is designed in large part to surround and contain India. Under the guise of building ports and roads for commerce, many Indians worry that China may reach secret agreements with India's neighbors to build dual-use facilities that can become Chinese naval bases later. In addition to the huge investment in the Gwadar port and connective roads in Pakistan, China is funding South Asia's largest port in Hambantota, Sri Lanka, and has started negotiations for a port project in Bangladesh. India has recently convinced both Sri Lanka and Bangladesh to walk back some of their cooperation with China. China also wants to build a military base off Djibouti's coast, on the strategically important Horn of Africa. Even without formal bases, these ports would allow Chinese navy ships to rest, get repairs, and take on new supplies, and thus allow China to maneuver easily throughout the Indian Ocean. If it had a naval base at Gwadar (there are *no* current plans for this), China would be in prime position to control the Straits of Hormuz near Iran, through which one-third of the world's oil supply transits.

Chinese naval ships have followed closely behind China's growing infrastructure and economic interests. The Chinese navy had no significant "blue water" capabilities (the ability to sail far beyond its coasts and still support its personnel) before 2000. It was absent from the Indian Ocean region until 2008, when a group of three ships sailed through the Malacca Strait to fight Somali pirates with other navies. Since these first antipiracy patrols, China has kept a near-constant presence in the western Indian Ocean, near Somalia, where twenty-five of its warships protect the Chinese merchant fleet. This doesn't worry India's admirals much.

However, in the past two years Chinese submarines have docked in Pakistan and Sri Lanka and have taken part of some antipiracy patrols. This set alarm bells ringing loudly in the Indian navy. Pirates use swarms of tiny, fast skiffs on the surface—so submarines with their torpedoes and missiles are not the right vessel for dealing with piracy. This makes India wonder what other reason the subs have for being there. In the very saline Indian Ocean, such submarines are also very difficult for Indian sonar to track, hence the reliance in part on India's fishermen to help their navy.

Indian journalist Pramit Pal Chaudhuri told me that when he questioned a Chinese admiral about China's new interest in the Indian Ocean, the admiral barked: "The Indian Ocean is not *India's* ocean." Unperturbed, Pramit shot back, "And the South China Sea is not *China's* sea." Economic relations between the two giants are so important that neither is yet ready to declare a cold war, but India is wary enough that it is arming to the hilt and seeking friends wherever it can.

★   ★   ★

Sitting in London, Washington, or Delhi, it is easy to see China as an unreasonable bully, stomping on the rights of small countries in its orbit. This is not at all how the People's Liberation Army (PLA) sees the world. China actually feels quite insecure. A Chinese diplomat recently showed me a picture that perfectly summed up these insecurities: a map of China's coastline facing east, as the Chinese do when they look out into the Pacific. Seen from this angle, there are hundreds of islands from Japan to Taiwan and the Philippines no more than two hundred nautical miles of China's coast, called the "first island chain." Most of these countries are hostile, or at least cool, toward China.

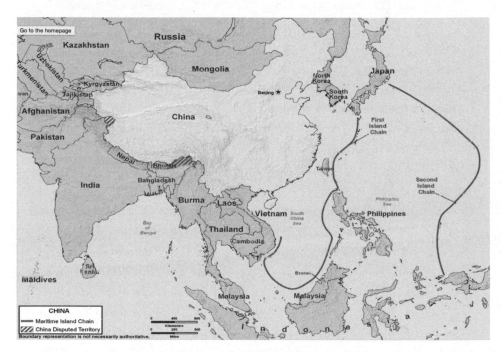

The "first island chain" China sees and feels
encircled by when it looks east at the Pacific.
photo credit: *Courtesy of the United States Department of Defense*

From China's vantage point, the "first island chain" seems menacingly close. In many areas the spaces between the islands where a Chinese ship could sail are quite narrow, so if an enemy controls these areas, it would be hard for Chinese commercial and military ships to pass. Japan and Taiwan are hostile to China. General MacArthur once famously called Taiwan an "unsinkable aircraft carrier." The Philippines is increasingly friendly to the United States, which recently added more troops to its military base there. As commentator Robert Kaplan explained in his thoughtful book

Monsoon, the first island chain allows the United States to radiate power very close to China's coast. It must feel awful for Chinese sailors to see U.S. Navy aircraft carrier groups sailing throughout their backyard.

This worry about the oceans is new. For centuries China was more concerned with land invasions. It built a four-thousand-mile Great Wall to keep out Turkic invaders. More recently, after the Sino-Soviet split in the 1960s, China worried about invasion from the Soviet Union, so Mao Zedong concentrated the country's defense budget on its army while largely neglecting the navy. China shares borders with fourteen countries and has unresolved border disputes with many of them, like India. These inland borders are mostly mountainous and cold, difficult to guard, and populated by ethnic minorities not particularly loyal to Beijing. China also struggles to contain strong separatist movements, especially in Tibet and Xinjiang, where Uighurs have recently resorted to some violence to promote independence.

Amid all these concerns, access to the open sea is the most critical for Beijing. China's massive energy and raw materials imports arrive by sea and its countless manufactured goods leave the same way to be sold around the world. China's navy sees itself as the protector of these ever-expanding economic interests, known in military-speak as "commercial sea-lanes of communication," or SLOC. It also watches over the soaring numbers of Chinese citizens who work abroad, expected to reach 100 million by 2020, who are building the infrastructure of the One Belt, One Road initiative. China's biggest military operation in recent memory was its evacuation of thirty thousand Chinese workers from war-torn Libya in 2011.

At the heart of China's interests at sea is "the Malacca dilemma." The Strait of Malacca, linking the Indian Ocean and the Pacific Ocean, is the shortest sea route between African and Persian Gulf oil suppliers and Asian consumers. Eighty percent of China's energy, including most of its seventy oil supertankers, in addition to much of its trade, moves through here. At its narrowest point, the strait is only 1.7 miles across. It is an increasingly critical chokepoint in Asia, with an estimated 15.2 million barrels per day transported through the strait in 2013, compared to only half that a decade earlier. If the Strait of Malacca were blocked, nearly half of the world's fleet would have to reroute around the Indonesian archipelago, thus raising shipping costs substantially. China's military views its growing energy needs and economic reach as a vulnerability that a future adversary could exploit.

In addition to these strategic needs, China feels insecure in part because—unlike India—it doesn't have any natural allies. Its relations with most of its direct neighbors range from tense (with India, Vietnam, the Philippines, and Korea) to hostile (Japan and Taiwan). A madman rules North Korea. China constantly worries that that country will implode and send millions of refugees across its borders. Pakistan is a friend. China has for several years supported Pakistan's military buildup by supplying submarines and fighter jets and is believed to have helped Pakistan develop its nuclear weapons program. Still, Pakistan has such all-consuming internal problems that it may not be much help in a real fight.

Russia and China talk a lot about their enduring friendship, but there is much distrust between them. After a major border clash on the Amur River border in 1968 and 1969, the Chinese side of the border was so bombed out it looked like a moonscape. Russia apparently asked the United States in secret if we would intervene to help China if Russia used nuclear weapons. (Russia didn't.) Xi and Putin show public unity by attending each other's military parades, including the spectacular one in Beijing in September 2015, while American and other western leaders sit out in protest.

Russia sells China weapons, mostly because it needs the hard currency and the two navies exercise together as they both try to deter U.S. influence in the region. They cooperate often, but not always, in international organizations like the UN. Bilateral trade is substantial, but Russia is too dependent on the European market and China on the American one to create a true trade bloc. Like the West, Russia worries about China's growing influence in Central Asia. Increasingly, a declining Russia is a junior partner to China: for example, it had to offer major concessions to sign a large gas deal with Beijing in 2014. Despite some aligned interests, many

Russians don't like the Chinese much. The distrust is mutual. This is more a partnership of convenience than an enduring alliance.

Finally, there are no security pacts in Asia—like NATO in Europe—that could tie these various dysfunctional relationships into a mutually beneficial whole.

Without close allies, how is China protecting its growing interests? The One Belt, One Road initiative is one way to make itself less vulnerable. When complete, it will diversify China's energy supply and create new land and sea routes for trade and for all those raw materials to reach China.

More worrying, however, is that China has ramped up military spending. It is working hard to modernize its forces and proudly showed its new equipment to the world at a spectacular military parade in September 2015. It is hard to find accurate numbers for China's defense budget. The Chinese government says it spends about $140 billion a year. SIPRI, an independent defense think tank, thinks the actual number was closer to $216 billion in 2014 and that overall spending has quadrupled since about 2005. This is still only about a third of America's defense budget, but much larger than any other country in Asia.

China is building navy ships and attack submarines at warp speed. Its navy has more than three hundred ships today, most of them in Asian waters, compared to 289 the U.S. Navy has scattered around the world. While American scholars point out that many of these new ships are of low quality, and a numbers comparison makes little sense, former U.S. Secretary of Defense Robert Gates quips, "at some point, quantity takes on a quality all if its own." Particularly worrying, in Gates's view, are China's new attack submarines. Their number has doubled since 2005, and the Pentagon estimates that China will have at least ten more submarines than the United States by 2020. They can fire antiship and ballistic missiles and are very hard for other militaries to track.

To support its new ships and submarines, China has developed sophisticated "anti-access/area denial" capabilities. This is military-speak for technology that would prevent foreign navies from getting close to China's coasts and helping Taiwan in a war with China, for example. These weapons could help China disable American satellites (which the

United States uses to guide its ships), or launch cyberattacks. Above all, China's highly accurate antiship missiles may be able to sink a U.S. aircraft carrier, and some of its ballistic missiles could even hit Hawaii or Alaska. A recent video/cartoon that went viral on the Internet and is rumored to have been created by the PLA shows all of these new Chinese toys successfully attacking U.S. ships and a base that looks like the American base in Okinawa, Japan. Even without the bravado, this new equipment is designed to eventually push the United States out far beyond China's first island chain. As the American navy has shrunk since the Cold War, China for the first time presents a challenge to U.S. dominance in the Pacific Ocean.

China's strategic needs are also leading it to bully its neighbors, especially those in the South and East China Sea. China says it wants the islands because they are historically Chinese (a much-disputed claim). Really, they will help China protect its sea-lanes. Some oil and gas reserves and important fishing grounds have also been found near the islands. The most spectacular example of this is in the South China Sea, where China claims a vast tongue-shaped area—the "nine dash line"—that sticks out more than a thousand miles from the Chinese mainland. The Philippines, Malaysia, Vietnam, and Indonesia each claim some of these islands, their fishing rights, and the oil that lies under their seabeds.

China is using a classic "salami-slicing" strategy. It is taking incremental steps, none of which alone would cause the world to punch back militarily, to gradually change the status quo in China's favor. In May 2014, China provocatively placed an oil rig near the Paracel Islands, which Vietnam claims as its own, and in February 2016 it deployed surface to air missiles on another disputed island (in fairness to China, other countries are also doing this). In the spring of 2015, IHS Jane's, a defense intelligence provider, published stunning satellite pictures of China's breakneck building on some of the nearby Spratly Islands. What months before was just a desolate, tiny strip of sand and coral with the fitting name of "Fiery Cross Reef," Chinese dredgers and cement ships had now built into an enormous airstrip and harbor. It is essentially a stationary aircraft carrier. China could deploy radar and missile systems there to force others out, and can land fighter jets or even large transport planes.

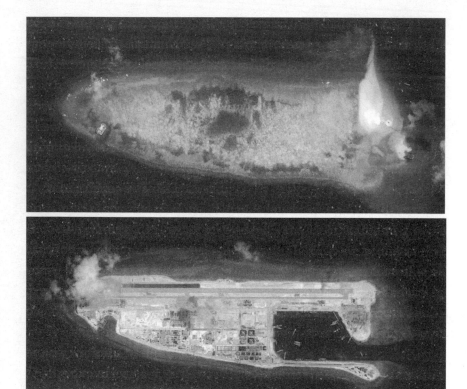

Before (August 2014) and after (September 2015) satellite
images of China's building of a military air strip and port on
the "Fiery Cross Reef," as first appeared in IHS Jane's.

photo credit: *CNES 2014, 2015. Distribution Airbus DS / IHS*

The Chinese are absolutely unabashed about their building spree. A
Chinese diplomat told me, since this is "China's land," building an airstrip
there is "like building a fountain in your own backyard."

China's actions have unleashed a mad scrum of activity. Boats from
many navies jostle for position. Various air forces "monitor" the situation
from the skies. In late 2015 and early 2016, the United States sailed a U.S.
destroyer within twelve miles of China's artificial islands to signal it does
not accept China's territorial claims. The Australian air force and some
private aircraft carrying journalists have also intentionally crossed over

the islands, and been yelled at by belligerent Chinese ground crews. So far no serious accidents have happened with these types of challenges. The incident between the U.S. ship *Impeccable* and Chinese fishing trawlers shows, however, how easy it would be to have an accidental collision. Fishermen would probably not interfere with the U.S. Navy without explicit go-ahead from the PLA. Chinese Coast Guard vessels repeatedly clash with Vietnamese boats and even hit them with water cannons. Robert Gates recalls that during his time in office, a Chinese fighter jet hotdogged within thirty feet of an American reconnaissance plane, nearly causing an accident. While the PLA may not have specifically sanctioned this, the pilot's rules of engagement must have led him to believe this was all right.

In the East China Sea, the long-contested area between China and Japan, the situation is even more explosive. Both China and Japan claim the uninhabited, desolate rocks called the Diaoyu islands by China, and Senkaku by the Japanese. While there is thought to be some oil near the islands, they are craggy rocks not well suited to becoming ports or military bases. The fight over who owns them is deeply emotional on both sides: for the Chinese because the trauma of Japanese atrocities during World War II is not forgotten, and for the Japanese because they fear encroachment by a rising China.

I have been at several conferences where the famously unemotional Chinese and Japanese participants had to be told to calm down and sit down—so heated were their discussions over these rocks. Transfer this emotion and petulance to naval officers and pilots and there is a real chance that an accidental collision could become an international crisis.

In 2012, the Japanese government escalated the standoff by buying some of the islands from their private Japanese owner, triggering Chinese public and diplomatic protests. Since then, Chinese government ships regularly challenge Japan by sending ships and aircraft near the islands. In late 2013, China created an Air Defense Identification Zone, covering a large swath of airspace over the East China Sea, which requires any aircraft in the zone to identify itself to Beijing air controllers and do their bidding. The United States flew two B-52 bombers through the zone without notifying China or responding to Chinese air controllers. Japan's biggest airlines are also defying the ban. China recently threatened to set up a similar zone in the South China Sea.

While no major accident has happened yet, military tensions in the entire region are high. Former U.S. Navy chief Gary Roughead explained to me that the problem is not the jostling of ships and planes, but the fact that China has no agreements in place, especially with other Asian powers, to handle unforeseen clashes. "During the Cold War," he explains, "we had many more dangerous incidents—from ships ramming each other, to near collisions of airplanes. The difference was that, in those days, only the chains of command on both sides knew about these problems. There were also procedures to quickly deescalate a conflict. Now any incident is splashed all over the news, which makes it much harder for political leaders not to react. Nationalism is ratcheted up on all sides, and since no one can control the information, any accident could immediately become a crisis."

Condoleezza Rice recalls that when a Chinese fighter jet collided with a U.S. spy plane in 2001, the crisis nearly spiraled out of control. The PLA fed misinformation to the Chinese leadership, and U.S. and Chinese leaders couldn't talk properly for several days. "We just couldn't get anyone on the phone," she adds, "and finally had to track a senior Chinese official down at a barbecue in Argentina. It created unnecessary danger."*

Even fifteen years later, China's willingness to communicate with other militaries to deescalate a crisis remains primitive. As defense secretary, Robert Gates got the Chinese to agree to a direct phone link with his Chinese counterpart, but no one has ever used it. Beijing and Tokyo also set up an emergency hotline recently to deescalate the situation in case there is an accident near their disputed islands. However, in practice, the Chinese minister of defense does not directly command Chinese military forces, so even with a direct phone link, it may be hard to deescalate quickly.

There are glimmers of hope. Members of the U.S. Pacific Command

---

* Similar communication difficulties occurred when the U.S. accidently bombed the Chinese Embassy in Belgrade, Serbia, capital of the former Yugoslavia, in 1999.

tell me that in the past few years, the interaction between the United States and Chinese fleet has expanded quite a bit. Commanders are starting to speak to each other directly, know each other personally, and be able to pick up the phone when there is a problem. This is quite helpful as the number of potential conflicts rises. More conversation is a real bright spot in an otherwise bleak military picture. While no one in the region wants a military conflict, an inadvertent clash could spiral out of control and have significant political and economic consequences.

Despite the rapid expansion of Chinese military power, the PLA is a very opaque institution. Even after cutting its manpower nearly in half, it is still estimated to be more than 2.2 million soldiers strong. President Xi just announced that he will cut another three hundred thousand soldiers. Ordinary conscripts in the PLA are mostly uneducated and from rural areas. They live simply: a military newspaper reported proudly about a decade ago that most barracks, but not all, now have year-round electricity and indoor plumbing. Some senior generals, by contrast, have built vast fortunes through corruption. One of the most notorious, Gu Junshan, was recently sentenced to life in prison for amassing several billion dollars, mostly by selling military land and taking kickbacks from the developers. At just one of Gu's many houses, police needed four military trucks to confiscate his loot. Among other things, the house was filled with four hundred kilograms of gold bars, expensive liquor, and a large solid gold bust of Mao Zedong.

Unlike U.S. or Indian soldiers, who swear to defend their country's constitution, Chinese conscripts swear allegiance to the Chinese Communist Party. Most PLA officers are Party members, and their training constantly reinforces China's not entirely accurate view of its own history: it was oppressed by the West in the nineteenth century, the courageous Communist Party routed the Japanese in World War II, and China has defeated every enemy handily since 1949 (the United States in the Korean War, India in 1962, and Vietnam in 1979). The writings of Confucius, the great Chinese military scholar Sun Tzu, and Mao Zedong are all part of their training. They teach lessons such as: the highest objective is to defeat the enemy without fighting, especially if your side is weaker, emphasize planning and deception where necessary, and mobilize the entire population for your cause.

Most PLA officers don't mingle much with Chinese civilian officials. They live in separate compounds and keep to themselves. Military officers also don't tend to move in and out of civilian life—to think tanks or other government jobs—in a way that is common in the United States. The officers I have met also don't converse freely with foreigners. Instead, I tend to hear Party-approved speeches that reflect, to an American ear, a deep nationalism and near paranoia about the intentions of the United States, Japan, and others toward China. This leads to many misunderstandings.

Years ago, when Americans visited Chinese bases, they were assigned "handlers" and observed stiff, unnatural show units, rather than actual military exercises. The PLA showed off its fancy equipment, which looked like they were trying to keep it pristine and unused. Many American military officials believe that the Chinese military, which hasn't fought in an actual war since 1979 against Vietnam, where it didn't do well, would not perform well in a real battle today. This is a problem the Chinese are aware of and are now starting to address.

Before Xi took over, the PLA also operated quite independently from its civilian leaders. Gates recalls that the Chinese air force chose a day he was visiting China to roll out its new J-20 stealth fighter jet, almost certainly to insult the U.S. visitor. When Gates jokingly pointed this out to then president Hu Jintao, it was clear that Hu had no idea what his military had done.

President Xi is aware of these problems and recently orchestrated the biggest shakeup of China's military in a generation. Starting in 2014, Xi quickly brought the military leadership under tighter control, both to stem high-level corruption, and force the separate services (army, navy, and air force) to work together more cohesively—a very difficult thing for any military.* In the past eight years or so, the PLA budget has doubled. In the summer of 2015, the PLA for the first time published a doc-

---

* In the United States, the Joint Chiefs of Staff was created right after World War II, but it took until the Goldwater-Nichols legislation in the mid-1980s for the army, navy, air force, and marine corps to abandon some of their turf battles and cooperate more effectively.

ument titled "China's Military Strategy." It strikes a much more confident tone than earlier documents, saying that China's "national strength . . . is increasing, [and it] enjoys growing international . . . influence." It states bluntly that China's biggest military concerns are America's rebalance to Asia, Japan's push to revise its military and security policies, and the "provocative actions [by the Philippines and Vietnam to] reinforce their military presence on China's reefs and islands that they have illegally occupied."

To deal with these perceived threats, the PLA will shift its focus from just defending Chinese territory to also "securing its overseas interests." To do this, it will end its traditional emphasis on land forces and instead continue to build a navy that can do more than guard Chinese shores and in addition be capable of "open ocean protection." The PLA will emphasize four key domains: cyber-warfare, defending China's interests in outer space, creating a reliable second-strike capability for its nuclear forces, and building a first-rate navy. The paper was a sobering read for all those who are already suspicious of China's peaceful intentions.

On December 31, 2015, President Xi announced sweeping changes to the PLA's structure to enable it to secure these overseas interests. The offices responsible for buying weapons systems, recruiting soldiers and others were slimmed down and brought under firm CMC (and thus Communist Party) command. As the strategy paper promised, Xi also changed China's powerful regional commands, upgraded the importance of the navy, and created a new command responsible for space and cyber-warfare. The new Chinese PLA means business.

The PLA is actively recruiting officers from outside its military academies who have real technical skills to put this plan into action. The anti-corruption campaign has snared more than two hundred senior officers and thousands of others already. It is breaking up some of the patronage chains where corruption is most rampant. As a side benefit, it is also breaking up some army cliques that oppose building naval, cyber, and space capabilities at the expense of the ground forces. Many analysts believe new promotions are also creating a new clique of officers loyal to Xi.

The United States worries most about the PLA's new, aggressive emphasis on cyber-warfare. Chinese government hackers with colorful aliases like "UglyGorilla" and "SuperHard" have been stealing America's most sensitive secrets. They tend to be men in their twenties who trained at PLA universities. The Chinese government doesn't pay well, so some moonlight as mercenaries who also sell their skills to state-owned and private companies. Secretive PLA cyber-unit 61398 is the most famous of these groups. It is housed in a nondescript building in Shanghai. American cyber firm Mandiant believes it employs hundreds, if not *thousands*, of malware authors and hackers, and that it is only one of twenty-five suspected hacker groups with ties to the PLA.

My former Pentagon colleagues say that they are under a constant barrage of attacks from China. China's cyber-warriors have hacked into everything from the systems of hundreds of American companies, to U.S. government personnel records (presumably to get information on individual American officials), to a frightening number of plans for U.S. weapons systems, including the F-35 joint strike fighter, drones, nanotechnology, and electronic warfare systems. China now has access to advanced U.S. designs that they could exploit to jam or otherwise disable U.S. systems in a conflict. It also accelerates China's ability to acquire advanced military technology, saving it billions in development costs.

China is also developing the capability to launch a serious cyber-attack on other countries' critical infrastructure, for example by shutting down an entire electricity grid. So far it has not used this against the United States or other major powers. The Chinese probably believe, accurately, that the country attacked would see this as sufficient provocation to retaliate with real military force. One could, however, imagine China using this weapon against a lesser power, as Russia recently did against Ukraine.

★   ★   ★

Not surprisingly, the reactions of China's neighbors and the United States range from anxious to terrified. China's actions threaten to undo the delicate political-military balance in the Asia-Pacific region, which the United States has dominated since World War II. There is a real threat that misunderstandings and distrust on all sides will lead to everyone arming to the hilt in a way that benefits no one. Many smaller countries are ramping up their own military spending and looking to the United States to help them push back against China.

In July 2015, Japan's parliament approved legislation that allows an expanded role for its military for the first time since the end of World War II. It is buying F-35 fighter jets, drones, and other equipment, and increased its military spending to record levels. Promptly after China announced the Air Defense Zone, U.S. defense secretary Chuck Hagel reaffirmed that the U.S.-Japan Mutual Defense Treaty applies to the Senkaku islands—meaning that a Chinese attack on the Japanese military there would bring the United States into a war with China. Japan, in turn, is collaborating more with the navies of the Philippines and Thailand.

The Philippines is spending more on defense, wants more exercises with the United States, and is buying warships and planes to help protect its troops in the South China Sea. Vietnam is increasing its military budgets by record numbers and expanding its relations with the United States, Japan, and India. An Indian admiral told me proudly that India is selling ships and antiship missiles to Vietnam. Even Malaysia, one of China's closest friends, wants to host U.S. spy planes for joint surveillance of the South China Sea. From 2011 to 2015 Asia bought nearly half of all global arms imports.

The most dramatic change is in India. Concerned about China's new focus on the Indian Ocean and the high Himalayas, India is ramping up defense spending, and looking everywhere for allies. India spends more than any other Asian country except China on its defense.

Prime Minister Modi has signaled his resolve to build a strong military, following (accurate) claims that India could not fight a two-front war against China and Pakistan. India largely ignored its navy for two decades, and it is not well prepared to confront China. So, in spite of a serious budget crunch, India increased its defense spending by 11 percent to $40 billion for the fiscal year 2015–16 (although spending is mostly flat for 2016–17). Ever ambitious, it plans to build a two-hundred-ship navy by 2027, and is also busily increasing its submarine fleet to around twenty-five, including several capable of firing nuclear missiles. It has asked the United States to help it build several modern aircraft carriers to compete with the Chinese efforts in this area. Delhi displayed some of its new machinery at a massive "Fleet Review" in February 2016, where helicopters and fighter jets roared while sailors stood at attention and black-clad commandos practiced raids. It was the largest show of India's military might in fifteen years, and was tellingly held on India's eastern coast, facing China.

By the numbers, India's military would be no match for China in an all-out war. China already has three hundred surface ships and around sixty modern submarines, including four capable for firing nuclear ballistic missiles. India just tested its first such submarine in late 2015. It gets worse: China has over two million troops compared to India's 1.3 million, and hundreds more fighter jets, tanks, surface ships, and on and on.

Defense expert Ashley Tellis believes that the Indian military is much stronger than these numbers suggest. Several American defense officials I spoke to agree. India has a volunteer army, which keeps morale fairly high. The rank and file is mostly young kids from rural areas without much education. They are glad to live in the simple but adequate accommodations (one Indian soldier assured me that all have electricity and running water). Noncommissioned officers, the leaders whom most enlisted men interact with daily, are competent. Indian officers are energetic and well educated. Until recently, the military was considered an excellent career for intelligent sons from families of modest means. Schools on military bases are quite good, and several of my friends who attended Harvard or other prestigious universities were Indian "army brats."

India's military is also one of the few institutions in the country that is not corrupt. Unlike the PLA, it is also a tested fighting force. From the many border skirmishes with Pakistan to near-constant patrol of the Indian Ocean, the Indian military is out and about rather than home showing off its new equipment in military parades. Tellis believes the Indian air force is number one in Asia—better than both Japan and China—and its navy is second to Japan's but better than China's. China is spending much on new equipment, but it will take years to learn to use these new toys effectively.

Realizing that the numbers are not in its favor, India is both trying to solidify its economic relations with China to avoid conflict, and casting around for allies in case there is one. When I served in the U.S. State Department in 2007, the Chinese government protested vociferously over a small joint military exercise by the United States, India, Japan, and Australia. We scaled back the event in subsequent years to avoid antagonizing China.

That delicate era of sparing China's feelings is long past. India now holds more military exercises with the United States than with any other country. With its eye firmly on China, in just six months in 2015, India held a flurry of bilateral and multilateral naval exercises with everyone from Australia, Japan, and Indonesia to Sri Lanka, Thailand, Myanmar, and Singapore. Interspersed with them were exercises with the United States, United Kingdom, and France. It is providing military assistance to Vietnam. It is even boosting its ties with tiny Mauritius, Maldives, and Seychelles, islands where China also hopes to have a greater presence.

* * *

Since World War II, the United States has been the predominant military power in the Pacific and Indian Ocean region. Whether America and its friends like it or not, that era is ending.

Nervous about this prospect, thoughtful American scholars such as Ashley Tellis, Bob Blackwill, and John Mearsheimer, among others, have called for more explicit balancing of China's military rise. This joint effort to balance against China has already begun, as we see increased military cooperation between India, Japan, Australia, the United States, and smaller Asian states. This strategy alone, however, will not shape China's rise in a way the United States would be comfortable with.

Whenever the United States says "balance" or "pivot to Asia," China hears only "contain." Former Australian prime minister Kevin Rudd points out that China's leadership recently circulated a document concluding that the United States' goals are to isolate, contain, diminish, and internally divide China, and to sabotage its leadership. This may seem far-fetched sitting in Washington, D.C., but it is in fact how Beijing sees the world, and it has real data to back it up.

Instead of pure balancing, managing China's military rise requires subtle policy making from like-minded countries. We should take a longer-term view of China: as its economic interests expand, it will continue to invest heavily in its military, as all rising powers have done. China will be a global military player because its economy requires it. India and the United States must carefully temper their desire to cooperate militarily with a real effort to avoid alienating China. Subtlety is not something democratic countries do particularly well, but here are some ideas for the elements of such a strategy:

First, the United States, India, and like-minded countries should be clear and consistent about what lines must not be crossed—for example China's land grabs and cyber-hacking. This means other militaries, including the United States, should continue multilateral regular freedom of navigation patrols in the western Pacific, so China does not overreach. This is not a call for a big step-up in defense spending. The United States is already reducing troop size and conventional military equipment, and investing more in special forces, drones, and cybersecurity to be ready for a full range of new threats. The United States should also make smart capital investments in its navy. India too is taking the right steps here— investing in some new equipment and technology for its navy to have a continued presence in the Indian Ocean.

Second, we should continue military exercises with other Asian nations, as long as we include China in as many of these as possible. For years, India, the United States, Japan, Australia, and others were reluctant to cooperate militarily on a large scale, out of a desire to spare China's feelings. China's recent bullying behavior means that patience is running thin. These exercises demonstrate to the PLA that its actions do have consequences. The United States should only avoid a few scenarios that China would see as very hostile: for example, major joint naval exercises with Japan and Korea, or congregating many U.S. aircraft carriers near China's Hainan Island.

If these first two points sound a lot like balancing, they are. We should moderate this tougher stance as best we can with the following others:

Third, the United States, India, and others should speak to the Chinese military as much as possible, on every conceivable issue. More communication can help everyone avoid misunderstandings. This has been difficult in the past. At times the PLA has been hesitant to speak to India on defense issues at all. The U.S. military felt that in many dialogues the PLA was just "going through the motions," rather than trying to resolve thorny disagreements on crisis management, cybersecurity, and other issues. The impetus for greater communication has to come from the political level. Robert Gates points out that military dialogues with China really only made progress when Presidents Obama and Xi told their militaries that they *had* to cooperate. Where the PLA is hesitant to engage, we should quietly (to let everyone save face) but insistently keep pushing for dialogue.

When there are political disagreements with China—and there will be many—we should try to internationalize them rather than be lured into a "USA versus China" dynamic. The United States says that it is neutral in the territorial disputes in the East and South China Seas, yet sometimes our vociferous (and rightful) defense of the rights of the smaller countries, such as our recent decision to cruise close to the islands China is building, makes China believe we have taken sides. Instead we should finally ratify the Law of the Sea Convention (the treaty we say we are defending in the South China Sea and elsewhere). We should ratchet down the rhetoric wherever possible, for example by having an independent body do a study of what the actual oil and gas reserves and fishing resources are, and which atoll has which territorial rights.

The most immediate goal of military dialogues should be to establish strict procedures for managing accidents at sea. An incident between one of the many planes and ships crowding disputed territory in the East and South China Seas is nearly inevitable. The important thing is to communicate quickly and clearly if this happens to prevent any political crisis from spinning out of control.

Cybersecurity is a second priority of these dialogues.

It is important to separate various strands of "cybersecurity" that tend to get jumbled in the press: cyber-spying on each other's governments and weapons systems is, for better or worse, something that all countries do and will continue to do. China's extensive stealing of American business secrets and technologies, however, is not just spying and most countries consider it unacceptable. President Xi acknowledged this in September

2015 when he and President Obama committed both countries to "not engage in or knowingly support online theft of intellectual properties."

Although it is understandably frustrated, the United States should think carefully about some of the tit-for-tat actions it has taken in response to Chinese cyber-espionage, such as indicting six Chinese hackers and threatening sanctions right before Xi's state visit in 2015. Such U.S. reactions at first achieved only Chinese retaliation, which makes it even harder for American businesses to operate in China. Talks that create real cyber-rules are likely more productive than indicting hackers who will never be turned over to the United States for prosecution.

In a promising sign, Beijing and Washington kicked off a first "high-level" dialogue on this issue in December 2015, and agreed to guidelines for helping each other prevent cyber-theft. China recently reached similar "no cyber-theft" pacts with the UK and Germany, and accepted this norm as part of the G20. These are excellent developments, and exactly the right approach. However, they will be hard to enforce even if the Chinese government is willing, because again, many of the Chinese hackers stealing foreign business secrets are moonlighting—they are paid by Chinese companies to do so.

Most important, there are as yet no rules of the road for offensive cyberattacks. What happens if Chinese hackers shut down our electrical grid? Or, more likely, India's or Japan's? Would the United States respond with bombs? Dialogues between all countries should seek to establish clear guidelines to avoid an accidental escalation. A quiet dialogue with China, the United States, Russia, India, and European nations (either together or each bilaterally with China) could do much to help keep everyone's cyber-activities in acceptable bounds.

Fourth, India, the United States, and others should *include* China in as many military exercises as possible, rather than exercising without them. The United States has been doing this recently by exercising with the Chinese navy near Florida and Shanghai, and by inviting China to the enormous RIMPAC naval exercises we conduct every year. Other than a few minor antipiracy patrols, interaction between *India* and China's militaries is minimal. This is mostly because the Chinese have been hesitant to cooperate. India, the United States, Europe, and the Asian powers must keep pushing China—again and again—to cooperate, exercise together, and talk more.

Finally, and most important, we all must find positive areas of collaboration. Most of these will *not* happen in the military sphere, which tends to be fraught with misunderstanding. Instead joint projects could focus on the environment, health care, joint aid to third countries, and the other issues discussed in earlier chapters. Even in military matters, however, the United States should seek to see India's and China's new power projection as an opportunity. By working closely with *both* militaries to avoid misunderstandings and increase confidence, we can help build China and India into partners. Jointly we can protect everyone's economic interests in key sea-lanes like the Straits of Malacca, respond to humanitarian crises like the Fukushima earthquake, and prevent piracy, to build a peaceful future for all.

CONCLUSION: OURS TO LOSE

WHEN NEW countries rise to power, the story often ends badly, sometimes in war. Many Americans worry about China's economic power and, understandably, about its military assertiveness. Pundits and presidential candidates often talk as if China were already an adversary of the United States. Few have focused on Asia's other giant, India. Instead of scaring the American people about one country and ignoring another, we need to get busy working with both on a new world system that accommodates all three. There is reason to hope that with thoughtful, steady policies agreed upon by the United States, China, and India, this time will be different.

One example makes me cautiously optimistic that the rise of China and India can be peaceful. I'll call it a tale of three powers. In the late nineteenth century, the British Empire stretched around the world. Its economic and military might were unparalleled. Yet some cracks were showing in the foundations. Steadily, two other powers encroached on Britain's dominance. Both these rivals had strong economies, were rapidly industrializing, and increasingly sought a place for themselves in the international order. One was a monarchy, Germany. The other, the United States, was a democracy that shared some, but not all, of Britain's values. Over several decades, Britain decided to accommodate the rise of the United States, believing that the United States would generally align itself with the rules of the international system Britain had established, and eventually help share the burden of supporting this order by keeping the seas free for navigation, and trade mostly open. Britain tolerated many missteps by the United States on the latter's way to great power status. The two avoided major conflicts and ultimately became allies in two world wars. While Britain made some friendly overtures to Germany as well, it treated Germany mostly as a rival to be balanced. Both countries rapidly built up their navies in the lead-up to World War I, and ultimately fought two devastating wars.

Many in the United States today call for us to repeat, in essence, the policy that Britain pursued in the late nineteenth century: to support the rise of India, a democracy, and other like-minded countries, as a counterweight against the growing power of authoritarian China. I believe that this strategy alone will not succeed, just as it did not succeed for Britain. Some American analysts argue that a show of strength will encourage China to play a positive rather than negative role on the international stage. The United States, India, and other Asian powers will certainly have to push back in some form against China's more provocative actions, such as its cyber-spying on foreign companies, and bullying of smaller neighbors in the South and East China Seas. The problem with the balance-only approach, however, is that it creates a typical security dilemma. If we treat China like the "other," including by allying more closely with India, China is more likely to feel insecure and friendless and to act like an opponent—just as Germany did in the late nineteenth and early twentieth centuries. India is also highly dependent on China's economy and is unlikely to want to ally formally with the United States against it.

Others believe that the United States has harmed itself by being too generous to China. They explain, accurately, that the United States has spent decades providing military stability in the Pacific and extending normal trade status to China and thus facilitated its rise, as well as that of India and other Asian powers. In this view, China has enjoyed a free ride and taken advantage of American generosity to grow into a major strategic challenger. The solution, so the argument goes, is to stop enabling China's rise and start opposing it. This populist argument is appealing, especially now that many Americans worry about their own future. While most experts don't argue this explicitly, variations on the theme pop up frequently, especially during U.S. presidential campaigns: we should stop exporting jobs to China; sanction the country for its cyber-activities; impose a 45 percent tax on all Chinese imports; cancel the summit with Xi Jinping, and declare it a currency manipulator on "day one."

Unfortunately for this school of thought, China (and India) will rise no matter what we do. Both will remain integrated in the world economic system even if we stop trading with them entirely, and such a move would harm American companies and workers. Even if American manufacturing jobs don't go to China or India, they still won't come back here. They will go to other inexpensive countries like Vietnam and Bangladesh, so we must help our workers adjust. Trying to punish China (or India) or keep them down will only ensure that neither evolves into a responsible power, and will help bring about the negative vision of 2030.

A third school believes that as China becomes more prosperous (through our help) it will eventually move toward democracy, or at least begin to share U.S. values internationally. An "inevitable" transition to democracy seems unlikely. There is no great call among China's population for elections, just for better governance. Most Chinese believe that their economic model provides a great alternative to western democracy—it is more efficient than any other system at rapidly raising people out of poverty. The Chinese Communist Party is trying something completely novel: opening up its economy while keeping an ever-tighter grip on politics. It is unclear if this plan will succeed, or end in an internal coup or revolution. In a best-case scenario, China will gradually make its domestic institutions more accountable and move toward rule of law. A move to a full democracy like India's is unlikely.

It is possible that China will begin to share many—but not all—western values as it becomes wealthier, as its companies innovate more, and as its interests force it to interact more with the rest of the world. It may yet become what former U.S. Deputy Secretary of State Robert Zoellick called a "responsible stakeholder" in the global community. This view assumes that if China benefits enough from the existing system, it will see no reason to undermine it. India already shares many of our values, but as it takes on a diplomatic role commensurate with its economic power, we may begin to have more conflicts with it. Neither country will become a "responsible stakeholder" automatically. It will require real compromise and much effort by the rest of the world to nudge both China and India in the right direction.

We can and must do better than simply balancing the power of China by supporting India and others, trying to prevent both from becoming economically and politically powerful, or hoping that our generosity and the giants' growth will magically lead them to uphold our values. If this relationship is mismanaged, China could develop like the autocratic, insecure, and bravado-filled Germany of the early twentieth century. Right now our relationship with India is positive, but mostly because India is equally worried about China. As India expands its global role, we may have more disagreements. We have a duty to do everything in our power to prevent either country from becoming a foe.

So what is the solution? Instead of handling China the way that Britain did Germany—mostly as an adversary to be watched and balanced against—we should treat *both* China and India with the subtlety that Britain used for the upstart United States. This doesn't mean we will have identical policies toward them. We should, however, through patient, constant interaction coax both "adolescent" powers to gradually accept a responsible international role.

Stanford scholar Kori Schake, one of the foremost experts on America's ascent, argues that in the last decades of the nineteenth century, Britain did just this for the United States. Much like the United States and China today, at that time Britain and the United States distrusted each other. They had recently fought two wars, while the United States and China have never fought directly. Yet Britain consistently behaved like the "adult" power to the U.S. "teenager." Britain was patient when we acted impetuously (as most new powers do), balanced us militarily if we did something they couldn't accept, and encouraged us—through sustained cooperation and conversation—gradually to accept much of the international order Britain had created.

The parallels between America's ascent and those of China and India are imperfect, as all historical analogies are. Where the United States and United Kingdom already shared many values, we have major differences with China in particular. We have very different relations with India and China. And we certainly don't want India, China, or anyone else to replace us as the world's leader.

Yet the analogy yields some valuable lessons. The United States is generally acting toward India as Britain did: we assume it is a friend and smooth over many disagreements to make this friendship a reality. Largely because of China's recent aggressive behavior, we are in danger of treating it ever more as an adversary.

A strategy of "coaching" both China and India on how to become great powers doesn't require us to ignore our interests, or accept without complaint when either one makes moves we find unacceptable. It also does not mean we will groom them to be successors to the United States as world leader. It does, however, rely on the following assumptions: First, a prosperous China and India are good for the United States. Like it or not, their economies are the engines of world growth, and their joint populations are approaching 3 billion people. To keep our own economy strong, we will need to trade with and invest in them. Second, a confident China and India are better than the alternative. Countries make bad decisions when they feel insecure or threatened. To extend a world order based on American values, we must make a sustained, long-term effort to bring China and India along rather than alienating one or both.

Given these assumptions, what concrete steps should we take to ensure the emergence of these new great powers benefits us all? Here I offer some ideas based on strategies we know succeeded in recent history.

Military relations are the most difficult to get right, and the most likely to lead to catastrophic consequences if the United States, China, or India mismanage them. The current trajectory is not good. Strategic distrust between China on one side, and the United States, India, and like-minded countries on the other, is very high. All militaries are paid to think about worst-case scenarios and then build the capabilities to protect the country in case these situations materialize. Right now this mind-set dominates, and unintentional tit-for-tat actions further erode trust. In our view, China departed from its policy of "peaceful rise" around 2008 and started pressuring smaller countries over the South and East China Seas and, more recently, India over its Himalayan border. The United States then "pivoted" to Asia, initially by adding troops and ships in the Pacific. This was not intended as a hostile act, but China very much perceived it as such. The United States conducts surveillance activities close to China's coasts and artificial islands. India is building up its navy. Military exercises between the United States, India, and other Asian powers often exclude China. From Beijing's perspective, everyone is ganging up on them.

This is quite different from the approach Britain used with the United States. As the United States rose in the nineteenth century, Britain tried to accommodate Washington's legitimate concerns and treated bilateral goodwill as a diplomatic priority. In 1895, when the United States rashly threatened to declare war on Britain over a Venezuelan border dispute, London immediately extended an olive branch. The British permitted the Americans to build and control the Panama Canal. This gave the United States easier access between its East and West Coasts. When the United States overreached, however, by encroaching on Mexican territory after 1845, the United Kingdom signaled that it would align with Mexico to stop the United States from bullying the smaller country. Throughout these and several other small crises, the British and American governments were in constant contact at both the diplomatic and military levels.

Similarly, the United States, India, and others must separate China's real strategic concerns—such as protecting its vital economic sea-lanes— from nationalistic combativeness. We tend to underestimate how much Chinese military bravado is based on their feelings of insecurity. Where possible, we should seek to take into account both powers' legitimate interests.

The United States has been better at this with respect to India than with China—and India makes it much easier to be helpful. Washington is even willing to reform its byzantine export controls in an attempt to sell India some of its most advanced weapons systems.

A similarly more nuanced policy toward China might involve a concerted effort to assure China of its maritime security while preserving open passage for all nations in the South China Sea, as former national security advisor Stephen Hadley has proposed. This would encourage the navies of China, India, the United States, and other countries such as the

Philippines and Vietnam to exercise and operate together to ensure the sea-lanes are open for everyone. A small effort like this began in 2004, and it is time to expand it. It would be even better if the United States could encourage China quietly behind the scenes to propose such exercises and let China take the credit, all as a gesture of goodwill.

Second, when we disagree with China—as we will often—we should not be lured into a "USA versus China" dynamic. It is more effective to push back against China as a group of like-minded countries, and we should press India, Japan, Australia, and European nations to also express their concerns about Chinese landgrabs and cyber-hacking, for example. China recently began to engage in talks on cyber-hacking, but not on the South or East China Seas. We should quietly (so Chinese leaders save face) but insistently keep pushing them to do so.

The United States and India must maintain strong navies and solid alliances with other Asian powers, and continue to be present in the western Pacific and Indian Oceans. There is also no reason to stop exercising with other Asian navies, as long as we include China in as many of these exercises as possible. Most important, the United States, India, and others need to encourage the PLA to speak to other militaries as much as possible, on every conceivable issue. The immediate goals should be to establish procedures to manage incidents at sea to avoid a political crisis, and a dialogue involving China, India, and possibly also Russia and Europe to create cyberwarfare "rules of the road." It will take political leadership from both sides to ensure these dialogues actually achieve something concrete.

These recommendations are not revolutionary, and we are implementing many of them. Yet we are often distracted by the Middle East, so engage only episodically. Sometimes the heated nationalist rhetoric in China, India, and the United States threatens to undermine these good, gradual steps. All three should, at a minimum, work to manage events without a blowup until better conditions exist, and at best, to develop real trust. We should treat goodwill as a major diplomatic and military priority.

On the **economic** side, we have much to celebrate, even while we have work to do on fighting cyber-crime and ensuring a level playing field for all companies. As both of the giants' economies grow and become more sophisticated, they support free trade in some but not all instances. They are more open to investment and are slowly beginning to support intellectual property protection. China's currency is even becoming more responsive to market forces.

During its rise, the United States was at times protectionist. It became more open to free trade as its industries matured and it could compete internationally. Britain gently but consistently nudged the United States toward open trade during the late nineteenth century. British companies invested heavily in the United States, and when their capital ran low, the United States began to invest in Britain. London also wisely stayed out of U.S. domestic disputes, understanding that pushy intervention by an outside power might push Washington in the opposite direction. For example, the British pound, based on the gold standard, was the global reserve currency. The United States debated in three presidential elections from the 1870s to 1890s about moving to a silver standard that would favor the dollar as the world's reserve currency, since the United States had many silver mines. Britain wisely stayed out of our domestic debate and the United States finally decided it was in its own interest to let the gold standard continue. It is a debate oddly reminiscent of the current one about the prospect of the renminbi becoming one of the world's international reserve currencies.

Similarly, we should keep encouraging both China and India to accept open investment and trade regimes. This is painstaking work. We have spent years negotiating bilateral investment treaties with both countries without yet signing a deal. As the Trans-Pacific Partnership (TPP) is implemented, we should press hard to continue our free trade talks with both India and China, and try to eventually include them in the TPP. India in particular would benefit from more access to America's and China's large markets, especially India's first-rate services sector and the skilled labor manufacturing it is working hard to establish. U.S. officials should encourage Delhi and Beijing to push economic reforms. This will help China stabilize its economy and help India to jump-start the growth it needs to benefit from its demographic dividend. It is a positive sign that we recently welcomed the renminbi as part of the IMF's basket of reserve currencies. Finally, we should encourage companies from all three countries to invest in each other. This creates jobs that benefit all three, and produces a strong constituency in each country for good relations with the others. It may take a decade or more, but this is the patient work that creates lasting partnerships.

These steps don't require us to ignore the current difficult business climate with China, and to a lesser extent with India. Edward Snowden's revelation of National Security Agency snooping caused many Chinese and Indian companies to distrust U.S. technology firms and buy less from them. India continues to exclude foreign investments in many sectors, and its complex license raj still makes it difficult to do business. China supports its national champions, insists on "secure and controllable" technology back doors, and throws up regulatory obstacles for foreign companies. Chinese (and some Indian) firms would argue that the United States also makes it difficult for them to invest in and sell to the United States. We all have a lot of work to do.

We can start by explaining to each of our publics that, in this interconnected world, all three giants have a mutual interest in the others' economic success. Negative press about China was so prevalent in the lead-up to President Xi Jinping's visit in September 2015 that when a handful of American CEOs posed with Xi for the *New York Times,* they were accused by some of currying favor with the Communist Party. This is ridiculous. We should encourage companies and governments from all three countries to speak openly and often to resolve differences.

American, Chinese, and Indian businessmen—and politicians—should more forcefully explain why economic cooperation is good for all three countries. Chinese investment in the United States is skyrocketing and has created jobs in four-fifths of all U.S. congressional districts. Chinese companies have invested more than $90 billion in the United States since 2005, and $42 billion of this investment was made in 2013–15 alone. Chinese investment has directly created more than 80,000 jobs in America, and U.S. exports to China indirectly support hundreds of thousands more. Indian investment in the United States is smaller but has more than doubled since 2008. Indian FDI is thought to have created at least 90,000 direct jobs, with other reports estimating the Indian tech industry alone indirectly supported more than 400,000 U.S. jobs in 2015.*

Our trade with and investment in each other is helping all three economies grow. The problems U.S. companies face in doing business in China and India, and vice versa, will only be solved if local constituents in each country make this case and support economic engagement.

China and India are rising into a world where the **institutional order** is fairly well developed. When the United States rose, by contrast, power wars were a normal occurrence, and countries only episodically committed to maintaining the global economy. So there is no direct historic parallel. However, Britain again went out of its way to establish some institutions that helped it cooperate with the United States, even if they disagreed on many issues. In the 1890s, for example, both countries together established an international court of arbitration to settle transnational commercial disputes.

Similarly, we should seek to cooperate with both China and India whenever that is feasible without compromising our core values. The United States cannot expect China and India to accept, without change, the institutions we helped create after World War II, such as the United Nations, the World Bank, and the international trading system. China, and to a lesser extent India, have worldviews that differ substantially from those of the West. This is another reason India must be a critical player in shaping China's rise: on issues such as sanctions on Iran or Syria, or aid to Afghanistan, it can act as a bridge between western and Chinese views.

Some have argued that the West should change these institutions to make real room for new players like China and India. If it is a matter of giving others a more prominent seat at the table, we should do so. This does not mean, however, that we should lower the standards related to transparency, labor relations, and the environment of these institutions.

---

* It is of course true that American investment in China and India has created many more direct jobs in those countries than they have so far created here. The point here is not to ignore that fact, but merely to point out that cross-border investment increasingly helps the United States as well.

President Xi says he shares this moderate view. He emphasized in his 2015 visit to the United States that developing countries want a more equitable international system, but they do not want to unravel the entire order. China does not intend to undermine the existing institutions, as some have warned, but it and India do want influence in the current system that matches their rising power.

To begin, we should join the Asian Infrastructure Investment Bank to lend support and shape its progress. If managed correctly, the AIIB is the first example of China trying to become a "responsible stakeholder" in the international system. It is voluntarily restraining its own economic clout. China could make massive infrastructure investments around the world on its own. Yet it has chosen to do much of it through the AIIB. The bank's new Chinese CEO is pushing for high transparency, environmental, and other standards, and wants to cooperate with the World Bank, Asian Development Bank, and others. We should encourage initiatives like this as much as possible.

The next U.S. president should also push hard to reform the World Bank and other institutions to make more room for developing countries like China and India. Over the next decade the UN Security Council will either be restructured to reflect the dramatic shift in world power or it will become obsolete. President Obama has wisely proposed India for a seat, which China quietly opposes. Eventually we will have to agree to a solution that will give China, India, and other developing countries a bigger say at the expense of the United States and Europe. It is preferable to have China and India inside a larger tent even if we often disagree, rather than on the outside creating an alternative order.

The new AIIB and BRICs development banks are warning shots: unless we reshape outdated postwar institutions, India and China will ignore or leave them. To build a positive vision for 2030, we need both of the world's largest countries engaged in international governance.

Cooperate, cooperate, cooperate. The most important step we can take to ensure good relations with China and India is not dramatic at all: it is to make cooperation the dominant element of our interaction. Cooperation is not automatic. It must be practiced at the level of diplomacy, business, and interpersonal relations to get everyone in the habit. Again, Britain did this in important ways with the United States in the nineteenth century. Instead of letting major quarrels (such as Britain's opposition to U.S. slavery and desire for more open trade) dominate their relationship, Britain worked to collaborate on many levels. British private capital contributed greatly to the westward expansion of U.S. railroads. In the late 1890s, the British government let the United States use the one existing trans-Pacific cable to get information to the U.S. fleet in the Philippines. The list continues.

Similarly, we should work on a long list of joint activities with China and India to make collaboration a habit. Prioritizing cooperation and goodwill does not mean that any of the three nations will surrender their national interests to each other. All three giants will often disagree on important issues from human rights to intellectual property to open sea-lanes. We will continue to compete for markets and resources. We will hedge against potentially aggressive military behavior. Our assumption should be, however, that we resolve conflicts in private and prioritize collaboration in public.

With India, we have already taken important steps in this direction. In 2005 the United States agreed to negotiate a civil nuclear energy agreement with India, something Delhi had long wanted to help solve its electricity shortages. It was a difficult step and the final outcome is still uncertain. Whether or not the agreement succeeds, it forced two governments that often distrusted each other to work together intensively, over several years, on a critical joint endeavor. By these means the United States demonstrated that it supports India's rise. The nuclear agreement has unlocked more cooperation on topics from defense sales to intelligence sharing to agricultural partnerships. These steps are just beginning. Throughout this book, I have suggested a number of areas for collaboration on issues large and small:

We must patiently continue our joint work to solve global challenges, from climate change and counterterrorism, to piracy controls in the Gulf of Aden. The nascent Chinese-American collaboration on climate change is a fantastic start. It has also helped prod India to take more dramatic action.

We must also work bilaterally and trilaterally to help with each other's internal challenges where we can. U.S. universities and community colleges can help India's education system. Chinese and American companies can set decent examples for promoting women in the workplace. Clean technology companies from all three countries can help solve some of the difficult environmental problems we all face. Chinese capital can help rebuild creaking infrastructure in the United States and India. The list is endless.

Finally, on the issues where we disagree, we must emphasize quiet, constructive dialogue over public grandstanding. China recently agreed not to commit economic espionage for commercial gains, and the United States and China are quietly negotiating to establish cyber "rules of the road." This is better than the public threats of sanctions that preceded President Xi's visit to the United States in September 2015. All three militaries disagree on much, but we are gradually talking more at every level.

By cooperating where we can and talking through areas of disagreement, we build a mature and enduring relationship. We will continue to have differences but they can be minimized and managed if we lift our eyes to focus on the positive goals in the distance.

Today, the U.S. presidential campaign is in full swing. The United States' anxiety about the rise of China at our expense seems to be going into overdrive. Presidential candidates on the left and right have claimed that we must "uncouple" from the Chinese economy or else it will bring us down, or that trade deals with Asia "are a major reason for the collapse of the American middle class." Listening to the candidates, we appear terrified of China and largely ignorant of the importance of India.

We do this at our peril. Yes, we face some large domestic problems that should be our priority. Yes, we will continue to have national interests that sometimes conflict with those of China and India. But whether we like it or not, China and India are the two great rising powers in the world order we still lead. They will rise whether or not we manage the relationship well. We will expend lots of time and resources on both relationships even if we manage them badly. During the Cold War, the United States spent more of its GDP on defense than we do today. The pessimistic scenario is unthinkable: a new cold war would result in increased military spending that would be better dedicated to helping our own citizens. Global problems would become unmanageable. Economic interactions would decline and thus harm all three countries.

These are not just tasks for diplomats and the next president. We all have a constructive role to play.

What can our politicians do? In addition to the military and diplomatic initiatives above, please be more honest and nuanced with your constituents. Explain that the rise of these two giants is not a black-and-white issue. After the United States has had nearly two decades as the world's dominant power, it will be difficult genuinely to accommodate new voices at the table. But the rise of China and India does not spell our demise. In fact, many problems can only be solved if we work on them together.

What can businesses do? Please continue to trade. Be honest with your employees and customers about how your business with China and India impacts people at home: yes, U.S. companies have moved blue-collar jobs to cheaper labor markets. Yet our trade with China and India makes many products we love much less expensive, and American companies' exports to China and India support many jobs here at home. Boeing, for example, which manufactures in America, sells more than a quarter of its commercial planes to China and India. If those markets were closed to us, the result would likely be tens of thousands of layoffs here. American businesses should acknowledge that this transition is hard, and not without losers, and perhaps do more for Americans whose jobs are being replaced. At the same time, they can help China and India solve some of their internal problems in health care, clean technology, elder care, education, and other issues, and thus help them succeed as our own businesses thrive.

What can ordinary citizens do? More than you may think. People-to-people relations will be the bedrock of all three relationships. Advocate for more exchanges with Chinese and Indian students at your high school or university. Host a student, scholar, teacher, or diplomat from either country in your home. Create a social media group about the environment, poverty, education, or whatever issue you care about, with people from all three countries to see if we can jointly tackle some of these problems. You will have many more ideas.

The United States, China, and India can create a positive, brave new world. To do so requires us to be patient and moderate. We should accommodate China's and India's legitimate interests wherever we reasonably can. We should communicate clearly when we plan to push back on aggressive behavior, and then do so jointly with other countries. We should look for opportunities to find common ground. If we prioritize collaboration, we can help solve global problems affecting us all, and the United States, China, and India can all enjoy increased peace and prosperity.

ACKNOWLEDGMENTS

M Y DEEPEST thanks go to Justine Isola, Rachel Gillum, and Tiffany Frisa, who spent many hours researching every last detail of every issue and editing my work, so we could be true experts before zooming out to the appropriate level for the reader. Thank you for your expertise and deep dedication to this book, which comes across in every page. This certainly would not have happened without you!

I am particularly indebted to the following people, who provided detailed insights and their own recollections of particular events or trends: Larry Lau, Gary Roughead, Susan Schwab, Karl Eikenberry, Sungmin Rho, Chong En Bai, Xiao Qiang, Atreyee Sen, Supriya Bhardwaj, David Zhou, Ashley Tellis, Montek Singh Ahluwalia, Pramit Pal Chaudhuri, Ajay Kela, Kori Schake, Condoleezza Rice, Stephen Hadley, Robert Gates, Nicholas Burns, and Richard Verma.

In addition, I am grateful for the collective wisdom of these experts and policymakers, who over the years have informed my views on China and India, including, in no particular order: S. Jaishankar, BJ Panda, Shivshankar Menon, Sachin Pilot, Raja Mohan, Kapil Sibal, Fan Gang, Liu Feitao, Liu Weimin, Xie Tao, Zhang Yesui, Chen Yonglong, Hu Angang, Wu Jiansheng, Lu Wei, Liu He and Wang Qishan's staffs, Hank Paulson, Jim Steinberg, Kevin Rudd, C. Fred Bergsten, Kevin Lynch, Robert Kaplan, Orville Schell, Joe Nye, Phil Zelikow, Bob Blackwill, John Podesta, David Sanger, Ash Carter, John Lipsky, Tom Fingar, David Shambaugh, James Kynge, Andrew Small, Rick Niu, Stapleton Roy, Yo Osumi, Adam Williams, Nandan Nilekani, Srikanth Nadhamuni, Romesh Wadhwani, Piyush Goyal, Arun Jaitley, Admiral RK Dhowan, Rajnath

Singh, Ram Madhav, NK Singh, Suresh Prabhu, Tarun Das, Ashok Malik, Satish Nambiar, Vishaka Desai, Jamshyd Godrej, Neeta Misra from Oxfam India, Josette Sheeran, Herro Mustafa, Jeremy Weinstein, Philip Reiner, Alyssa Ayres, Evan Feigenbaum, Tofer Harrison from China Beige Book, Ian Thomas from Boeing, Kai Fu Lee and his portfolio CEOs, Gary Reischel, Jim Mc-Gregor, Paul Haenle, Bill Bishop, Dan Rosen, Dan Twining, Richard Fontaine, Michelle Flournoy, Steve Orlins, Richard Cooper, Ken Lieberthal, Jonathan Tepperman, Mirko Wormuth, Christian Hansmeyer, Jing Gussin, Awais Khan, Parag Khanna, Ankhi Das, Martin Roscheisen, Sebastian Thrun, several U.S. and Chinese intelligence officials, members of the U.S. Pacific Command, Chinese, Indian, and American businessmen, and many well-informed members of the Chinese, Indian, and U.S. diplomatic corps. Many others in China and India are too shy to be mentioned here but were kind enough let me interview them for additional color or generously spoke to me about their experiences working or living in or studying the two Asian giants.

I am privileged to call Condoleezza Rice, Stephen Hadley, and Robert Gates my business partners. They believed in this book from the beginning and encouraged me to tackle it, despite the many hours that it would take me away from our firm. They also weighed in with their own recollections and edited my work, thus giving me the benefit of their wisdom and decades of experience. The RHG team could not have been more supportive—thank you in particular Tiffany and Catherine for your help with the launch, Georgia and Keith for your invaluable advice on press, Aysha, Rebekah, Marilyn, Caroline, and the Hoover team for your professionalism and grace under pressure.

Nicholas Burns has been a mentor and friend since I worked for him more than a decade ago at the U.S. State Department. I could not have been luckier. He has been a constant source of support for many years, and gave me valuable edits on the entire manuscript despite being one of the busiest people I know.

My agent, Andrew Wylie, was kind to believe in this project after meeting me only once, and tirelessly worked with me to shape the proposal, providing guidance and encouragement throughout the whole publishing process.

Alice Mayhew's legendary reputation is well-deserved, and I feel very privileged to have had the opportunity to work with her. She took a chance on me as a first-time book author, and was an indispensible ally and sounding board throughout. The top-notch team at Simon & Schuster has no equal: Stuart

Roberts, thank you for patiently answering my endless inquiries; Phil Metcalf and Tom Pitoniak for your tireless copyediting and production help (and Tom for telling me you really enjoyed the book just when I needed a serious confidence boost). Larry Hughes and Nicole McCardle, thank you for holding my hand through the bewildering process of book publicity and marketing. Emily Loose, thank you for editing and re-editing my initial proposal. Anthony Garrett, your wisdom and advice on book marketing was invaluable.

To the great team at the Aspen Strategy Group, especially Jonathan Price, thank you for letting me participate in the many dialogues over the years that have so informed my views on India. The Ditchley Foundation provided several invaluable experiences bringing Chinese, American, and European government officials and scholars together to speak frankly and quietly in the most beautiful surroundings one could imagine. The China Institute of International Studies, Asia Society, and German Marshall Fund have also sponsored my visits and conversations with officials in China and India. I appreciate your generosity. CNAS, and especially its leaders Michele Flournoy and Richard Fontaine, have been a great sounding board over the years.

To my former colleagues in the U.S. Government, especially State, the NSC, and Defense: you work tirelessly for little pay trying to solve the most difficult issues the world can throw at us, and often get too little acknowledgement. Thank you for your dedication and service—all of us in the private sector are lucky to have you on the front lines.

Café du Soleil, its owner Mustapha, and its always-smiling staff became my home away from home, with great lattes and music while I was working my way through these chapters.

None of this would have happened without the "writers group." Kathleen Janus, you first persuaded me to start this project over a glass of wine, got our little group together, and backed me throughout, including by taking the photo for the cover! Thank you. This truly would not have happened without your friendship. Along with Kathleen, I am grateful to Sarah Thornton, Kori Schake, and Ana Homayoun for your perfect combination of unflagging encouragement, great advice, and tough-love edits.

My family and close friends—you all know who you are—put up with far more than your fair share of exchanging ideas about the book, reading passages, and helping me come up with particularly juicy anecdotes. You supported me even when I must have been insufferable. A special shout-out for book-related help well beyond the call of duty goes to Josh Davis and my dad Kirk Miller for your edits, my mom Christina for your faith in me and your loving care for the kids when I was working on yet another weekend, and the self-designated "launch ladies."

And, of course, Greg. Twenty-one years ago we began staying up all night in the quad at Stanford because we could not stop talking—about life, travels, philosophy and, yes, foreign policy. Thank you for being my closest friend, my strongest supporter, the love of my life, and the best father that Alexei and Alia could ever have.

BIBLIOGRAPHIC NOTE

THIS BOOK is the product of more than a decade of working on and studying the relations between the United States and the new Asian giants, first at the U.S. State Department, and then through my clients at Rice-HadleyGates LLC, and as a lecturer at Stanford University. I have been lucky enough in my travels and business dealings to meet some of the people—politicians and businessmen—who are shaping the future of China, India, and the United States' policy toward both. In researching and writing the book, I conducted dozens of interviews and many more informal and "off the record" conversations, and read the notes and writings that some interviewees were kind enough to pass on to me.

Reliable statistics can be hard to find, especially for China. I did my best to rely on high-quality sources for all current statistics, and predictions of future trends, such as the IMF and World Bank databases, SIPRI, IHS Jane's, the International Energy Agency, Freedom House, the United Nations, and others.

For news, I relied on the impressive reporting of the *Economist*, BBC, *Financial Times*, the *New York Times*, *Wall Street Journal*, *Hindustan Times*, *Times of India*, *Caixin*, and the *Diplomat*, as well as the Sinocism blog, *China Digital Times*, and the China Leadership Monitor.

The following books and articles were among my "go-to" sources for background and history:

Antholis, William. *Inside Out, India and China*. Washington, DC: Brookings Institution Press, 2014.

Bose, Sugata, and Ayesha Jalal. *Modern South Asia: History, Culture, Political Economy*. London and New York: Routledge, 2011.

Li, Cheng. "Leadership Transition in the CPC: Promising Progress and Potential Problems." Brookings Institution, 2015.

Luce, Edward. *In Spite of the Gods: The Rise of Modern India*. London: Anchor, 2008.

Osnos, Evan, *Age of Ambition*. New York: Farrar, Straus & Giroux, 2014.

———. "Born Red." *New Yorker,* April 6, 2015.

Schell, Orville, and John Delury. *Wealth and Power: China's Long March to the Twenty-First Century*. New York: Random House, 2014.

Spence, Jonathan. *The Search for Modern China*. New York: Norton, 2012.

Wolpert, Stanley. *A New History of India*. New York: Oxford University Press, 2008.

NOTES

INTRODUCTION

1 *"China Flexes Its Military Muscle"*: Jeremy Page and Chun Han Wong, "China Flexes Its Military Muscle at World War II Parade," *Wall Street Journal*, September 23, 2015; Corrie Driebusch, Kwanwoo Jun, and William Kazer, "China Fears Sink Markets Again," *Wall Street Journal*, September 1, 2015; "It's Time to Get Tough on China and President Xi," editorial, *Washington Post*, September 23, 2015; Aaron Friedberg and Gabriel Schoenfeld, "China, a Wounded Tiger, Could Lash Out," *Los Angeles Times*, September 14, 2015.

2 *surpass the combined power*: "Global Trends 2030: Alternative Worlds," National Intelligence Council, December 2012, http://www.dni.gov/index.php/about /organization/global-trends-2030.

3 *world's largest economy*: "China 2030: Building a Modern, Harmonious, and Creative Society," World DataBank, World Bank, March 26, 2013, http://databank .worldbank.org/Data/Views/reports/tableview.aspx. The International Monetary Fund reports that China's GDP was $19.5 trillion in current international dollars based on purchasing-power-parity (PPP) in 2015. U.S. GDP (PPP) was $18 trillion. World Economic Outlook, October 2015.

3 *coverage of China is filled with breathless statistics*: China had six megacities of more than 10 million people in 2014: Shanghai, Beijing, Chongqing, Guangzhou, Tianjin, and Shenzhen. (India came in second with three megacities: Delhi, Mumbai, and Kolkata.) "World Urbanization Prospects: The 2014 Revision," United Nations Department of Economic and Social Affairs, Population Division, 2015, http://esa.un.org/unpd/wup/FinalReport/WUP2014-Report.pdf. As of 2009, China has promised retirement benefits to some 325 million Chinese. Mark Frazier, "No Country for Old Age," *New York Times*, February 18, 2013. As of 2014, China pumps 10 billion tons of CO_2 equivalent into the atmosphere each year, followed by the United States at 5.3 billion, and India 2.3 billion. Jos G. J. Olivier, Greet Janssens-Maenhout, Marilena Muntean, and Jeroen A. H. W. Peters, "Trends in Global CO_2 Emissions, 2015 Report." PBL Netherlands Environmental Assessment Agency and European Commission Joint Research Center, November 2015, http://edgar.jrc.ec.europa.eu/news_docs/jrc-2015-trends-in -global-co2-emissions-2015-report-98184.pdf. As of 2014 (latest data available across countries), China had 641 million Internet users compared to the United States, with 280 million internet users, and the EU's 401 million. "China Inter-

net Users," Internet Live Stats, May 2015, http://www.internetlivestats.com/in
ternet-users/china/. Internet Live Stats reports that China's number of Internet
users is 718 million as of November 2015. (More recent data not available across
other countries.) Two million internet monitors: "2014 Report to Congress of
the U.S.-China Economic and Security Review Commission," November 2014,
http://origin.www.uscc.gov/sites/default/files/annual_reports/Complete%20
Report.PDF.

3   *Many still doubt the relevance of India*: Sources for this paragraph are, for popula-
tion: The United Nations projects that India's population will be 1.5 billion and
China's 1.4 billion in 2030. United Nations World Population Prospects, 2015
Revision, accessed October 6, 2015, http://esa.un.org/unpd/wpp/. *middle class*:
"Hitting the Sweet Spot: The Growth of the Middle Class in Emerging Markets,"
Ernst and Young, 2013. *Energy demand*: "World Energy Outlook 2013 Factsheet,"
International Energy Agency, 2013, http://www.worldenergyoutlook.org/media
/weowebsite/factsheets/WEO2013_Factsheets.pdf. *Carbon emissions*: "India
Can Triple CO2 Emissions Under New Climate Commitment," Institute for En-
ergy Research, October 6, 2015, http://instituteforenergyresearch.org/analysis
/india-triple-co2-emissions-new-climate-commitment/. *Share of global investment*: The World Bank estimates that in 2030 China will account for 30 percent
of global gross investment, the United States for 11 percent, and India for 7 percent. "Capital for the Future: Saving and Investment in an Interdependent World,"
World Bank, 2013, http://econ.worldbank.org. *Size of economy*: "Real GDP (2010
Dollars) Projections." *U.S. Department of Agriculture*, December 2014. USDA
explains data comes from World Bank World Development Indicators, International Financial Statistics of the IMF, IHS Global Insight, and Oxford Economic
Forecasting, as well as estimated and projected values developed by the Economic
Research Service all converted to a 2010 base year. http://www.ers.usda.gov
/data-products/international-macroeconomic-data-set.aspx.

1   LONG MEMORIES

15 *As an Italian journalist*: Tiziano Terzani, *Behind the Forbidden Door: Travels in Un-
known China* (New York: Henry Holt, 1986).

16 *The life of Confucius*: Michael Schuman, *Confucius: And the World He Created* (New
York: Basic Books, 2013); Jeffrey Riegel, "Confucius," *The Stanford Encyclopedia
of Philosophy* (Summer 2013 Edition), ed. Edward N. Zalta, http://plato.stanford
.edu/entries/confucius/.

16 *President Xi and other party leaders*: "Xi Underlines Morality During Confucius
Site Visits," Xinhua, November 28, 2011.

17 *Why this sudden interest*: Schuman, *Confucius*.

17 *Hinduism is present*: "PM Narendra Modi: Hinduism Not A Religion but a Way
of Life," *Times of India*, April 17, 2015; "Narendra Modi Tells About His Sleeping
Habits and Secret of Energy," YouTube, August 31, 2012, http://www.youtube
.com/watch?t=70&v=fkzwi3kpd2c.

18 *dozens gathered around television sets*: William Dalrymple, "All Indian Life Is Here,"
Guardian, August 22, 2008.

18 *many secular, liberal Indians*: Mugdha Variyar, "RSS Chief Bhagwat Repeats India Is

a Hindu Nation, Congress Calls Him Hitler," *International Business Times*, August 18, 2014; "Analysis: RSS Aims for a Hindu Nation," BBC News, March 10, 2003; Robert Kaplan, "India's New Face," *Atlantic*, April 2009; Victor Mallet, "Hindu Nationalist Flex Muscles in Narendra Modi's India," *Financial Times*, August 25, 2014.

19 *Some sources say*: Kaplan, "India's New Face."

19 *While Hinduism is a native religion*: Robert Kaplan, *Monsoon: The Indian Ocean and the Future of American Power* (New York: Random House, 2010), p. 28; Stanley Wolpert, *A New History of India*, 8th ed. (Oxford: Oxford University Press, 2008), p. 109.

20 *Indian Islam today*: "Why India's Muslims Are So Moderate," *Economist Explains*, September 7, 2014.

20 *While most Indians*: "Census: Hindu Share Dips Below 80%, Muslim Share Grows but Slower," *Indian Express*, January 24, 3015.

20 *During his first visit*: "Chinese President Xi Jinping Speaks on China-India Relations," CCTV.COM, September 19, 2014.

21 *Over the centuries*: Sugata Bose and Ayesha Jalal, *Modern South Asia: History, Culture, Political Economy* (Delhi: Routledge, 2011).

21 *one senior Indian politician*: "Address by the Defence Minister Pranab Mukherjee at the Carnegie Endowment for International Peace, Washington, DC on India's Strategic Perspectives," June 27, 2005.

22 *As historian Jonathan Spence explains*: Jonathan Spence, *The Search for Modern China* (New York: Norton, 1991), p. 7.

22 *to dramatize China's role*: "Chinese Trade in the Indian Ocean," Asia Society, 2015.

22 *Deng also used Zheng*: Tami Blumenfield and Helanie Silverman, *Cultural Heritage Politics in China* (New York: Springer Science & Business Media, 2013), p. 269.

23 *"Instead of establishing colonies"*: Xuejun Tian, Ambassador of the People's Republic of China in the Republic of South Africa, "Friendship and Cooperation for a Better Future of China-Africa Relations," Forum on China-Africa Cooperation, July 17, 2012, http://www.focac.org/eng/zxxx/t951978.htm.

23 *China then accounted for*: "Xi Jinping and the Chinese Dream," *Economist*, May 2, 2013.

23 *The Chinese do not*: Spence, *The Search for Modern China*, p. 122.

24 *cash crop*: "World Drug Report 2008: A Century of International Drug Control," United Nations Office on Drugs and Crime, p. 174.

24 *Civil society groups*: Dong Wang, *China's Unequal Treaties: Narrating National History* (Lanham, MD: Lexington Books, 2008).

25 *"Fifty years after"*: Soutik Biswas, "'Opium Financed British Rule in India,' interview with Amitav Ghosh," BBC, June 23, 2008.

25 *This made it attractive*: Bose and Jalal, *Modern South Asia*.

26 *His country, he said*: "Select Speeches and Writings of Nehru," Jawaharlal Nehru Commemorative International Conference, 2014, http://www.nehruinternationalconference2014.com/nehru_speech30.aspx.

27 *It is telling that Chinese*: Sulmann Wasif Khan, "Cold War Co-operation: New Chinese Evidence on Jawaharlal Nehru's 1954 Visit to Beijing," *Cold War History*, February 18, 2011, http://www.tandfonline.com/doi/pdf/10.1080/14682745.2010.494300.

27 *"I have been especially interested"*: "Chinese President Xi Jinping Speaks on China-India Relations," CCTV.com, September 19, 2014.

28 *"Under the leadership"*: Xiyun Yang, "People, You Will See This Film. Right Now," *New York Times,* June 24, 2011.

28 *Others reacted cynically*: Li Chen, "Communist Party Drags China to Propaganda Film Flop, Netizens React," *Tech Asia,* July 6, 2011.

29 *Many in today's Chinese elite*: John Garnaut, "The Creation Myth of Xi Jinping," *Foreign Policy,* October 19, 2012; Joseph Kahn, "Bo Yibo, Leader Who Helped Reshape Chinese Economy, Dies at 98," *New York Times,* January 17, 2007.

29 *One asked him*: Adam Century, "Retracing Mao Zedong's Long March—by Motorcycle," *Atlantic,* January 10, 2014.

29 *Japanese soldiers killed*: Rana Mitter, *China's War with Japan, 1937–1945: The Struggle for Survival* (London: Allen Lane 2014).

29 *More than one hundred thousand*: Nicholas Kristof, "China's Films: More Propaganda, Less Art," *New York Times,* August 1, 1991.

30 *One widely used textbook*: Howard French, "China's Textbooks Twist and Omit History," *New York Times,* December 6, 2004.

30 *In September 2015*: Didi Kirsten, "Excerpts from Xi Jinping's Speech," *New York Times,* September 3, 2015.

31 *Some students say*: Author conversation with Beida students. See also Joseph Khan, "Where's Mao? Chinese Revise History Books," *New York Times,* September 1, 2006.

32 *They merely wanted*: Wolpert, *A New History of India,* p. 267; Bose and Jalal, *Modern South Asia.*

34 *More than a million people*: Ramachandra Guha, *India After Gandhi: The History of the World's Largest Democracy* (New York: Houghton Mifflin Harcourt, 2007), p. 31.

35 *Later China also gave*: Bruce Riedel and Pavneet Singh, "U.S.-China Relations: Seeking Strategic Convergence in Pakistan," Brookings Institution, January 2010, http://www.brookings.edu/~/media/research/files/papers/2010/1/12%20us%20china%20relations%20riedel/0112_us_china_relations_riedel.pdf.

2 THE NATIONS THEY BUILT

37 *As Xi himself explains*: Jinping Xi, "Full Text of Xi Jinping's Speech on China-U.S. Relations in Seattle," Xinhua, September 23, 2015.

38 *Disguised as a Sikh*: "When NaMo, Swamy Played Hide and Sikh," *Times of India,* June 27, 2015.

38 *They, along with national ministers*: Kenneth Lieberthal and Michael Oksenberg, *Policy Making in China: Leaders, Structures, and Processes* (Princeton, NJ: Princeton University Press, 1988).

39 *As writer Evan Osnos reported*: Evan Osnos, "Born Red," *New Yorker,* April 6, 2015; John Garnaut, "The Creation Myth of Xi Jinping," *Foreign Policy,* October 19, 2012; Edward Wong, "Tracing the Myth of a Chinese Leader to Its Roots," *New York Times,* February 16, 2011.

39 *It became the famous*: Patricia Buckley Ebrey, *The Cambridge Illustrated History of China* (Cambridge: Cambridge University Press, 2010).

40 *The Communist Party*: A useful resource on China's complex government structure

is Susan Lawrence, "China's Political Institutions and Leaders in Charts," Congressional Research Service, November 12, 2013.

40 *Security guards and staff*: Barbara Demick, "China Leaders' Summer Retreat to Beidaihe Shrouded in Secrecy," *Los Angeles Times,* August 16, 2012.

40 *People are promoted to*: Victor Shih, Christopher Adolph, and Mingxing Liu, "Getting Ahead in the Communist Party: Explaining the Advancement of Central Committee Members in China," *American Political Science Review,* February 2012, http://faculty.washington.edu/cadolph/articles/ChinaRank.pdf.

41 *From the Politburo*: John Dotson, "The China Rising Leaders Project, Part 2: Outcomes of the Chinese Communist Party's 18th National Congress," U.S.-China Economic and Security Review Commission, December 21, 2012, http://www.uscc.gov/sites/default/files/Research/18th-CCP_PartyCongress_Overview.pdf.

41 *The NPC's nearly three thousand members*: "China's Internet Bigwigs Turn to Politics," *China Daily Mail,* April 8, 2103.

41 *A law is only*: Kevin O'Brien, *Reform without Liberalization: China's National People's Congress and the Politics of Institutional Change* (Cambridge: Cambridge University Press, 2008); "China's State Organizational Structure," Congressional Executive Commission on China, 2015, http://www.cambridge.org/us/academic/subjects/politics-international-relations/comparative-politics/reform-without-liberalization-chinas-national-peoples-congress-and-politics-institutional-change.

42 *Xi Jinping grew up*: Damian Grammaticas, "Xi Jinping: Cave Dweller or Princeling?" BBC News, February 14, 2012.

42 *He adds that*: Osnos, "Born Red."

42 *Without elections or other checks*: Kerry Brown, *The New Emperors: Power and the Princelings in China* (London: Tauris, 2014).

42 *The elder Xi*: Osnos, "Born Red."

42 *Xi Jinping's elite birth*: Ibid.

42 *While Xi was shocked*: Ibid.

43 *In the 1970s*: "Xi Jinping: One of China's Top Future Leaders to Watch," Brookings Institution, 2015, http://www.brookings.edu/about/centers/china/top-future-leaders/xi_jinping.

44 *Many Chinese derisively*: Dexter Roberts, "China's Civil Service Loses Luster Amid Graft Crackdown," *Bloomberg Business,* December 1, 2014.

44 *Two senior military leaders*: Susan Lawrence, "China's Political Institutions and Leaders in Charts," Congressional Research Service, November 12, 2013, http://www.fas.org/sgp/crs/row/R43303.pdf.

44 *No part of the government*: Michael S. Chase et al., "China's Incomplete Military Transformation," RAND Corporation, February 2015.

45 *Unlike in federalist*: William Antholis, *Inside Out, India and China* (Washington, DC: Brookings Institution Press, 2014), pp. 22–23.

45 *Chongqing, small by Chinese standards*: "Chongqing," Deutsche Bank Research, January 2016.

46 *But when he veered*: John Garnaut, *The Rise and Fall of the House of Bo* (Melbourne: Penguin Books, 2012); Rachel Lu, "Bo Xilai, The Man Chinese Cyberspace Could Not Forget," *Foreign Policy,* April 2, 2015; Angus, "Chavez and Bo Xilai Gone: Death of a Political Model?" *Tea Leaf Nation,* March 12, 2013; Kevin Lu, "The Chongqing Model Worked," *Foreign Policy,* August 8, 2012.

46   *While Bo was convicted*: Wang Xiaopeng, "Commentary: CPC Will Not Tolerate Defiance of Discipline," Xinhua, January 25, 2013.

47   *These days leaders remain*: Barbara Demick, "China Leaders' Summer Retreat to Beidaihe Shrouded in Secrecy," *Los Angeles Times,* August 16, 2012; Cary Huang, "Communist Party Leaders Gather in Beidaihe for Annual Policy Summit," *South China Morning Post,* August 6, 2014.

47   *Yet China scholars*: Alice Miller, "The Trouble with Factions," Hoover Institution, 2015, http://www.hoover.org/sites/default/files/research/docs/clm46am.pdf.

48   *It defines "security" as everything*: "National Security Law of the People's Republic of China," unofficial translation by China Law Translate. The law passed on July 1, 2015.

48   *The "populists" often*: Cheng Li, "Rule of the Princelings," Brookings Institution, 2013, http://www.brookings.edu/research/articles/2013/02/china-xi-jinping-li.

49   *When they see Xi*: Osnos, "Born Red."

49   *According to one source*: Author conversation with Chinese official at Ditchley Conference, June 2015.

49   *The Standing Committee's*: Lawrence Sullivan, *Historical Dictionary of the People's Republic of China* (Lanham, MD: Scarecrow Press, 2007), p. 399.

49   *Most Chinese jaws dropped*: "How China Is Ruled," BBC News, 2015.

50   *To make this point*: Author conversation with Chinese official at Ditchley Conference, June 2015.

50   *The most infamous*: Alice Miller, "The CCP Central Committee's Leading Small Groups," Hoover Institution, 2015, http://www.hoover.org/sites/default/files/uploads/documents/CLM26AM.pdf.

51   *The government announced*: Gabriel Wildau, "China Pension Reform Targets Civil Servant Privileges," *Financial Times,* January 15, 2015; Mi Jiayi, "Reform of China's Pension System has 40 Million Civil Servants Wary," CCTV America, January 28, 2015.

51   *Recently the government*: Huaxia, "China's Legislature Passes Toughest Food Safety Law Amendment," Xinhua, April 24, 2015.

51   *The forum is China's*: Edward Tse, *China's Disruptors: How Alibaba, Xiaomi, Tencent, and Other Companies Are Changing the Rules of Business* (New York: Penguin, 2015).

51   *At the 2013 forum*: Author conversation and emails with participant in Yabuli Forum who does not want to be named, June 20–25, 2015. See also Tse, *China's Disruptors;* "Freaking Out: Is Private Enterprise Under Attack," *Economist,* September 14, 2013.

52   *They were made to*: "China Media Bulletin: Issue No. 93," *Freedom House,* September 20, 2013 ; Lily Kuo, "Business and Politics Aren't Mixing Well for China's Billionaire Entrepreneurs Turned Civil Activists," *Quartz,* January 23, 2014 ; Josh Chin, "Outspoken Chinese Businessman Reappears After Long Hiatus," *Wall Street Journal,* April 21, 2015.

52   *"This means some people"*: Author conversation with Chinese diplomat, June 20, 2015.

54   *Party officials often*: Edward Luce, *In Spite of the Gods: The Rise of Modern India* (London: Anchor, 2008), pp. 215–17.

55   *The BJP proudly announced*: Parth M. N. and Shashank Bengali, "India's Ruling

Bharatiya Janata Party Claims Title of World's Largest," *Los Angeles Times,* March 30, 2015.

55 *Narendra Modi was drawn*: For many of the details of Modi's early life and career, I rely on Andy Marino, *Narendra Modi: A Political Biography* (Delhi: HarperCollins, 2014).

56 *She banned opposition groups*: "Emergency Taught Me Some Compromises Are Not Possible: Arun Jaitley," *Indian Express,* June 25, 2014; Shamik Ghosh, "Who Is Rajnath Singh," NDTV, February 20, 2014.

56 *India's constitution also*: Stanley Wolpert, *A New History of India* (Oxford: Oxford University Press, 2008), p. 377; Marino, *Narendra Modi*, p. 48.

57 *His annual "Vibrant Gujarat" business*: William Antholis, *Inside Out, India and China* (Washington, DC: Brookings Institution Press, 2014), p. 98.

57 *CEO after CEO took*: Author conversation with Nicholas Burns, former U.S. undersecretary of state for Political Affairs, December 2013.

57 *While Andhra Pradesh*: See "U/S Burns in Hyderabad: A New Consulate, More Visas And Limitless Growth," WikiLeaks, 2015.

58 *Rates of child hunger*: Christophe, "Gujarat Elections: The Sub-Text of Modi's 'Hattrick'—High Tech Populism and the 'Neo-middle Class,'" *Studies in Indian Politics* 1, no. 1 (2013): 79–95. See also Antholis, *Inside Out, India and China*, p. 99; "Of Secrecy and Stunting," *Economist,* July 2, 2015.

59 *In the Rajya Sabha*: Author conversation with senior U.S. State Department official, July 30, 2015; author interview with Pramit Pal Chaudhuri, foreign editor of *Hindustan Times,* November 9, 2015; author interview with Montek Singh Ahluwalia, October 13, 2015.

59 *More than four hundred thousand aspirants*: "Understanding the Competition in Civil Services Examination," Civil Service India, 2015.

3 ECONOMIC TAKEOFF

63 *The "unequal treaties"*: John Delury, "How 19th Century History Explains Present-Day China," *Atlantic,* September 6, 2013.

63 *Mao Zedong and his colleagues*: Angus Maddison, "Chinese Economic Performance in the Long Run," OECD Development Center, 1998.

64 *The economic dislocation*: "Average GDP growth increased from approximately 4 percent prior to reform to 9.5 percent during 1978-2005." Loren Brandt and Thomas G. Rawski, eds., *China's Great Economic Transformation* (New York: Cambridge University Press, 2008). According to economist Angus Maddison, China's actual average annual real GDP between the end of the Revolution and Cultural Revolution was about 4.4 percent. See also Wayne M. Morrison, "China's Economic Rise: History, Trends, Challenges, and Implications for the United States," Congressional Research Service, June 14, 2015, https://www.fas.org/sgp/crs/row/RL33534.pdf. From 1952 to 1978, China's per capita GDP rose by 3 percent per year. Xiaodong Zhu, "Understanding China's Growth: Past, Present, and Future," *Journal of Economic Perspectives,* October 23, 2012, http://homes.chass.utoronto.ca/~xzhu/paper/JEP2012.pdf.

64 *By the end of the Cultural Revolution*: Zhu, "Understanding China's Growth."

64 *After proposing reforms*: "China Mourns Death of Ex-Leader's wife, Communist Stalwart," CNN, August 10, 2009.

65 *Deng's team kick-started*: Larry Lau, "What Makes China Grow," Chor Talk Distinguished Lecture on Global Economics and Finance, November 24, 2014, p. 21.

65 *At the end of the season*: David Kestenbaum and Jacob Goldstein, "The Secret Document That Transformed China," NPR, January 20, 2012.

65 *Rural per capita income*: Carl Riskin, *China's Political Economy* (New York: Oxford University Press, 1987), p. 292.

66 *As Deng gradually opened the economy*: "Town and Village Enterprises (TVE)," Washington State University, 2015, http://public.wsu.edu/~hallagan/EconS391 /weeks/week5/TVE.pdf.

67 *China's economic boom*: Economist Park and Lau argue that Chinese growth between 1965 and 1995 was over 80 percent due to growth in tangible capital (investments in infrastructure, factories, machines etc.) and virtually not at all due to technical progress. Lau, "What Makes China Grow," p. 26.

68 *When asked later*: McGregor, Richard, *The Party: The Secret World of China's Communist Rulers* (New York: Harper Perennial, 2011), p. 226. *See also* Chong-En Bai, Chong-En, Chang-Tai Hsieh, and Zheng Song, "Crony Capitalism with Chinese Characteristics,." University of California, San Diego, May 2014., http://china .ucsd.edu/_files/pe2014/10062014_Paper_Bai_Chong.pdf.

68 *Many of these local*: Benjamin Kang Lim, Matthew Miller, and David Stanway, "Exclusive: China to Lay off Five to Six Million workers, Earmarks at Least $23 Billion," Reuters, March 3, 2016.

68 *In contrast to the past*: Author interview with Chong-En Bai, economics professor at Tsinghua University, April 15, 2015.

69 *Chinese economists I speak to*: For public sources, see for example World Bank World Development Indicators, 2013, http://data.worldbank.org/indicator /GC.DOD.TOTL.GD.ZS; Richard Dobbs, Susan Lund, Jonathan Woetzel, and Mina Mutafchieva, "Debt and (Not Much) Deleveraging," McKinsey Global Institute, February 2015, http://www.mckinsey.com/insights/economic_studies /debt_and_not_much_deleveraging.

69 *This means that by 2030*: "China 2030: Building a Modern, Harmonious, and Creative Society," World DataBank, World Bank, March 26, 2013, http://databank .worldbank.org/Data/Views/reports/tableview.aspx. The share of China's population age sixty and over will rise from 12 percent in 2010 to almost 25 percent in 2030, and to more than 33 percent by 2050, http://www.worldbank.org/con tent/dam/Worldbank/document/China-2030-complete.pdf.

69 *China's rotting rivers*: Beina Xu, "China's Environmental Crisis," Council on Foreign Relations, April 25, 2014, http://www.economist.com/node/21538687.

70 *China's environmental degradation*: "Conservation," Paulson Institute, 2015.

70 *Headlines call China*: Gordon Chang, "The Doomed Dragon: Is China's Economy Headed for a Crash Landing?" *National Interest*, November 6, 2014; Henry Blodget, "Yes, at Some Point China Will Implode," *Business Insider*, June 17, 2013; Trefor Moss, "5 Signs of the Chinese Economic Apocalypse," *Foreign Policy*, July 2, 2012; Robert J. Samuelson, "Will China Crash?" *Washington Post*, September 6, 2015. See also Heather Stewart, "Global Investors Brace for China Crash, Says IIF," *Guardian*. October 1, 2015; "Productivity Brief 2015," Conference Board Productivity Brief, 2015.

71   *As a result*: These favorable fundamentals help China grow in the long term, but they are not sufficient. They existed even when China's growth stagnated between 1949 and 1978. During that time, as we saw earlier, China's economy was artificially inefficient due to central planning. Lau, "What Makes China Grow," pp. 12–14 and chart 12.

71   *In inland cities*: Leland Miller, China Beige Book, December 15, 2015. China Beige Book conducts a comprehensive survey of over two thousand Chinese firms every quarter, so their data is usually more accurate and comprehensive than the economic figures generated by China's central government. See also Malcolm Scott, "China Beige Book Shows Disturbing Economic Deterioration," *Bloomberg News*, December 17, 2015.

72   *Chinese households with one child*: Keyu Jin, "China's Two Child Consumption Engine," Project Syndicate, January 6, 2016.

72   *It is growing health-care spending*: Franck Le Deu, Rajesh Parekh, Fangning Zhang, and Gaobo Zhou, "Health Care in China: Entering 'Unchartered' Waters," McKinsey & Company, November 2012.

72   *There are some signs*: Lau, "What Makes China Grow," pp. 35–36. China's economy grew around 7.4 percent in 2014, and consumer spending grew around 12 percent. See also Alexandra Stevenson, "As Growth Slows, China Pins Hopes on Consumer Spending," *New York Times*, January 19, 2015; Gabriel Wildau, "China's New Normal for Consumption," *Financial Times*, October 28, 2014.

72   *The services industry*: Gabriel Wildau, Tom Mitchell, and Jamil Anderlini, "China Growth Lowest Since 2009 as Property and Manufacturing Drag," *Financial Times*, April 15, 2015; Mark Magnier, "China Surprises with 7% Growth in Second Quarter," *Wall Street Journal*, July 21, 2015; Eswar Prasad, "The Path to Sustainable Growth in China," Brookings Institution, April 22, 2015; Daniel H. Rosen, "A Deeper Assessment of China's 2014 Growth," Center for Strategic and International Studies, January 2015.

73   *Chinese consumers*: Everett Rosenfeld, "Apple's Cook on China to Cramer: Seeing Strong Growth in China Through July, August," CNBC, August 24, 2015.

74   *Local governments are privatizing*: "Developments in the Reform of China's State-Owned Enterprises," Franklin Templeton Investments, June 9, 2015.

74   *In March 2016*: Benjamin Kang Lim, Matthew Miller, and David Stanway, "Exclusive: China to Lay off Five to Six Million workers, Earmarks at Least $23 Billion," Reuters, March 3, 2016.

75   *Innovation fever is gripping*: "A Question of Utility," *Economist*, August 8, 2015.

76   *In the eighteenth century*: Ilhan Niaz, *Old World Empires: Cultures of Power and Governance in Eurasia* (London: Routledge, 2014), p. 139. See also Douglas M. Peers, *India Under Colonial Rule: 1700–1885* (Oxford: Taylor & Francis, 2006), p. 16; Gurcharan Das, *India Grows at Night: A Liberal Case for a Strong State* (London: Penguin Global, 2012).

76   *Economist Angus Maddison*: J. Bolt and J. L. van Zanden, "The World Economy," Maddison Project, 2014, http://www.ggdc.net/Maddison/other_books/HS-8_2003.pdf.

77   *There is evidence*: Neeladri Bhattacharya, *Pastoralists in a Colonial World*, in David Arnold and Ramachandra Guha, eds., *Nature, Culture, Imperialism: Essays on the Environmental History of South Asia* (Delhi: Oxford University Press, 1998), pp. 49–85; Anand Swamy, "Land and Law in Colonial India," Williams

College, December 2010, http://web.williams.edu/Economics/wp/Swamy
LandAndLawInColonialIndia.pdf.

77   *As Britain became more efficient*: See, for example, David Clingingsmith and Jeffrey G. Williamson, "India's De-Industrialization Under British Rule: New Ideas,
New Evidence," National Bureau of Economic Research, June 2004, http://www
.nber.org/papers/w10586. This explanation for deindustrialization was a potent weapon in the Indian nationalists' critique of colonial rule. See, for example,
Romesh Dutt, *The Economic History of India* (Delhi: Government of India Pub-
lications Division, 1960) and Jawaharlal Nehru, *The Discovery of India* (London:
Meridian Books, 1947).

77   *The government protected*: Sugata Bose and Ayesha Jalal, *Modern South Asia: History, Culture, Political Economy* (London: Routledge, 2011), p. 175; "The Indian
Economy Since Independence," Florida Atlantic University, 2015, http://home
.fau.edu/sghosh/web/images/India%20talk.pdf.

77   *The government hamstrung*: Stanley Wolpert, *A New History of India* (Oxford: Oxford University Press, 1991–99).

78   *Its share of world trade*: *India's Economy at the Midnight Hour*, East Asia Analyti-
cal Unit, Department of Foreign Affairs and Trade, Commonwealth of Australia,
1994, p. 10.

78   *In the midst of this crisis*: Wolpert, *A New History of India*.

78   *From 1991 to 2011*: Elvis Picardo, "India Is Eclipsing China's Economy as Brightest BRIC Star," Investopedia.com.

78   *The stock market boomed*: Kartikay Mehotra and Unni Krishnan, "One Year in, Modi
Euphoria Fades Along with Indian Stocks," *Bloomberg Business,* May 12, 2015.

78   *This opening*: For a detailed account of this, see Thomas L. Friedman, *The World Is
Flat: A Brief History of the Twenty-First Century* (New York: Farrar, Straus & Giroux, 2007).

80   *More than a third of GDP*: Das, *India Grows at Night*.

80   *Since Modi came*: The 2015 budget allocated $20 billion, and the 2016 budget al-
located 32.7 billion to infrastructure. The full text of Modi's 2016 budget speech is
available in "Union Budget 2016: Full Text of Arun Jaitley's Budget Speech," *Times
of India*, February 29, 2016.

81   *This is a good start*: Richard Abadie and Manish Agarwal. "Gridlines—The Opportunity and Challenge of India's Infrastructure," *PWC India*, 2015; Beina Xu and
Eleanor Albert. "Governance in India: Infrastructure," Council on Foreign Relations, October 1, 2014.

81   *To make India attractive*: "Ease of Doing Business Index (1=Most Business-Friendly Regulations)," World Bank, 2015.

81   *India's power minister*: Piyush Goyal, power, coal, and renewables minister, speech
to Aspen Strategy Group, January 2015.

82   *He made the land acquisition*: William Antholis, *Inside Out, India and China: Local
Politics Go Global* (Washington, DC: Brookings Institution, 2013), p. 98.

82   *Yet recent surveys*: "IGCC Business Monitor 2014—Key findings Among German
Investors in India," Indo-German Chamber of Commerce, April 30, 2014, http://
indien.ahk.de/fileadmin/ahk_indien/Bilder/2014_IGCC_Business_Monitor
/IGCC_Survey_2014_Report_-_CNC_2nd_Draft__30_04_2014_.pdf.

82   *State bureaucracies*: K. Alan Kronstadt, "India's New Government and Implications for U.S. Interests," Congressional Research Service, August 7, 2014.

84 *As former U.S. Treasury secretary*: For a detailed version of this argument, see Henry Paulson, *Dealing with China: An Insider Unmasks the New Economic Superpower* (New York: Grand Central Publishing, 2015); "United States Exports to China," *Trading Economics*, 2015.

84 *Chinese companies invested*: Thilo Hanemann and Cassie Gao, "Chinese FDI in the US: 2015 Recap," Rhodium Group, January 19, 2016.

84 *Chinese investment has directly*: "New Neighbors: Chinese Investment in the United States by Congressional District," National Committee on US-China Relations and Rhodium Group, May 2015.

85 *Indian foreign direct investment*: A NASSCOM report in September 2015 claims that Indian IT companies alone created 156,000 direct and 255,00 indirect jobs in the United States in 2015. "Contributions of India's Tech Industry to the US Economy," *NASSCOM*, 2015.

85 *Trade between the two giants*: Data from India's Ministry of Commerce April 2014 to May 2015, http://commerce.nic.in/eidb/. Data for 2000 was reported on website of Indian embassy in China "Economic and Trade Relations," accessed October 5, 2015, http://www.indianembassy.org.cn/DynamicContent.aspx?MenuId=97&SubMenuId=0.

85 *China is already*: According to CIA *World Factbook* data for 2013, 31 countries count the United States as their largest exports partner, 26 countries count the United States as their largest imports partner. *World Factbook*, CIA, 2015.

4 SHARING THE WEALTH

89 *In India the 1.5 million waste pickers*: Author interview with Supriya Bhardwaj, January 9, 2015. For another estimate of the number of waste-pickers, see Tom Szaky, *Outsmart Waste: The Modern Idea of Garbage and How to Think Our Way Out of It* (San Francisco: Berrett-Koehler, 2014).

91 *"It is positive peer pressure"*: Author interview with Supriya Bhardwaj and Mohammad Asif, January 9, 2015.

91 *In total, almost 65 million Indians*: Author's calculation based on data for "Population" and "Poverty headcount ratio at $1.25 a day (PPP) (% of population)" for 2012 (latest available) from World Bank World Development Indicators database, last updated December 19, 2014, http://databank.worldbank.org/data/home.aspx. Many countries have their own definitions of poverty. I use the World Bank data to make it easier to compare across countries. The World Bank anchors its international poverty lines to the national poverty lines used in the poorest countries.

91 *Almost a third of the rural Indians*: Government of India Planning Commission, *Report of the Expert Group to Review the Methodology for Measurement of Poverty*, June 2014, http://planningcommission.nic.in/reports/genrep/pov_rep0707.pdf.

92 *By contrast, China's economic juggernaut*: World Data Bank, World Bank, 2014. Author's calculation based on data for 2011 (latest available) from World Bank World Development Indicators database, last updated December 19, 2014, http://data bank.worldbank.org/data/home.aspx.

92 *While the GDP per person*: "All the Parties in China," *Economist*, February 24, 2011.

92 *Until recently the government*: Author interview with Sungmin Rho, March 3, 2015. Estimates vary, but expert Sungmin Rho cites data released by China's National

Health and Family Planning Commission in November 2015 that there are approximately 220 million migrant workers living in China's cities today. One academic paper published in 2011 reports the size of the rural migrant labor pool is growing, from about 50–60 million in the early 1990s to exceed 150 million in 2009. Experts assume it is higher today. Kam Wing Chan, "China, Internal Migration," University of Washington. http://faculty.washington.edu/kwchan/Chan-migration.pdf.

93 *The* Economist *estimates that 61 million*: "Pity the Children," *Economist,* October 17, 2015.

95 *A manufacturing industrial revolution*: Hemal Shah, "Transition to Labor Law Reform: State-Level Initiatives & Informal Sector Labor Relations," *Indian Journal of Industrial Relations* 50, no. 1, July 2014, https://www.questia.com/library/journal/1G1-382085723/transition-to-labor-law-reform-state-level-initiatives.

97 *According to some experts*: Sugata Bose and Ayesha Jalal, *Modern South Asia* (New York: Oxford University Press, 2004), p. 10.

97 *The most famous*: Author interview with Pramit Pal Chaudhuri, foreign editor of the *Hindustan Times*, November 9, 2015.

97 *Indian columnist Shikha Dalmia*: Shikha Dalmia, "The Tragic Truth About India's Caste System," Reason.com, January 24, 2012. http://reason.com/archives/2012/01/24/the-tragic-truth-about-indias-caste-syst.

98 *In spite of a "reservation" system*: 7.5 percent of university places are reserved for Scheduled Tribes, 15 percent reserved for Scheduled Castes, and an additional 27 percent reserved for Other Backward Classes. Sheetal Sekhrit, "Affirmative Action and Peer Effects: Evidence from Caste Based Reservation in General Education Colleges in India," University of Virginia, March 2011, http://people.virginia.edu/~ss5mj/Peereffects_April12_2011.pdf.

98 *While this is an improvement*: Kanchan Srivastava, "Dalits in India Are Poorer than Muslims: Government Report," DNAIndia.com, November 7, 2014.

98 *The previous Congress Party government budgeted*: Raymond Zhong, "This Is Why India Has to Shrink the Subsidy Raj," *Wall Street Journal,* July 7, 2014.

99 *In 2016 the Modi government*: "Union Budget 2016: Full Text of Arun Jaitley's Budget Speech," *Times of India,* February 29, 2016.

99 *In addition, the National Rural Employment Guarantee Act (NREGA)*: Government of India, "The National Rural Employment Guarantee Act, 2005," September 7, 2005, http://nrega.nic.in/rajaswa.pdf. According to the government's data, spending on NREGA for fiscal year 2015–16 (April to March) was 33700.00 Crore ($5 billion USD) of total expenditure. http://indiabudget.nic.in/ub2015-16/bag/bag8.pdf.

99 *In spite of these large investments*: "Social Spending Is Falling in Some Countries, but in Many Others It Remains at Historically High Levels," Organisation for Economic Co-operation and Development, November 2014, http://www.oecd.org/els/soc/OECD2014-Social-Expenditure-Update-Nov2014-8pages.pdf (using data from 2012). These numbers are notoriously hard to measure, because not everyone has the same definition of "social spending." The Asian Development Bank calculated in 2009 that India's spending on social protection expenditures as a percent of GDP was 1.7 percent and China's was 5.4 percent for that year. This data includes spending on social insurance, social assistance, and labor market programs, and includes food subsidies. "The Social Protection Index, Assessing Results for

Asia and the Pacific," Asian Development Bank, 2013, http://www.adb.org/sites/default/files/publication/30293/social-protection-index.pdf.

99 *To reduce infant mortality*: Government of India Planning Commission, "Twelfth Five Year Plan (2012–2017) Social Sectors," vol. 3, 2012, http://planningcommission.gov.in/plans/planrel/fiveyr/12th/pdf/12fyp_vol3.pdf.

99 *Currently, Indian public spending*: World Bank, "Health Expenditure, Public (% of GDP)," World Development Indicators, accessed December 2015, http://data.worldbank.org/indicator/SH.XPD.PUBL.ZS. World Bank data for "Health expenditure, total % of GDP"—which includes both public and private spending on health care—was 5.4 percent for China, 4.0 percent for India, and 17.9 percent for United States in 2012. http://data.worldbank.org/indicator/SH.XPD.TOTL.ZS. The Planning Commission's twelfth Five Year Plan reported: "Public expenditure on Core Health (both plan and non-plan and taking the Centre and States together) was about 0.93 per cent of GDP in 2007–08. It has increased to about 1.04 per cent during 2011–12. It needs to increase much more over the next decade." "Twelfth Five Year Plan (2012–2017) Social Sectors," Planning Commission, Government of India, vol. 3, 2012, http://planningcommission.gov.in/plans/planrel/fiveyr/welcome.html.

99 *Under it the government*: Aditya Kalra, "Modi Govt Puts Brakes on India's Universal Health Plan," Reuters, March 27, 2015.

100 *It covers three-fourths of rural*: Joshua Meltzer, "Improving Indian Food Security: Why Prime Minister Modi Should Embrace the WTO," Brookings Institution, May 16, 2014, http://www.brookings.edu/research/opinions/2014/05/16-world-trade-organization-india-food-security-meltzer; Avinash Kishore, P. K. Joshi, and John Haddinott, "A Novel Approach to Food Security," International Food Policy Research Institute, 2013, http://www.ifpri.org/gfpr/2013/indias-right-to-food-act#fn10, citing V. P. Sharma, "Food Subsidy in India: Trends, Causes, and Policy Reform Options, Working Paper 2012-08-02," Ahmedabad, India, Indian Institute of Management, 2012.

100 *Yet according to its own data*: Raymond Zhong and Vibhuti Agarwal, "India Clings to Disputed Food Subsidies," *Wall Street Journal*, October 1, 2014.

100 *Because of corruption*: Government of India Ministry of Women and Child Development, "Rapid Survey on Children 2013–2014," http://wcd.nic.in/issnip/National_Fact%20sheet_RSOC%20_02-07-2015.pdf.

101 *At the lowest end of the income scale*: "All-India Report on Evaluation of NREGA: A Survey of Twenty Districts," Institute of Applied Manpower Research, March 8, 2009; Findings from All-India Report on Evaluation of NREGA: A Survey of Twenty Districts, December 2008 (data pertains to the year 2006–07), http://planningcommission.gov.in/reports/genrep/rep_NREGA_03-08-2009.pdf.

101 *The Modi government*: "Pradhan Mantri Jan Dhan Yojana," Department of Financial Services, Government of India, accessed January 22, 2016, http://pmjdy.gov.in.

101 *Instead of having state energy firms*: Manoj Kumar, "Modi's Welfare Reforms May Need to Be Bigger and Bolder," Reuters, October 8, 2014.

101 *Massive income disparities existed*: Yu Xie and Xiang Zhou, "Income Inequality in Today's China," *Proceedings of the National Academy of Sciences*, February 20, 2014, http://www.pnas.org/content/111/19/6928.full.

102 *Not surprisingly, many peasants fled*: Jason Young, *China's Hukou System: Mar-

kets, Migrants and Institutional Change (New York: Palgrave Macmillan, 2013), pp. 36–39.

102   *However, because of poor administration*: Hsiao-Hung Pai, *Scattered Sand: The Story of China's Migrants* (London: Verso, 2013), p. 4. This is an excellent work on the history of China's rural-urban migration, the hukou system, and the problems migrants face today.

102   *Most Chinese say*: "China's Imaginary Middle Class," *Wilson Quarterly*, http:// wilsonquarterly.com/stories/chinas-imaginary-middle-class/; Kam Wing Chan, "Crossing the 50 Percent Population Rubicon: Can China Urbanize to Prosperity?" *Stanford Social Innovation Review*, p. 71.

103   *Migrants who do not work in factories*: See photojournalism and essay by Sim Chi Yin, http://viiphoto.com/articles/chinas-rat-tribe/.

103   *While nearly all rural residents*: World Bank, *China 2030: Building a Modern, Harmonious, and Creative Society* (Washington, DC: World Bank, 2013), p. 276.

103   *In 2011, the government*: "China's Twelfth Five Year Plan (2011–2015)," http://www.britishchamber.cn/content/chinas-twelfth-five-year-plan-2011 -2015-full-english-version. See also Celia Hatton, "Taking Stock of China's Five Year Economic Model," BBC, October 30, 2015.

103   *Chinese health minister Li Bin optimistically*: Michael Woodhead, "Health Insurance Cover for 95% of Chinese? More like 30%," *China Medical News*, November 12, 2014, http://www.chinesemedicalnews.com/2014/11/health-insurance-cover-for -95-of.html.

103   *Yet the rural insurance*: "Ending Apartheid," *Economist*, April 19, 2014. The only migrants who have urban health insurance are those with formal job contracts, but not even one in five enjoys that privilege. A Chinese government survey of more than six hundred migrant workers found that only a third had health insurance where they lived. Even in their hometown, only about 60 percent of migrant workers had health coverage, because—even where there were clinics available—the poorly educated residents weren't aware that they are permitted to use these services and could not fill out the complex paperwork they needed. See also Woodhead, "Health Insurance Cover for 95% of Chinese?"

104   *It is worried that migrants*: "The Great Transition," *Economist*, March 22, 2014.

104   *In late 2015 the government*: "Reform meeting tables healthcare, environmental, hukou proposal," *Xinhuanet*, December 10, 2015.

104   *It also said it would grant*: Chun Han Wong and Laurie Burkitt, "China Moves to Normalize the Status of Millions of People on Margins," *Wall Street Journal*, December 11, 2015.

105   *Critics of the proposed reforms note*: Elizabeth Economy, "Time for Xi To Reform His Reforms," *Forbes*, June 2, 2015.

105   *Many migrant workers are surprisingly suspicious*: "China's Hukou Reform Plan Starts to Take Shape," *Wall Street Journal*, August 4, 2014. The *Journal* reports that an August 2014 survey found that 90 percent of migrant workers don't want an urban hukou.

105   *The Chinese government is also working hard*: For a more detailed discussion, see World Bank, *China 2030: Building a Modern, Harmonious, and Creative Society* (Washington, DC: World Bank, 2013).

105   *Xi pledged in November 2015*: Zhuang Pinghui, "China's Poverty Relief 'Grading Scheme' Will Rate Top Officials Based on How Much They Improve Life for the Poor," *South China Morning Post*, February 17, 2016.

106 *The United States continues to give*: In China, spending by the U.S. Agency for International Development (USAID) for 2015 was $12.85 million for clean environ-
ment, disaster readiness, economic opportunity, higher education, HIV/AIDS,
private sector competitiveness, rule of law and human rights, and social assistance.
India: USAID spending for 2015 was $83.59 million for agriculture, basic educa-
tion, clean environment, family planning, and reproductive health. http://beta
.foreignassistance.gov/explore/country/China; http://beta.foreignassistance.gov
/explore/country/India.

106 *And these corporations*: Angel Gurria, "Promoting a Fair and Sustainable Welfare
System in China," Organisation for Economic Co-operation and Development,
March 23, 2014. "A growing number of companies are doing their part by en-
rolling their workers in government programs that grant industrial injury benefits, maternity leave and unemployment benefits." http://www.oecd.org/social
/promoting-a-fair-and-sustainable-welfare-system-in-china.html.

107 *In 2010, farmers in the PepsiCo program*: "Partnership with Farmers," PepsiCo
India, http://www.pepsicoindia.co.in/purpose/environmental-sustainability
/partnership-with-farmers.html.

107 *In particular, research has shown*: For this argument, see for example, Ann Tutwiler
and Matthew Straub, "Making Agricultural Trade Reform Work for the Poor,"
International Food & Agricultural Trade Policy Council, June 2005, http://
www.agritrade.org/Publications/Position%20Papers/Making%20Trade%20
Work%20for%20the%20Poor.pdf.

108 *Whenever the United States*: Raymond Zhong and Vibhuti Agarwal, "India Clings
to Disputed Food Subsidies," *Wall Street Journal,* October 1, 2014, http://www
.wsj.com/articles/india-clings-to-disputed-food-subsidies-1412188174. ("At a
WTO meeting in March, the U.S. presented a two-page briefing on its own experiences with farm subsidies, saying that for much of the 20th century, it too stock-
piled grain to support growers' incomes and protect them from price shocks. But
beginning in the 1970s, the paper said, 'difficult political decisions were made to
reform an agricultural policy that was ineffective, costly and difficult to administer.'
The Indian delegation was 'nonplussed,' according to a person present at the meeting. This person paraphrased India's reaction as: 'Nobody has asked to hear this
paper. Why are you even putting it in front of us?' ")

5 BANISHING BRIBES

111 *A scheme uncovered in India*: "Indian Government Hit by Corruption Scandals,"
Reuters, February 18, 2011.

111 *In China, one estimate*: Minxin Pei, "Corruption Threatens China's Future," Carnegie Endowment for International Peace, October 2007, http://carnegieendow
ment.org/files/pb55_pei_china_corruption_final.pdf.

112 *At least seventy detainees*: Anderlini, Jamil. "Profile: Wang Qishan, China's anticorruption tsar." *The Financial Times,* August 5, 2014.

113 *Former U.S. Treasury Secretary Henry Paulson*: Author conversation with former
U.S. Treasury Secretary Henry Paulson, December 2014, and emails, October
2015. See also Jamil Anderlini, "Profile: Wang Qishan, China's Anti-Corruption
Tsar," *Financial Times,* August 5, 2014.

113   *Under Wang Qishan's leadership*: "Wang Qishan Work Report to the Sixth Plenary
      Session of the Standing Committee," Xinhua News Agency, January 12, 2016,
      http://www.ccdi.gov.cn/xwtt/201601/t20160124_73389.html.

113   *In October 2014*: "Xu Caihou Confesses to Taking Bribe," Xinhua, October 28,
      2014.

114   *"The PLA was always"*: Author conversation with senior official of Chinese Foreign
      Ministry in Washington, D.C., November 2014.

114   *In June 2015*: For details of Zhou's corruption, see, for example, Matt Schiavenza,
      "With Zhou Yongkang's Downfall, Xi Jinping Becomes Most Powerful Chinese
      Ruler In Decades," *International Business Times*, July 29, 2014; "China Corruption:
      Life Term for Ex-Security Chief Zhou," BBC, June 11, 2015.

114   *Caixin ran lengthy*: See, for example, "Zhou's Dynasty," Caixin Online, 2014.

115   *The* New York Times: David Barboza, "Billions in Hidden Riches for Family of
      Chinese Leader," *New York Times*, October 25, 2012; William Wan, "China Blocks
      New York Times Web Site After Report on Leader's Wealth," *Washington Post*, Oc-
      tober 26, 2012.

115   *For example, after the 2015*: Sophia Yan, "Top China banker implicated in corrup-
      tion probe," CNN. November 3, 2015.

116   *It begins with*: Jeremy Page, "China Spins New Lesson from Soviet Union's Fall,"
      Wall Street Journal, December 10, 2013.

116   *An article in the Party-run journal*: The original *Seeking Truth* article appears in Chi-
      nese at http://www.qstheory.cn/zl/bkjx/201401/t20140123_315814.htm.

117   *The U.S. government*: U.S. Attorney's Office Northern District of Illinois, "Six De-
      fendants Indicted in Alleged Conspiracy to Bribe Government Officials in India to
      Mine Titanium Minerals," April 2, 2014.

117   *He argues that*: Jagdish Bhagwati, "Getting Corruption Right," Project Syndicate,
      December 29, 2010.

117   *Indians reacted angrily*: Jim Yardley, Jim. "India Arrests Former Chief of Common-
      wealth Games," *New York Times*, April 25, 2011.

117   *broadband licenses were sold*: Alan K. Kronstadt, Paul K. Kerr, Michael F. Martin,
      and Bruce Vaughn, "India: Domestic Issues, Strategic Dynamics, and U.S. Rela-
      tions," Congressional Research Service, September 2011, p. 43. India's defense
      budget for 2011–12 was $36.1 billion. "India's Defense Budget 2011–2012," *De-
      fense Review Asia*, May 3, 2011, http://www.defencereviewasia.com/articles/98
      /INDIA-S-DEFENCE-BUDGET-2011-12.

117   *In the "coalgate" scandal*: Vikas Bajaj and Jim Yardley, "Scandal Poses a Riddle: Will
      India Ever Be Able to Tackle Corruption?" *New York Times*, September 15, 2012.

118   *A court recently*: Niharika Mandhana and Saurabh Chaturved, "Indian Court Sum-
      mons Ex-Prime Minister in Coal Corruption Probe," *Wall Street Journal*, March 11,
      2015.

118   *Although Hazare has*: Jason Burke, "Anna Hazare: The Divisive Face of a New
      India," *Observer*, August 20, 2011.

119   *The most successful parties*: Author conversation with Baijayant "Jay" Panda, mem-
      ber of Indian Parliament in the Lok Sabha, January 10, 2015.

121   *"They are less worried"*: Author conversation with Nandan Nilekani as part of
      Aspen Strategy Group, January 13, 2013.

121   *The program has been*: Unique Identification Authority of India, Dashboard Sum-

mary, https://portal.uidai.gov.in/uidwebportal/dashboard.do, accessed November 17, 2015.

121 *He explained how*: Author conversations and review of case studies with Srikanth Nadhamuni, former Aadhaar chief engineer, January–May 2014, September 2015.

122 *This reduced his actual pay*: "A Cost-Benefit Analysis of Aadhaar," National Institute of Public Finance and Policy, 2012, http://planningcommission.nic.in/reports /genrep/rep_uid_cba_paper.pdf.

122 *The World Bank said*: "World Development Report 2016: Digital Dividends," The World Bank Group, 2016, http://www-wds.worldbank.org/external/default /WDSContentServer/WDSP/IB/2016/01/13/090224b08405ea05/2_0/Ren dered/PDF/World0developm0000digital0dividends.pdf.

123 *Four decades ago*: For additional details of Hong Kong's anticorruption reforms, see for example Tony Kwok Man-wai, "Comprehensive & Effective Approach to Anti-Corruption: "The Hong Kong ICAC Experience, with a View on New Approaches in the Fight Against Corruption," http://www.kwok-manwai.com /articles/Comprehensive_Effective.html. See also Augusto Lopez-Claros, "Six Strategies to Fight Corruption," World Bank, May 14, 2014; "Hong Kong: The Facts," Information Services Department, Hong Kong Special Administrative Region Government, September 2014, http://www.gov.hk/en/about/abouthk /factsheets/docs/icac.pdf.

124 *The ICAC commission*: Diego Laje, "What China Can Learn from Hong Kong in Its Fight Against Corruption," CNN, October 15, 2013.

124 *While most anticorruption*: Ugo Panizza, "Public Sector Wages and Bureaucratic Quality: Evidence from Latin America," *Economía* (2012), pp. 2, 97; Alberto Ades and Rafael Di Tella. "The New Economics of Corruption: A Survey and Some New Results," *Political Studies* 45 (1997): 496–515; Daniel Treisman, "The Causes of Corruption: A Cross-National Study," *Journal of Public Economics* 76 (2000): 399–457; Daniel Treisman, "What Have We Learned About the Causes of Corruption from Ten Years of Cross-National Empirical Research?" *Annual Review of Political Science* 10 (2007): 211–44.

124 *China is experimenting*: "China's millions of government workers to get huge 60% pay raise," *Market Watch*, January 22, 2015.

124 *Various studies have found*: See, for example, Lopez-Claros, "Six Strategies to Fight Corruption."

125 *The efforts to move*: Beina Xu, "Governance in India: Corruption," Council on Foreign Relations, September 4, 2014.

125 *From one of the most corrupt*: Jose Ugaz, "Corruption Is Threatening Economic Growth for All," Transparency International, 2014, http://www.transparency .org/cpi2014/results.

125 *Although both countries*: Austin Ramzy, "U.S. Repatriates Fugitive Businessman Long Sought by China," *Wall Street Journal*, September 18, 2015.

126 *Although the effort*: "India, U.S. to Collaborate on 'Digital India' Initiative to Enhance E-governance and E-services," Indian News Service, January 17, 2015.

126 *U.S. laws have already*: Tencent conducts its own internal audits to battle corruption and recently voluntarily gave information on an employee's wrongdoing to Chinese police. Paul Carsten and Arathy S Nair, "Former Tencent employees, including Alibaba exec, held in China graft probe," Reuters, July 10 2015.

6 THE YOUNG AND THE OLD

129 *In 2008, President Hu Jintao*: Condoleezza Rice, *No Higher Honor* (New York: Crown Publishers, 2011).

129 *Almost 200 million*: Many of the details and statistics about China's rapidly aging population come from Mark Frazier, *Socialist Insecurity: Pensions and the Politics of Uneven Development in China* (Ithaca, NY: Cornell University Press, 2010). See also his shorter article, "No Country for Old Age," *New York Times*, February 18, 2013; and Robert Pozen, "Tackling the Chinese Pension System," Paulson Institute, July 2013. For U.S. data, see http://www.aoa.acl.gov/aging_statistics/fu ture_growth/future_growth.aspx#gender.

129 *China's working-age*: A comprehensive analysis of China's demographic shift can be found in "Global Trends 2030: Alternative Worlds," National Intelligence Council, December 2012, http://www.dni.gov/index.php/about/organization /global-trends-2030. See also "China 2030: Building a Modern, Harmonious, and Creative Society," World DataBank, World Bank, March 26, 2013, http://data bank.worldbank.org/Data/Views/reports/tableview.aspx. The share of China's population age sixty and over will rise from 12 percent in 2010 to almost 25 percent in 2030, and to more than 33 percent by 2050. http://www.worldbank.org /content/dam/Worldbank/document/China-2030-complete.pdf.

130 *Indian Prime Minister Modi*: "Regional Economic Outlook: Asia and Pacific," International Monetary Fund, 2012, http://www.imf.org/external/pubs/ft /reo/2012/APD/eng/areo0412.html.

130 *In 2030, almost 70*: "Asia Pacific: Managing Spillovers and Advancing Economic Rebalancing," International Monetary Fund, April 2012, http://www.imf.org /external/pubs/ft/reo/2012/APD/eng/areo0412.pdf.

130 *After he spoke*: Author meeting with Arun Jaitley, Indian finance minister, January 10, 2015.

131 *When I ask why*: Author interviews with David "Yunheng" Zhou, December 2–3, 2014, and March 8, 2015.

132 *It is a patchwork*: For statistics in this paragraph, see Mark W. Frazier, "No Country for Old Age," *New York Times*, February 18, 2013, and Mark Frazier, *Socialist Insecurity: Pensions and Politics of Uneven Development in China*. (Ithaca: Cornell University Press, 2010).

133 *In 2011, government workers*: For statistics in this paragraph, see Ren Ro, "China Turning Gray Over Pension Reform Stress," China File, January 12, 2015.

133 *The employees' individual accounts*: When unpaid pensioners recently launched fierce protests, the local governments "borrowed" from the individual accounts in order to pay the benefits for current retirees. In some provinces up to 90 percent of individual accounts have been raided this way. Zuo Xuejin, "Designing Fiscally Sustainable and Equitable Pension Systems in China," International Monetary Fund, January 9–10, 2013, http://www.imf.org/external/np/seminars /eng/2013/oapfad/pdf/zuo.pdf.

133 *Accurate numbers*: Frazier, *Socialist Insecurity*.

133 *This gap will rise*: CAAS study, http://www.nisd.cass.cn/news/734589.htm.

133 *Almost 400 million*: "China 2030: Building a Modern, Harmonious, and Creative Society," World DataBank, World Bank, March 26, 2013, http://www.worldbank .org/content/dam/Worldbank/document/China-2030-complete.pdf.

133 *As China scholar Mark Frazier*: Frazier, *Socialist Insecurity.*

134 *The government made*: "China Will Set Plan for Raising Retirement Age Next Year: Media," Reuters, February 28, 2016.

134 *There was no dedicated*: Gabriel Wildau, "China Pension Reform Targets Civil Servant Privileges," *Financial Times*, January 15, 2015; "Reform of Pension System Worries Public Sector Workers," *Sina English*, January 19, 2015.

135 *Even if they are aware*: For all statistics on China's health-care system in the following paragraphs, see *China 2030: Building a Modern, Harmonious, and Creative Society* (Washington, DC: World Bank, 2013), p. 302. For U.S. numbers, see "National Health Expenditures 2013 Highlights," Centers for Medicare & Medicaid Services, accessed March 2015, http://www.cms.gov/Research-Statistics-Da ta-and-Systems/Statistics-Trends-and-Reports/NationalHealthExpendData /downloads/highlights.pdf.

135 *On average, households*: Americans in 2014 on average spent 6.4 percent of their total income on healthcare. "Consumer Expenditures (Annual) News Release," Bureau of Labor Statistics, 2015, http://www.bls.gov/news.release/cesan.htm. https:// www.whitehouse.gov/assets/documents/071009_FINAL_Middle_Class _Task_Force_report2.pdf. In India, averages vary depending on source—one Princeton paper cited that health accounts for 9–15 percent of household expenditure. "Catastrophic Health Expenditure and Poor in India: New Evidence from a Nation-wide Survey," Princeton University, accessed March 2015, http:// paa2012.princeton.edu/papers/121467.

136 *It needs to nearly double*: The World Health Organization reports that in 2011 (latest WHO data available), China only had 1.49 physicians—including both general practice and specialists—per 1,000 people. For comparison, in the same year, the United States had 2.45. This lack of physicians can lead to incredibly long waits and rushed appointments leading to sub-standard care for Chinese patients. The author calculates that with 1.2 billion people China would need to train about one million doctors to reach the same ratio as the U.S. Global Health Observatory data repository, World Health Organization, 2015. http://apps.who.int/gho/data/node.main.A1444.

136 *The insurance industry*: David Taylor, "Special Report: The Chinese Insurance Market," Insurance Echo, http://cdn.crccasia.com/files/Insurance-Echo.pdf. See also "'Ticking Time Bombs': China's Health Care System Faces Issues of Access, Quality and Cost," Wharton School, University of Pennsylvania, June 26, 2013, http:// knowledge.wharton.upenn.edu/article/ticking-time-bombs-chinas-health-care -system-faces-issues-of-access-quality-and-cost/.

137 *As the population gets wealthier*: For details of how other countries have taken advantage of their demographic dividend, see "Malawi's Pathway to a Demographic Dividend," Population Reference Bureau, 2014, http://www.prb.org/pdf14 /malawi-demographic-dividend-2014.pdf; John Ross, "Understanding the Demographic Dividend," Policy Project, September 2004, http://www.policyproject .com/pubs/generalreport/demo_div.pdf.

139 *India spent*: For India data, see World Bank, "Expenditure on Education as % of Total Government Expenditure," World Development Indicators, accessed March 2015, http://data.worldbank.org/indicator/SE.XPD.TOTL.GB.ZS. For data on China and the United States, see, "Education at a Glance 2011," Organisation for Economic Co-operation and Development, 2013, http://www.oecd.org/educa tion/skills-beyond-school/48677215.pdf.

139 *Children from the poorest*: "Right to Education Act," India Development Gateway, accessed November 8, 2015, http://www.indg.in/primary-education/policies andschemes/right-to-education-bill.

139 *According to UNICEF*: Unicef India, http://www.unicef.org/india/education .html.

139 *which means an impressive*: "ASER 2014: Annual Status of Education Report," ASER, January 2015, http://img.asercentre.org/docs/Publications/ASER%20 Reports/ASER%202014/National%20PPTs/aser2014indiaenglish.pdf.

139 *The state governments*: "Global Initiative on Out-of-School Children: South Asia Regional Study," UNICEF Regional Office for South Asia, 2014, http://www .unicef.org/education/files/SouthAsia_OOSCI_Study__Executive_Summa ry_26Jan_14Final.pdf.

139 *He added that*: Author conversation with Kapil Sibal, Indian minister of communications and information technology, January 2012. Statistics confirmed at "India Has One of the Lowest Teacher-Student Ratios: Expert," *Economic Times*, November 9, 2009. See also Vikas Pota, "Why Modi Needs to Focus on Education," *Hindu Business Online*, August 8, 2014.

140 *Even when there are teachers*: Author interview with Supriya Bhardwaj, Chintan employee, January 2015. For information on Indian teachers, see Pota, "Why Modi Needs to Focus on Education."

140 *Only about a third*: "Education at a Glance 2012," Organisation for Economic Co-operation and Development, May 2012, http://www.oecdilibrary.org/doc server/download/9612041ec005.pdf?expires=1423697003&id=id&accname= guest&checksum=2E848FE098F4CE468D8595ED339DC111.

140 *Muslim and lower-caste boys*: Omkar Goswami and Kabir Malik, "A Shocking Divide," *India Today*, August 14, 2006.

141 *As many as 83 percent*: Neerja Jetley, "India's Lost Generation: A Systemic Risk," CNBC, September 17, 2014; Geeta Anand, "India Graduates Millions, but Too Few Are Fit to Hire," *Wall Street Journal*, April 5, 2011.

141 *Kela himself is a graduate*: Author interview with Ajay Kela, February 27, 2015.

142 *The foundation has researched which jobs*: Author interviews with Ajay Kela and Romesh Wadwani, June 2011, June 2013, July 2014, and February 2015.

143 *She is diminutive*: Author interview with Suman Singh, March 25, 2014. See also notes from Wadhwani Foundation case study about her experience. In this case, the Haryana state Education Ministry used and implemented the courses provided by the Wadhwani Foundation.

144 *This means training*: "Faster, Sustainable and More Inclusive Growth: An Approach to the 12th Five Year Plan," draft, National Planning Commission of India, August 2011, p. 127.

144 *In addition, it is consolidating*: Arun Jaitley, "Budget 2015: National Skills Mission to Consolidate Initiatives of Different Ministries," *Economic Times*, February 28, 2015; Apeksha Kaushik, "Budget 2015: Jaitley's 10 Initiatives for Skilling India," *Economic Times*, March 2, 2015.

144 *In February 2016*: "Union Budget 2016: Full Text of Arun Jaitley's Budget Speech," *Times of India*, February 29, 2016.

145 *The U.S. government is already*: "U.S.-India Higher Education and Skills Development Cooperation," U.S. Department of State, September 30, 2014. http://www .state.gov/r/pa/prs/ps/2014/09/232334.htm.

145   *This is by far*: Author interview with Sebastian Thrun, September 23, 2015.

145   *The Khan Academy*: Rozelle Laha, "Khan Academy Launches Hindi Math Tutorials in India," *Hindustan Times*, December 7, 2015.

7 HALF THE SKY

147   *"I tried to run on the mud path"*: I interviewed Atreyee Sen, associate professor of anthropology at the University of Copenhagen, on April 28, 2015. Banwari Devi was interviewed by Sen in 2009. Some of Sen's primary research and interviews are also published at Atreyee Sen, "Women's Vigilantism in India: A Case Study of the Pink Sari Gang," Encyclopedia of Mass Violence, published December 20, 2012, accessed June 1, 2015, http://www.massviolence.org/Women-s-Vigilantism-in -India-A-Case-Study-of-the-Pink-Sari.

148   *Their fame has spread around the world*: "Gulabi Gang," http://www.gulabigang.in; Shweta Desai, "Gulabi Gang: India's Women Warriors," Al Jazeera, March 4, 2014.

148   *During the colonial period*: The custom was outlawed by India's British rulers in 1829 following demands by Indian reformers; however, the practice continues in remote areas in the country. In 1987 a new law had to be passed to again ban this medieval practice, Commission of Sati (Prevention) Act, 1987 (No. 3 of 1988).

149   *India's 1949 constitution*: Constitutional and Legal Provisions for Women in India, National Legal Research Desk, http://nlrd.org/womens-rights-initiative/legis lations-laws-related-to-women/constitutional-and-legal-provisions-for-women -in-india; Beina Xu, "Governance in India: Women's Rights," Council on Foreign Relations, June 10, 2013, http://www.cfr.org/india/governance-india-womens -rights/p30041; "Sexual Harassment of Women at Work Place Act, 2013," *Gazette of India*, April 13, 2013, http://ncw.nic.in/PDFFiles/SexualHarassmentofWom enatWorkPlaceAct2013.pdf.

150   *two percentage points*: "Economic Survey of India 2014," Organisation for Economic Co-operation and Development, 2014, http://www.oecd.org/economy /economic-survey-india.htm. Scholars generally agree that increased women's participation in the labor force can boost GDP. B. Loko and Mame A. Diouf, "Revisiting the Determinants of Productivity Growth: What's New?" IMF Working Paper, 2009 09/225; D. Cuberes and M. Teignier, "Gender Gaps in the Labor Market and Aggregate Productivity," Sheffield Economic Research Paper SERP 2012017, 2012; DeAnne Aguirre, Leila Hoteit, Christine Rupp, and Karim Sabbagh, *Empowering the Third Billion. Women and the World of Work in 2012* (San Francisco: Booz, 2013).

151   *The entire factory*: Author interview with Sungmin Rho (PhD, Stanford), assistant professor at Graduate Institute of International and Development Studies at Geneva, May 14, 2015.

151   *Mao Zedong's Communist Party*: Frances Conway, "Women in the Chinese Revolution," Marxist Fourth International, August 1951, https://www.marxists.org /history/etol/newspape/fi/vol12/no04/conway.html.

151   *While there are some powerful*: Laurie Burkitt, "No Consensus: China Debate on Women's Roles," *Wall Street Journal*, September 13, 2013.

151   *Overall, almost 70 percent*: Steve Crabtree and Anita Pugliese, "China Outpaces India for Women in the Workforce," Gallup, November 2, 2012, http://www.gallup

.com/poll/158501/china-outpaces-india-women-workforce.aspx. For U.S. statistics, see "Women in the Labor Force: A Databook," BLS Reports, May 2014, http://www.bls.gov/opub/reports/cps/womenlaborforce_2013.pdf.

152 *China also has 29 million female entrepreneurs*: "The Sky's the Limit," *Economist*, November 26, 2011.

152 *She took a crowded train home*: Author interview with Sungmin Rho, May 14, 2015.

153 *In addition, due to unofficial*: Didi Tatlow, "Women in China Face Rising University Entry Barriers," *New York Times*, October 7, 2012.

153 *In contrast to China*: Crabtree and Pugliese, "China Outpaces India for Women in the Workforce." See also "Economic Survey of India 2014," Organisation for Economic Co-operation and Development, 2014, http://www.oecd.org/economy/economic-survey-india.htm.

153 *Many women in India*: Divya Arya, "Why Motherhood Makes Indian Women Quit Their Jobs," BBC News, April 23, 2015.

153 *Women currently run many of India's*: Palash Ghosh, "Shattered Glass Ceiling: Indian Female Executives Thriving in Banking Industry, but Ordinary Women Need Greater Access to Loans," *International Business Times*, February 26, 2014. ("Arundhati Bhattacharya . . . heads the State Bank of India . . . Vijayalakshmi R. Iyer serves as chairwoman of Bank of India; Archana Bhargava is the boss at United Bank of India; while Shubhalakshmi Panse reigns as chairwoman of Allahabad Bank. According to *Business Today* . . . state-owned banks headed by women control 45 percent of all of India's public sector bank deposits and 50 percent of all loans. Within the private sector, Chanda Kochhar is chairwoman and managing director of ICICI Bank, India's largest private bank and second-largest of all banks by assets; while Shikha Sharma heads the Axis Bank. In addition, Indian women lead the local subsidiaries of foreign-based banking giants like JPMorgan Chase & Co., Morgan Stanley, Bank of America Corp., and Royal Bank of Scotland.")

154 *Most of these women*: "Women-Owned Businesses in India," International Finance Corporation, 2014. http://www.ifc.org/wps/wcm/connect/a17915804336f2c29 b1dff384c61d9f7/Womenownedbusiness1.pdf?MOD=AJPERES. As a result, more than 90 percent of India's 90 million plus microfinance clients are women.

154 *The government provided*: Nupur Acharya, "India Inaugurates First Women's-Only Bank," *Wall Street Journal*, November 19, 2013.

154 *Chinese Internet giant Alibaba*: Catherine Chu, "Alibaba Affiliate Ant Credit Launches $80M Financing Program for Female Entrepreneurs in China," *TechCrunch*, January 27, 2015.

154 *So far, women's empowerment*: Mohammed Uzair Shaikh, "Narendra Modi at Facebook Townhall: Women Equal Partner in Development of India," India.com, September 27, 2015.

155 *By 2030, studies suggest*: Nicholas Eberstadt, "The Demographic Future," https://www.foreignaffairs.com/articles/2010-11-01/demographic-future.

155 *Young men also prefer to work*: Author interview with Sungmin Rho, May 14, 2015.

155 *Studies estimate the figure*: Beina Xu, "Governance in India: Women's Rights," Council Foreign Relations, June 10, 2013, http://www.cfr.org/india/governance-india-womens-rights/p30041.

156 *In 2014, there were 900 girls*: World Factbook, Central Intelligence Agency, https://www.cia.gov/Library/publications/the-world-factbook/fields/2018.html.

156 *The pink ladies like Banwari*: Rhitu Chatterjee, "Abortion in India Is Legal Yet Women Are Still Dying," NPR, October 2, 2014.

156 *Wealthier and better-educated*: Prabhat Jha et al., "Trends in Selective Abortions of Girls in India: Analysis of Nationally Representative Birth Histories from 1990 to 2005 and Census Data From 1991 to 2011," *Lancet*, May 24, 2011, http://www .thelancet.com/journals/lancet/article/PIIS0140-6736(11)60649-1/abstract.

156 *While China doesn't officially*: Leta Hong-Fincher, *Leftover Women: The Resurgence of Gender Equality in China* (New York: Zed Books, 2014).

157 *In it, a thirty-three-year old woman*: Ibid. See also http://www/pri.org/sto ries/2013-01-28/china-investing-big-convincing-leftover-women-get-married.

157 *Many of her girlfriends*: Author conversations with Gong Ting, December 1–3, 2014.

157 *Divorce has been legal in China*: "Marriages and Crude Marriage Rates, by Urban /Rural Residence: 2007–2011," UN Stats, http://unstats.un.org/unsd/demo graphic/products/dyb/dyb2011/Table23.pdf and Table 25.

157 *In India divorce is still rare*: Muneeza Naqvi, "India's Divorce Rate Rising," *Huffington Post*, April 12, 2012; Sukrit Sabhlok, "What's Responsible for Rising Divorce Rates," Indian Link, October 16, 2014. http://www.indianlink.com.au/whats-re sponsible-for-rising-divorce-rates/.

158 *More than two-fifths of Indian women*: "Improving Children's Lives; Transforming the Future," UNICEF, http://www.unicef.org/publications/files/Improving _Children_s_Lives_-_Transforming_the_Future_9_Sep_2014.pdf.

158 *According to a government survey*: For government statistics, see "National Family Health Survey, India," International Institute for Population Sciences, http:// www.rchiips.org/nfhs/nfhs3.shtml. See also Yugantar Education Society, "A Study of Nature, Extent, Incidence and Impact of Domestic Violence Against Women in the States of Andhra Pradesh, Chhattisgarh, Guhrat, Madhya Pradesh and Maharashtra," Planning Commission, Government of India, http://planning commission.nic.in/reports/sereport/ser/stdy_demvio.pdf.

159 *The amounts can be oppressive*: "Marriage," Country Studies, http://countrys tudies.us/india/86.htm; Nishita Jha, "The Despicable Persistence of the Dowry in India," *Daily Beast*, August 4, 2014.

159 *The Indian government estimates*: "India Court Says Women 'Misusing' Dowry Law," BBC News, July 3, 2014.

159 *After her husband's death*: Dean Nelson, "Indian Entrepreneur Found Hanging After 'Dowry Harassment' Complaint," *Telegraph*, October 30, 2012.

159 *Again, the Indian government*: "India Court Says Women 'Misusing' Dowry Law," BBC News, July 3, 2014. The Dowry Prohibition and the Protection of Women from Domestic Violence Act are also often misused by women filing false cases. "The simplest way to harass is to get the husband and his relatives arrested under this provision. According to the National Crime Records Bureau statistics, nearly 200,000 people, including 47,951 women, were arrested over dowry offences in 2012, but only 15% of the accused were convicted, the court said."

159 *Even if she could leave*: Author interview with Atreyee Sen, associate professor, Department of Anthropology, University of Copenhagen, Denmark, April 28, 2015.

159 *A 2014 study reported*: Gina Duclayan, "New Study from Population and Development Review Finds That Indian Women with More Resources than Their Husbands Face Heightened Risk of Violence," Population Council, March 25, 2014.

http://www.popcouncil.org/news/new-study-from-population-and-develop
ment-review-finds-that-indian-women-wi.

160 *Dowry-related violence*: "Dowry-Related Violence," Advocates, http://www
.stopvaw.org/dowry-related_violence; Carol Williams, "India 'Dowry Deaths'
Still Rising Despite Modernization," *Los Angeles Times,* September 5, 2013.

160 *The news coverage and chauvinist comments*: "Protests in India After Delhi Gang-
Rape Victim Dies," BBC, December 29, 2012; Julie McCarthy, "Indian Rape
Case Ignites National Debate on Abuse of Women," NPR, December 28, 2012,
("The president's son, Abhijit Mukherjee, ignited new anger Thursday when he
described the women protesting the rape as 'dented and painted,' as if they were a
damaged car"); "Ban Skirts as School Uniform: BJP Legislator," Hindustan Times,
December 29, 2012, (a legislator in Rajasthan suggested banning skirts as a uniform for girls in schools, citing it as the reason for increased cases of sexual harassment and rape).

160 *The four rapists*: Terrence McCoy, "The Chilling Reason the Delhi Bus Gang-Rapist
Blames His Victim," *Washington Post,* March 3, 2015. (Mukesh Singh, one of the
five convicted of the crime, in an interview maintained the rape was the victim's
fault. She was out too late and was asking for trouble. "A decent girl won't roam
around at nine o'clock at night," he told Udwin. "A girl is far more responsible for
rape than a boy. Housework and housekeeping is for girls, not roaming in discos
and bars at night doing wrong things, wearing wrong clothes. About 20 percent of
girls are good.")

161 *Studies estimate that between*: Simon Denyer, "Battered Women in China Could Finally Get a Measure of Legal Protection," *Washington Post,* March 6, 2014.

161 *Kim spent hours and hours waiting*: Louisa Lim, "American Woman Gives Domestic Abuse a Face, and Voice, in China," NPR, February 7, 2013, http://www.npr
.org/2013/02/07/171316582/american-woman-gives-domestic-abuse-a-face
-and-voice-in-china.

161 *In early 2015*: Andrew Jacobs, "Chinese Women's Rights Activists Fall Afoul of
Officials," *New York Times,* April 5, 2014.

162 *Human Rights Watch*: "China: Submission by Human Rights Watch to the National People's Congress on the Draft Anti-Domestic Violence Law," Human
Rights Watch, September 25, 2014.

162 *Several of India's powerful chief ministers*: Anandiben Mafatbhai Patel is the in-
cumbent chief minister of Gujarat; Vasundhara Raje, chief minister of Rajasthan
since 2013; Mamata Banerjee, chief minister of West Bengal since 2011; and Selvi
J. Jayalalithaa, chief minister of Tamil Nadu since 2015.

162 *Only 12 percent of India's parliamentarians*: "Women in National Parliaments,"
Inter-Parliamentary Union, May 1, 2015, http://www.ipu.org/wmn-e/classif
.htm. In the 1990s, India's government introduced a quota of 33 percent women
in small, local elected bodies called *panchayats*. This significantly improved governance at these local levels and helped to train a new generation of potential female
politicians.

162 *Studies from the United States show*: "Why Women Matter: Lessons About Women's
Political Leadership from Home and Abroad," White House Project's Why Women
Matter Summit, Washington, D.C., March 3, 2003, http://scholar.harvard.edu/
shaunashames/files/whp_wwm_briefing_book_post_conf.pdf; Rosa Linda T.
Miranda, "Impact of Women's Participation in Decision Making," United Nations,

December 2005, http://www.un.org/womenwatch/daw/egm/eql-men/docs /EP.7_rev.pdf. See also "Politics and Leadership," Women in the World Foundation, April 22, 2013, http://womenintheworld.org/solutions/track/politics -and-leadership.

163 *"They felt so threatened"*: Author conversation with Margaret Alva, April 2013; "Women Reservation Bill Will Be Tabled in Parliament After Careful Consideration: Government," NDTV, April 23, 2015.

163 *Global research has found*: Anja Manuel and Justine Isola, "Beyond Malala: Progress for Pakistan's Women," *Daily Beast,* May 8, 2013.

164 *In May 2015, Alibaba started*: Susan Wang, "Alibaba Women's Conference: The Buzz from Female Leaders," Alizila, May 20, 2015, https://www.alizila.com/ali baba-womens-conference-buzz-female-leaders.

164 *After some research*: Author conversation with Sebastian Thrun, October 25, 2015.

164 *Ernst & Young started*: Astrid Tuminez, "Rising to the Top?" Asia Society, April 2012, http://sites.asiasociety.org/womenleaders/wp-content/uploads/2012/04 /Rising-to-the-Top-Final-PDF.pdf.

165 *Political science research shows*: Craig Volden, University of Virginia; Alan E. Wiseman, Vanderbilt University; and Dana E. Wittmer, Colorado College, "When Are Women More Effective Lawmakers than Men?" *American Journal of Political Science,* 2013.

8 ENERGY VS. THE ENVIRONMENT

168 *In January 2013*: Jonathan Kaiman, "Chinese Struggle Through 'Airpocalypse' Smog," *Observer,* February 16, 2013.

168 *And recent research*: Rebecca Morelle, "Asian Air Pollution Strengthens Pacific Storms," BBC, April 24, 2014; Yuan Wang et al., "Assessing the Effects of Anthropogenic Aerosols on Pacific Storm Track Using a Multiscale Global Climate Model," *Proceedings of the National Academy of Sciences* 111, no. 19 (May 13, 2014), http://www.pnas.org/content/111/19/6894.full.

169 *Pictures of protesters*: "Environmental Protest in China: Volatile Atmosphere," *Economist,* April 4, 2014.

169 *A government report*: The latest official State of the Environment report recorded 712 cases of "abrupt environmental incidents [protests]" in 2013, up 31 percent from the previous year. http://www.mep.gov.cn/zhxx/hjyw/201406 /W020140605385940287254.pdf.

169 *The World Health Organization*: They are New Delhi, Patna (in the state of Bihar), Gwalior (Madhya Pradesh), and Raipur (Chhattisgarh). World Health Organization. "Ambient (Outdoor) Air Pollution in Cities Database 2014," 2014, http:// www.who.int/phe/health_topics/outdoorair/databases/cities/en/.

170 *We finally concluded*: No new reactors have yet been built under the agreement because the Indian parliament has not yet passed a law that ensures those building the power plants are not liable in case of an accident—as all U.S., French, and Russian builders have insisted. Prime Minister Modi and President Obama announced that they had fixed this liability problem at their summit in January 2015, but there are still some disagreements.

172 *Life expectancy in China's north*: Yuyu Chen, Avraham Ebenstein, Michael Green-
     stone, and Hongbin Li, "Evidence on the Impact of Sustained Exposure to Air
     Pollution on Life Expectancy from China's Huai River Policy," *Proceedings of the
     National Academy of Sciences* 110, no. 32 (August 6, 2013), http://www.pnas.org
     /content/110/32/12936.abstract; Robert A. Rohde and Richard A. Muller, "Air
     Pollution in China: Mapping of Concentrations and Sources," *PLOS One* 10, no. 8
     (August 20, 2015), http://journals.plos.org/plosone/article?id=10.1371/jour
     nal.pone.0135749.
172 *A different study*: For specifics, see "Ambient Air Pollution Among Top Global
     Health Risks in 2010," Health Effects Institute, March 31, 2013. See also Adrija
     Brose, "Air Pollution Killed 35,000 People in the Past 9 Years," *Huffington Post,* July
     8, 2015; "Catching up with China," *Economist,* October 10, 2015.
172 *China is the world's*: U.S. Energy Information Administration, "China," February 4,
     2014, http://www.eia.gov/countries/country-data.cfm?fips=CH.
172 *India's new energy minister*: Author conversation with Energy Minister Piyush
     Goyal as part of Aspen Strategy Group, January 10, 2015.
174 *The supply per person*: Sonia Luthra and Amrita Kundu, "India's Water Crisis:
     Causes and Cures: An Interview with Kirit S. Parikh," National Bureau of Asian Re-
     search, 2013; "China and the Environment: The East Is Grey," *Economist*, August
     10, 2013. For slightly different estimates, see "Catching up with China," *Economist,*
     October 10, 2015; Bappa Majumdar and Sunil Mungara, "Delhi Groundwater
     May Run Dry in 3–5 Yrs: Study," *Economic Times*, December 19, 2012.
175 *The Modi government's current plan*: Adam Jourdan, "Overcrowding on Farms
     Behind Mystery of China's Floating Pigs," Reuters, April 24, 2013; Miao Hong,
     "China Battles Pollution Amid Full-Speed Economic Growth," Embassy of the
     People's Republic of China in the United Kingdom, September 29, 2006, http://
     www.chinese-embassy.org.uk/eng/zt/Features/t274443.htm.
176 *It set out detailed directives*: "Five Year Plan—Transforming Growth Pattern, Cre-
     ate a New Scenario for Scientific Development," CBI China, 2015, http://www
     .cbichina.org.cn/cbichina/upload/fckeditor/Full%20Translation%20of%20
     the%2012th%20Five-Year%20Plan.pdf; "Report on China's Implementation of
     the Millennium Development Goals," Ministry of Foreign Affairs of the People's
     Republic of China, 2015, http://www.fmprc.gov.cn/mfa_eng/zxxx_662805
     /W020150730508595306242.pdf.
177 *When a former Chinese*: Liam Fox, *Rising Tides: Facing the Challenges of a New Era*
     (London: Heron Books, 2013), p. 293.
177 *Engineers would need*: "South Asia's Water: Unquenchable Thirst," *Economist*, No-
     vember 19, 2011.
178 *Powerful state chief ministers*: "India has an elaborate set of laws relating to environ-
     mental protection that dates back to the Water Act in 1974. The central govern-
     ment, through the Ministry of Environment and Forests (MOEF) and the Central
     Pollution Control Board (CPCB), is in charge of planning and formulating na-
     tional policies and standards. Their implementation and enforcement are decen-
     tralized and are the responsibility of the State Pollution Control Boards." Stefania
     Lovo, "The Effect of Environmental Decentralization on Polluting Industries in
     India," Centre for Climate Change Economics and Policy Working Paper No. 160,
     Grantham Research Institute on Climate Change and the Environment Working
     Paper No. 143, January 2014.

178 *Swami Nigamananda*: Padmaparna Ghosh, "A River Runs Through It," *India Today*, June 18, 2011.

179 *local party bosses*: Nat Green, "Positive Spillover? Impact of the Songhua River Benzene Incident on China's Environmental Policy," Wilson Center, March 2009, http://www.wilsoncenter.org/publication/positive-spillover-impact-the-song hua-river-benzene-incident-china-s-environmental.

179 *Since January 2014*: Beina Xu, "China's Environmental Crisis," Council on Foreign Relations, April 25, 2014, http://www.cfr.org/china/chinas-environmental-cri sis/p12608.

180 *The new law*: Guizhen He et al., "Revising China's Environmental Law," *Science* 341, no. 133 (2013); Liu Jianqiang, "China's New Environmental Law Looks Good on Paper," ChinaDialogue, April 24, 2014, https://www.chinadialogue .net/blog/6937-China-s-new-environmental-law-looks-good-on-paper/en. See also "Implementation of China's Environmental Law Vital: Vice Minister," *China-Daily*, April 29, 2014, citing Pan Yue, vice minister, China Ministry of Environmental Protection, stating that although the law is " 'the most powerful legislation in the environmental category' . . . it could still fail without ironclad enforcement." http://www.chinadaily.com.cn/bizchina/greenchina/2014-04/29/content _17473705.htm.

180 *For example, Conoco Phillips paid*: Lucy Hornby, "CNPC Settles China Oil Spill Lawsuit," *Financial Times*, June 26, 2015. See also "Landmark Case on Lead Poisoning in Children Begins in China," *Guardian*, June 12, 2015. (Of the more than fifty residents who originally sued a chemical plant, only eleven remain. Some plaintiffs had withdrawn under pressure from local government officials.)

180 *With surging numbers*: Kenneth Rapoza, "Within Four Years, China to Consume More Oil than U.S.," *Forbes*, August 25, 2013.

180 *While China will lead*: International Energy Agency, "World Energy Outlook Fact Sheet," 2013, http://www.worldenergyoutlook.org/media/weowebsite/fact sheets/WEO2013_Factsheets.pdf.

180 *We are the top three*: Jos G. J. Olivier et al., "Trends in Global CO2 Emissions, 2015 Report," PBL Netherlands Environmental Assessment Agency and European Commission Joint Research Centre, November 2015, http://edgar.jrc.ec.europa .eu/news_docs/jrc-2015-trends-in-global-co2-emissions-2015-report-98184 .pdf.

180 *It is promising*: China increased its CO2 emissions by only 0.9 percent in 2014 compared to 2013, down from 12 percent annual growth a decade earlier. Emissions increased by 7.8 percent in India. Netherlands Environmental Assessment Agency and European Commission Joint Research Centre, "Trends in Global CO2 Emissions: 2015 Report," 2015, http://edgar.jrc.ec.europa.eu/news_docs /jrc-2015-trends-in-global-co2-emissions-2015-report-98184.pdf.

180 *On current pace*: Most scientists agree that the planet needs to cut *total* world greenhouse gas emissions to 15 billion tons of CO2 to stay within the goal of the planet warming by 2 degrees centigrade or less. Even in optimistic scenarios, China will emit 11 billion and India between 4 and 7 billion tons of CO2 by 2030. This very general estimate is the subject of considerable debate, but it provides a useful benchmark. See, for example, Malte Meinhausen, "Greenhouse Gas Emission Targets for Limiting Global Warming to 2 degrees C," *Nature*, April 30, 2009; William Atholis, *Inside Out, India and China* (Washington, DC: Brookings

Institution Press, 2014); Kathy Chen and Stian Reklev, "China Plan to Cap CO2 Emissions Seen Turning Point in Climate Talks," Reuters, June 3, 2014; Sanjoy Majumder, "India Emissions Triple by 2030," BBC, September 2, 2009, "Catching up with China," *Economist,* October 10, 2015.

181 *Xie Zhenhua*: Fiona Harvey, "Paris Climate Change Agreement: The World's Greatest Diplomatic Success," *Guardian,* December 14, 2015.

181 *Senior Indian policymakers*: See, for example, Antholis, *Inside Out, India and China,* p. 154. For data on global emissions see, "Trends in Global CO2 Emissions 2015 Report," European Commission Joint Research Center, 2015, http://edgar .jrc.ec.europa.eu/news_docs/jrc-2015-trends-in-global-co2-emissions-2015 -report-98184.pdf.

181 *While India has not agreed*: Ellen Barry and Coral Davenport, "India Announces Plan to Lower Rate of Greenhouse Gas Emissions," *New York Times,* October 1, 2015; Joshua Busby and Sarang Shidore, "Now Comes the Hard Part: India's Scope for Emissions Mitigation," *Council on Foreign Relations,* December 22, 2015.

182 *Promisingly, India recently removed*: "Catching Up with China," *Economist,* October 10, 2015.

182 *In 2016 the government*: "Union Budget 2016: Clean Environment Cess to In-flate Coal Price, Power Tariffs," February 29, 2016, http://www.india.com /budget-2016/union-budget-2016-clean-environment-cess-to-inflate-coal-price -power-tariffs-993554/ (Accessed March 4, 2016).

182 *Unfortunately, for all the ambitious pronouncements*: Author conversations with En-vironment Minister Prakash Javadekar and Energy Minister Piyush Goyal as part of Aspen Strategy Group, January 9–10, 2015.

182 *Indian Energy Minister Piyush Goyal*: Author conversation with Energy Minister Piyush Goyal as part of Aspen Strategy Group, January 10, 2015.

182 *In fact, even as India*: Krishna N. Das and Tommy Wilkes, "India says Paris climate deal won't affect plans to double coal output," *Reuters,* December 14, 2015.

182 *The renewables strategy*: "Detailed Report on India's National Solar Mission Phase II Batch I," Renewable Energy World, November 5, 2013, http://www.renewable energyworld.com/rea/blog/post/2013/11/detailed-report-on-indias-national -solar-mission-phase-ii-batch-i; D. S. Arora et al., "Indian Renewable Energy Sta-tus Report Background Report for DIREC 2010," Direc2010.gv.in, October 2010, http://www.direc2010.gov.in/pdf/Indian-Renewable-Energy-Status-Report .pdf.

182 *They frequently describe*: Author conversations with officials from China's National Development and Reform Commission, Center for Renewable Energy Develop-ment, December 1–3, 2014.

182 *Temperatures are rising*: Sean Gallagher, *Meltdown: China's Environmental Crisis* (Washington, DC: Pulitzer Center, 2013), p. 57.

183 *The 2012 Five Year Plan*: People's Republic of China, "China's Policies and Ac-tions for Addressing Climate Change," National Development and Reform Commission, 2013, http://en.ndrc.gov.cn/newsrelease/201311/P0201311086 11533042884.pdf.

183 *The government has pledged*: Elizabeth Economy, "China and Climate Change: Three Things to Watch After Paris," *Diplomat,* December 19, 2015.

183 *Coal still generates*: "China," U.S. Energy Information Administration, February 4, 2014, http://www.eia.gov/countries/country-data.cfm?fips=CH.

183 *This means it added*: Of 63 gigawatts, 27 GW were from fossil fuels, and 36 GW from renewables: 7.9 wind, 3.6 solar, 2.2 nuclear, and 22.3 hydroelectric. National Energy Administration of China, December 4, 2013, http://www.nea.gov.cn/2013 -12/04/c_132939619.htm. For 2014 numbers, see http://www.carbonbrief.org /blog/2015/02/official-data-confirms-chinese-coal-use-fell-in-2014/.

183 *In 2015 alone*: "A Year for the Record Books: Tracking the Energy Revolution," *Clean Energy Canada*, February 2016. Available at http://cleanenergycanada.org /wp-content/uploads/2016/02/A-Year-for-the-Record-Books_final.pdf.

183 *Many environmentalists also worry*: For example, flooding land for hydroelectric reservoirs often destroys forest, wildlife habitat, agricultural land, and scenic lands. In developing the Three Gorges Dam in China, entire communities had to be relocated to make way for reservoirs.

183 *The United States was*: "Renewables 2014: Global Status Report," Renewable Energy Policy Network for the 21st Century, http://www.ren21.net/portals/0/doc uments/resources/gsr/2014/gsr2014_full%20report_low%20res.pdf.

184 *"My goal is"*: Notes from Greg Manuel attendance at dinner. See also Katie Fehrenbacher, "Hong Kong Company Shunfeng Buys Majority Share of Solar Startup Suniva," *Fortune*, August 13, 2015; Ehren Goossens, "Property Tycoon Reveals $20 Billion Solar-Led Portfolio," Bloomberg, September 29, 2014.

185 *By increasing the production*: Victor David, "Nuclear Power for India Is Good for Us All," Freeman Spogli Institute, Stanford University, March 26, 2006, http:// fsi.stanford.edu/news/nuclear_power_for_india_is_good_for_us_all_says_ pesd_director_david_victor_20060317/.

185 *President Obama personally*: Coral Davenport, "Bill Gates Expected to Create Billion-Dollar Fund for Clean Energy," *New York Times*, November 27, 2015.

186 *These creative steps*: Ellen Barry, "India Announces Plan to Lower Rate of Green-house Gas Emissions," *New York Times*, October 1, 2015; Coral Davenport and Ellen Barry, "Narendra Modi Could Make or Break Obama's Climate Legacy," *New York Times*, November 30, 2015.

9 MANAGING DISCONTENT

187 *He left the comfort*: Author interview with Xiao Qiang, April 24, 2015.

188 *The government went to great lengths*: Megan Garber, "There Are 64 Tiananmen Terms Censored on China's Internet Today," *Atlantic*, June 4, 2014.

189 *Scholar Louisa Lim*: Louisa Lim, *The People's Republic of Amnesia: Tiananmen Revisited* (New York: Oxford University Press, 2014), p. 29.

190 *The Party even controls*: Yuwei, "The End of Reform in China," *Foreign Affairs*, May/ June 2015.

190 *Political scientists argue*: See, for example, Samuel Huntington, *The Third Wave* (Norman: University of Oklahoma Press, 1992), p. 276, and Guillermo O'Donnell and Philippe C. Schmitter, *Transitions from Authoritarian Rule* (Baltimore: Johns Hopkins University Press, 1986), p. 11.

191 *A staggering 180,000*: Will Freeman, "The Accuracy of China's 'Mass Incidents,'" *Financial Times*, March 2, 2010 (citing Sun Liping study). According to the *Financial Times*, "mass incidents are officially defined as any kind of planned or impromptu gathering that forms because of 'internal contradictions,' including mass public

speeches, physical conflicts, airing of grievances or other forms of group behavior that may disrupt social stability. In practice, there is no agreement on the definition of a 'mass incident.' Police generally use a wider definition which enables them to document how effective their enforcement is; government officials tend to use a narrower definition to minimize the apparent scale of the problem."

191 *His most recent data*: Even the Chinese Police Academy acknowledged that the number of protests has increased more than tenfold in the past two decades, from approximately 8,700 in 1993 to 90,000 in 2006. Xiaobing Li and Xiansheng Tian, eds., *Evolution of Power: China's Struggle, Survival, and Success* (Lanham, MD: Lexington Books, 2014).

191 *Research by the Chinese Academy of Social Sciences*: Lin Li and He Tian, "The Annual Report on China's Rule of Law No.12," Sciences Academic Press, February 2014, http://casseng.cssn.cn/research/research_publications/research _books/201403/t20140324_1040769.html. See also Xi Chen, *Social Protest and Contentious Authoritarianism in China* (Cambridge: Cambridge University Press, 2012), arguing that China has experienced a notable increase in social protests since the early 1990s and that demands are mainly around workers' welfare, including laid-off workers, health insurance, punishing corrupt officials, environmental pollution, land expropriation, house demolition, and migration.

192 *"Everyone thinks my people"*: Author conversation with Condoleezza Rice, May 2015. For an in-depth study of Uighur grievances, see Gardner Bovingdon, *The Uyghurs: Strangers in Their Own Land* (New York: Columbia University Press, 2013).

192 *The local government*: Author interview with Sungmin Rho, May 14, 2015. For another account of the Guangdong protests, see Tom Orlik, "Unrest Grows as Economy Booms," *Wall Street Journal,* September 26, 2011.

193 *He thus has*: Author interview with Xiao Qiang, April 15, 2015, and September 22, 2014. See also "The Politburo's Predicament: Confronting the Limitations of Chinese Communist Party Repression," Freedom House, January 2015, https://free domhouse.org/sites/default/files/12222014_FH_ChinaReport2014_FINAL .pdf.

194 *He adds*: Author interview with Xiao Qiang, April 15, 2015. The National People's Congress is China's three-thousand-member legislature, a largely symbolic body with no real legislative power. Its members are elected for five-year terms by subnational party congresses. It formally elects the president (Xi Jinping) and confirms the premier (Li Keqiang). However, it serves as a rubber-stamp parliament—meeting for only two weeks a year to approve proposed legislation.

195 *The law passed*: Huaxia, "China's Legislature Passes Toughest Food Safety Law Amendment," Xinhua, April 24, 2015, http://news.xinhuanet.com/english /2015-04/24/c_134182342.htm.

195 *Rather than a real way*: This is a common tactic of authoritarian regimes. See Lust-Oskar, Ellen, *Structuring Conflict in the Arab World: Incumbents, Opponents and Institutions* (Cambridge: Cambridge University Press, 2005); Blaydes, Lisa, *Elections and Distributive Politics in Mubarak's Egypt* (New York: Cambridge University Press, 2011).

196 *As journalist Eric Fish*: Eric Fish, "The Education of Detained Chinese Feminist Li Tingting," China File, March 16, 2012, http://www.chinafile.com/library /excerpts/education-detained-chinese-feminist-li-tingting.

196 *One student insists*: Didi Tatlow, "In China, Supporters of Detained Feminists Come Under Pressure," *New York Times*, March 25, 2015.

197 *One post about*: Patrick Boehler, "China's Case Against a Civil Rights Lawyer, in Seven Social Media Posts," *New York Times*, December 14, 2015.

197 *His arrest was*: For these and other examples, see "China, Freedom in the World 2015," Freedom House, https://freedomhouse.org/report/freedom -world/2015/china#.VPY68EK4lE4. For details of arrests of Christians, see Robert Marquand, "China's Arrest of Southern Christians Intensifies," *Christian Science Monitor*, September 25, 2015. See also Teng Biao, "A Chinese Activist: Out of Prison but Not Free," *Washington Post*, September 7, 2014. Finally, a Beijing lawyer was sentenced to four years in prison for organizing small protests just to urge officials to disclose their assets—a policy fully in line with the government's anticorruption crackdown.

197 *Freedom House, an American nonprofit organization*: "China, Freedom in the World 2015," Freedom House, https://freedomhouse.org/report/freedom-world /2015/china#.VPY68EK4lE4.

197 *A new draft law*: "Uncivil Society," *Economist*, August 20, 2015.

197 *For years*: Michael Forsythe, "China's Spending on Internal Policing Outstrips Defense Budget," *Bloomberg Business*, March 5, 2011. In the United States, by contrast, *all* federal, state, and local spending on police, prisons, and the judicial system is only approximately half of what the government spends on the military. Michael Martina, "China Withholds Full Domestic-Security Spending Figure," Reuters, March 4, 2014.

198 *Chinese propaganda officials*: Author conversation with Yo Osumi, political minister, Japanese Embassy London, and photos of damage to Panasonic factory, June 26, 2015; William Wan, "Beijing Both Encourages and Reins in Anti-Japan Protests, Analysts Say," *Washington Post*, September 17, 2012.

198 *Japanese foreign direct investment*: Data for January–June 2013 and 2014 is from China's Ministry of Commerce, http://english.mofcom.gov.cn/article/statistic /foreigninvestment/?. See also Tetsuya Abe, "Japanese Investment in China Falls 16% in First Half," *Nikkei Asian Review*, July 21, 2015.

198 *President Xi poignantly*: Edward Wong, "Xi Jinping's News Alert: Chinese Media Must Serve the Party," *New York Times*, February 22, 2016.

199 *It is now available*: "China Central TV: Champion of the People With a Blurred Picture," *Financial Times*, November 20, 2013; "CCTV News, Your Link to Asia," CCTV English.

199 *Even foreign journalists*: Tania Branigan, "New York Times Blocked in China Over Wen Jiabao Wealth Revelations," *Guardian*, October 26, 2012.

199 *Evan Osnos wrote*: Evan Osnos, *Age of Ambition* (New York: Farrar, Straus & Giroux, 2014), p. 156.

199 *By 2016, this had ballooned*: "China Internet Users," Internet Live Stats, January 2016, http://www.internetlivestats.com/internet-users/china/.

199 *They are also public relations*: Author interview with Sungmin Rho, May 15, 2015.

199 *The Chinese government*: "2014 Report to Congress of the U.S.-China Economic and Security Review Commission," November 2014, http://origin.www.uscc .gov/sites/default/files/annual_reports/Complete%20Report.PDF.

200 *Five years ago*: Author conversation with Xiao Qiang, April 24, 2015.

200 *The Central Propaganda Department*: Johan Lagerkvist, "New Media Entrepre-

neurs in China: Allies of the Party-State or Civil Society," *Journal of International Affairs* 65, no. 1 (Fall/Winter 2011): 169–82.

200 *It also issues*: Jonathan Stray, "What China Is Censoring This Week," JonathanStray .com, May 5, 2009, http://jonathanstray.com/what-china-is-censoring-this-week.

200 *They instantly delete*: Gary King, Jennifer Pan, and Margaret E. Roberts, "How Censorship in China Allows Government Criticism but Silences Collective Expression," *American Political Science Review* 107, no. 2 (May 2013): 1–18, http:// gking.harvard.edu/publications/how-censorship-china-allows-government-crit icism-silences-collective-expression. The government also blocks the accounts of "super users" with many followers. In 2013, the government criminalized "online rumors" and cracked down on social media. For example, popular blogger Charles Xue (who had 12 million Sina Weibo followers) was detained on the trumped-up charge of allegedly soliciting prostitutes and forced to apologize on government TV for inappropriately influencing public opinion on his blog. See also "The Politburo's Predicament: Confronting the Limitations of Chinese Communist Party Repression," Freedom House, January 2015, https://freedomhouse.org/sites /default/files/12222014_FH_ChinaReport2014_FINAL.pdf.

200 *Xiao says his algorithm*: Xiao Qiang, "Fear and Anger on the Chinese Internet: The Struggle Between Censors and Netizens," U.S.-China Economic and Security Review Commission, May 15, 2014, http://www.uscc.gov/sites/default/files /Xiao_Testimony.pdf. Researchers have observed that censored keywords can vary considerably across sites, which suggests individual companies have some flexibility in how they interpret government instructions.

203 *It ranks a low*: "Harsh Laws and Violence Drive Global Decline: Freedom of the Press, 2015," Freedom House, April 2015, https://freedomhouse.org/sites/de fault/files/FreedomofthePress_2015_FINAL.pdf.

203 *China scored an abysmal*: "Privatizing Censorship, Eroding Privacy: Freedom on the Net, 2015," Freedom House, October 2015, https://freedomhouse.org/sites /default/files/FOTN%202015%20Full%20Report.pdf.

203 *So far, Modi's government*: Nita Bhalla, "Charities Warn India's Modi That Crackdown Will Hurt the Poor—TRFN," Reuters, May 8 2015.

204 *In 2014 in Srinagar*: For details of these incidents, see, for example, "Arrests Over India Journalist Murder," BBC, June 22, 2015; "Journalists Attacked in Kashmir While Covering Elections," Reporters Without Borders, April 28, 2014, http:// en.rsf.org/india-journalists-attacked-in-kashmir-28-04-2014,46206.html; "India: Amnesty Urges Journalist Death Probe," BBC, June 11, 2015.

204 *The law criminalizes*: See Section 66A of the Information Technology (Amendment) Act of 2008, http://deity.gov.in/sites/upload_files/dit/files/downloads /itact2000/it_amendment_act2008.pdf. See also "Facebook Trouble: 10 Cases of Arrests Under Sec 66A of IT Act," *Hindustan Times*, March 24, 2014.

204 *In an interview*: "Shreya Singhal on Her Fight for Free Speech Online and What Led Her Petition Against SEC 66A of IT Act," IBN Live, April 2, 2015.

205 *Different protesters shut down*: "India Caste Unrest: Ten Million Without Water in Delhi," BBC, February 22, 2016.

205 *Some whisper that*: Didi Kirsten Tatlow, "In Book, Xi Jinping Taints Ousted Rivals with Talk of Plots," *New York Times*, January 27, 2016.

206 *Only about a third*: Michael Albertus and Victor Menaldo, "Aftermath of Revolution," *New York Times*, February 14, 2013.

206 *Such an evolution*: Mainstream political scientists agree that evolution leads to more enduring and stable democratic change. See Huntington, *The Third Wave*, and O'Donnell and Schmitter, *Transitions from Authoritarian Rule*. Huntington concludes. "It seems more plausible to hypothesize that a consensual, less violent transition provides a better basis for consolidating democracy than do conflict and violence" (p. 276). O'Donnell and Schmitter reach a similar conclusion in their book on transitions from authoritarianism (see p. 11).

10 THE NEW MERCANTILISTS

211 *India had spent*: Ashlyn Anderson, "Economics of Influence: China and India in South Asia," Council on Foreign Relations, August 7, 2015, http://www.cfr.org/economics/economics-influence-china-india-south-asia/p36862.

211 *While China has given*: Zhao Huasheng, "What Is Behind China's Growing Attention to Afghanistan?," Carnegie Middle East Center, March 8, 2015; Joshua Partlow, "Afghan Minister Accused of Taking Bribe," *Washington Post*, November 18, 2009.

212 *As scholar Steve Levine put it*: Steve LeVine, "China Is Building the Most Extensive Global Commercial-Military Empire in History," *Quartz*, June 9, 2015.

213 *For decades after independence*: According to the *Economist*, "Between 1951 and 1992 India received about $55 billion in foreign aid, making it the largest recipient in history." Michael Kirkham, "Charity Begins Abroad," *Economist*, August 13, 2011; Shyam Kamath, "Foreign Aid and India: Financing the Leviathan State," *Cato Policy*, May 6, 1992, http://www.cato.org/pubs/pas/pa-170.html.

213 *India now gives*: This is according to Indian government figures. Based on OECD numbers, India remains a net aid recipient. Lorenzo Piccio, "In Latest Indian Budget, Aid Spending Dwarfs Aid Receipts," Devex, February 24, 2014, https://www.devex.com/news/in-latest-indian-budget-aid-spending-dwarfs-aid-receipts-82915.

213 *In 2015, it gave*: Lorenzo Piccio, "India's 2015-16 Foreign Aid Budget: Where the Money Is Going," Devex, March 9, 2015, https://www.devex.com/news/india-s-2015-16-foreign-aid-budget-where-the-money-is-going-85666.

213 *In addition to direct grants*: "Annual Report 2014-2015," Export-Import Bank of India, April 27, 2015, http://www.eximbankindia.in/sites/default/files/English%20Annual%20Report_0.pdf.

213 *India was one of the*: "U.S., India and Qatar Contribute to U.N. Democracy Fund," press release, Consulate General of the United States in Kolkata, India, March 9, 2006. http://kolkata.usconsulate.gov/wwwhipr031006a.html.

213 *Eighteen thousand Indians died*: For details, see for example, Brandon Cramer, "Tsunami's Impact on India," *Evergreen*, 2005, http://academic.evergreen.edu/g/grossmaz/cramerbd/. See also Edward Bryant, *Tsunami: The Underground Hazard* (Chicago: Springer, 2014), p. 120.

214 *More than sixteen thousand*: According to the United Nations Office for the Coordination of Humanitarian Affairs, total contributions to date (as of 2015) are China, $62 million, and India, $23 million. "Indian Ocean—Earthquake/Tsunami," Financial Tracking Service, September 11, 2015, https://fts.unocha.org/reports/daily/ocha_R24_E14794____1508191707.pdf. See also "Tsunami Aid: Who's Giving What," BBC News, January 27, 2005.

214   *Why would India*: According to UN data from February 2015, India has a fourth of the world's poor. Vibhuti Agarwal, "India Hits Its U.N. Poverty-Cutting Target, but Misses Others," *Wall Street Journal*, February 5, 2015.

214   *China, by contrast*: "World Investment Report 2015," United Nations Conference on Trade and Development, 2015, http://unctad.org/en/PublicationsLibrary /wir2015_en.pdf; Anant Kala, "India Attracts Enough FDI to Join Global Top Ten," *Wall Street Journal*, June 25, 2015.

215   *Jaguar had been operating*: Ashutosha Kumar Jha et al., "Case Study, Strategic Management,"August 10, 2010, http://www.slideshare.net/Lordnikhil/tata-jlr-acqui sition-case-study.

215   *The company has created*: "Jaguar Land Rover Annual Report, 2014–15," 2015, http://www.jaguarlandrover.com/media/75843/jaguar-land-rover-annual-r eport-2014-15-web_final.pdf; "Company Information," 2015, http://www.jaguar landrover.com/media/23076/jlr_company_information.pdf.

215   *Some Indian companies*: Author calculation based on data on bilateral Indian FDI flows for 2012 from United Nations Conference on Trade and Development database, based on data from the Reserve Bank of India. Indian FDI flows to developed economies were $4.2 billion in 2012 and total flows were $11 billion.

215   *China has invested*: Data from China Global Investment Tracker, compiled by the American Enterprise Institute and the Heritage Foundation, accessed January 25, 2016, https://www.aei.org/china-global-investment-tracker/. Foxconn, from neighboring Taiwan, by contrast, plans to spend $5 billion to create a dozen new manufacturing facilities in India and employ up to one million workers.

215   *He announced proudly*: The Chinese company Beiqi Futon Motor is partnering on the construction of a 1,250-acre industrial park near Pune, Maharashtra, and China Development Bank is helping finance an industrial park in Gujarat. http:// www.mea.gov.in/bilateral-documents.htm

215   *Prime Minister Modi*: Author interview with Susan Schwab, August 13, 2015, and October 18, 2015.

215   *So Modi talks*: Joshua Meltzer, "Make in India," Brookings India, 2015, http:// www.brookings.in/in-focus/for-modis-india-a-new-trade-policy/#_ednref4.

216   *In July 2014*: Randy Schnepf, "Agriculture in the WTO Bali Ministerial Agreement," Congressional Research Service, November 13, 2014, https://www.fas .org/sgp/crs/misc/R43592.pdf.

216   *India's controversial food*: Raymond Zhong, "India Clings to Disputed Food Subsidies," *Wall Street Journal*, October 1, 2014; Nita Bhalla, "How Much of a Winner Is India in WTO Trade Facilitation Agreement?" RT Network, December 12, 2014.

216   *It took intense midnight negotiations*: Author conversation with senior Obama administration official, August 17, 2015.

217   *In 2014 its trade with Asia*: Author calculation based on data from India's Ministry of Commerce, April 2014–May 2015, http://commerce.nic.in/eidb/.

217   *The two traded*: Data from ibid.

217   *It is the largest*: "China Outpacing Rest of World in Natural Resource Use," United Nations Environment Programme, August 2, 2013; "China," International Energy Data and Analysis, May 14, 2015. http://www.eia.gov/beta/international/analy sis.cfm?iso=CHN.

217   *The Chinese government*: "Promoting China-Japan Relations Through Culture,"

China.org, June 18, 2014, http://www.china.org.cn/opinion/2014-06/18/con tent_32690843.htm.

217 *The CIA World Factbook*: *World Factbook*, CIA, 2015, https://www.cia.gov/library /publications/the-world-factbook/.

217 *Even using the*: According to CIA World Factbook data for 2014 (latest available estimate), 53 countries count China as their largest import trade partner; 43 countries count China as their largest exports partner; 24 countries count the United States as their largest imports partner; 32 countries count the United States as their largest exports partner. World Factbook, CIA, site accessed January 25, 2016, https://www.cia.gov/library/publications/the-world-factbook/.

218 *It is most astounding*: Jamil Anderlini, Geoff Dyer, and Henny Sender, "China's Lending Hits New Heights," *Financial Times*, January 18, 2011.

218 *It also has plans*: Scott Kennedy and David Parker, "Building China's 'One Belt, One Road,'" Center for Strategic and International Studies, September 10, 2015.

218 *Because of these initiatives*: Steve LeVine, "China Is Building the Most Extensive Global Commercial-Military Empire in History," Reuters, June 9, 2015; "West China's International Railway Development," Maxxelli Consulting, 2015, http://www.maxxelli-consulting.com/west-chinas-international-railway -development/.

218 *One Belt, One Road will be*: "One Belt, One Road: China's Great Leap Outward," European Council on Foreign Relations, June 2015, http://www.ecfr.eu/page /-/China_analysis_belt_road.pdf.

218 *The China Development Bank reportedly*: Mercy A. Kuo and Angelica O. Tang, "China's 'One Belt, One Road' Initiative: Outlook for OBOR and the US Rebalance: Insight from Erica Downs," *The Diplomat*, December 3, 2015; Bert Hofman, "China's One Belt One Road Initiative: What We Know Thus Far," World Bank blog, December 4, 2015.

219 *China reiterates over and over*: Tian Shaohui, "Vision and Actions on Jointly Building Belt and Road," Xinhua, March 28, 2015, http://news.xinhuanet.com/en glish/china/2015-03/28/c_134105858.htm.

220 *Third, China has*: Qiao Yu, "Relocating -China's Foreign Reserves," Brookings Institution, November 21, 2013, http://www.brookings.edu/research/papers /2013/11/21-relocating-foreign-reserves.

220 *Amid sentimental pronouncements*: Huaxia. "Pakistanis Hail Ironclad Friendship with China Ahead of Xi's Visit," Xinhua, April 20, 2104; Irfan Haider, "Details of Agreements Signed During Xi's Visit to Pakistan," *Dawn*, April 20, 2015.

221 *Chinese contractors reportedly say*: Author conversation with Andrew Small, August 15, 2015.

221 *Almost four-fifths of Pakistanis*: "How Asians View Each Other," Pew Research Center, July 14, 2014, http://www.pewglobal.org/2014/07/14/chapter-4-how -asians-view-each-other/.

222 *In recent years*: Alan K. Kronstadt, "Pakistan-U.S. Relations: Issues for the 114th Congress," Congressional Research Service, May 14, 2015, http://www.fas.org /sgp/crs/row/R44034.pdf.

222 *China has a broader*: Paul Callan, Jasmin Blak, and Andria Thomas, "Breaking Down China's Foreign Aid and Investment," Dalberg, April 12, 2013, http://dal berg.com/blog/?p=1778. See also Charles Wolf, Xiao Wang, and Eric Warner,

"China's Foreign Aid and Government-Sponsored Investment Activities," RAND Corporation, 2013, http://www.rand.org/content/dam/rand/pubs/research _reports/RR100/RR118/RAND_RR118.pdf.

222 *More than 80 percent*: Wolf, Wang, and Warner, "China's Foreign Aid and Government-Sponsored Investment Activities."

222 *Instead its development banks*: Author interview with Andrew Small, August 14, 2015; author interview with Awais Khan, CEO of U.S. Pakistan Foundation, September 2, 2015. See also Andrew Small, *The China-Pakistan Axis: Asia's New Geopolitics* (Chicago: C. Hurst, 2015). See also "Agreements Signed Between Pakistan and China," *Express Tribune,* April 26, 2015.

223 *He believes China*: Author interview with Parag Khanna, senior research fellow in the Centre on Asia and Globalization at the Lee Kuan Yew School of Public Policy at the National University of Singapore, August 27, 2015.

223 *The government is looking*: "Handover of Gwadar Port," *Dawn,* April 14, 2015; Gwadar Port Authority. "Information About Gwadar," 2015, http://www.gwadar port.gov.pk/gwadar.html.

223 *China is lavishing*: Jamil Anderlini, Geoff Dyer, and Henny Sender., "China's Lending Hits New Heights," *Financial Times,* January 18, 2011.

224 *The* New York Times: Gregor Aisch, Josh Keller, and Rebecca Lai, "The World According to China," *New York Times,* July 24, 2015.

224 *More than a third*: Author calculation based on data from 2009 to 2015 from the China Global Investment Tracker, compiled by the American Enterprise Institute and the Heritage Foundation.

224 *When James Kynge*: James Kynge, "Uganda Turns East: Chinese Money Will Build Infrastructure, Says Museveni," *Financial Times,* October 21, 2014; author conversation with James Kynge, June 20, 2015.

225 *China's white papers*: Hui Lu, "China's Foreign Aid," Xinhua, July 7, 2014, http:// news.xinhuanet.com/english/china/2014-07/10/c_133474011.htm.

225 *A research firm*: Grisons Peak is the research firm. See coverage in James Kynge, "Chinese Overseas Lending Dominated by One Belt, One Road Strategy," *Financial Times,* June 18, 2015.

225 *Over the past two years*: "Export-Import Bank of the United States," EXIM Bank Advisory Committee, June 2015, http://www.exim.gov/sites/default/files/re ports/EXIM%202014CompetReport_0611.pdf. This reports also explains that China gives lenient interest rates and long repayment terms to countries that buy big Chinese projects, such as hydropower or water treatment plants. The United States and European countries have rules preventing them from making economically unsound loans to countries that then won't be able to repay. Developed countries have also placed voluntary limits on benefits they can give to emerging economies in loans given to buy western products. China and Russia aren't governed by these rules and thus are able to offer more lenient financing that are more attractive than U.S./developed country terms. In 2014 only 34 percent of the world's export credits came from countries that abide by these international rules—compared to 100 percent in 1999. China was the source of more than half of that unregulated credit.

225 *Second, while these loans*: Author conversation with James Kynge, June 19, 2015; Kynge, "Chinese Overseas Lending Dominated by One Belt, One Road Strategy." An earlier book on China's aid to Africa describes China's interest-free loans:

David Shinn and Joshua Eisenman, *China and Africa: A Century of Engagement* (Philadelphia: University of Pennsylvania Press, 2012).

225 *Scholar Parag Khanna*: Author interview with Parag Khanna, senior research fellow in the Centre on Asia and Globalisation at the Lee Kuan Yew School of Public Policy at the National University of Singapore, August 27, 2015.

225 *Especially a decade ago*: See, for example, Rebecca Ray, Kevin Gallagher, Andres Lopez, and Cynthia Sanborn, "China in Latin America," Boston University, April 2015, http://www.bu.edu/pardeeschool/files/2014/12/Working-Group-Final-Report.pdf.

226 *They are trying*: Author conversation with Russian-American businessman in mining sector, August 4, 2015.

226 *In another example*: Euan Rocha, "CNOOC Closes $15.1 Billion Acquisition of Canada's Nexen," Reuters, February 25, 2013.

227 *China replaced India*: For statistics in this paragraph, see Alyssa Ayres and Ashlyn Anderson, "Economics of Influence: China and India in South Asia," Council on Foreign Relations, August 7, 2015, http://www.cfr.org/economics/economics-influence-china-india-south-asia/p36862. Also, author conversation with Alyssa Ayres, senior fellow for India, Pakistan, and South Asia at the Council on Foreign Relations, August 14, 2015.

228 *This does not yet match*: "World Investment Report 2015," United Nations Conference on Trade and Development, 2015, http://unctad.org/en/Publications Library/wir2015_en.pdf; Anant Kala, "India Attracts Enough FDI to Join Global Top Ten," *Wall Street Journal*, June 25, 2015.

229 *At United Nations meetings*: "President Xi Jinping's UN Speech in 6 Key Words," Xinhua, September 29, 2015, http://news.xinhuanet.com/english/china/2015-09/29/c_134672436.htm.

11 THE WORLD THEY WILL MAKE

232 *In the late 1940s*: Estimates from Angus Maddison, *Contours of the World Economy, 1–2030 AD* (Oxford: Oxford University Press, 2007).

234 *Getting an answer from authoritarian Beijing*: Author conversation with Susan Schwab, former U.S. trade representative, August 13, 2015, and October 17, 2015.

235 *America and China are pursuing*: "America's Big Bet," *Economist*, November 10, 2014.

235 *The agreement manages its members' trade*: Adam Hersh, "The Trans-Pacific Free Trade Charade," Project Syndicate, October 2, 2015.

235 *TPP's emphasis on high standards*: "Trans-Pacific Partnership (TPP)," Office of the United States Trade Representative, 2015, https://ustr.gov/tpp.

236 *If TPP is implemented*: Peter A. Petri and Michael G. Plummer, "The Economic Effects of the Trans-Pacific Partnership: New Estimates," The Peterson Institute for International Economics, January 2016.

236 *In addition, the TPP*: Meltzer, "Make in India."

236 *For example, the New York Times*: Keith Bradsher, "Trans-Pacific Partnership's Potential Impact Weighed in Asia and U.S," *New York Times*, July 8, 2015.

236 *Together the RCEP*: Based on data from International Monetary Fund's World Economic Outlook estimates for 2015, accessed January 20, 2016.

236 *The RCEP has lower labor*: Murray Hiebert, "ASEAN and Partners Launch Regional Comprehensive Economic Partnership," Center for Strategic and International Studies, December 7, 2012, http://csis.org/publication/asean-and -partners-launch-regional-comprehensive-economic-partnership.

237 *It could also help India*: Bipul Chatterjee and Surendar Singh, "Why RCEP Is Vital for India," *Diplomat*, March 3, 2015, http://thediplomat.com/2015/03/why -rcep-is-vital-for-india/.

237 *This is not likely*: Author interview with Susan Schwab, August 13, 2015.

237 *China insists*: Li Shengjiao, "U.S.-China Trade Rivalry in Asia Is Overhyped," *Huffington Post*, March 4, 2015.

237 *Research has shown*: "Protectionism—the case against." OECD, site accessed December 7, 2015, http://www.oecd.org/trade/protectionism-thecaseagainst.htm. *See also* Ann Tutwiler and Matthew Straub, "Making Agricultural Trade Reform Work for the Poor," *International Food and Agricultural Trade Policy Council*, June 2005, http://www.agritrade.org/Publications/Position%20Papers/Making%20 Trade%20Work%20for%20the%20Poor.pdf.

237 *Other economic surveys*: See, for example, "Seizing the Benefits of Trade for Employment and Growth," Organisation for Economic Co-operation and Development, International Labor Organization, World Bank, World Trade Organization, Report prepared for submission to the G-20 Summit meeting Seoul, Korea, November 11–12, 2010, http://www.oecd.org/tad/benefitlib/46353240.pdf.

238 *The so-called BRICS . . . represent more than*: IMF World Economic Outlook data for 2015: GDP, current prices in U.S. dollars. Compared world total to emerging market and developing economies total. Raj Desai and James Raymond Vreeland, "What the New Bank of BRICS Is All About," *Washington Post*, July 17, 2014.

238 *IMF officials were frustrated*: Author conversation with former senior IMF official, September 22, 2015.

238 *Christine Lagarde, the IMF's chief*: Christine Lagarde. Author conversation at private dinner. September 2014. *See also* Robin Harding, "Christine Lagarde Warns U.S. Over IMF Reform Failings." *Financial Times*, December 12, 2014.

239 *Rebecca Liao*: Rebecca Liao, "Out of the Bretton Woods," *Foreign Affairs*, July 27, 2015, https://www.foreignaffairs.com/articles/asia/2015-07-27/out-bret ton-woods.

239 *Influential Chinese bloggers*: Indian Finance Minister Arun Jaitley told the IMF in April 2015: "We are greatly disappointed that the 2010 Quota and Governance Reforms have not become effective in spite of the strong support of the global community for the reform" and called the reforms "imperative to maintain [the IMF's] relevance." http://www.financialexpress.com/article/economy/india -disappointed-over-non-implementation-of-imf-reforms-arun-jaitley/64938/. In China, one much-liked comment on social media said, "The IMF can't be trusted. It's just a puppet of the U.S." A Weibo blogger vented that this "illustrates the parochialism and rascality of the U.S." http://www.wsj.com/articles/chinas -resistance-to-reform-may-grow-with-imf-rejection-1440076190.

239 *As a finger in the eye*: It differs from the AIIB in that its founding members are just the BRICS (although membership will be open to all UN member states) and it will fund projects in BRICS countries, not just Asia. The combined capital share of the founding members can't be lower than 55 percent. William Engdahl, "AIIB, BRICS Development Bank and an Emerging World," *New Eastern Outlook*, Octo-

ber 4, 2015, http://journal-neo.org/2015/04/10/aiib-brics-development-bank
-and-an-emerging-world/.

240 *a reserve currency*: Author conversation with Richard Cooper, Maurits C. Boas
Professor of International Economics at Harvard University and former chairman
of the Federal Reserve Bank of Boston, October 19, 2015; Ian Talley and Lingling
Wei, "Momentum Builds to Label Chinese Yuan a Reserve Currency," *Wall Street
Journal*, April 1, 2015.

241 *China realizes that its unilateral*: "Rich but Rash," *Economist*, January 29, 2015.

241 *The AIIB is cooperating*: Quotes from Jin Liqun are from a speech he gave at the
World Internet Conference in Wuzhen, China, on December 15, 2015, which
the author attended. Devon-Douglas Bowers, "The Truth About BRICS,"
Foreign Policy Journal, August 21, 2015, http://www.foreignpolicyjournal
.com/2015/08/21/the-truth-about-brics/; Chen Jia, "AIIB, World Bank Planning Closer Project Cooperation," *China Daily*, July 17, 2015.

242 *China voted with the United States*: "Voting Coincidence with the United
States," U.S. Department of State, July 15, 2015, http://www.state.gov/p/io/rls
/rpt/2014/practices/244927.htm.

242 *The Economist reports*: "Xi and the Blue Helmets," *Economist*, October 3, 2015.

242 *In 2014, India voted*: "Voting Coincidence with the United States," U.S. Department of State, July 15, 2015. http://www.state.gov/p/io/rls/rpt/2014/prac
tices/244927.htm.

242 *It contributes a paltry*: China contributed $139,694,305, India $18,072,340. Total
Budget for 2015 is $2.771 billion. "Contributions Received for 2015 for the
United Nations Regular Budget," Committee on Contributions, October 7, 2015,
http://www.un.org/en/ga/contributions/honourroll.shtml; "United Nations
Financial Situation 'Generally Sound,' Top Management Official Tells Budget
Committee," United Nations, May 6, 2015, http://www.un.org/press/en/2015
/gaab4153.doc.htm.

243 *For example, India's representative*: "Security Council Approves 'No-Fly Zone'
over Libya, Authorizing 'All Necessary Measures' to Protect Civilians, by Vote of
10 in Favour with 5 Abstentions," United Nations, March 17, 2011, http://www
.un.org/press/en/2011/sc10200.doc.htm; Indrani Bagchi, "India Abstains from
UNSC Vote on Libya No-Fly Zone," *Times of India*, March 19, 2011.

243 *Cynics say, however*: Heather Timmons and Neha Thirani Bagri, "Poor Nations
Fight, Rich Nations Pay," *India Ink*, April 10, 2013.

243 *UN diplomats say with irritation*: Chris McGreal, "What's the Point of Peacekeepers When They Don't Keep the Pace," *Guardian*, September 17, 2015, http://
www.theguardian.com/world/2015/sep/17/un-united-nations-peacekeep
ers-rwanda-bosnia.

243 *As a reflection of India's growing*: Office of the Press Secretary, "Remarks by the
President to the Joint Session of the Indian Parliament in New Delhi, India,"
White House, November 8, 2010, https://www.whitehouse.gov/the-press-of
fice/2010/11/08/remarks-president-joint-session-indian-parliament-new-del
hi-india.

243 *China opposes a permanent seat*: Atul Aneja, "China Falls Short of Backing India for
a Permanent U.N. Seat," *Hindu*, April 13, 2015.

243 *The United States and Russia*: Elizabeth Roche, "US Committed to a Permanent
Seat for India in a Reformed UN Security Council," *Live Mint*, August 15, 2015.

245 *During recent BRICS summits*: Author conversation with senior U.S. State Department official October 5, 2015. See also "PM Narendra Modi's Full Statement at BRICS Summit," NDTV, July 15, 2014, http://www.ndtv.com/india-news /pm-narendra-modis-full-statement-at-brics-summit-588814.

245 *According to press reports*: Jayanth Jacob, "Brics Bank the Next India-China Flashpoint," *Hindu Times,* July 7, 2014; "Is This Victory for India at BRICS Summit?" DNA India, July 16, 2014.

12 THE NEXT MASTER AND COMMANDER

247 *Chinese and Indian soldiers shove*: See, for example, "Chinese Incursion in India Caught on Tape," Fox News–YouTube, 2013, https://www.youtube.com /watch?v=AW_9ZEO5y7I.

247 *issuing these devices to two hundred thousand fishing boats*: Vijay Sakhuja, "India Reinforces Maritime Domain Awareness but Challenges Remain," Center for International Maritime Security, December 2, 2014, http://cimsec.org/india-rein forces-maritime-domain-awareness-challenges-remain/13789.

247 *Chinese fishing boats are also getting into the act*: Author conversation with Gary Roughead, former U.S. chief of naval operations, September 8, 2015. See also "U.S. Protests 'Harassment' of Navy Ship by Chinese Vessels," *Washington Post,* March 9, 2009.

249 *concerned mostly with a potential threat from Pakistan*: Indo-Pakistan wars occurred in 1947, 1965, 1971, and 1999. Details of Pakistani terrorist groups operating in India can be found at Global Terrorism Database, 2015, http://www.start.umd .edu/gtd/; Mapping Militant Organizations, "Lashkar-e-Taiba," August 3, 2012, http://web.stanford.edu/group/mappingmilitants/cgi-bin/groups/view/79.

249 *In late 2008*: Stephen Tankel, "Lashkar-eTaiba: Past Operations and Future Prospects," New America Foundation, April 27, 2011, http://newamerica.net/publi cations/policy/lashkar_e_taiba; "Harakat ul-Mudjahidin," National Consortium for the Study of Terrorism and Responses to Terrorism, University of Maryland, http://www.start.umd.edu/start/data_collections/tops/terrorist_organiza tion_profile.asp?id=50.

249 *The dispute originated when*: For details on the 1962 war, see, for example, John Garver, "China's Decision for War with India in 1962," Harvard University, 2015, https://web.archive.org/web/20090326032121/http://www.people.fas.har vard.edu/~johnston/garver.pdf. For India's decision to develop nuclear weapons, see Mika Kerttunen, *A Responsible Nuclear Weapons Power: Nuclear Weapons and Indian Foreign Policy* (Helsinki: National Defence University Department of Strategic and Defence Studies, 2009), p. 152, http://www.nti.org/country-profiles /india/nuclear/.

250 *China's tidal wave of infrastructure projects*: Gordon Fairclough, "India-China Border Standoff: High in the Mountains, Thousands of Troops Go Toe-to-Toe," *Wall Street Journal,* October 30, 2014; Gordon Fairclough, "India Races to Bolster Border Infrastructure, Chasing China," *Wall Street Journal,* October 30, 2014.

251 *feuding over shared water supplies*: See, for example, Amit Ranjan, "Beijing's Threat to India's Water Security," Yale Global Online, November 15, 2010, http:// yaleglobal.yale.edu/content/beijings-threat-indias-water-security; Sudha Rama-

chandran, "Water Wars: China, India and the Great Dam Rush," *Diplomat,* April 3, 2015.

251 *"run of the river"*: John Vidal, "China and India 'Water Grab' Dams Put Ecology of Himalayas in Danger," *Guardian,* August 10, 2013. See also Simon Denyer, "Chinese Dams in Tibet Raise Hackles in India," *Washington Post,* February 7, 2013.

251 *Chinese "string of pearls"*: See, for example, Prem Mahdevan, "China in the Indian Ocean: Part of a Larger PLAN," CSS Analyses in Security Policy, June 2014, http://www.css.ethz.ch/publications/pdfs/CSSAnalyse156-EN.pdf.

251 *Chinese navy ships*: For details of China's moves in the Indian Ocean and India's response to them, see, for example, "The Maritime Great Game India, China, US & The Indian Ocean," IPCS Special Focus, 2015, http://www.ipcs.org/pdf_file/issue/SR150-IPCSSpecialFocus-MaritimeGreatGame.pdf; Ashley Tellis, "U.S. and India Should Collaborate to Counter China in the Indian Ocean," Carnegie Endowment for International Peace, April 22, 2015. http://carnegieendowment .org/2015/04/22/us-and-india-should-collaborate-to-counter-china-in-indian -ocean/i7pr; Ridzwan Rahmat, "PLAN to Deploy Range of Warships in Indian Ocean, Says China's Defence Ministry," *Jane's 360,* January 29, 2015, http://www .janes.com/article/48464/plan-to-deploy-range-of-warships-in-indian-ocean -says-china-s-defence-ministry.

252 *questioned a Chinese admiral*: Author conversation with Pramit Pal Chaudhuri, foreign editor of the *Hindustan Times,* November 9, 2015.

253 *From China's vantage point*: For this argument, see, for example, Robert D. Kaplan, *Monsoon: The Indian Ocean and the Future of American Power* (New York: Random House, 2010), p. 285. See also Peter Dutton, Robert Ross, and Øystein Tunsjø, *Twenty-First Century Seapower: Cooperation and Conflict at Sea* (Chicago: Routledge, 2013).

254 *China was more concerned with land invasions*: Kaplan, *Monsoon,* p. 282.

254 *China shares borders*: "China's Geography and Security Goals," Columbia University, 2015, http://afe.easia.columbia.edu/special/china_1950_china_geo sec.htm.

254 *China's navy sees itself as the protector*: Mathieu Duchatel and Bates Gill, "Overseas Citizen Protection: A Growing Challenge for China," Stockholm International Peace Research Institute, 2015, http://www.sipri.org/media/newsletter/essay /february12. In addition, there are estimated to be 200 million Chinese tourists per year by 2020. Nyshka Chandran, "Chinese Tourists to Double by 2020: CLSA," CNBC, January 21, 2014.

254 *Eighty percent of China's energy*: "China: International Energy Data and Analysis," U.S. Department of Energy, May 14, 2015, http://www.eia.gov/beta/in ternational/analysis.cfm?iso=CHN; "International Energy Data and Analysis," U.S. Department of Energy, 2015, http://www.eia.gov/countries/analysisbriefs /World_Oil_Transit_Chokepoints/wotc.pdf; "World Oil Transit Chokepoint," U.S. Department of Energy, November 10, 2014, http://www.eia.gov/beta/inter national/analysis_includes/special_topics/World_Oil_Transit_Chokepoints /wotc.pdf; "The South China Sea Is an Important World Energy Trade Route," U.S. Department of Energy, April 4, 2013, http://www.eia.gov/todayinenergy /detail.cfm?id=10671.

255 *supported Pakistan's military buildup*: "China's Nuclear Exports and Assistance to Pakistan," Center for Nonproliferation Studies, Monterey Institute of Inter-

national Studies, August 1999, http://cns.miis.edu/archive/country_india /china/npakpos.htm; "Declassified Documents Show That, for Over Fifteen Years, Beijing Rebuffed U.S. Queries on Chinese Aid to Pakistani Nuclear Program," National Security Archive, March 2004, http://nsarchive.gwu.edu /NSAEBB/NSAEBB114/press.htm.

255 *After a major border clash*: Author interview with Robert Gates, former United States secretary of defense, August 27, 2015.

256 *thinks the number was closer to*: "Sipri Milex Data Launch 2015," Stockholm International Peace Research Institute, 2015, http://www.sipri.org/research/arma ments/milex. The government announced 144.2 billion U.S. dollars in its national defense budget in 2015, but most analysts believe it is actually higher. "The 15 Countries With the Highest Military Expenditure in 2014," Stockholm International Peace Research Institute, 2014, http://www.sipri.org/googlemaps/milex _top_15_2014_exp_map.html.

256 *Its navy has more than three hundred ships*: Office of the Secretary of Defense, "Annual Report to Congress: Military and Security Developments Involving the People's Republic of China 2015," April 17, 2015, http://www.defense.gov/Por tals/1/Documents/pubs/2015_China_Military_Power_Report.pdf; "Report to Congress on the Annual Long-Range Plan for Construction of Naval Vessels for FY2015," Deputy Chief of Naval Operations, 2000, http://navylive.dodlive.mil /files/2014/07/30-year-shipbuilding-plan1.pdf.

256 *Gates quips*: Author conversation with Robert Gates, August 27, 2015.

256 *"anti-access/area-denial" capabilities*: Teshu Singh, "China: Contextualizing the Anti-Access Area-Denial Strategy," Institute of Peace and Conflict Studies, April 30, 2013, http://www.ipcs.org/article/china/china-contextualising-the-anti-ac cess-area-denial-strategy-3902.html.

257 *A recent video/cartoon*: Michael Ballaban, "This Is the Insane Video China Just Put Out Showing It Attacking the U.S," FoxTrotAlpha, September 3, 2015.

257 *help China protect its sea-lanes*: Author interview with Gary Roughead, September 8, 2015.

257 *"salami-slicing" strategy*: Ronald O'Rourke, "Maritime Territorial and Exclusive Economic Zone (EEZ) Disputes Involving China: Issues for Congress," Congressional Research Service, August 28, 2015, https://www.fas.org/sgp/crs/row /R42784.pdf.

257 *China watchers were stunned*: James Hardy and Sean O'Connor, "China's First Runway in Spratlys Under Construction," *IHS Jane's Defence Weekly*, April 16, 2015, http://www.janes.com/article/50714/china-s-first-runway-in-spratlys-under -construction.

258 *Chinese diplomat told me*: Author conversation with Chinese Embassy official, June 18, 2015.

259 *yelled at by … Chinese ground crews*: Rupert Wingfield Hayes, "Flying Close to Beijing's New South China Sea Islands," BBC, December 14, 2015, http://www.bbc .com/news/magazine-35031313.

259 *Robert Gates recalls*: Author conversation with Robert Gates, August 27, 2015. For details on other incidents, see, for example, Jane Perlez, "Chinese Oil Rig Near Vietnam to Be Moved," *New York Times*, July 15, 2014.

259 *China created an Air Defense Identification Zone*: Ian Rinehart and Elias Bart, "Chi-

na's Air Defense Identification Zone (ADIZ)," Congressional Research Service, January 30, 2015, http://www.fas.org/sgp/crs/row/R43894.pdf. "An ADIZ . . . essentially extends a country's airspace, allowing it more time to respond to foreign, and possibly hostile, aircraft. While there is no international law that specifically governs ADIZs, the United States and Japan contend that China's ADIZ in the East China Sea is contrary to international law, and specifically the law of the sea and norms of freedom of navigation. The ECS ADIZ also overlaps with pre-existing ADIZs held by Japan, South Korea and Taiwan."

260 *Former U.S. Navy chief*: Author interview with Gary Roughead, September 8, 2015.

261 *interaction between the United States and Chinese fleet has expanded*: Conversation with member of U.S. Pacific Command, September 22, 2015.

261 *2.2 million soldiers*: Susan Lawrence, "China's Political Institutions and Leaders in Charts," Congressional Research Service, November 12, 2013, https://www.fas.org/sgp/crs/row/R43303.pdf.

261 *Ordinary conscripts in the PLA*: Alison Kaufman, "Field Guide: The Culture of the Chinese People's Liberation Army," CAN China, 2009, http://www.dtic.mil/dtic/tr/fulltext/u2/a495052.pdf.

261 *one of the most notorious*: For details, see, for example, Wang Wei, "How General Used His Military Service to Amass Fortune," Caixin, August 21, 2015; "Gold-Obsessed' Chinese Officer's Graft Case Worth $5 Billion: Magazine," Reuters, December 8, 2014.

261 *Chinese conscripts swear allegiance*: Kaufman, "Field Guide."

262 *would not perform well in a real battle*: Author conversation with Robert Gates, August 26, 2015.

263 *PLA for the first time published*: The entire text of China's Military Strategy can be found at China White Paper, Part I: National Security Situation, "National Security Situation" and "Part IV: Building and Developing China's Armed Forces," Ministry of National Defense, May 26, 2015, http://eng.mod.gov.cn/Database/WhitePapers/2015-05/26/content_4586688.htm.

263 *On December 31, 2015*: Li Jing, "President Xi Jinping lays down the law to the Chinese army in first 'precept' speech since Mao Zedong," *South China Morning Post*, January 4, 2016; "Xi's new model army," *The Economist*, January 16, 2016; John Costello, "China finally Centralizes its Space, Cyber, Information Forces," *The Diplomat*, 20 January 20, 2016.

263 *anticorruption campaign has snared*: Charles Clover, "Xi Warns China Military Amid Anti-Corruption Purge," *Financial Times*, July 20, 2015.

263 *breaking up some army cliques*: Kevin McCauley, "President Xi Clears the Way for Military Reform: PLA Corruption, Clique Breaking and Making, and Personnel Shuffle," Jamestown Foundation, February 4, 2015.

263 *Chinese government hackers*: "Exposing One of China's Cyber Espionage Units," Mandiant, 2014, http://intelreport.mandiant.com/Mandiant_APT1_Report.pdf. For details on unit 61398 see also Edward Wong, "U.S. Case Offers Glimpse into China's Hacker Army," *New York Times*, May 22, 2014.

264 *China's cyber-warriors have hacked*: "Task Force Report: Resilient Military Systems and the Advanced Cyber Threat," Department of Defense Science Board, January 2013, http://www.acq.osd.mil/dsb/reports/ResilientMilitarySystems.Cyber

Threat.pdf. In their recent well-researched novel, *Ghost Fleet*, U.S. scholars Pete Singer and August Cole imagine what a war with China would look like now that the Chinese military has access to all this information.

265 *Indian admiral told me*: Author conversation with Admiral R. K. Dhowan, chief of naval staff, as part of speech to Aspen Dialogue, January 12, 2015. See also http:// news.usni.org/2014/09/04/india-sell-high-speed-anti-ship-missile-vietnam -venezuela. For details on other countries' actions, see, for example, Mark Manyin, "Vietnam Among the Powers: Struggle & Cooperation," Asan Forum, October 17, 2014; Jim Gomez, "Philippines Seeks U.S. Help to Protect Troops in Disputed Sea," *Military Times*, August 26, 2015; Josh Rogin, "Malaysia and U.S. in Talks to Ramp Up China Spying," *Bloomberg View*, September 3, 2015.

265 *increasing its defense spending*: Laxman Behera, "India's Defence Budget 2015–16," Institute for Defence Studies and Analyses, March 2, 2015, http://www.idsa.in /issuebrief/IndiasDefenceBudget2015-16_lkbehera_020315.html. For details on shipbuilding, see David Tweed and N. C. Bipindra, "Submarine Killers: India's $61 Billion Warning to China," *Bloomberg Business*, July 28, 2015; Manu Pubby, "As Sightings of Chinese Submarines Become Frequent, Navy Steps Up Guard in Indian Ocean Region," *Economic Times*, August 8, 2015; Richard Sisk, "U.S. to Provide India Help to Develop Aircraft Carrier Fleet," *Military*, June 4, 2015; "Military and Security Developments Involving the People's Republic of China 2015," Annual Report to Congress, 2015, p. 51, http://www.defense.gov/Portals/1 /Documents/pubs/2015_China_Military_Power_Report.pdf.

265 *From 2011 to 2015*: Aude Fleurant, Sam Perlo-Freeman, Pieter D. Wezeman, and Siemon T. Wezeman, "Trends in International Arms Transfers, 2015," Stockholm International Peace Research Institute. February 2016.

266 *By the numbers*: International Institute for Strategic Studies, *The Military Balance*, 2012, https://www.iiss.org/en/publications/military%20balance/issues /the-military-balance-2012-77da; Alan Kronstadt, "U.S.-India Security Relations: Strategic Issues," Congressional Research Service, January 24, 2013, https://www .fas.org/sgp/crs/row/R42948.pdf; "Military Power Comparison Results for India vs. China," GFP, February 17, 2015.

266 *Tellis believes that the Indian military is much stronger*: Author conversation with Ashley Tellis, scholar at Carnegie Endowment for International Peace, October 5, 2015.

266 *protested vociferously*: The 2007 edition of the Malabar exercises in the Bay of Bengal were expanded to include Japan and Australia. However, Beijing lashed out at what looked like the so-called quadrilateral security dialogue, or "quad," between the United States, Australia, Japan, and India operating at sea.

267 *thoughtful American scholars*: Robert Blackwill, "Revising U.S. Grand Strategy Toward China," Council on Foreign Relations, April 2015, p. 29, http://www.cfr .org/china/revising-us-grand-strategy-toward-china/p36371; John Mearsheimer, "Why China's Rise Will Not Be Peaceful," University of Chicago, September 17, 2004, http://mearsheimer.uchicago.edu/pdfs/A0034b.pdf.

267 *China hears only*: Kevin Rudd, "How to Break the 'Mutually Assured Misperception' Between the U.S. and China," *World Post*, June 20, 2015, http://www.huff ingtonpost.com/kevin-rudd/us-china-relations-kevin-rudd-report_b_7096784 .html.

268 *continue to invest heavily in its military*: The exception is Japan after World War II, but that is only because it fell under the United States' military umbrella.

270 *Xi . . . and President Obama committed*: "Remarks by President Obama and President Xi of the People's Republic of China in Joint Press Conference," White House, Office of the Press Secretary, September 25, 2015, https://www.whitehouse.gov /the-press-office/2015/09/25/remarks-president-obama-and-president-xi-peo ples-republic-china-joint.

CONCLUSION: OURS TO LOSE

274 *Some American analysts argue*: See, for example, Robert Blackwill and Ashley Tellis, "Revising U.S. Grand Strategy Toward China," Council on Foreign Relations, April 2015, http://www.cfr.org/china/revising-us-grand-strategy-toward-china /p36371. As Ashley Tellis and Raja Mohan describe it in a separate article, we should create a "crescent of countervailing power centers to China, with India as one bookend, and Japan the other." Ashley Tellis and C. Raja Mohan, "The Strategic Rationale for Deeper U.S.-Indian Economic Ties," Carnegie Endowment, 2015, p. 28, http:// carnegieendowment.org/files/US_India_TellisMohan_Final.pdf.

276 *Stanford scholar Kori Schake*: Author interview with Kori Schake, research fellow at Stanford University, September 20, 2015. The background on British-U.S. relations in the nineteenth century comes from Schake's book manuscript: "Safe Passage: The Transition from British to American Hegemony."

281 *created jobs in four-fifths of U.S. congressional districts*: "New Neighbors: Chinese Investment in the United States by Congressional District," National Committee on US-China Relations and Rhodium Group, May 2015, http://rhg.com/wp-con tent/uploads/2015/05/NewNeighborsExSum.pdf.

281 *invested more than $90 billion*: Data from China Global Investment Tracker compiled by the American Enterprise Institute and the Heritage Foundation, accessed October 6, 2015, https://www.aei.org/china-global-investment-tracker/; Thilo Hanemann and Cassie Gao, "Chinese FDI in the US: 2015 Recap," Rhodium Group, January 19, 2016.

281 *Indian investment in the United States*: A NASSCOM report in September 2015 claims that Indian IT companies alone created 156,000 direct and 255,000 indirect jobs in the United States in 2015. "Contributions of India's Tech Industry to the US Economy," NASSCOM, 2015.

286 *Boeing*: Author interview and email correspondence with Ian Thomas, president of Boeing China, October 10, 2015. In 2015 alone, Boeing delivered 117 planes, or more than $10 billion in goods, to China. The U.S. Commerce Department estimates that each billion of exports support almost 6,000 jobs, so this would support almost 60,000 U.S. jobs.

INDEX

ABOUT THE AUTHOR

Anja Manuel is cofounder and partner with former Secretary of State Condoleezza Rice, National Security Advisor Stephen Hadley, and Secretary of Defense Robert Gates, in RiceHadleyGates LLC, a strategic consulting firm. She served as an official at the U.S. Department of State from 2005 to 2007, responsible for South Asia policy. She has traveled extensively across China and India, and with her business clients, regularly experiences tough government negotiating and managing unruly subsidiaries in cities from Beijing to Bangalore. A graduate of Harvard Law School and Stanford University, Manuel now lectures at Stanford. When she is not on a plane, she lives in San Francisco with her husband and two young children.